as it was

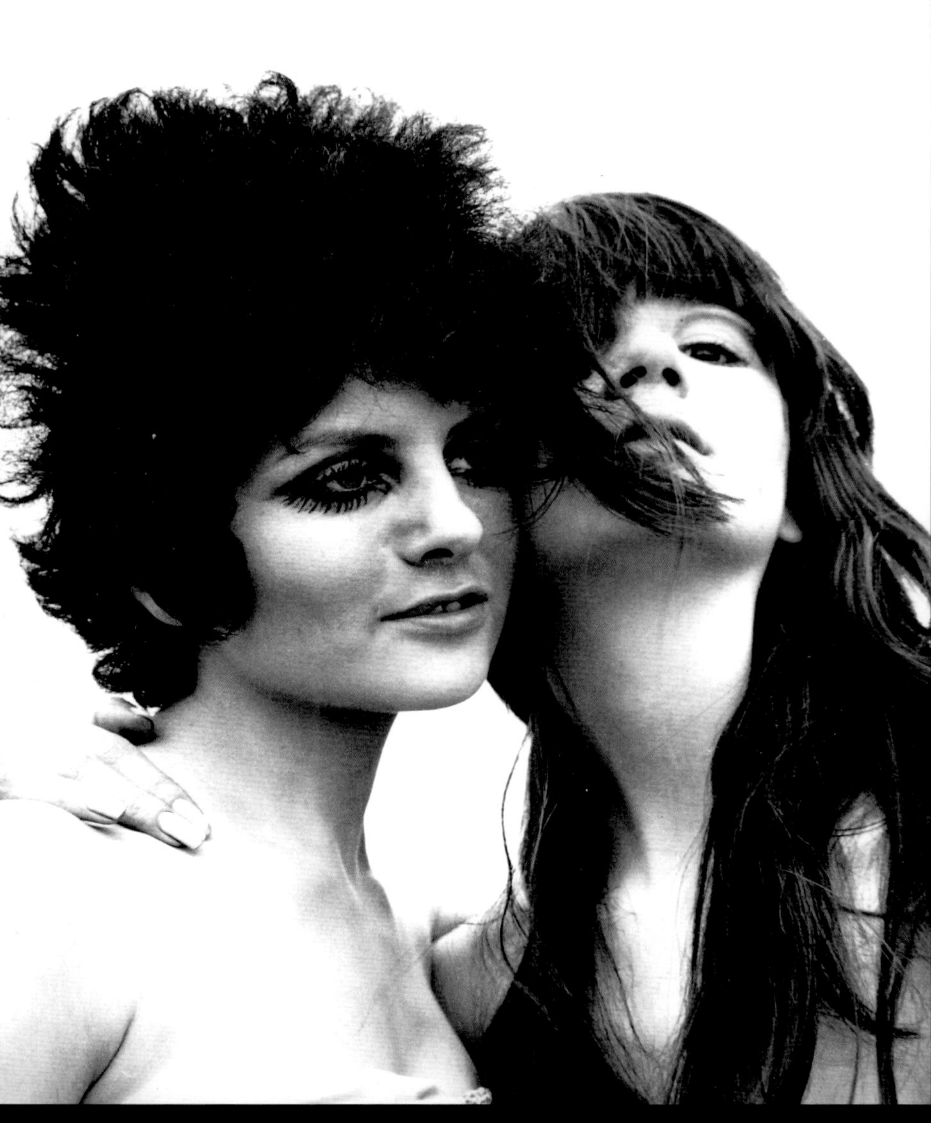

a revision of a legendary decade

HATJE
CANTZ

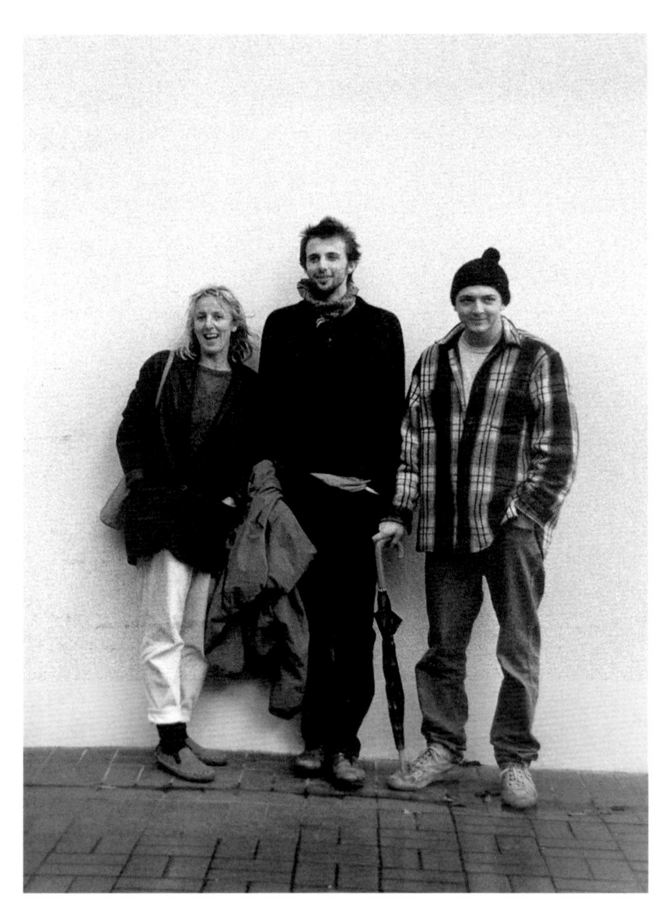

as it was

For Christine, Florian, and Sebastian

My heartfelt thanks go to all named
and unnamed friends illustrating
these pages, on earth or in heaven.

Foreword

Decades have passed and this is not my first attempt at juxtaposing images and words, attempting to explore some of the hidden corners of my past. In London and Paris there were the three of us: a Leicaflex, a Rolleiflex, and me—witnessing and being part of that immortal decade: the Sixties. I kept a visual diary of my human surroundings, fueled with devotion and curiosity.

My memories have not faded. Often, I still find myself living in that Sixties bubble, with undiluted memories of the time. I had no awareness then that one day I would pass on my visual account with personal notes to future generations.

Time waits for no one.

Thinking of great photographers that inspired me, I instinctively relate to the images of Edward Steichen's Magnum exhibition, *The Family of Man.*

The timeless images of black-and-white photographs gathered from celebrated photographers that were exhibited in the mid-fifties worldwide still remain a hallmark of my life. "With all beings and all things we shall be as relatives." This quotation of a Sioux Native American became a reflection of my inner self. The images still being a counterweight in a global environment with an ever-changing reality fueled my senses.

To me, photography became an everlasting love affair with images and people: to preserve passing moments through the lens of a camera during the current changing of times. To capture the humble and contrasting sides of life and recognizing the moment when it presents itself. Fueled by a natural born curiosity, and regretting time going by.

The tendency is to favor the natural shot—images should not depend on a certain formula, but rather on feelings—and my perspective and the mood I want the picture to convey.

I have never been preoccupied with heavy-handed technique for technique's sake. The reproductions in this book have been made from my originals, many of which were printed in my kitchen darkroom. We strive for perfection with the blessings of technology, losing orientation of the truth of today. Is there a place left for dreams? We are increasingly difficult to amaze. We've experienced it all. It's a welcome sensation when it does occur, however plain it might be. ☞

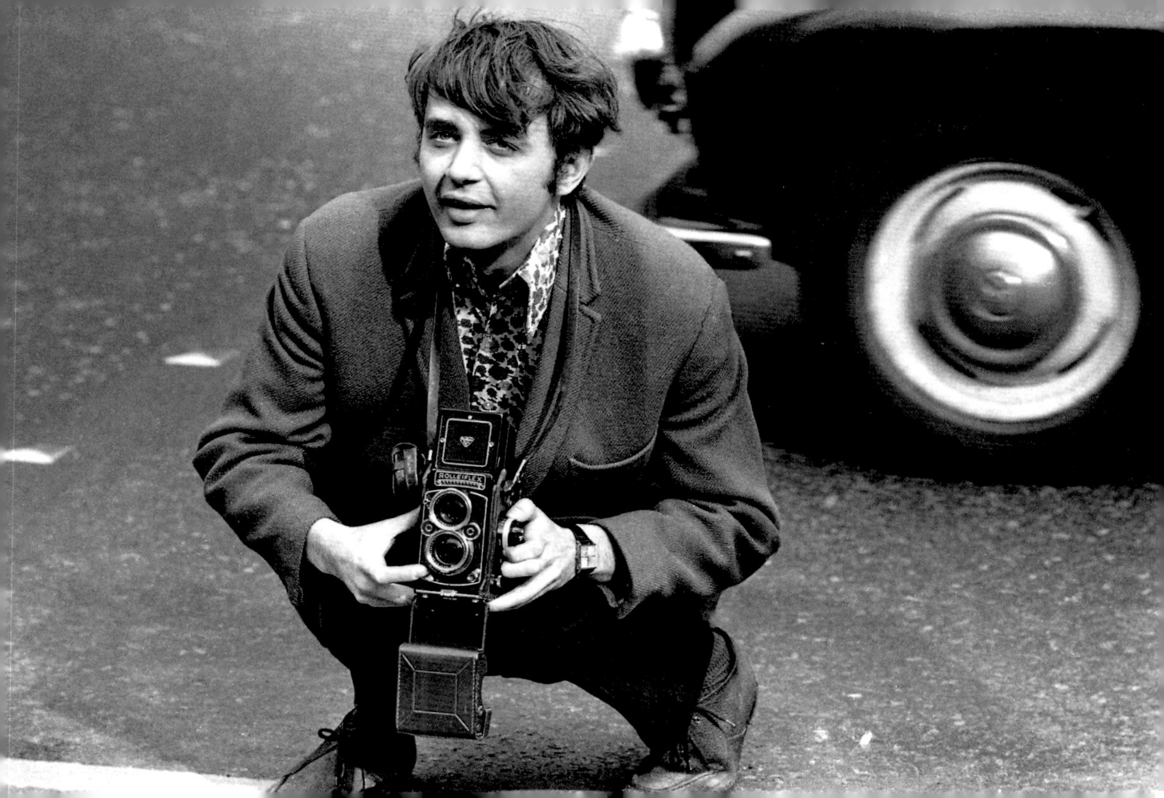
ROLLEIFLEX

Swimming against the tide and breaking conventions in relation to images and juxtapositions, I froze realities and fantasies in a real and unreal world—simply as I saw it or as I wanted it to be. Nor is the boundary between real and fake very exact.

Photographers may bond people to their inner vision, dramatizing the wealth and confusion that man has created. Antoine de Saint-Exupéry resorted to a world of fables. The Grimm Brothers wrote their plots. Lewis Carroll hovered in a world of fantasy.

The lines of beauty and ugliness run very close together. If you dip your finger into ice cold or extremely hot water you can hardly tell one temperature from the other.

I captured London without its traditional landmarks while searching for what happened behind the scenes. Looking for what hides behind the human soul, observing the contradictions, absurdities, the abstract, the surreal, the mystical, the frailties, being astounded by life's complexities, juxtaposing and blurring reality and fantasy, capturing togetherness, despair, rebellion, isolation, joy and sadness, surrounded by beauty and drama.

I was privileged to access the diverse extremes of our society, capturing the in between moments on movie sets, the artists, the innocence of street children, the poor being confused in towering cities, the wealthy parading their good fortunes. My approach was seemingly down-to-earth and never intimidating. The quality of the subject matter counts, and not necessarily the information contained within it.

We all have different perceptions and interpretations for what is presented to us in a never-ending flood of images.

The process of communication matters, the attempt to render life into a situation by fusing observer and observed. In life there is no thorough explanation for anything. The photographic image should strike a chord somewhere in the observer's subconscious. Some of the finest pictures I feel cannot be readily described or discussed. They are deeply felt, and may look at the humble details of life. Too much analysis kills emotion.

Art is only definable by its own terms. The images being a compilation of reality versus fantasy, representing a personal portfolio of my work through the Sixties.

The present melting into the past, still remaining the present.

Frank Habicht

Frank Habicht

Our young pop revolution

Our young pop revolution started in the very quarry of British life, ethics, traditions, and energy: in the working classes, the petite bourgeoisie, and the industrial North. Remember skiffle? Remember teddy boys? Remember ton-up boys? Remember mods and rockers? Remember that northern little band of slim, running jumping Beatles? It started as a great fistful of vigor and sap thrust through the socialist gloom of the kitchen-sink boys of the "fifties," the Angry Young Men and the Brechtomanes just off rations.

So "roll over Beethoven and don't step on my blue suede shoes" (Beatles' iconoclastic reference to the Rock of Elvis Ages) . . . The yeah-yeah generation of the Sixties has both created and been created by the new economic boom, by post-war affluence. This paradox is easily unraveled: this generation is a giant consumer by sheer dint of numbers (the post-war baby boom grown into teenagers and young working twenties), which have therefore created a need. In fact, it was originally the brain-child of an older generation of "rebels without causes" of Angry Young Man vintage, The Dick Lesters, the John Michaels, the John Stephens, the Mary Quants, the Time-lifers, the record company boys of greying eminence. An amorphous generation did not suddenly shape up and cry, "We are! . . . we are swinging London"; their immediate elders initially promoted their image, while they themselves gave it real life and form. But this new-blast generation was ultimately responsible for creating its own image. It was the first generation ever to wrest the communications and propaganda media into its own hands (though not exclusively); witness Radio Caroline and disc jockeys such as Emperor Rosco, Dave Symonds, Jimmy Young, ad-men and journalists and TV personalities such as David Frost, who holds a job usually held by a man twice his age. The remaining, older media boys have jumped on the bandwagon and never tire of talking about "dolly girls" and "mini-skirts."

The new blasts were brought up in a term of educational and social upheaval in the early, stumbling years of the Welfare State. They were taught to think and be aware of the world around them with socially keen eyes. Parents whose youth was curtailed by the last war, and who in turn had bad parents who had also aged prematurely through the first one, brought youngsters up to a better world. Like all parents, they did not want the same deprivations to be visited upon their children. And they weren't. As Satchmo [Louis Armstrong] says, "a man wants a chance to give his kids a better life." And this they have got. All things being equal, and all ages equal, the younger generation could have enjoyed their better world undisturbed had their fame/infamy not been created by precisely those channels that gave rise to their image and affluence—communications media. They had to fight that un-articulated prejudice that young people are not supposed to enjoy themselves, which springs not from "generations gap" and "old men forget" attitudes but from the fact that, till fairly recently, if young people were not habitually at war through need and near-historical custom, they were hard at work from their tenderest years. It also seems that many would have students behave like middle-aged parents rich in the weight of experience; they object to students' new activism and political awareness ("Interference").

But young people have always broken out of the chrysalis into adulthood with many a long and loud shout. We do not have to look far back to remind our patriarchs of their own lusty youths in the politically and socially boisterous and animated "twenties and thirties." It was, after all, as a result of those angry and hungry militants that the Welfare State was born, relieving many problems but also cunningly preserving systems which the revolutionaries wished to obliterate. The new activists of [the] London School of Economics and the New Universities are not only a product of a system created and condoned by their elders but also a continuation of that very fine vital British tradition of "stand up and be counted" from Jack Straw and company on down the ages. If one wishes to look for precedents one need only glance at the manners and riotously active student life led by Renaissance students. The young generation is fiercely aware of the world it lives in, and it also gives vent to all the hopes and fears young people and old alike always will have: will we have a long and prosperous and happy life . . . we'll jolly well see that we do, thank you. Nor is it that students mature younger now. Age means little. It is the society we change and not our blood and vitality. ☞

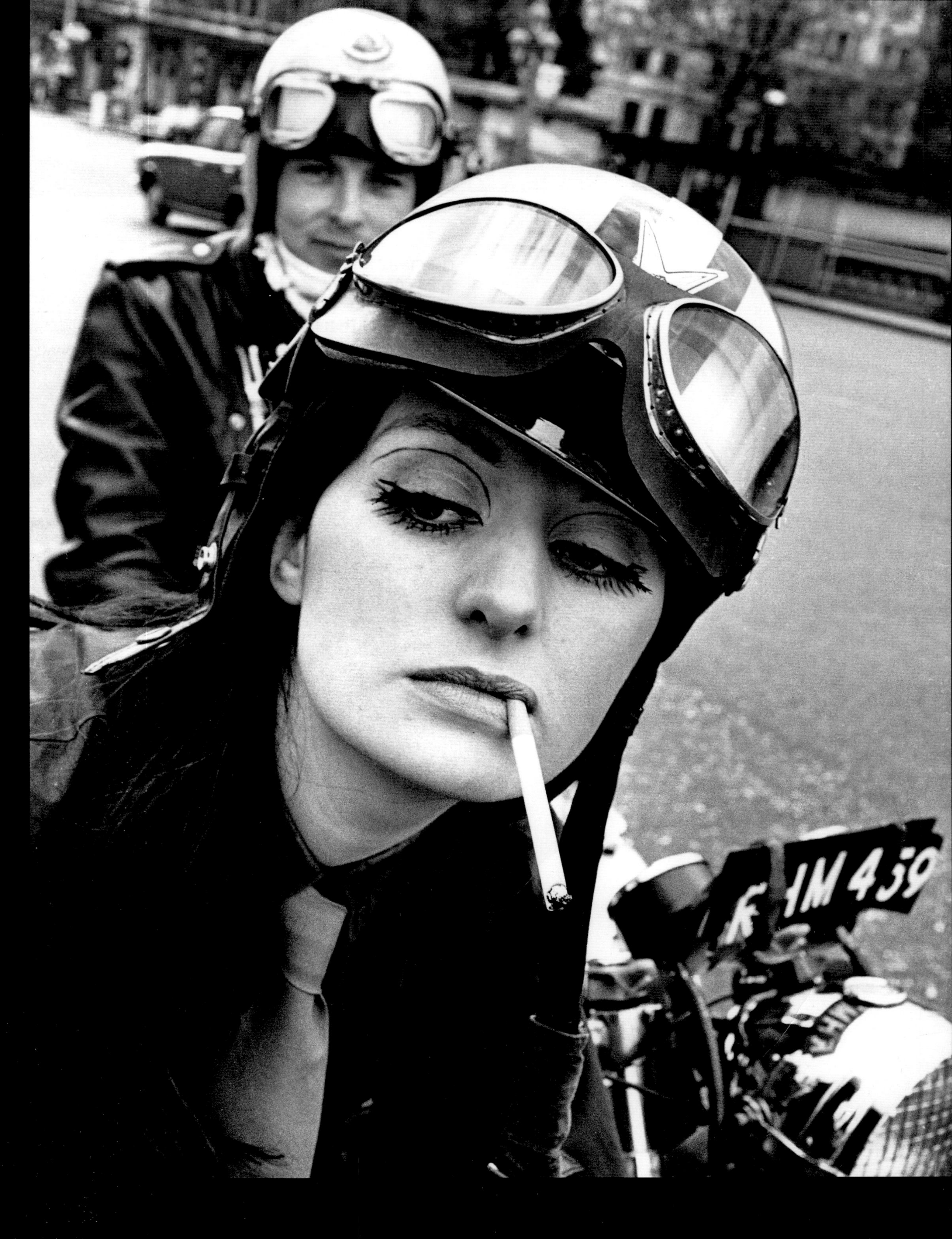

Live it to the hilt – Renee, Westminster Bridge, 1968

“I’ll give you all I’ve got to give . . . tell me you want the kind of things that money just can’t buy” (Beatles). In any case the young revolution did not, as it rarely does, start in the universities. It came from the outside-in and was taken up by every single walk of British society. It came from the young people who have “a hard day’s night,” who have been “working like dogs,” from young workers. This is why Young London, Young Britain, has caused such a stir—because it earned enough and could afford all the records, clothes, jewelry, beads, Indian silks, kaftans, Greek shepherds’ coats, cigarettes and beer, discotheque prices and accessories that change constantly in a near-monthly fashion cycle. It has made a good many sharp youngsters rich—and a good many more elders. During the day these boys and girls work hard in factories, mills, restaurants, shops, offices, banks, hairdressers. They rush home to transform themselves into the wondrously attired magical-mystery tourists of life in London town, dancing themselves into the open-eyed dawns of another salaried day.

An almost unique generation which has not been caught up, as most have been since the end of the professional armies, in the awful bittersweet excitement of war, in the grand illusion of glory and battle-fire, a generation which has not had Kitchener’s or Lloyd George’s or Winston Churchill’s fingers pointing at them, which has not lied about the tenderness of its years to enlist and die for its country and markets and standards.

And yet . . . and yet on many flanks it senses the vacuum. It has deflected those energies traditionally dissipated in proving manhood by show of arms into making Britain prosperous and joining in the economic Battle of Britain and the world. “Back Britain” itself, with its immediate Carnaby Street echoes of laughter-making fun Union Jacks (in which to throw your rubbish), is inversely the fighting banner of the make-love generation. And the laughter is healthy and vigorous. The gods toppled are but emergency gods set up to discipline the reconstructing millions to stick to rations and to the slap-on-the-back-never-had-it-so-bad-Uncle-Jack-men.

Make Love and not War. The urge to win adulthood through arms has romped into another ironical inversion by cocking the same finger at you out of posters which advertise “Lord Kitchener’s Valet” shops, selling, as do the junk-boys in Portobello Road, military and any uniforms that are to be sported, tendered, and paraded through London’s peaceable, decorative streets ablaze with colour and cornucopias of flowers and the quaint peace-loving daisy.

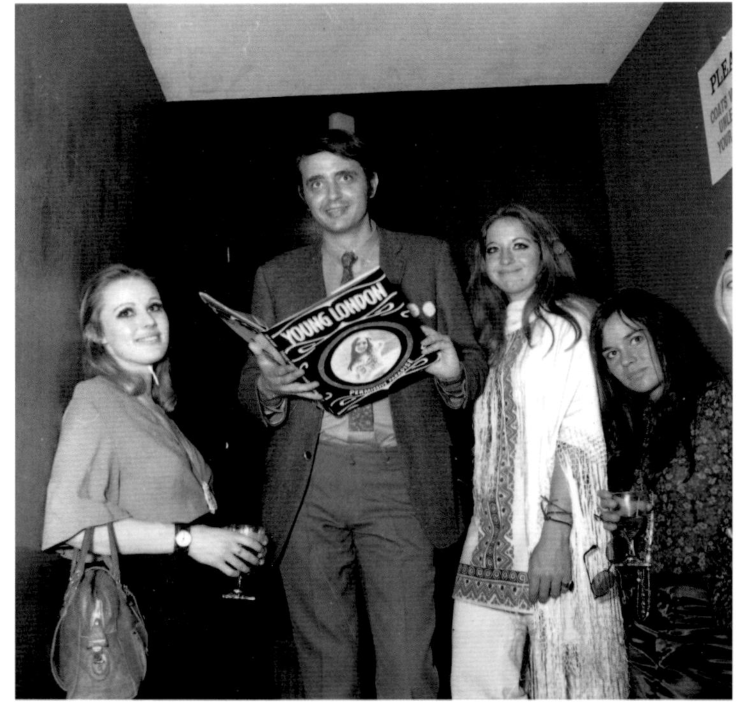

Flower power, flower people, love people, hippies bearing flowers and love buttons, heralding their presence with prayer-bells, incense, and mirth, bask in the reflected glory of the bright windows down the King’s Road boutiques, in the yellows and blues of “Count-Down,” the cool thirties silverings of Drug Store, the Bauhaus shell of Just Looking. They jangle and prance on a Saturday, job-free morning down Portobello Road in Finch’s, pushing an old H.M.V. phonograph, blasting out the scratched roars of old-time Charlestons.

English life has never, in fact, appeared more truly traditional than it does today and has done for the last six years or so. An ironical incident gives weight to this audacious claim. Fortnum and Mason have resuscitated a Mr. Fortnum and a Mr. Mason in the full splendor of eighteenth-century attire to walk about the established shop and assist customers. The comments, which have largely been leveled at them by establishments, have been, “Well! . . . I’ve seen youngsters dress wildly . . . but this is the limit!”

The limit? Should it really seem odd to those who boast of a Hepplewhite or a Chippendale or a piece of Brighton chinoiserie in their drawing-rooms? No, they are merely antique clothes of a booming, affluent Britain of those “those were the days” Regency times. And what about mini-skirts and golliwog hairdos and “permissive behavior” (a term culled from *Time Life* again and applicable to the land to which our Puritans had to flee from our wicked shores!)?

If one scrutinizes present fashions one will see glimmerings of bygone lovely-days, rip-roaring twenties, flapper-girls, bright young things. And what about all those exotically clad men with long hair and bell bottoms and beards? Remember the Oxford bags days, Blasted Wyndham Lewis, Augustus John’s Chelsea, the Six Bells, and remember our traditional taste for the exotic, our love affairs with the East and India.

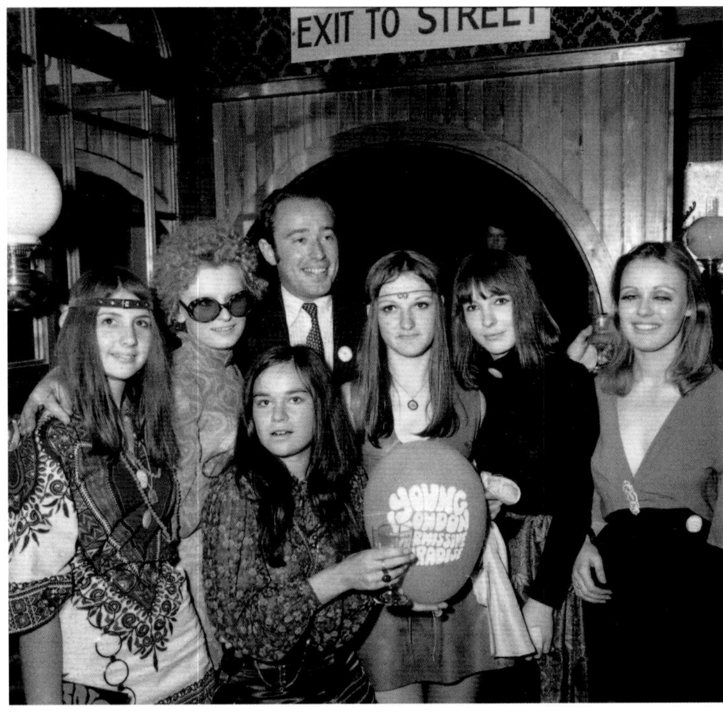

But what about this mysticism and transcendental meditation and this Maharishi Yogi (Verichichi Yogi Bear, as Private Eyes insists on dubbing him)? Well, they ring truly of Vedanta and the Western World, Isherwood, Richard Burton, Lawrence, Foster, Fitzgerald, Kipling, Yeats, Tambimuttu.

Then what about all the drugs and psychedelia?

Remember some of our better poets and artists: Blake, Coleridge, de Quincey, the eclectic and basically Celtic Art Nouveau designs of MacIntosh and Macmurdo and Aubrey Beardsley. The so-called emphasis on "sex" rings louder bells the further back one reaches: It girls, Theda Bara, Clara Bow, Jean Harlow, the Freud mania of the thirties, the Bloomsbury set, not to mention the courts, salons, and customs of all civil civilizations. That nothing is held sacred, that divinities tumble older people grumble, that new gods rise instead—these are all part and parcel of Britain's oft forgotten and forgetful heritage: satire, wit, bohemian manners, tastes, ways of life, morals and dress (Henry VIII, Buckingham, Charles II, Georgian England, Cavaliers, Byron, Oscar Wilde, Sitwells, Huxleys). For always everywhere under the sun, drizzle, and rain has the lovely lusty spirit of the Wife of Bath, Falstaff, Moll Flanders, Tom Jones piped to the Herrick tunes that lead us down the Primrose Hill to Carnaby Street and King's Road.

Young London has rediscovered essential, live Britain and restored its full vigour. It had literally created the Sixties boom. The Beatles were honoured by the Queen for having given the rest of the world a new real image of a live and lusty Britain.

In terms of artistic achievements this generation has invented and discovered something poets and artists have been searching for throughout this century in their Wastelands, Magic Mountains, Diamonds As Big as the Ritz, Metamorphosing Castles, and Lonely Long-distance Runs: a series of metaphors and symbols to capture postindustrial modern society and the personification and symbols have come tumbling out in a surge of pro-life ease of definition fully endowed with the breath of life recognizable on your own street-corner: "Lady Madonna" a calendar of hours and days in the life of a young hippy mother and child of the laddered stocking and Welfare State maternity clinic: *Rita, Rita Meter Maid, The G.P., Oh, Mr. Postman, The Man from Xanadu, The Man on the Hill,* (mod. Lear), pop Neo-Surrealism of the Magical Mystery Tour, of the new soap-box painters and pop poets and underground film-makers. The themes remain the same: love, fear, hope, desire, need, expectancy, what-is-man, whither-goest-thou, what's it all about anyway-man.

We are all strong, young, lusty, lively in love, hard-working, having fun, wanting everything that man, woman, and child have ever wanted: love, security, families, well-paid jobs, prospects, the promise of the long, sweet daisy-open-free life for all—eccentric, square, self-laughing, amusing, amused, creative, industrious, economically active, British shopkeepers that we are.

And all of Britain and all its cultural ramifications blown to the exotic corners of the earth and back home again have contributed to this rediscovery and renewed outburst of energy. The Chelsea-Kensington-King's Road shopping secretary in her bed-sit and share–a–flat, the Australians and New Zealanders of Kangaroo Row Earl's Court, the west Indian and the African, the Pakistani and the Indian, the Greek Cypriot, the Irish militant, the North Country Boys and girls, The East End barrow boys, the South Londoners and Central Londoners, the Etonians and Roedeanians, and the Shopkeepers, the Celts, the Yanks, the Welshmen, have all given their bang to the Wizz Age of Oz, Private Eye, It, auto-destructive art, Round house raves, the Revolution, Annabelle's, the Speak-Easy, Radio One, Radio Caroline, TV, cinema, experimental art, galleries, pop, music, fashion; to garlic, rosemary and thyme, to wine and roses and angry arts, to the mass sum total of a creative, active, British arts-in-life (and not apart, alienated, observant, aloof, anti- and even abdicated from life). It is in life and about and of and to life in London that Young London dedicates itself in this new British blast.

Heather Cremonesi
Introduction to *Young London: Permissive Paradise,* London, 1969

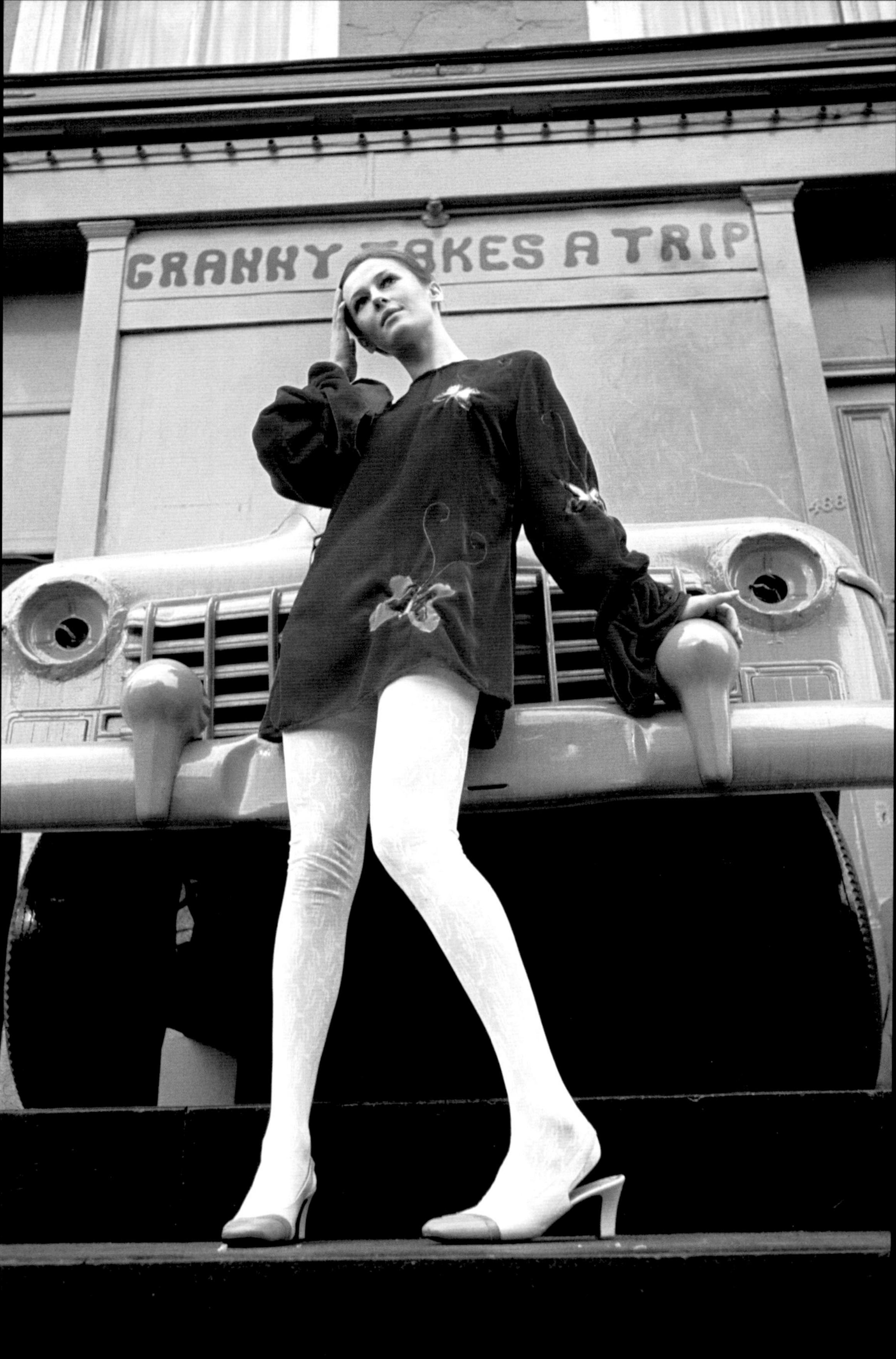

tte Lang at the famous Sixties boutique, King's Road, 1967

A Celebration in Photographs

Frank Habicht is a young German photographer whose hypersensitivity tuned in to Young London. He is, in his way, enraptured by London. To young people, he says, it offers a freedom and scope for the expression lacking in other capitals "where what matters is the kind of car you're running or your role in the rat race."

Young London s far from being William Morris's Earthly Paradise: "And dream of London, small, white and clean. The clear Thames bordered by its gardens green." Yet Frank Habicht's photographs touch a pulse of energy and youth not to be suppressed.

London without her people would be dead indeed. Habicht finds not the clothes but the men and women who wear them; not the places, but those who live and work within the city. In the contrasting textures of skin and water, trees and hair, soft body curves against metal and stone, he traces an intricate pattern of the London heart and its restlessness. His people have time not to hurry. They stand outside the bustle that notices nothing. Their self-consciousness asks to be seen, gathers a simple theatricality around eccentric clothes, flowing hair, no clothes at all. They are all still very young.

Frank Habicht, photographer, is in love with the London scene, but not blindly so. He sees the young at the same time celebrating their youth and worrying about the future, walking the tightrope of tolerance, which to slipping feet gives way to apathy.

Out in Epping Forest, London's large woodland, Frank's people meet the ghost of Dick Turpin, the spring nightingale around Connaught Water. Back in town to cluster round the market stalls, they relish variety: fur coats for winter, pots and pans for fun, flags for a joke of lost empire. They act their parts in costumes self-imposed. To wear the second-hand is not second-best. Nostalgically, old clothes supply a link with the past, like uniforms from battles long since fought; they fill the gap in an empty present, seem to afford protection against an incalculable future.

Painters, statesmen and poets of the past would find a London changed beyond recognition. It is no longer the painter Canaletto's city of sunlit spires. Cars have replaced the hansom cabs, Disraeli's "gondolas of London." It is probably more "populous and smoky" than could have been imagined by the poet Shelley who saw the city as a symbol of hell with London as: the great sea whose ebb flow at once is deaf and loud, and on the shore vomits its wrecks, and still howls on for more.

Undeafened and unblinded by thundering traffic and towering office blocks, Frank Habicht, photographer, feels his way along the paths of an open air London whose youth treats each day as a desert island adventure.

Valerie Mendes
Metropolis Magazine, 1969

Young London

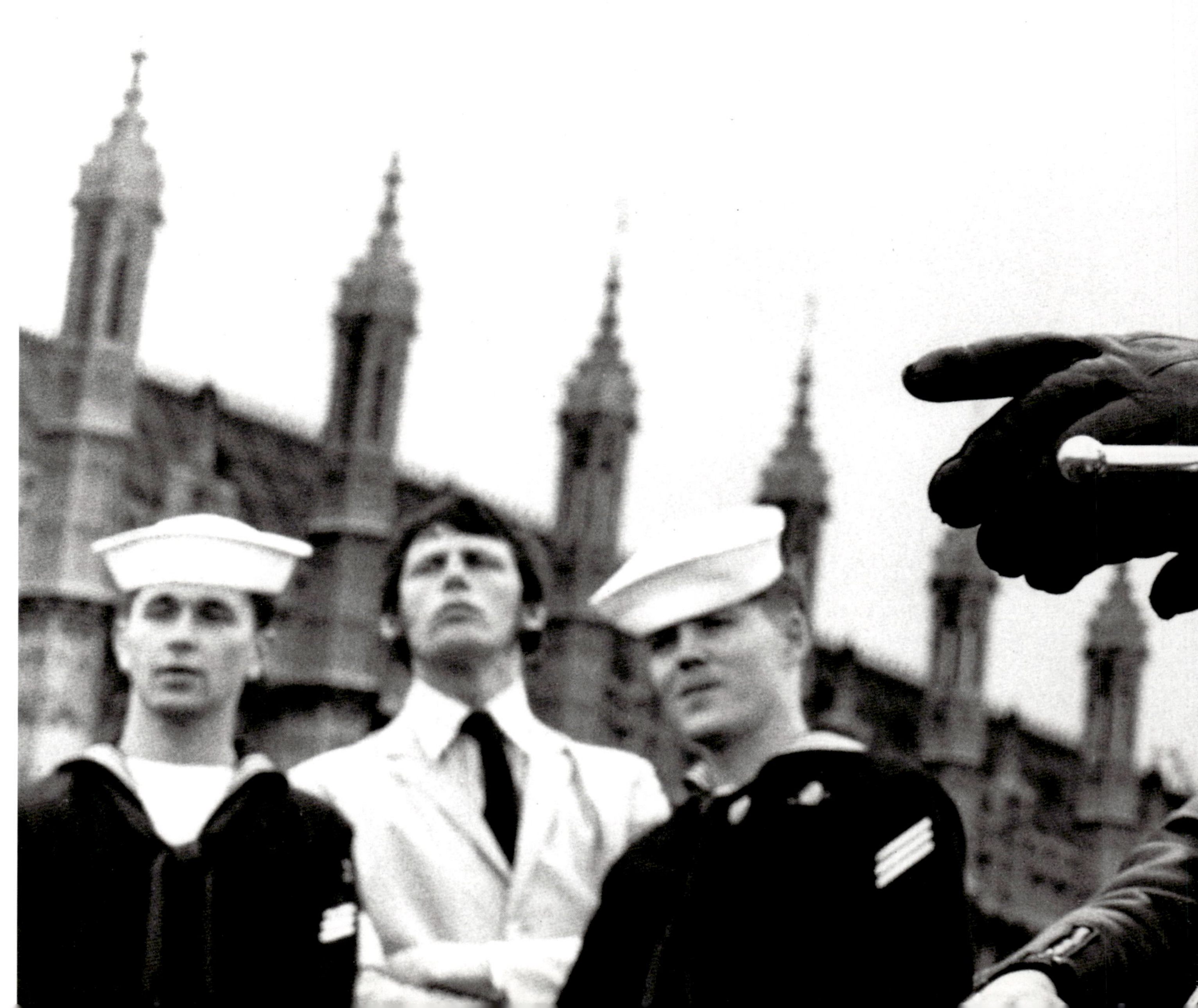

Gone by times –
Renee, Westminster Bridge

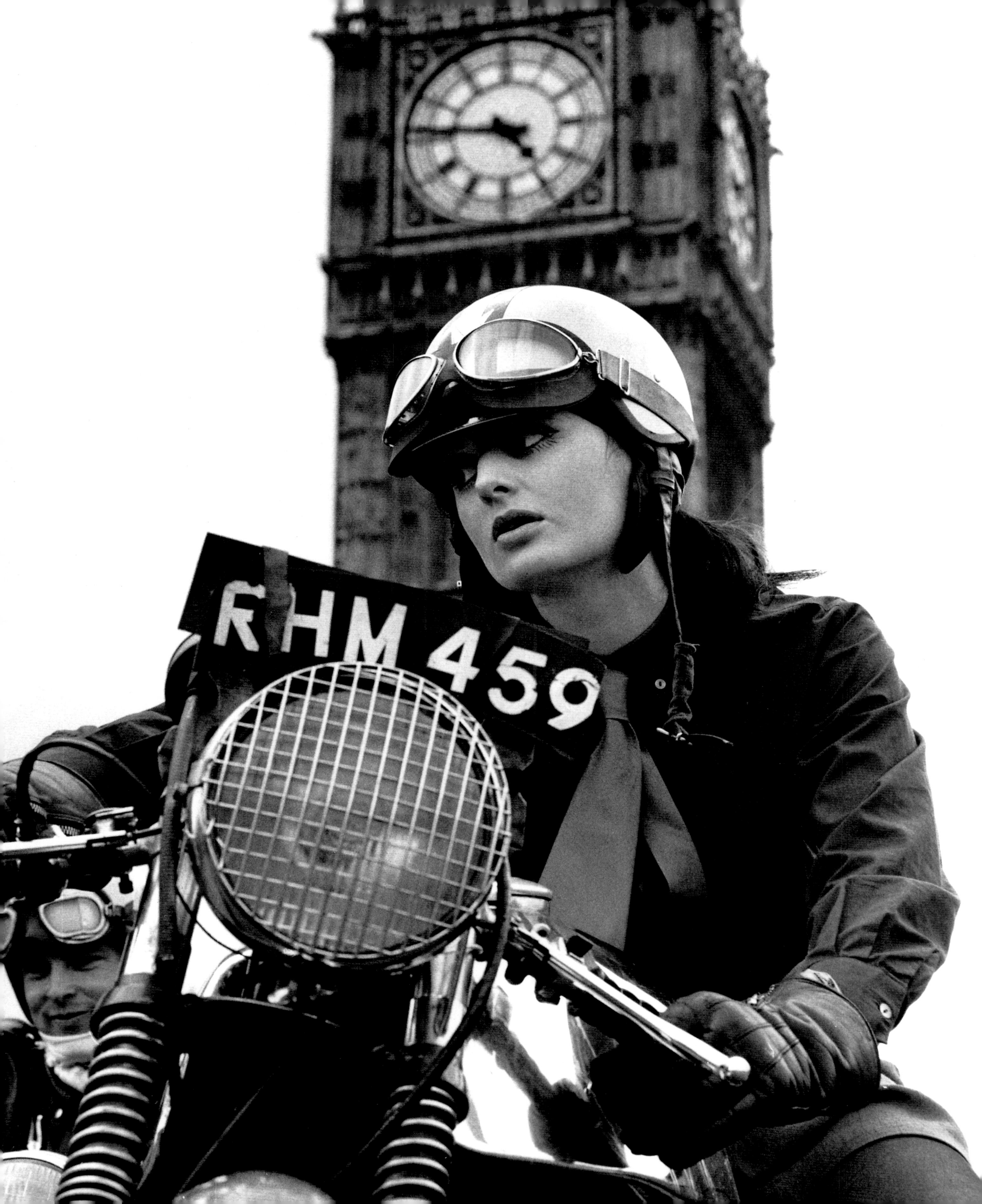
RHM 459

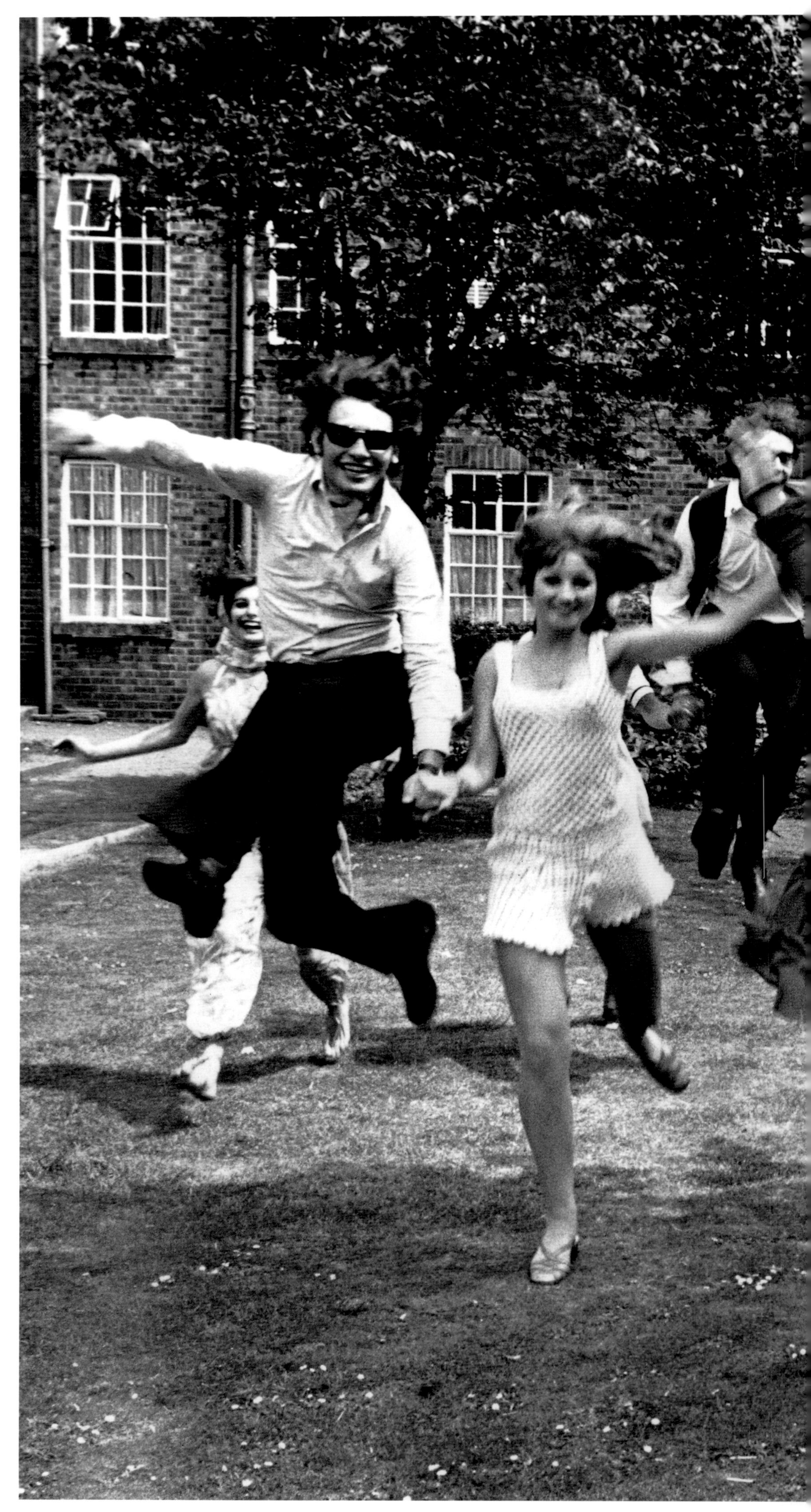

We are, we were, the children of the world, 1964

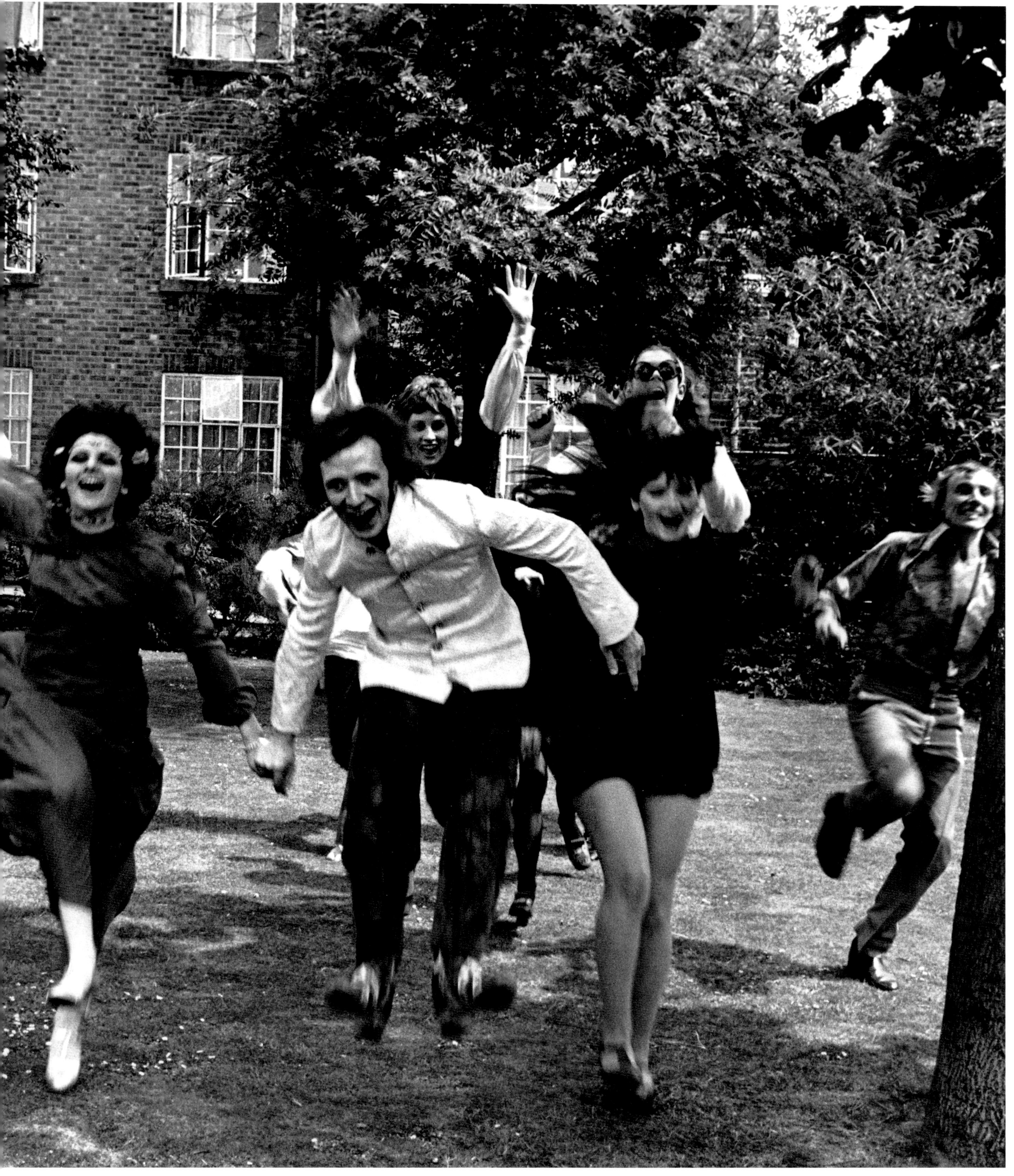

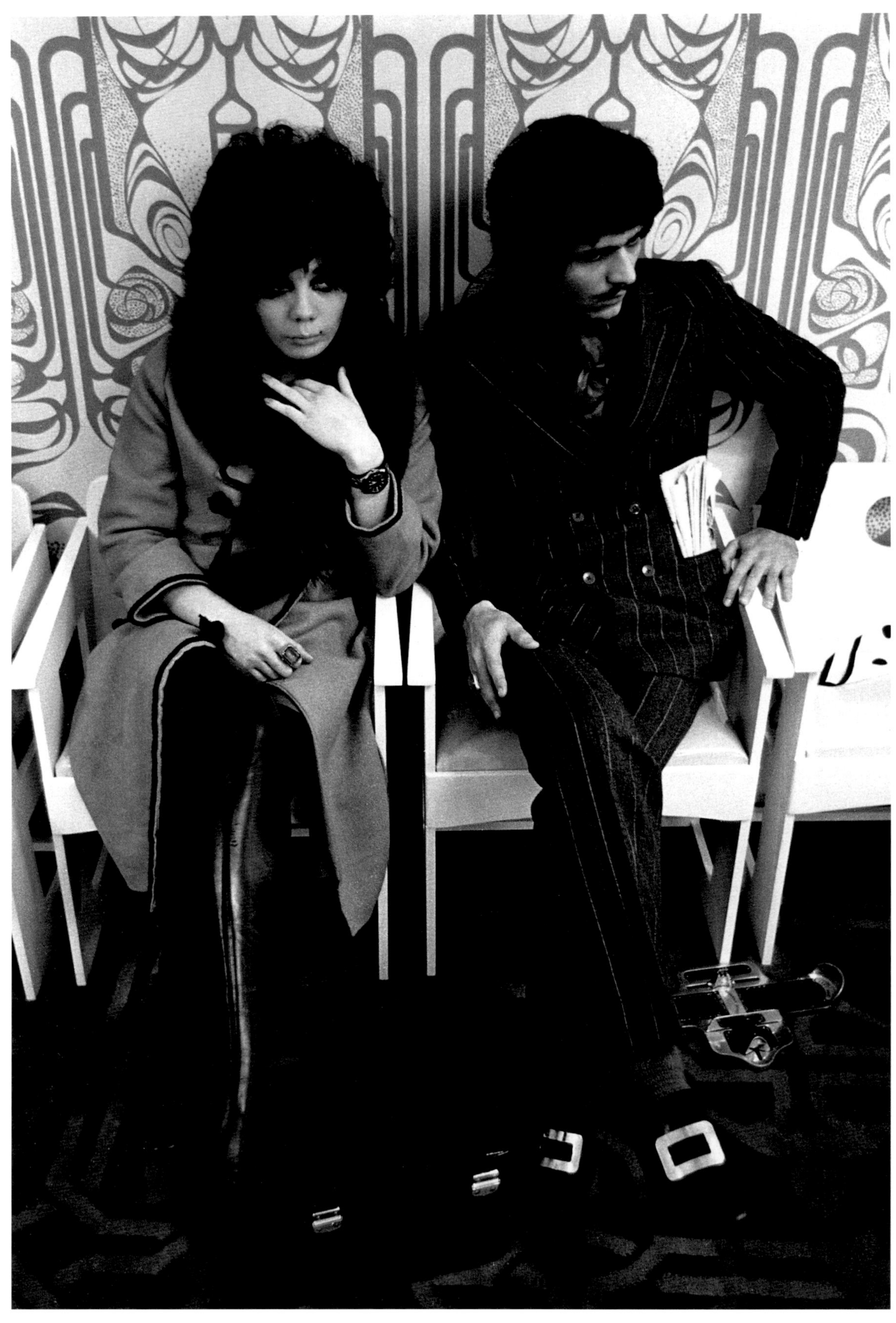

If the shoes fit – Carnaby Street

How kind of you to come – Carnaby Street

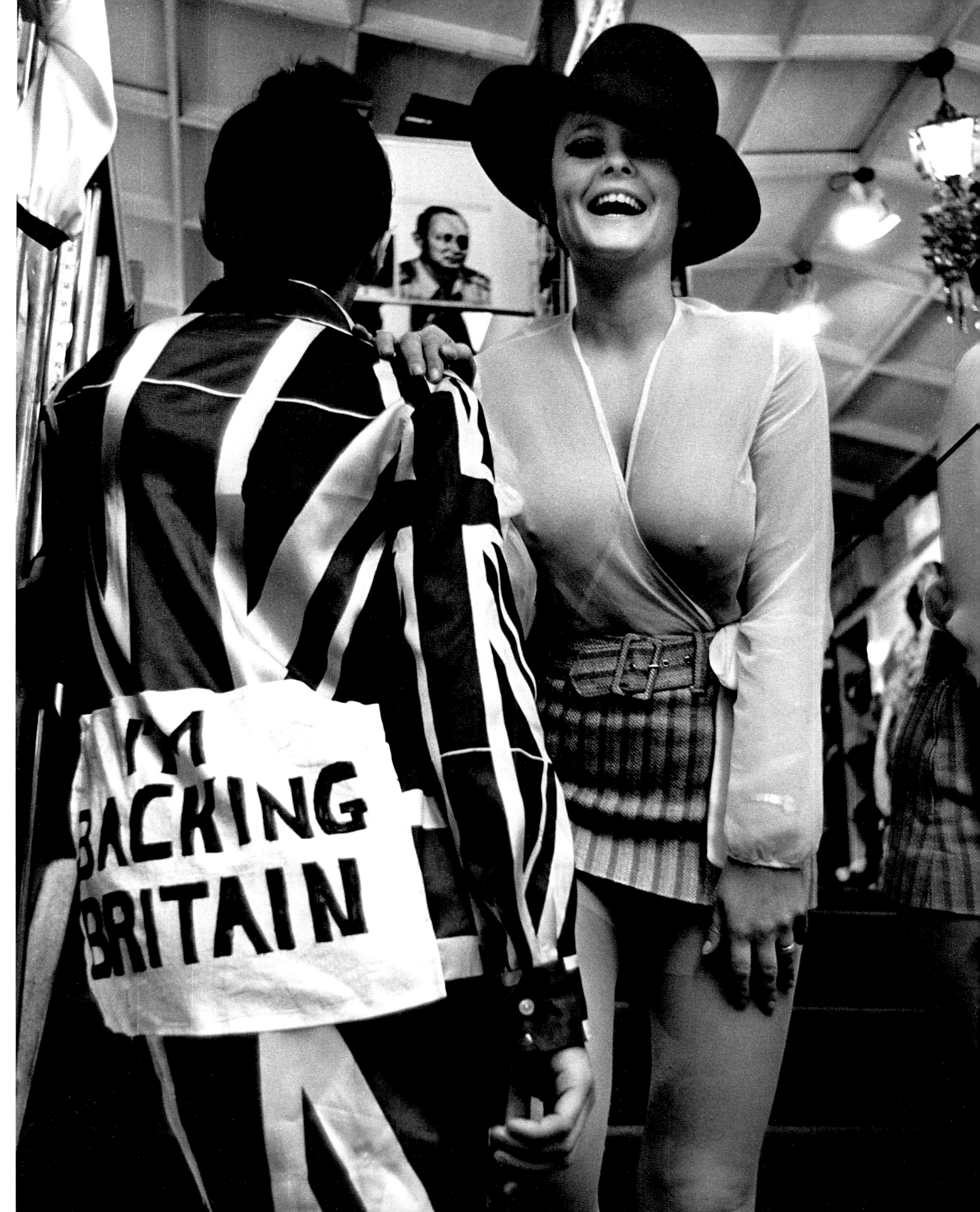
I'M
BACKING
BRITAIN

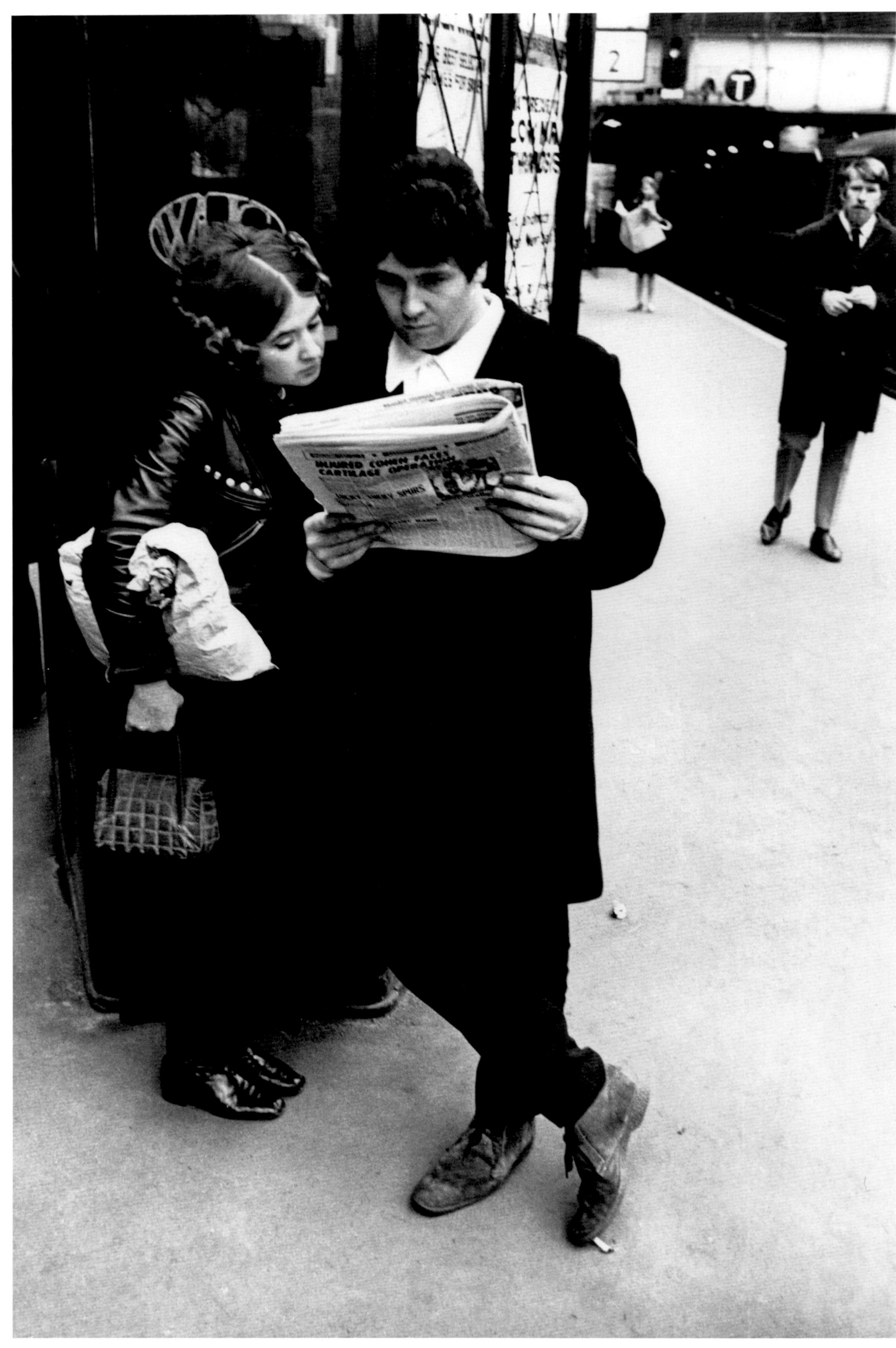

Total absorption – Earl's Court Tube Station

Come and join us – Salvation Army, Sloane Square, 1967

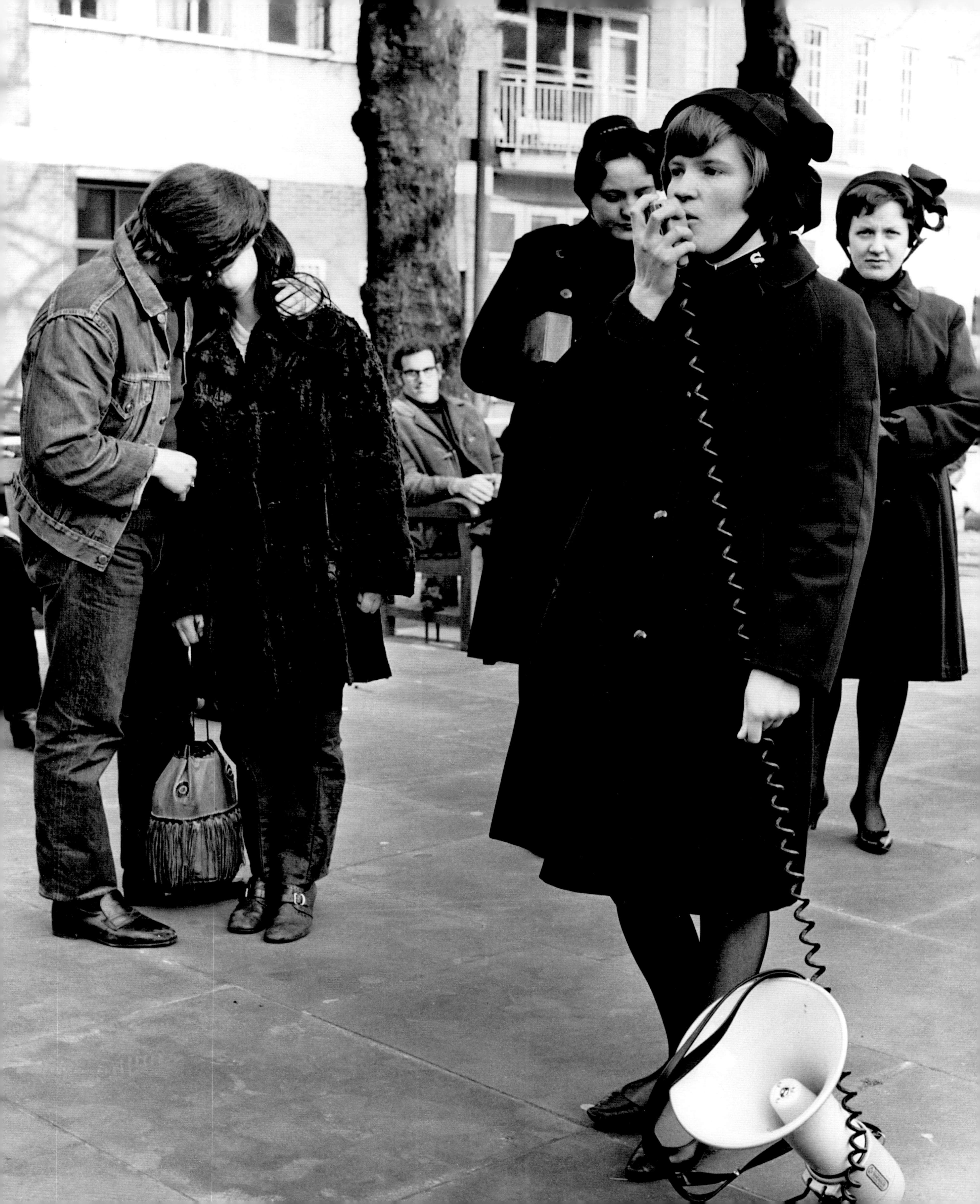

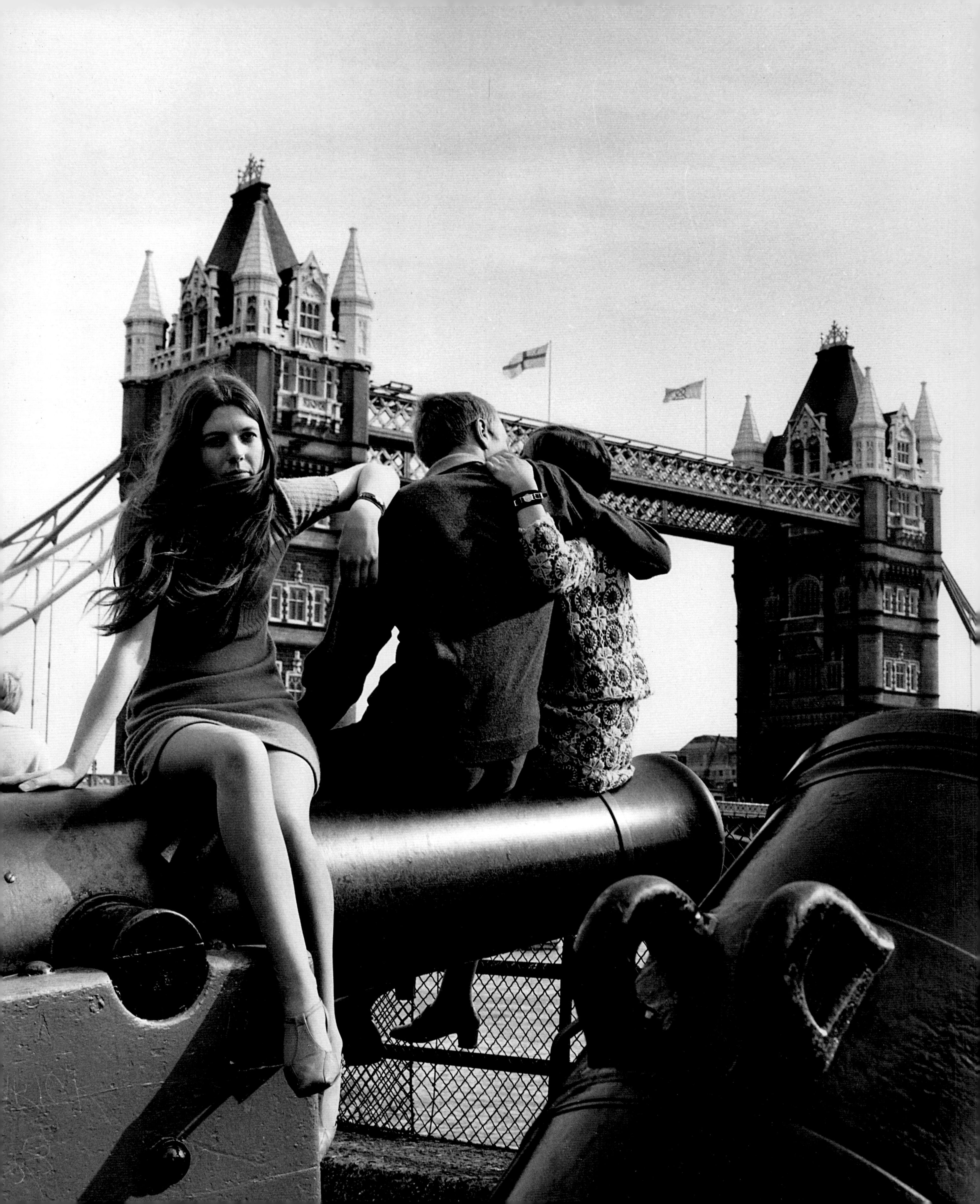

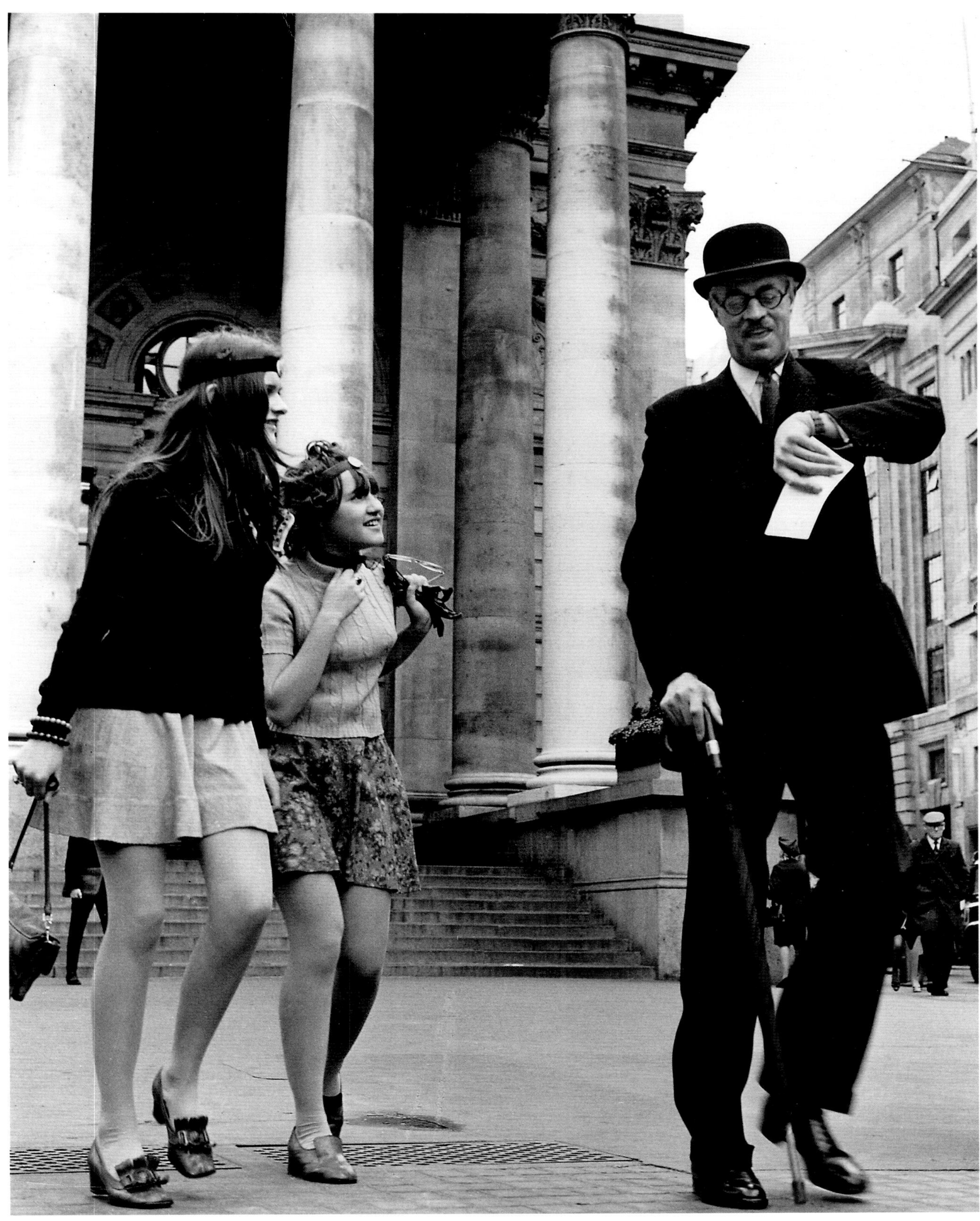

Three's a crowd – Tower Bridge

Time gentleman please – City of London, 1967

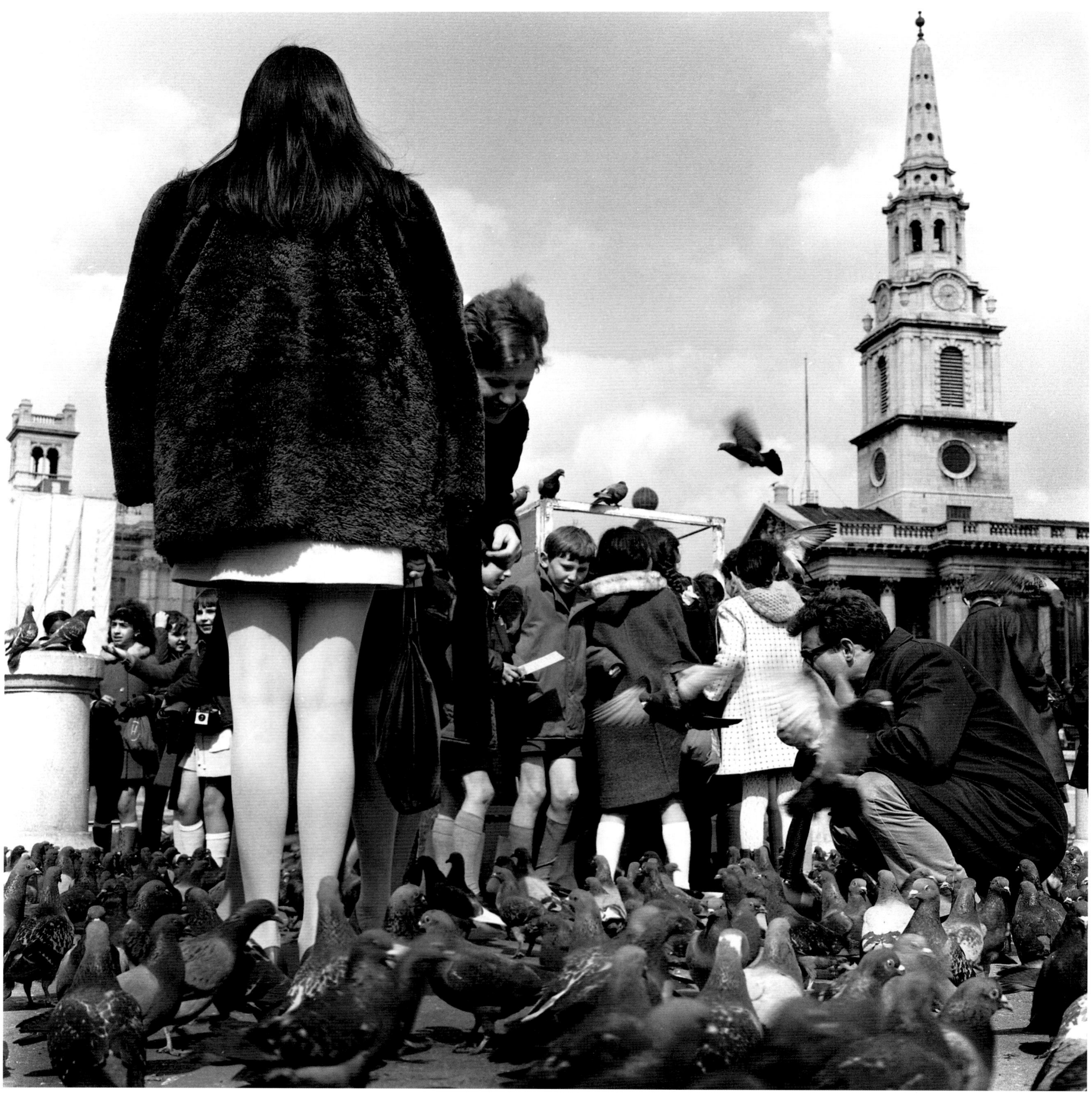

Fashion statements – Trafalgar Square

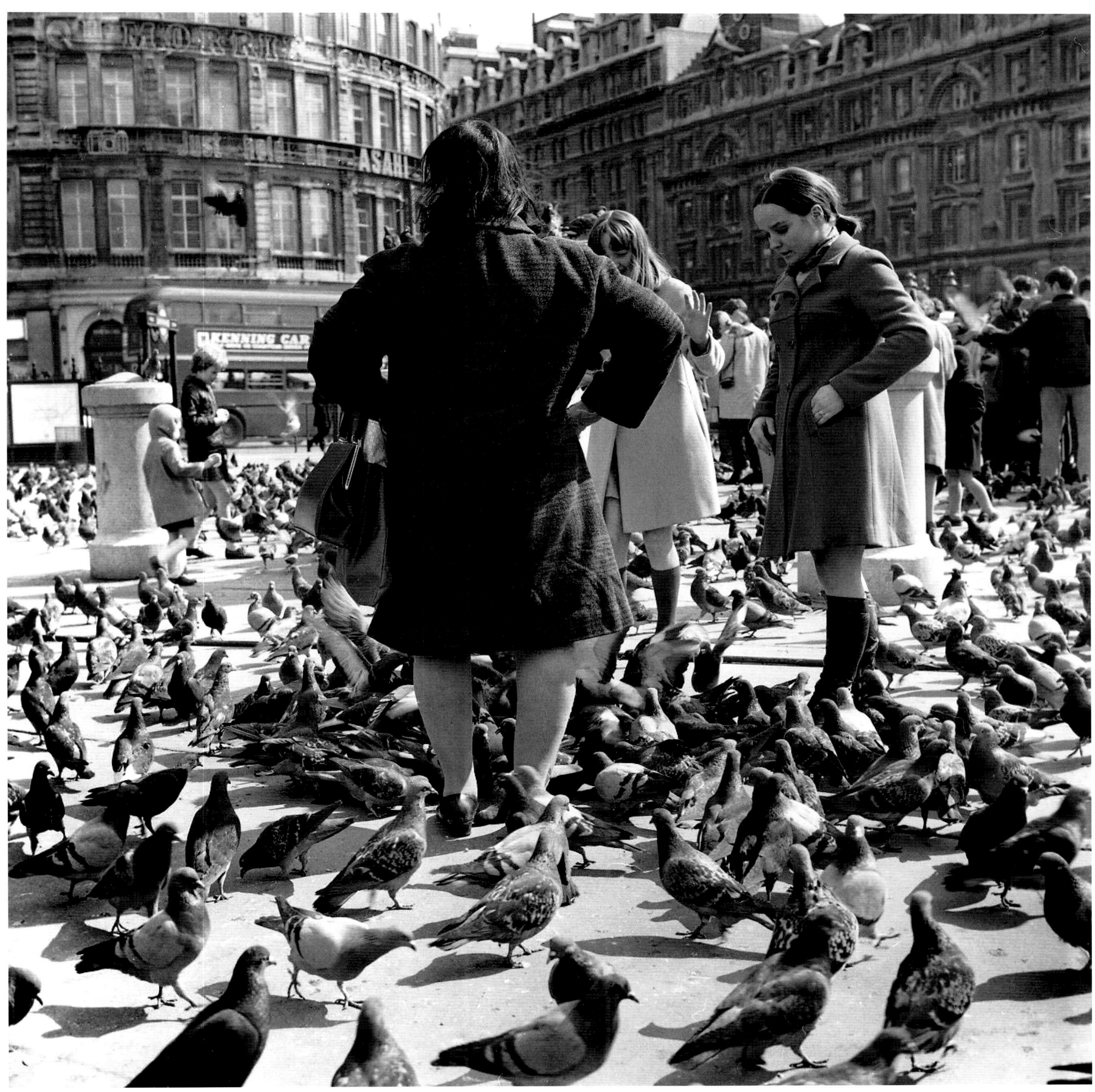
ASAHI
KENNING CAR

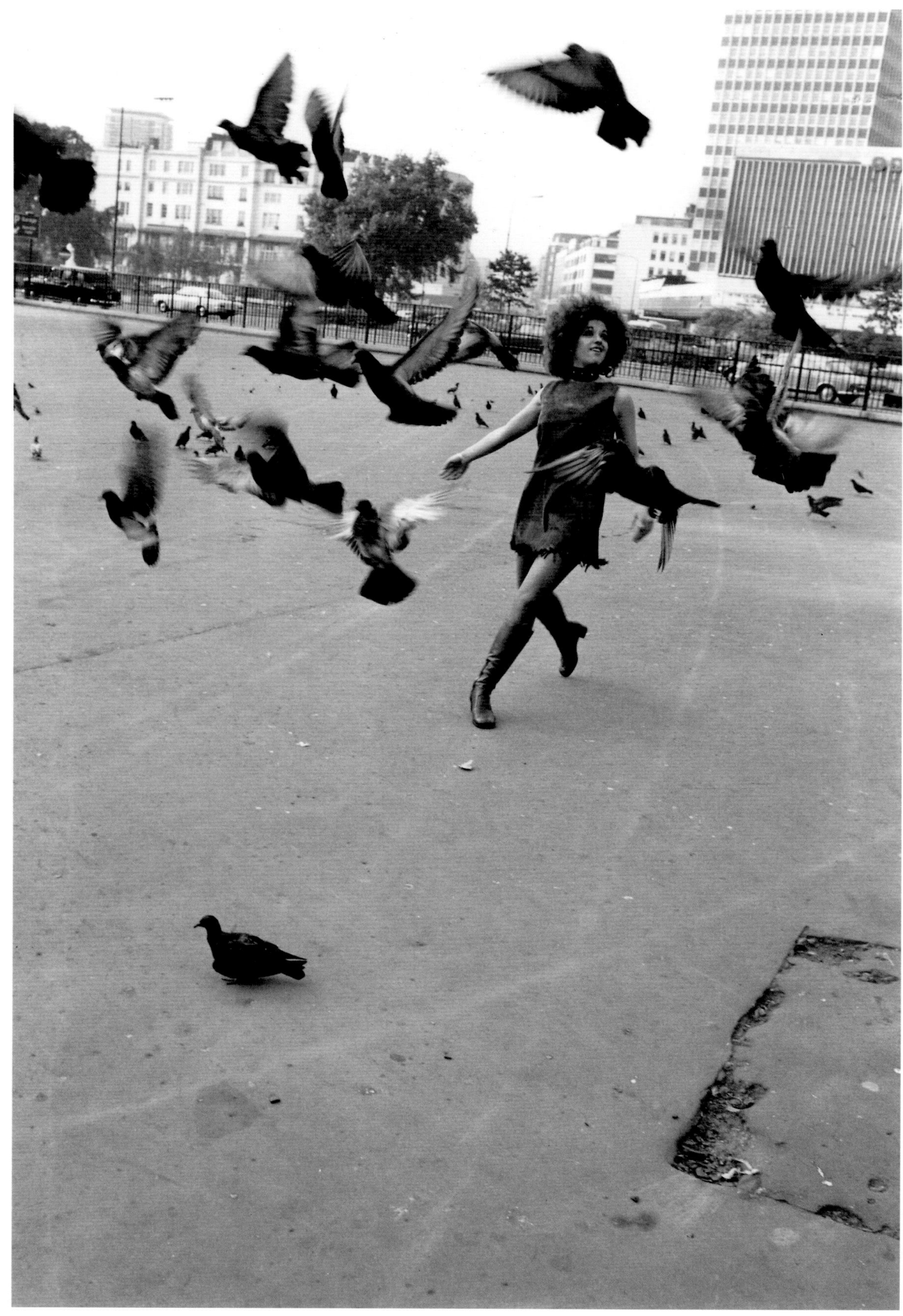

As free as a bird – Liz Krause, Marble Arch

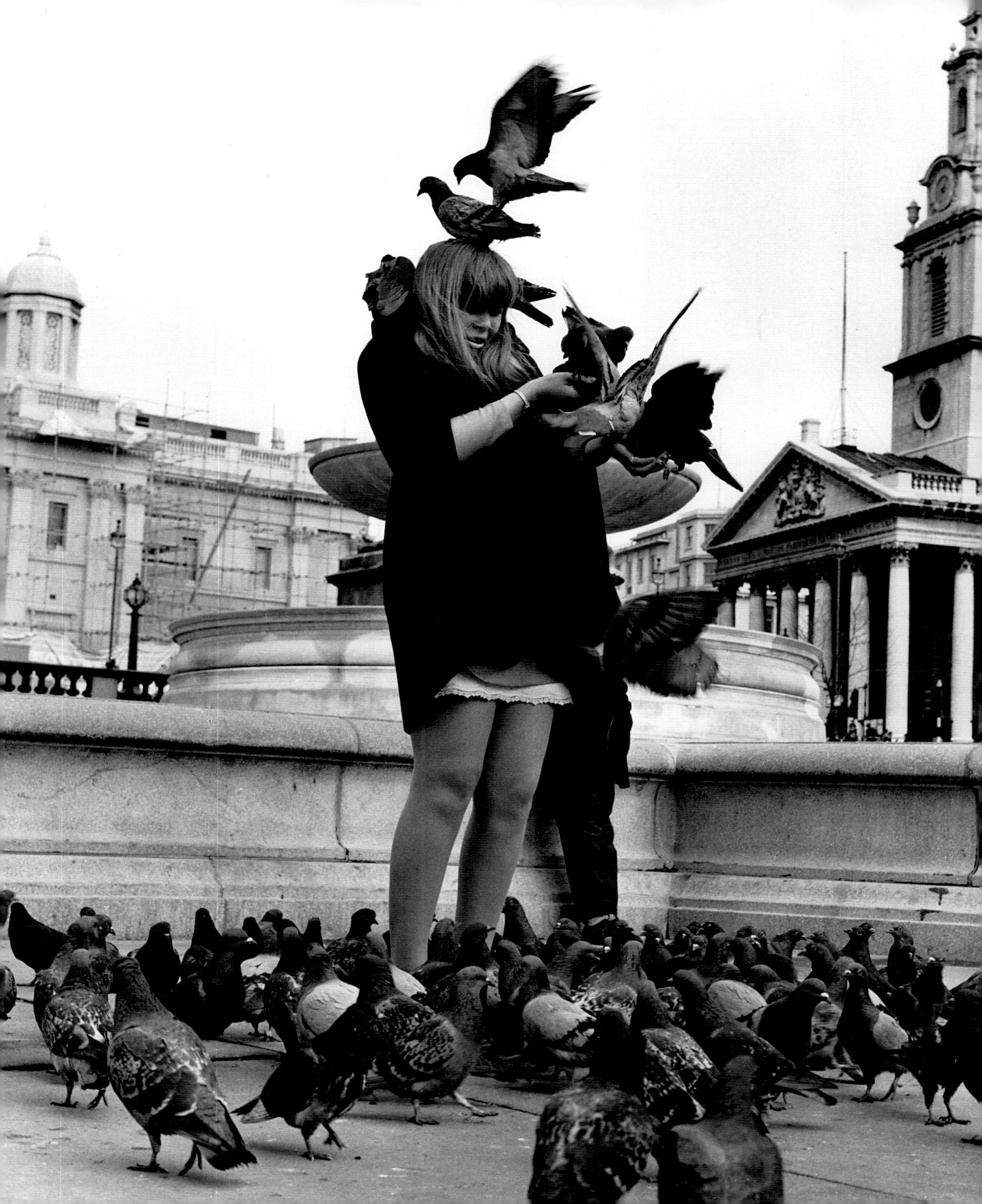

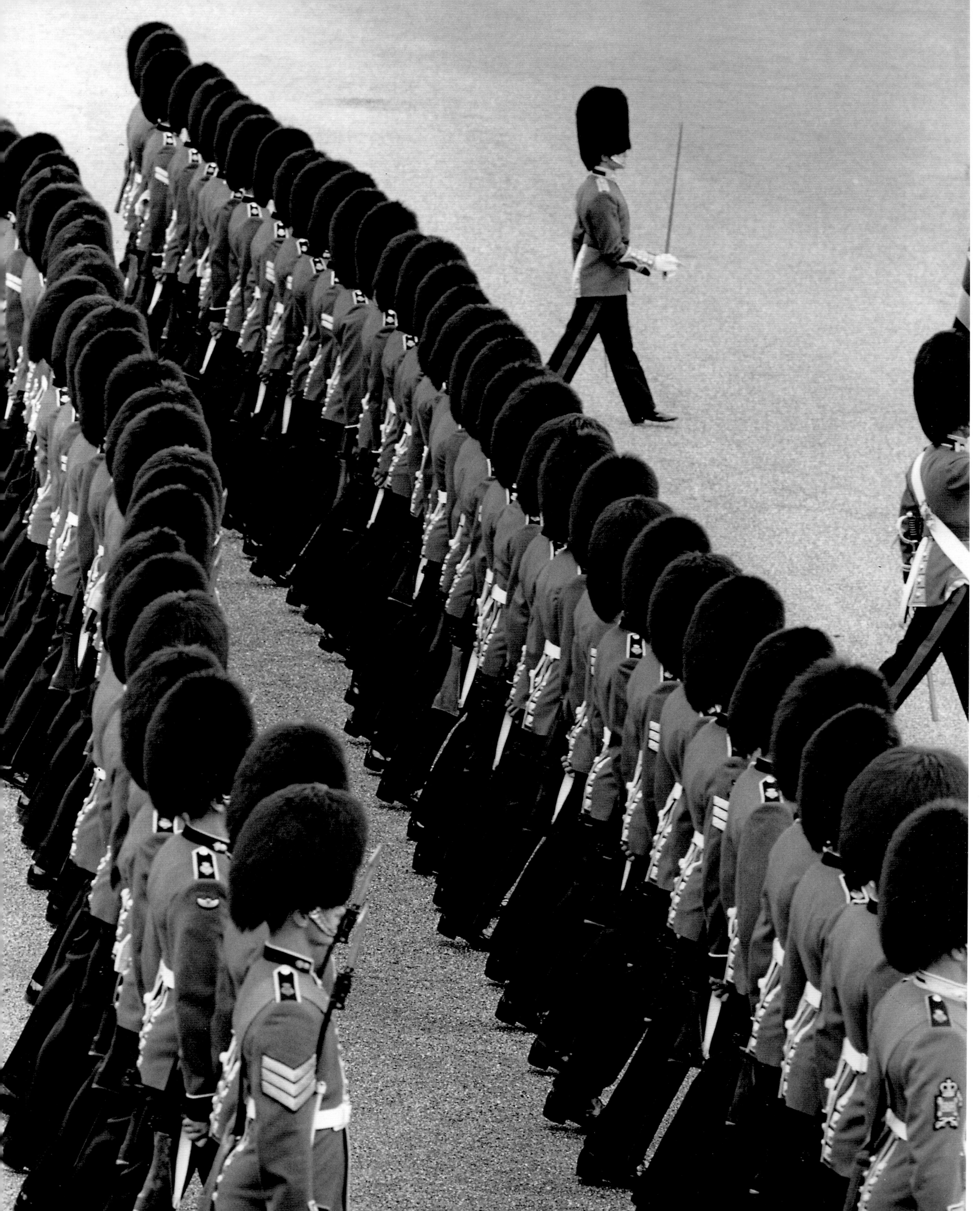

In straight lines – Queen's Birthday Parade, 1968

And who won? – Horse Guards Parade, 1968

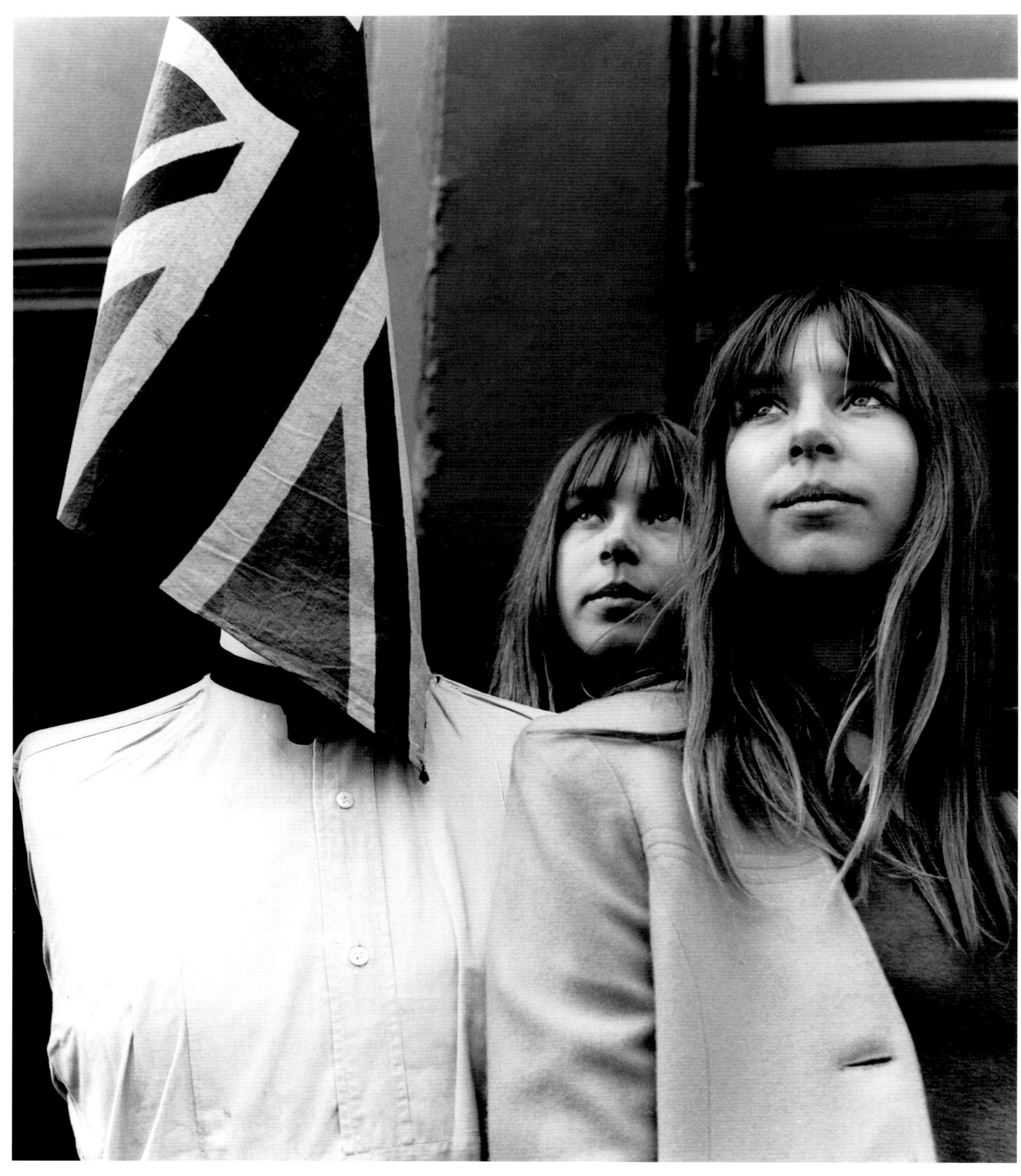

"God save our gracious Queen" – Horse Guards Parade

Uniformity – Royal Guards, Horse Guards Parade, 1968

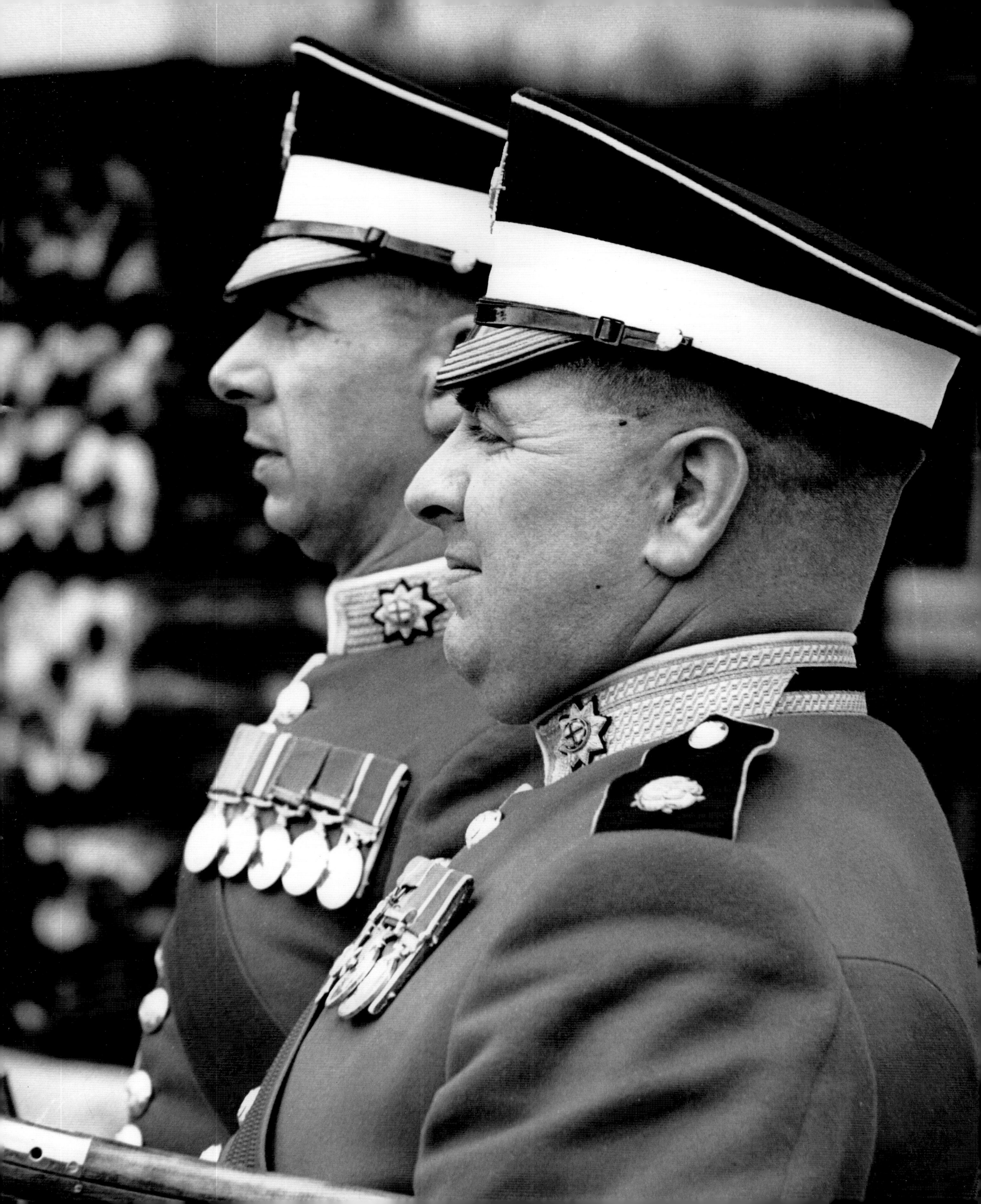

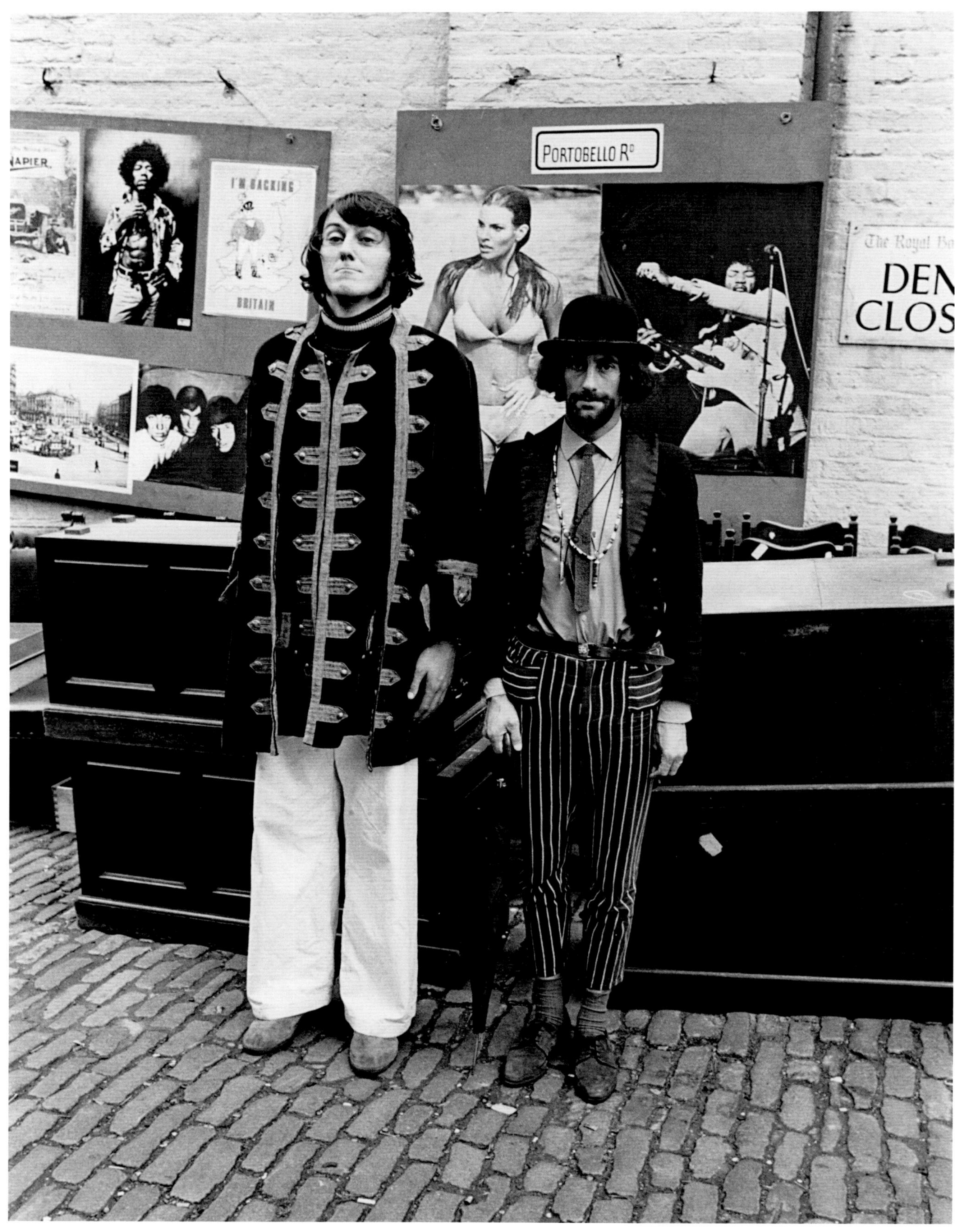

In our different ways – Street buskers, Portobello Road, 1965

To be seen, Snap – Marcia White, Marble Arch

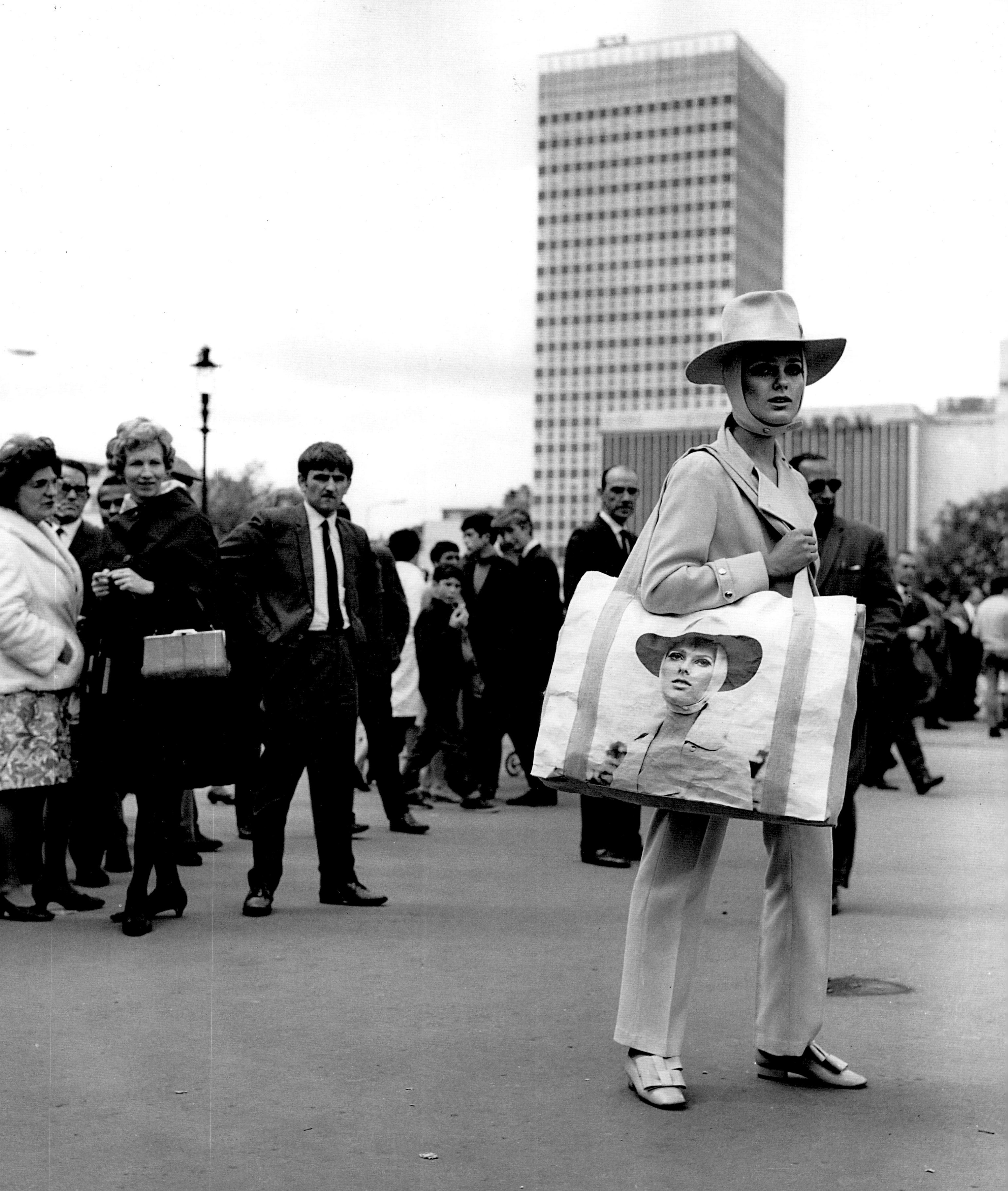

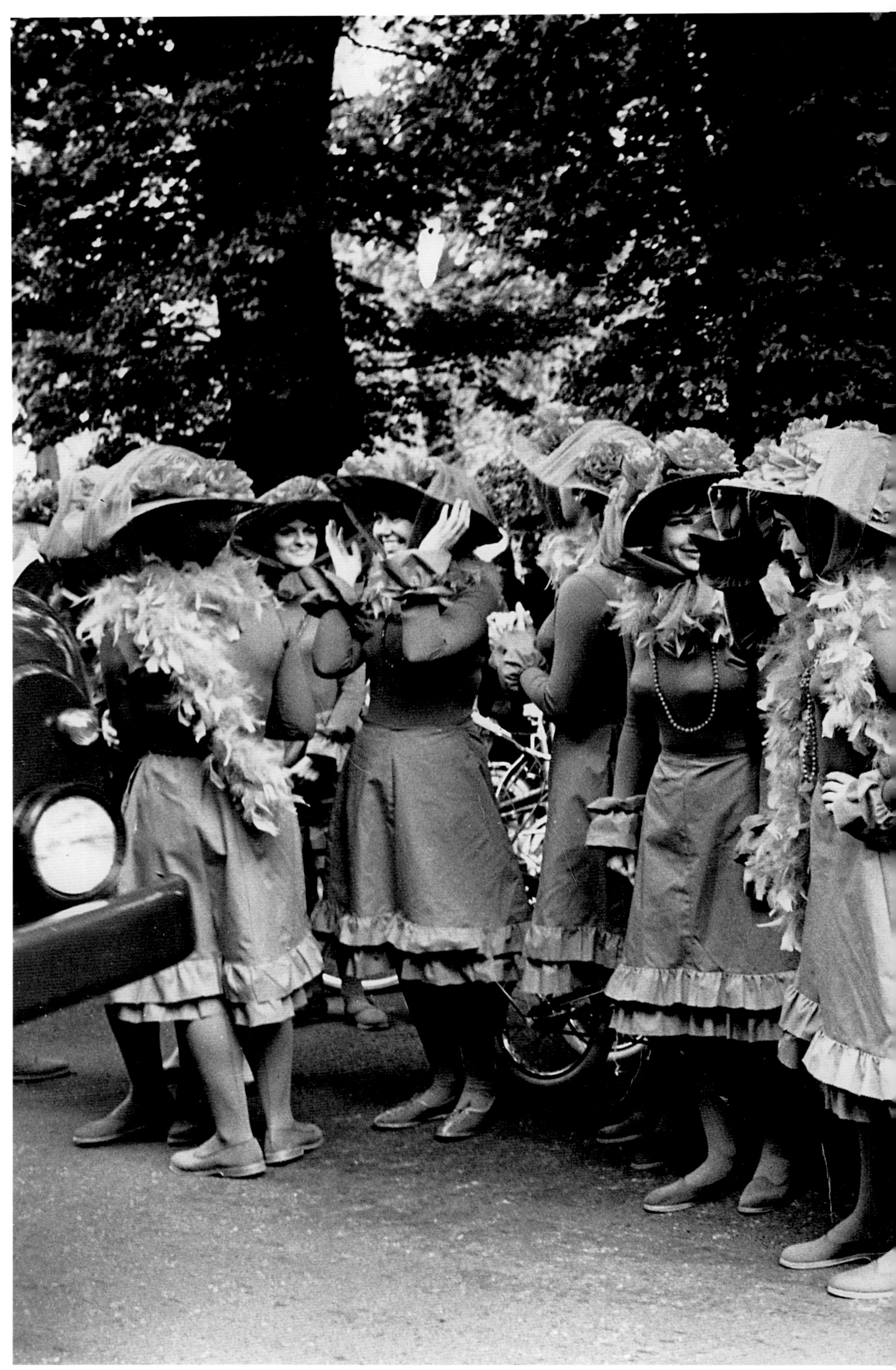

Street carnival, Marble Arch, 1964

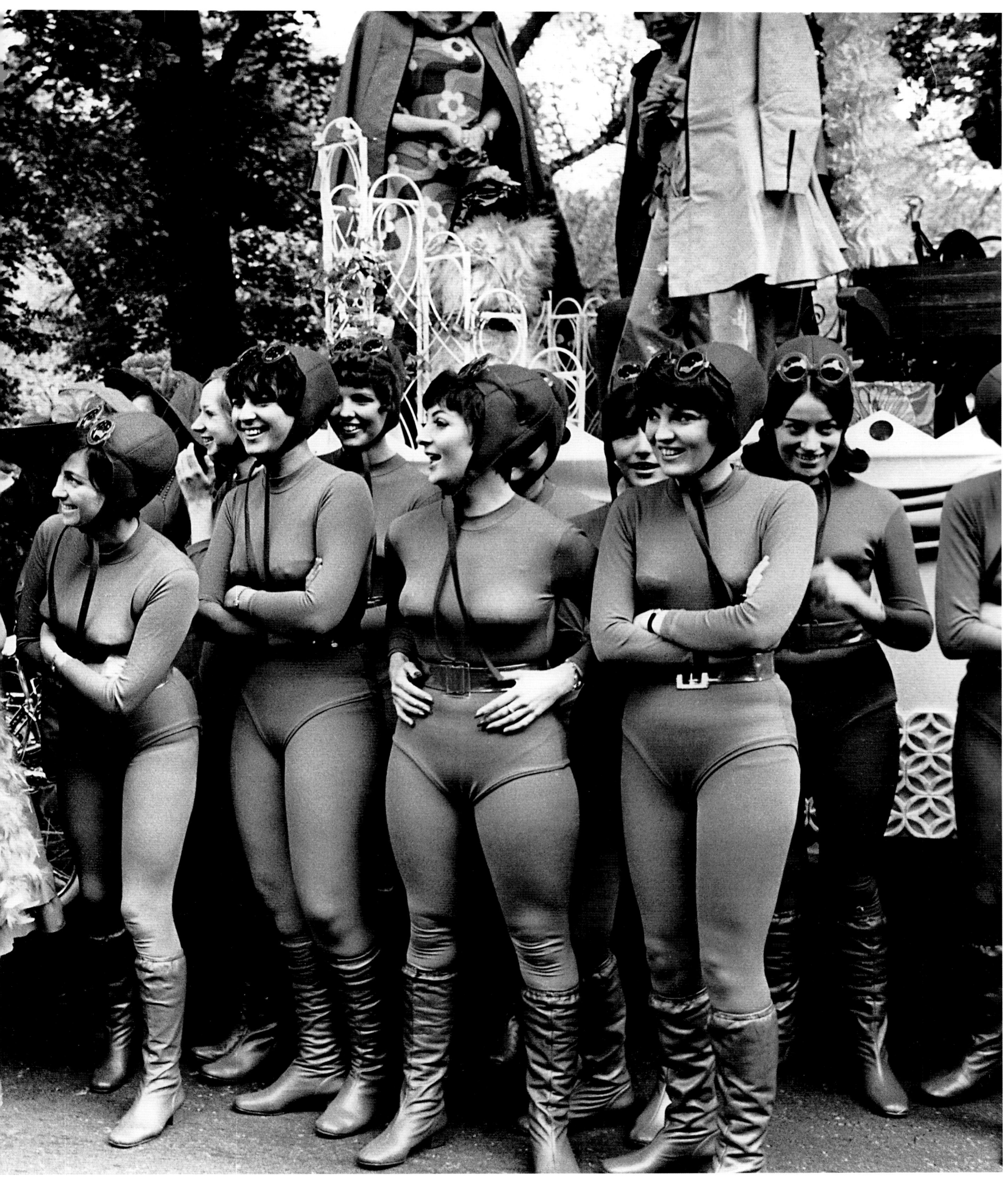

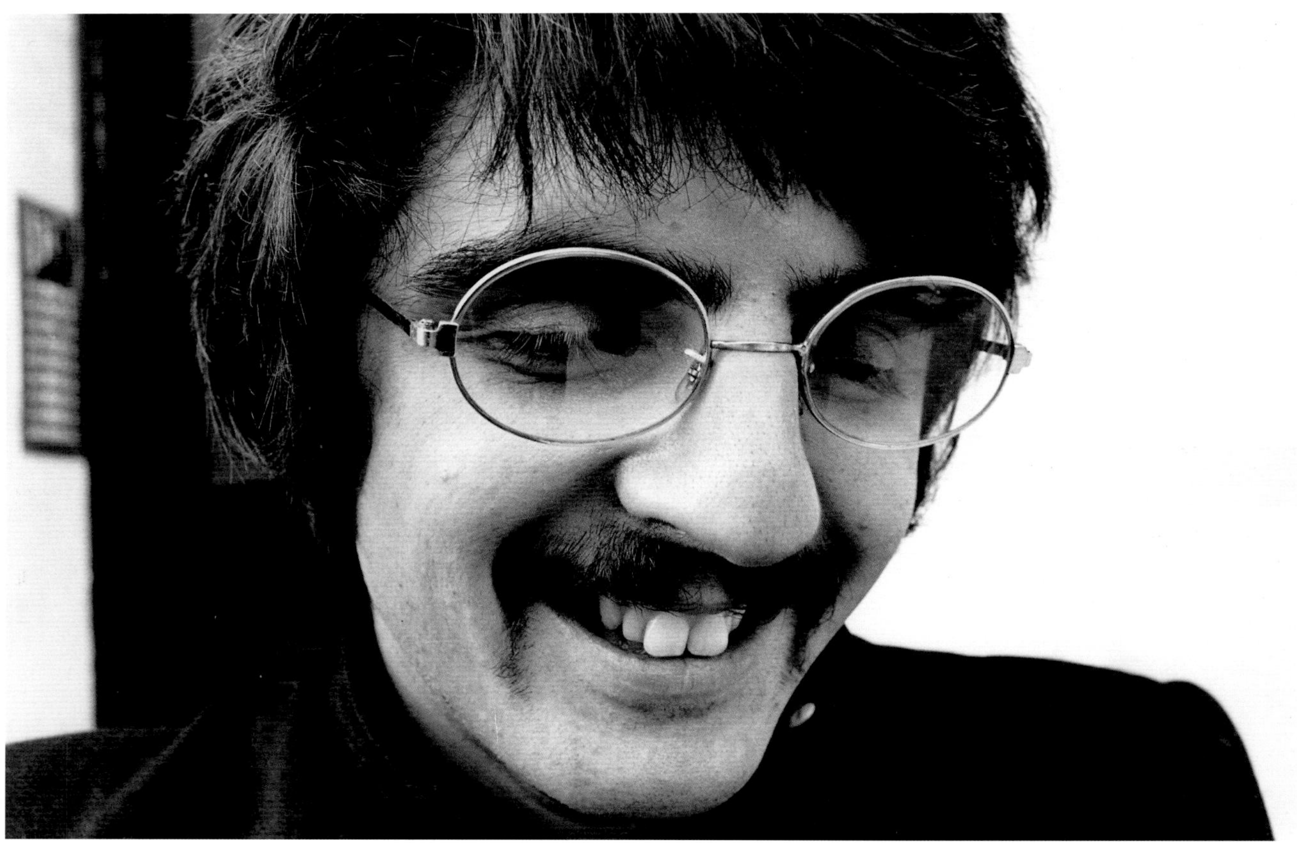

The Giocondo look – Harry, Hyde Park

Reluctant debutante – Miss Selfridges, Hyde Park, 1968

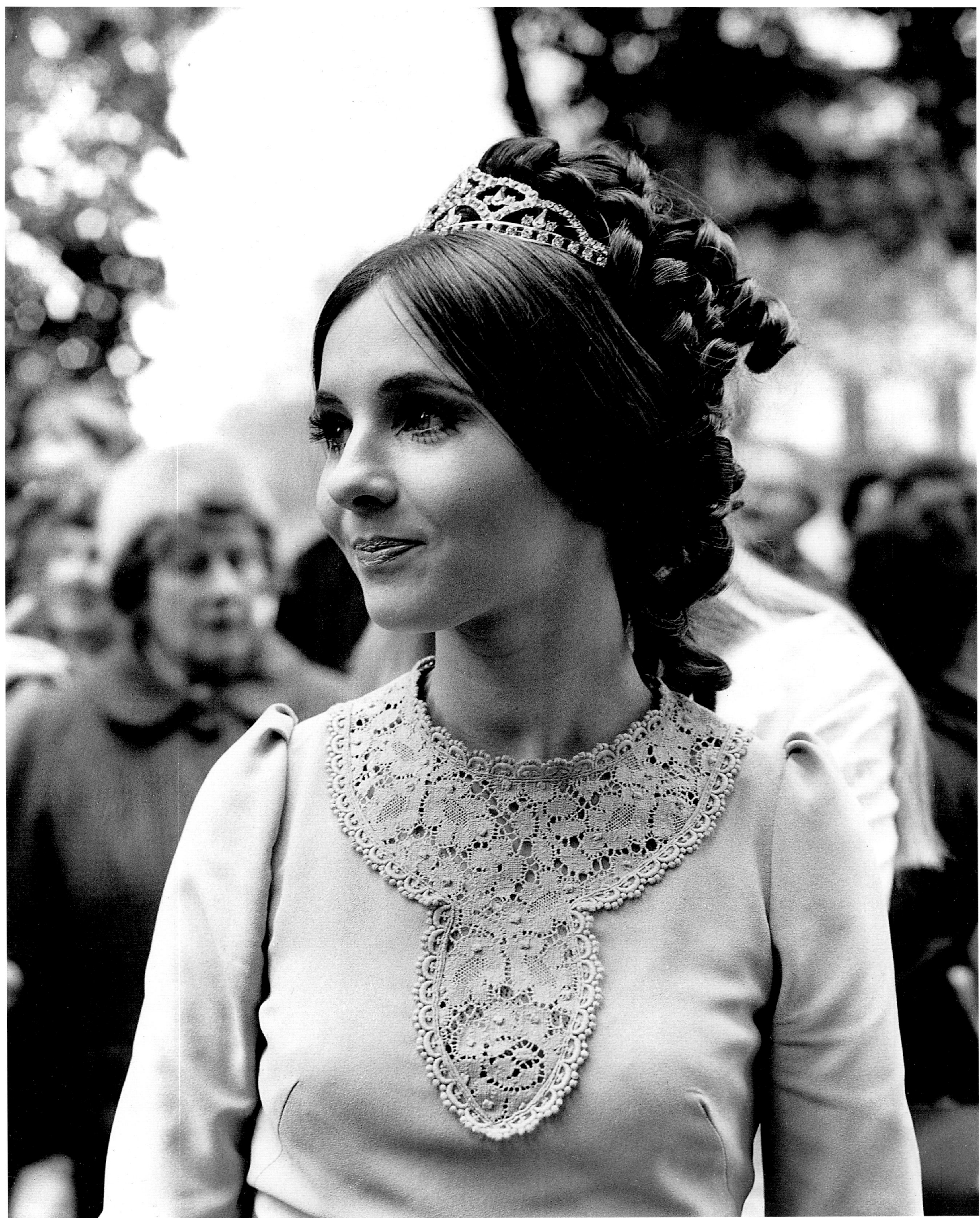

Station of the heart – Tottenham Court Tube Station, 1967

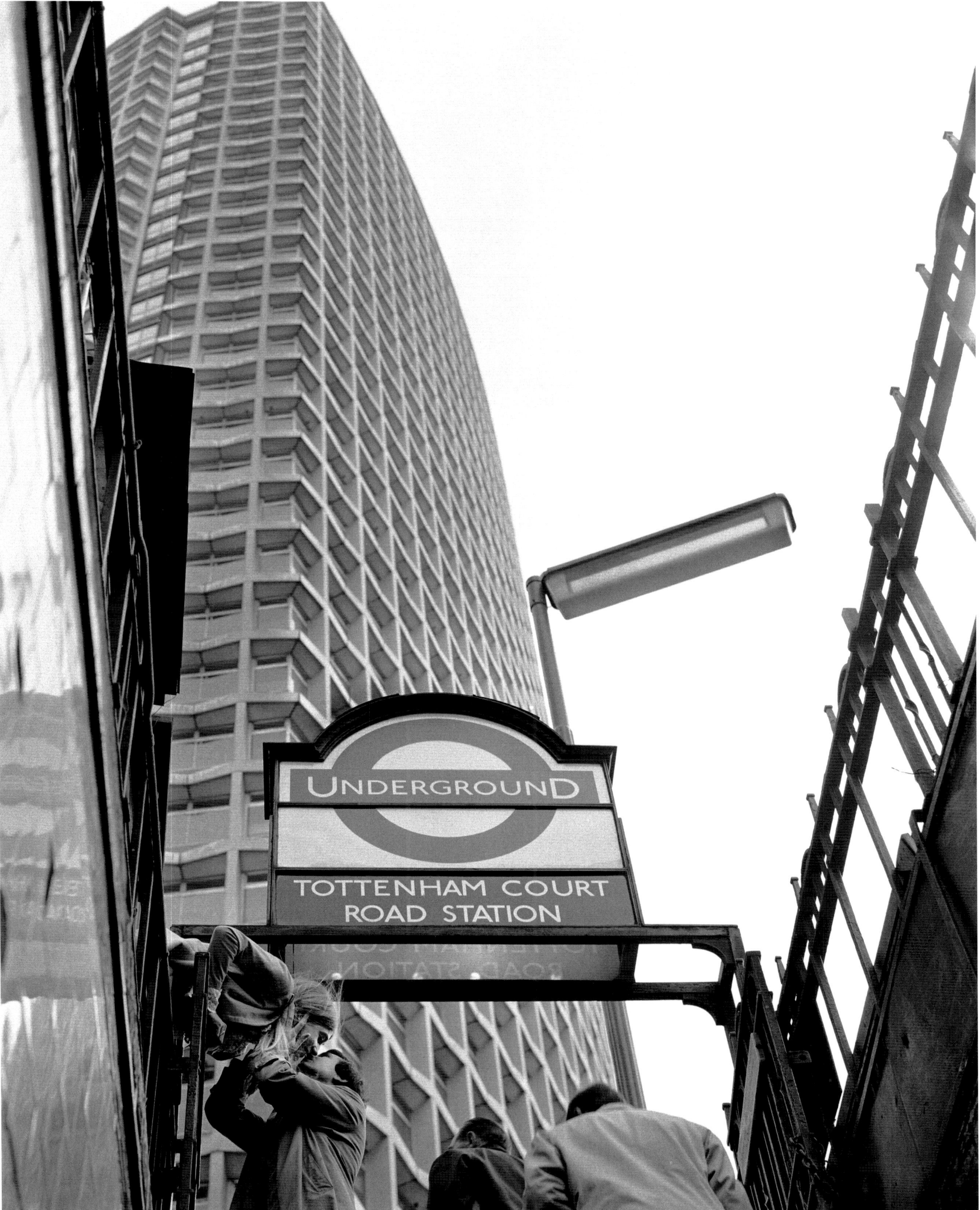
UNDERGROUND
TOTTENHAM COURT
ROAD STATION

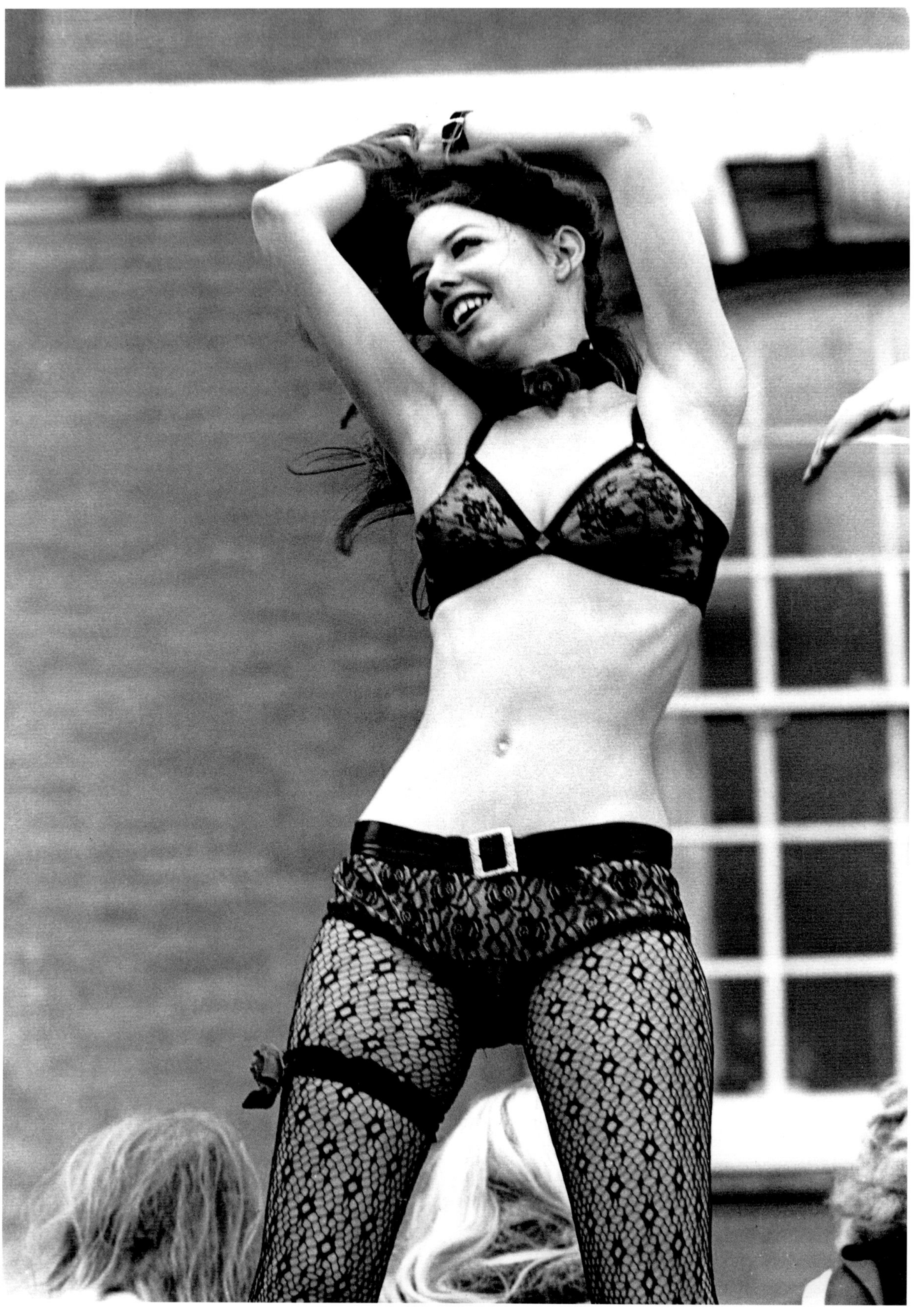

I kept my smile for you – Student Carnival Chelsea, 1964

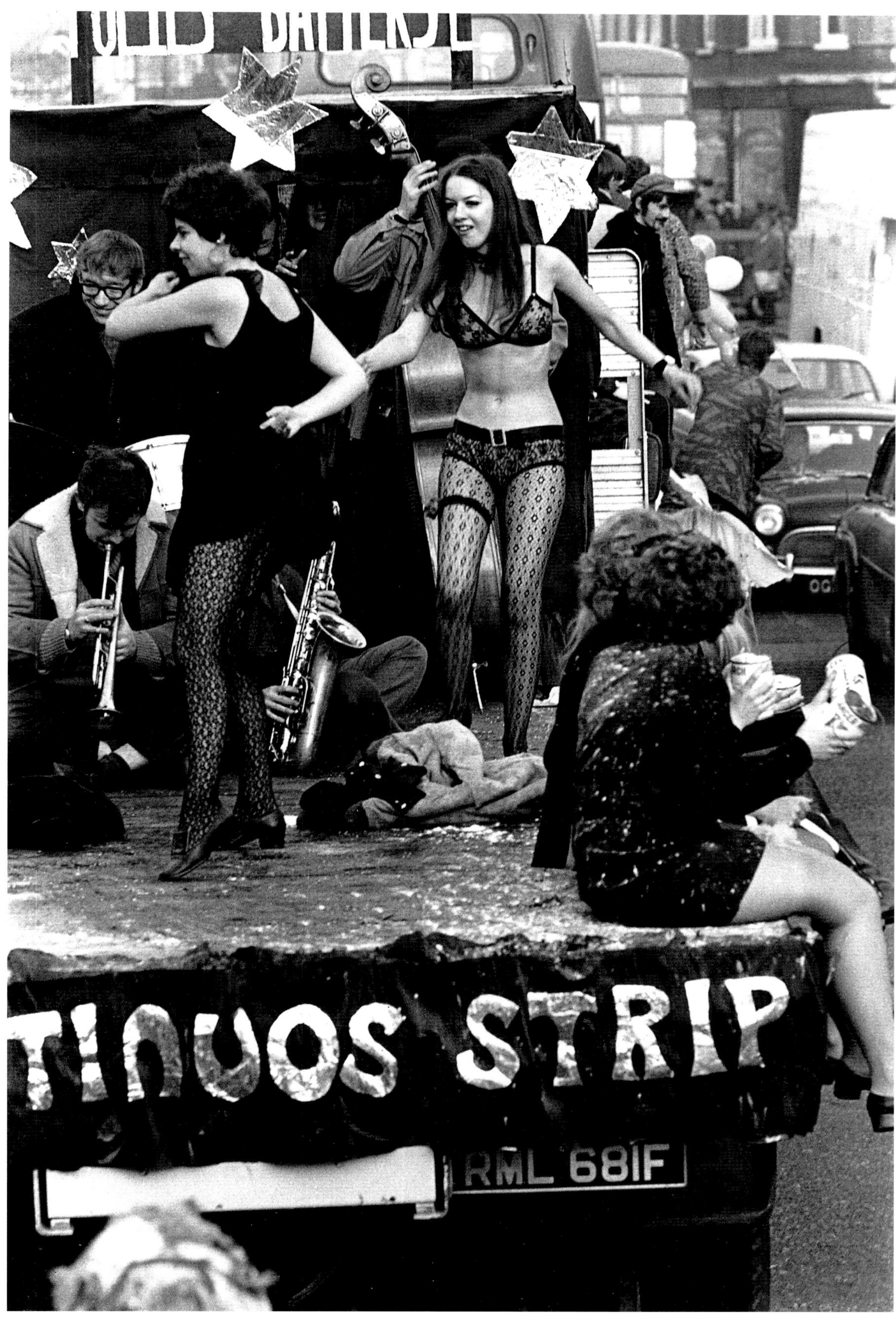

Rain, rain stay away – Student Carnival Chelsea, 1964

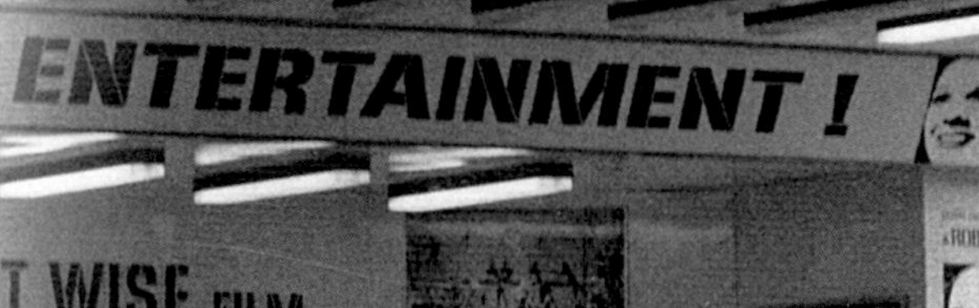
ENTERTAINMENT !
ERT WISE FILM
JULIE ANDREWS

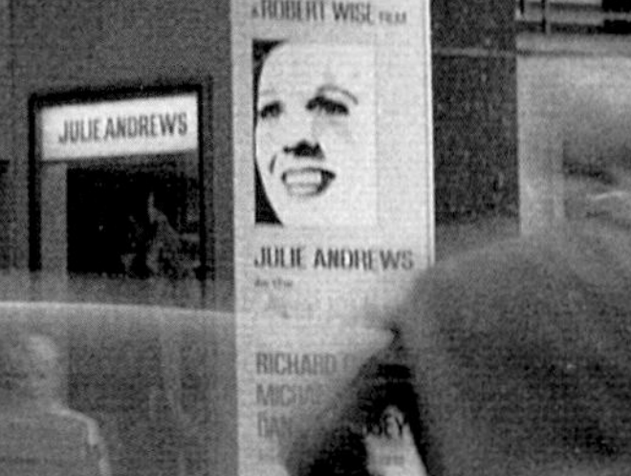
A ROBERT WISE FILM
JULIE ANDREWS

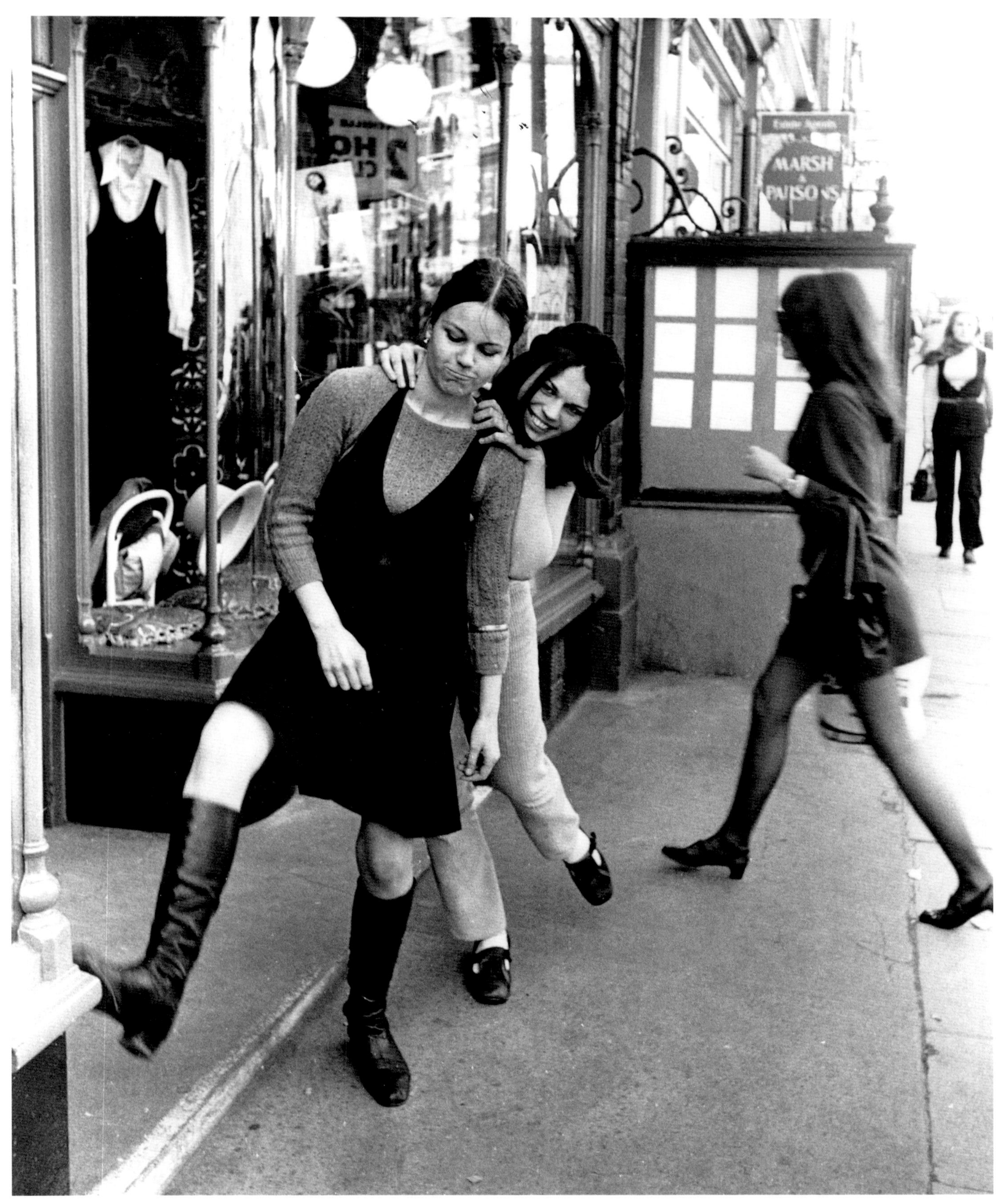

Lost in London Town – Dominion Theatre, West End

Having Fun – Biba Boutique, Church Street, Kensington, 1967

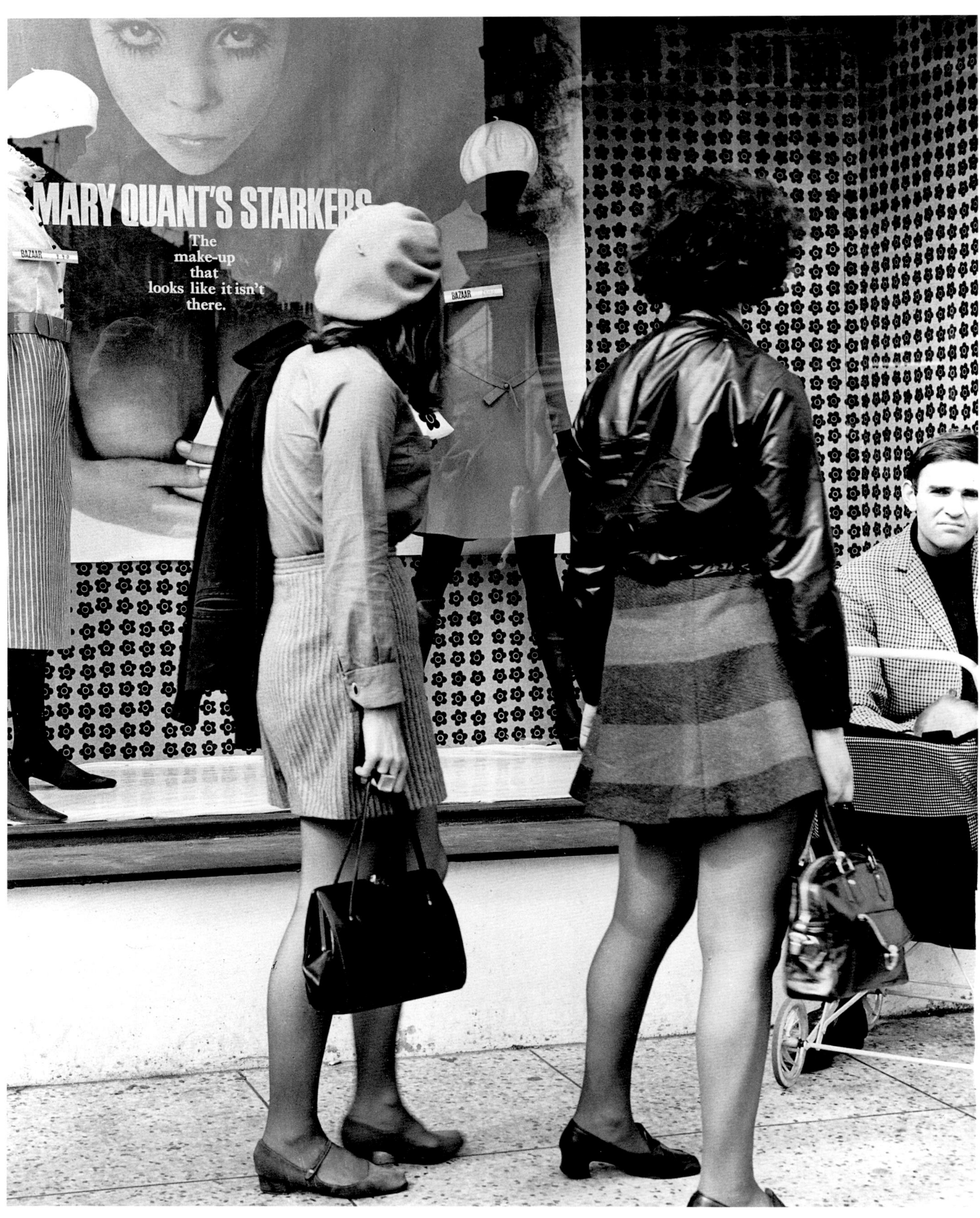

The "In" Look – Mary Quant Boutique, King's Road, 1966

Hold it please – Portobello Road

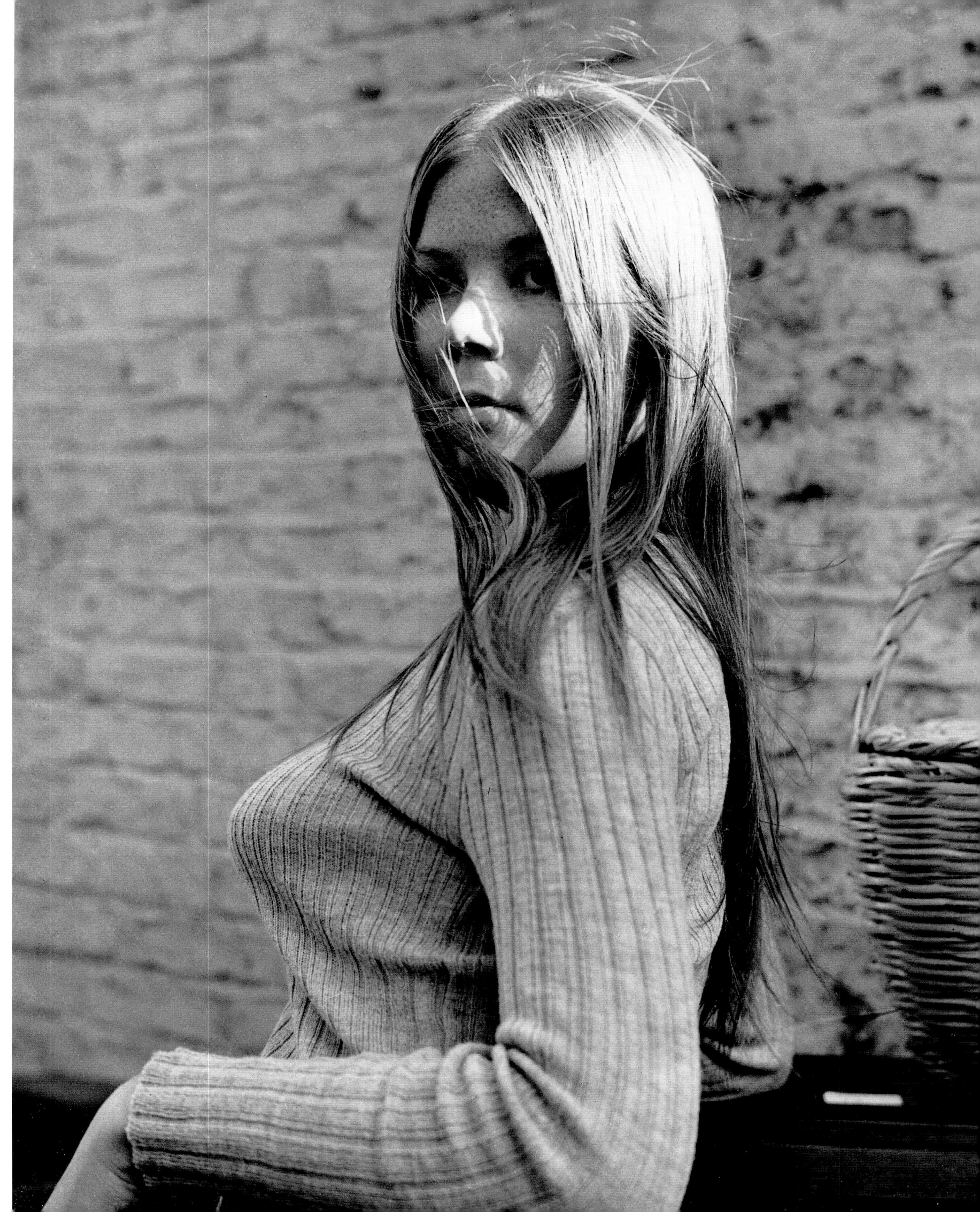

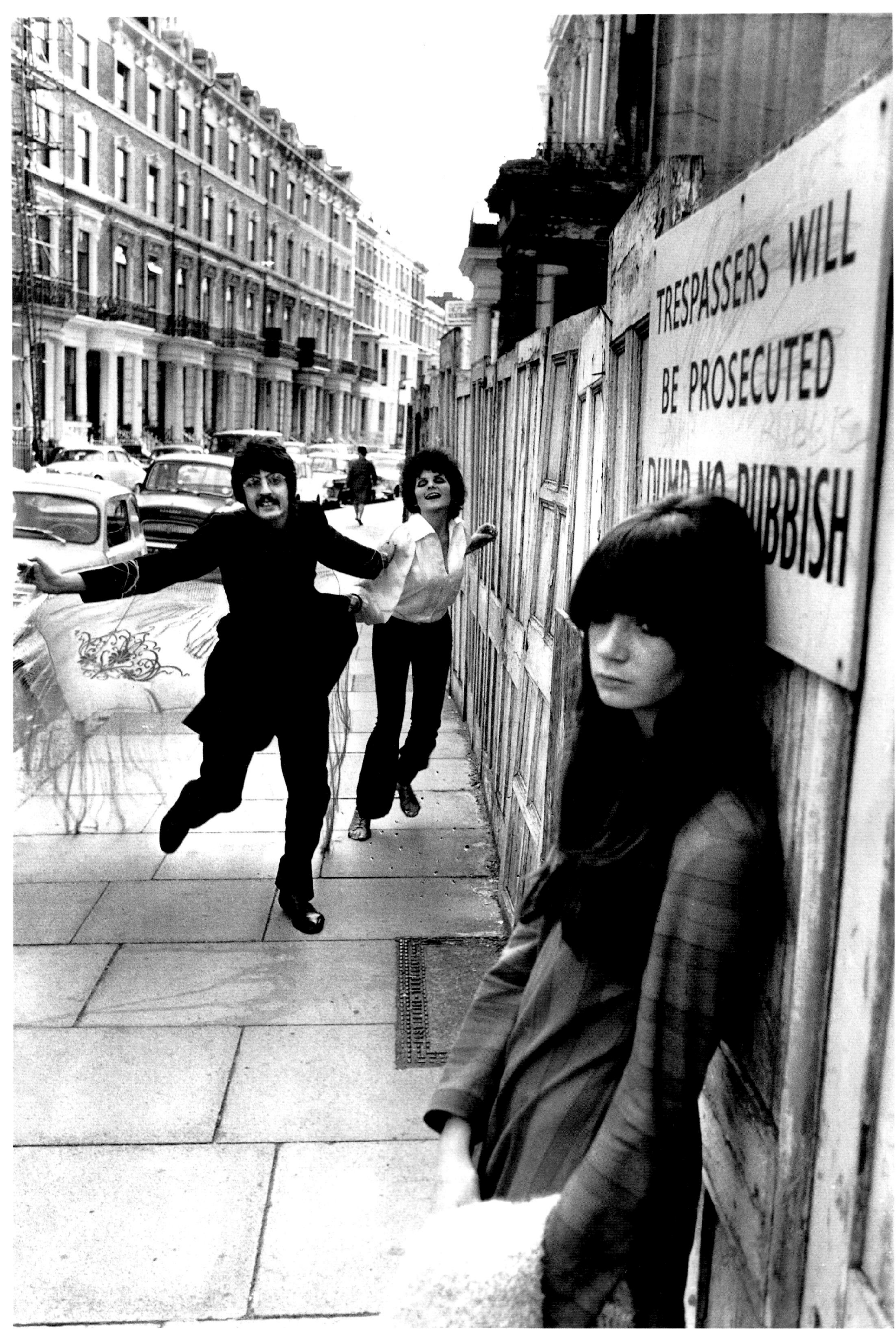

The Joy of Living – Hogarth Road, Earl's Court

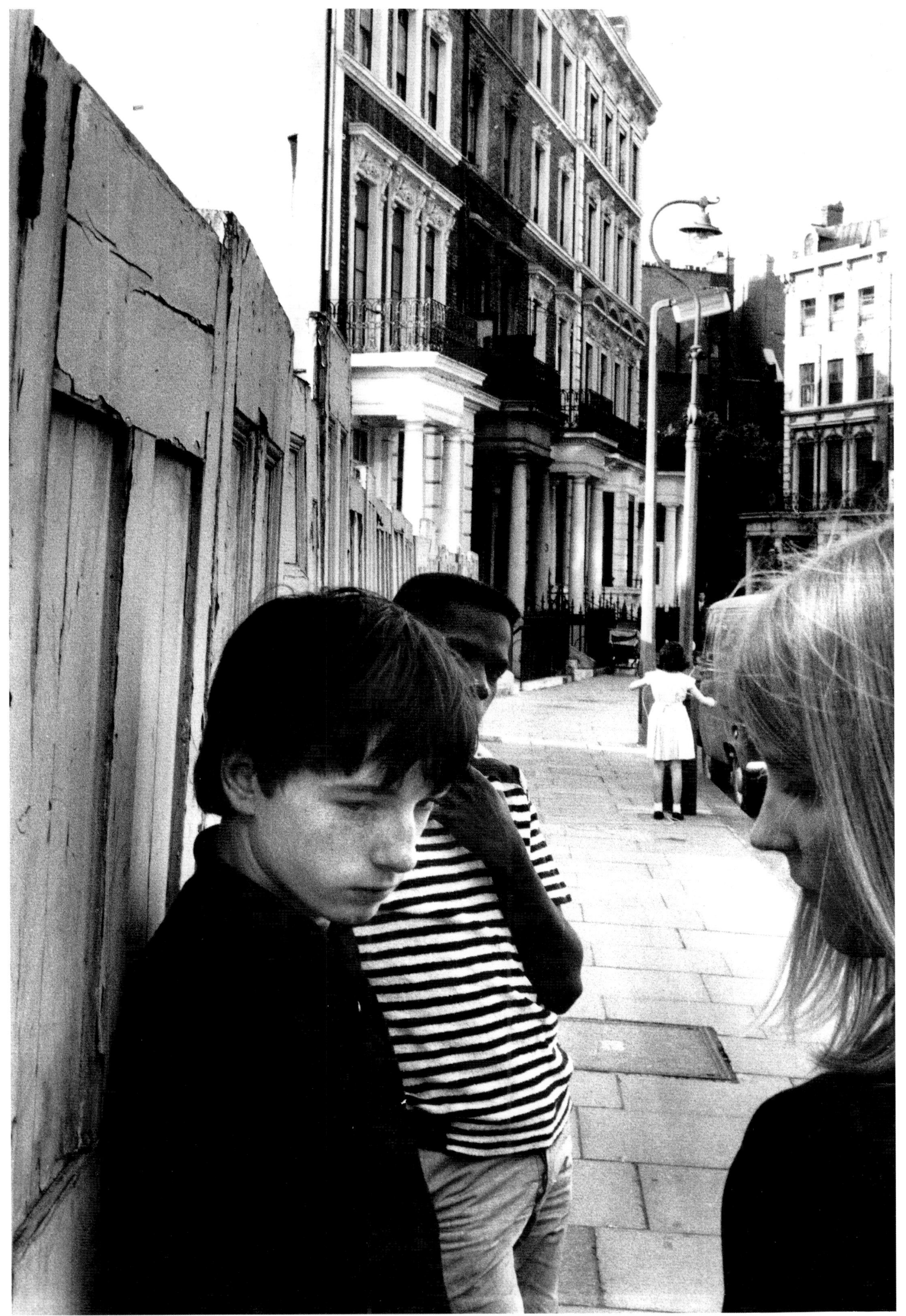

Distances – Hogarth Road, Earl's Court

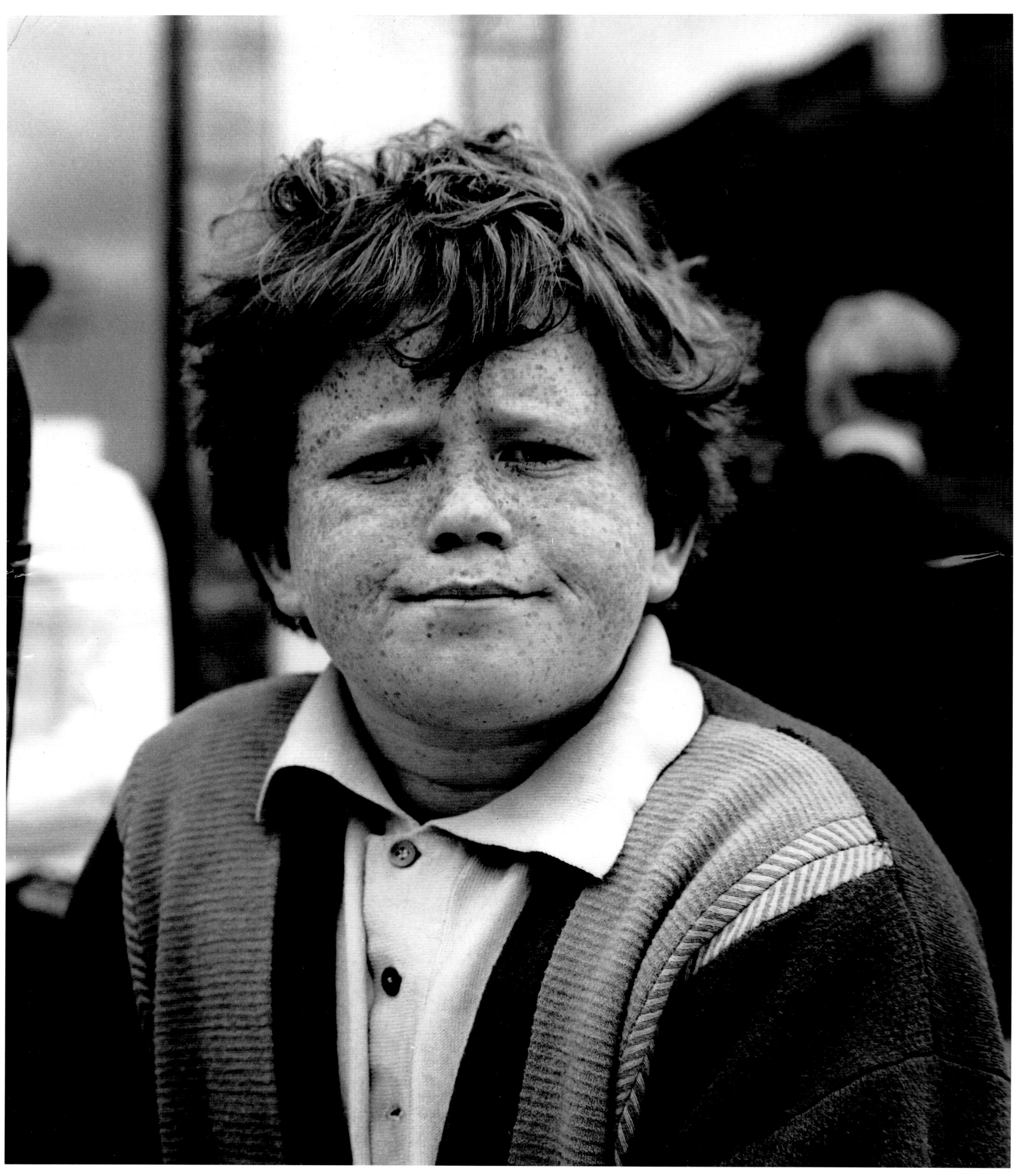

Isn't life strange? – Stallholder, Portobello Market

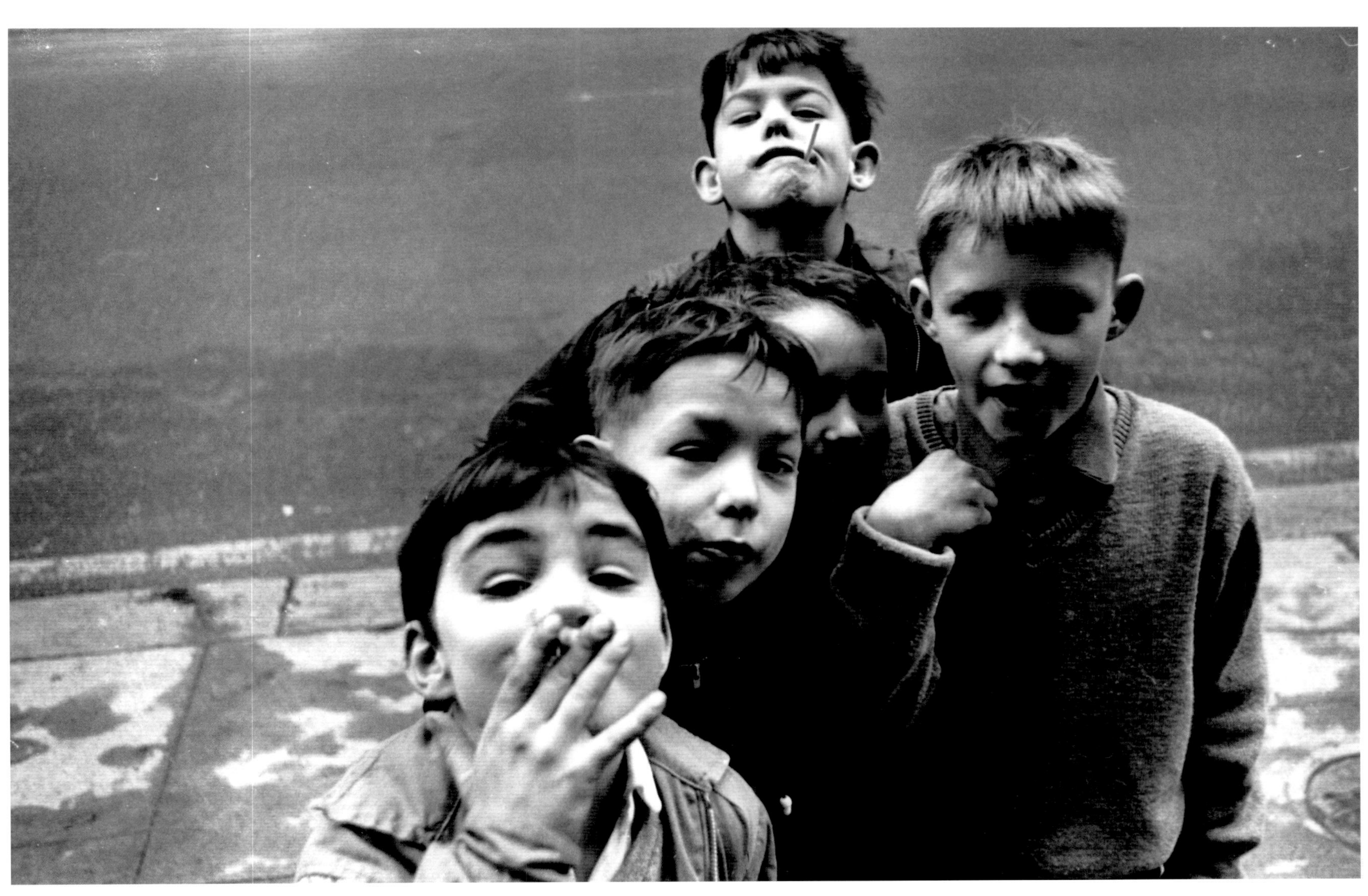

Forbidden Fruit – Street Kids, London East End

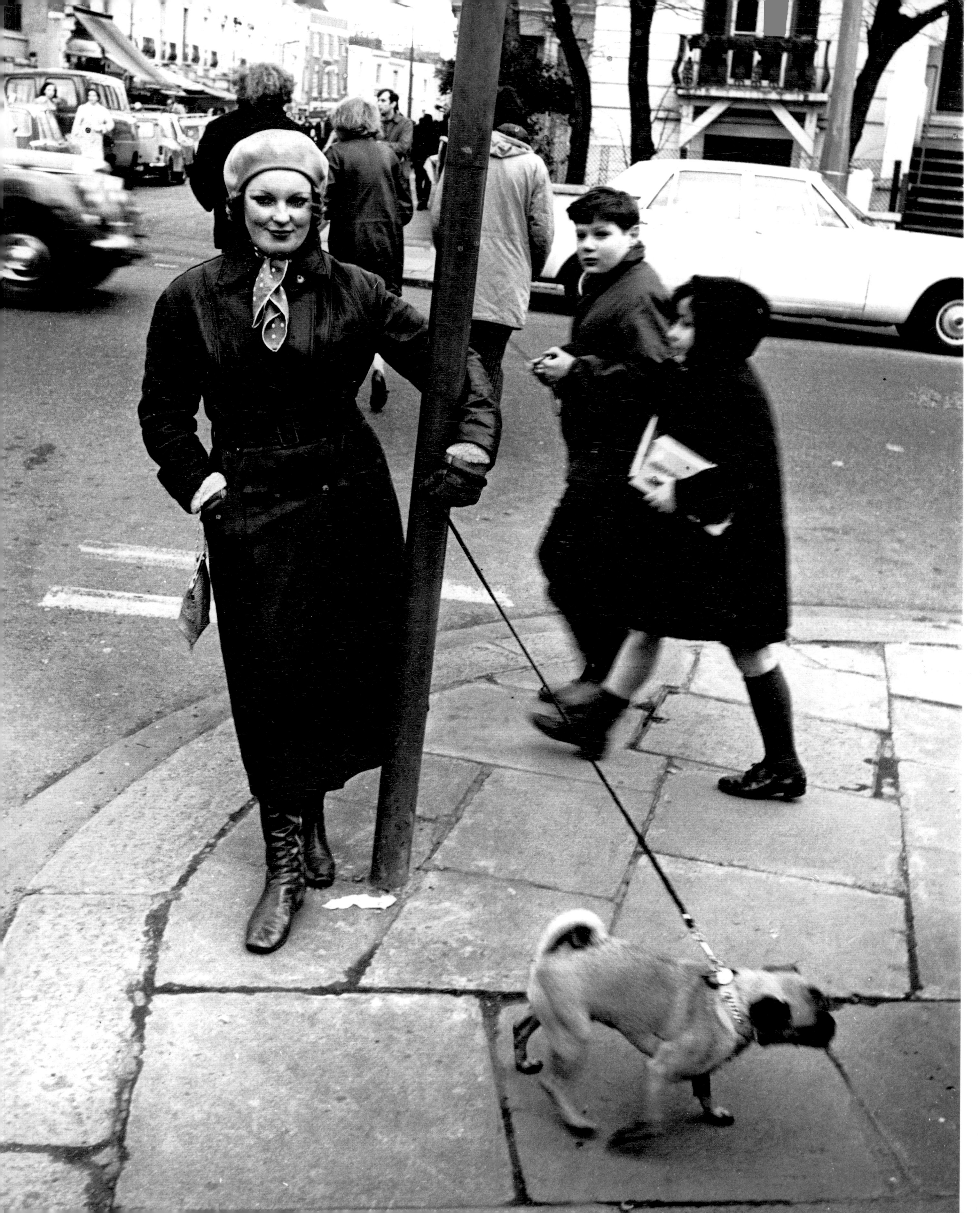

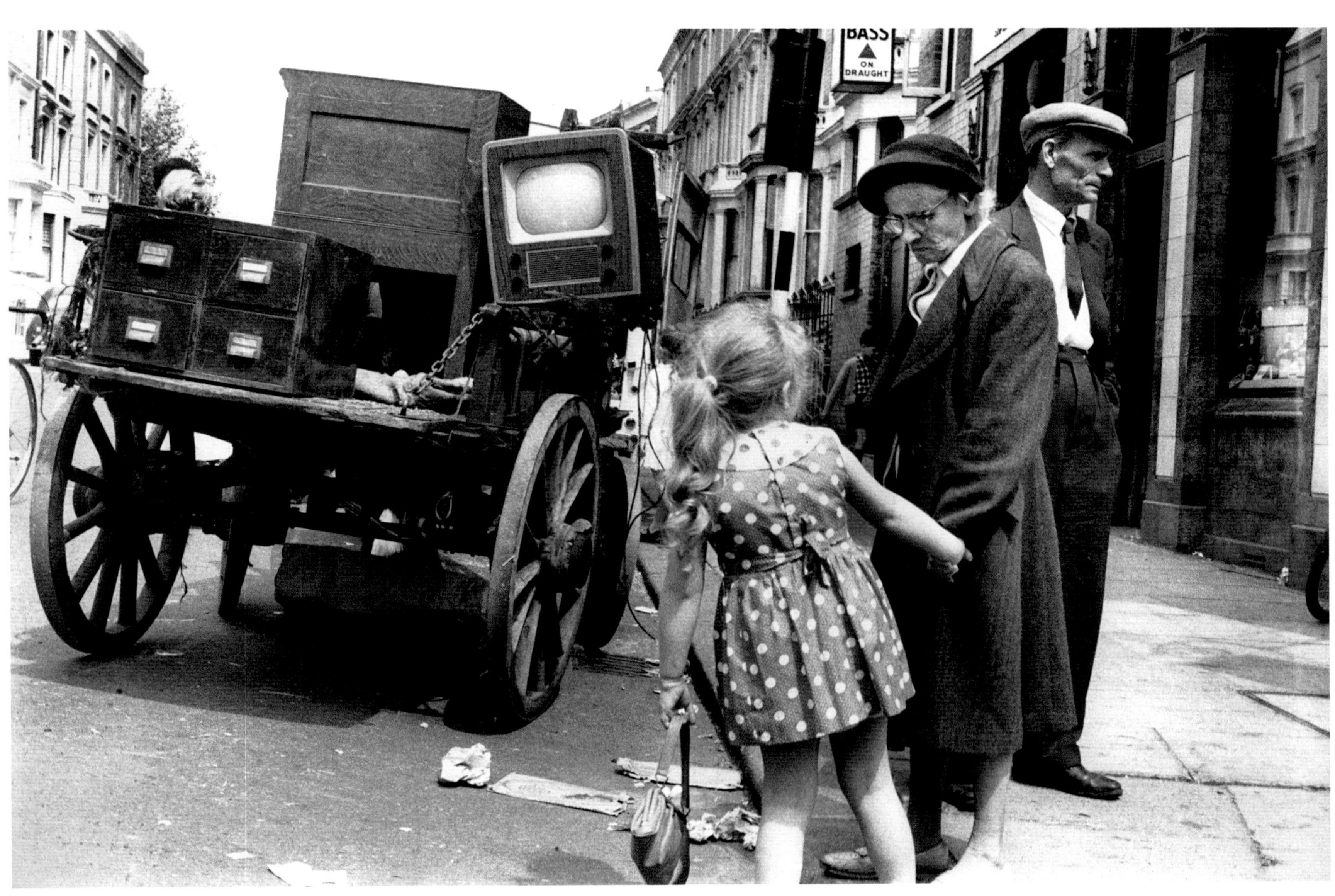

Saturday morning – Portobello Road

Where time stood still – near Portobello Road, 1963

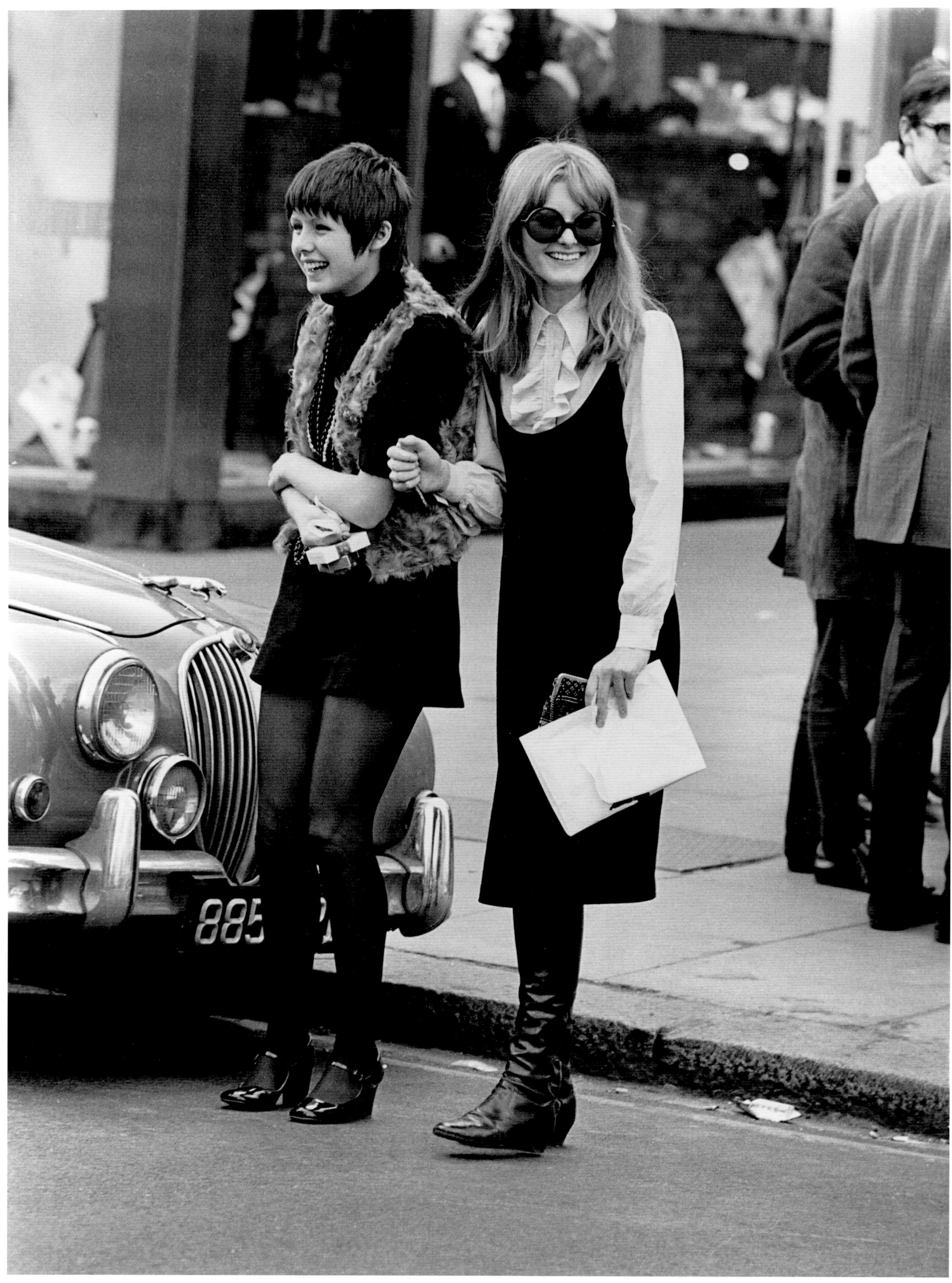

What is in, What is out – King's Road, Chelsea

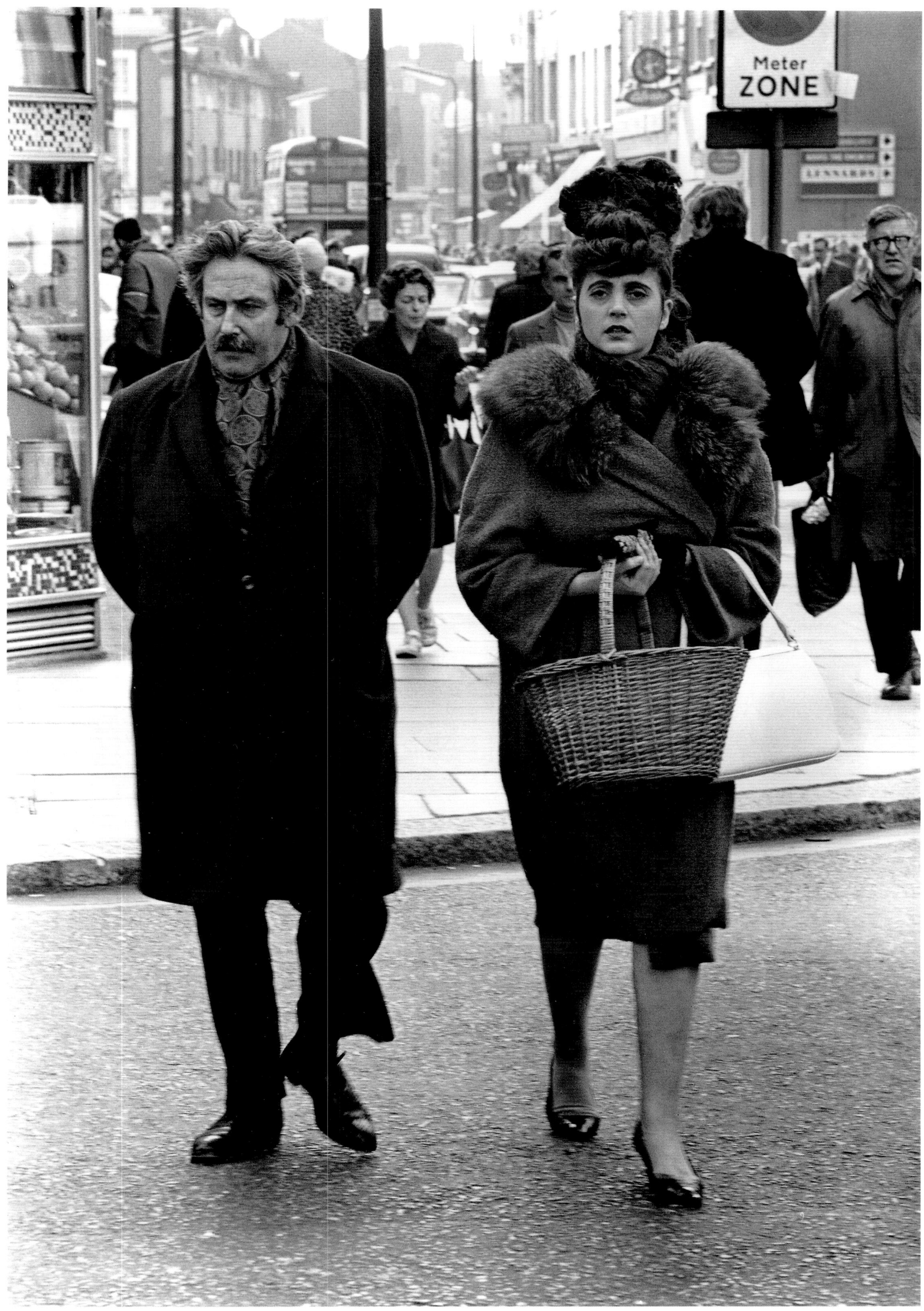

Keeping up appearances – King's Road, Chelsea

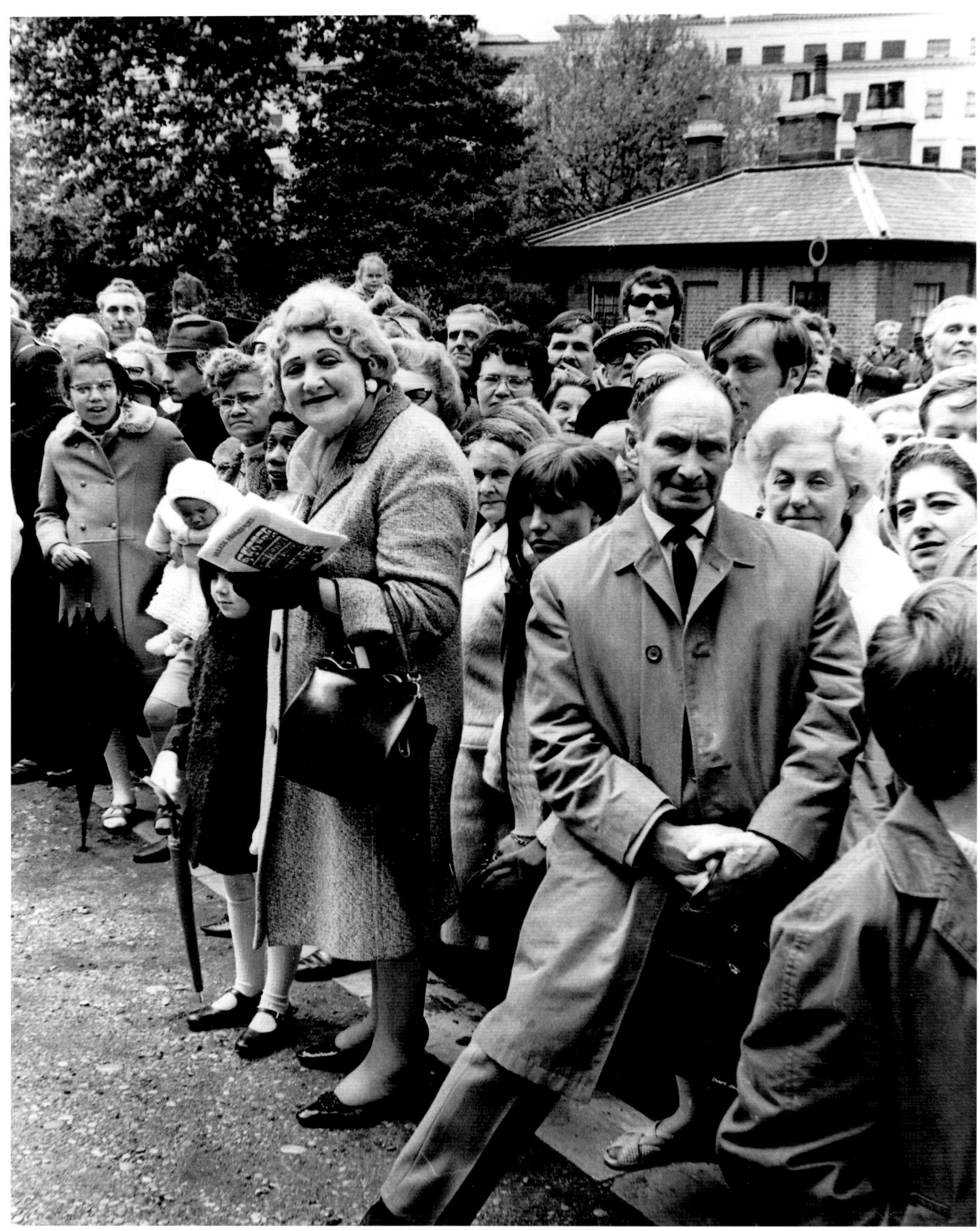

What's around the corner – Near Marble Arch

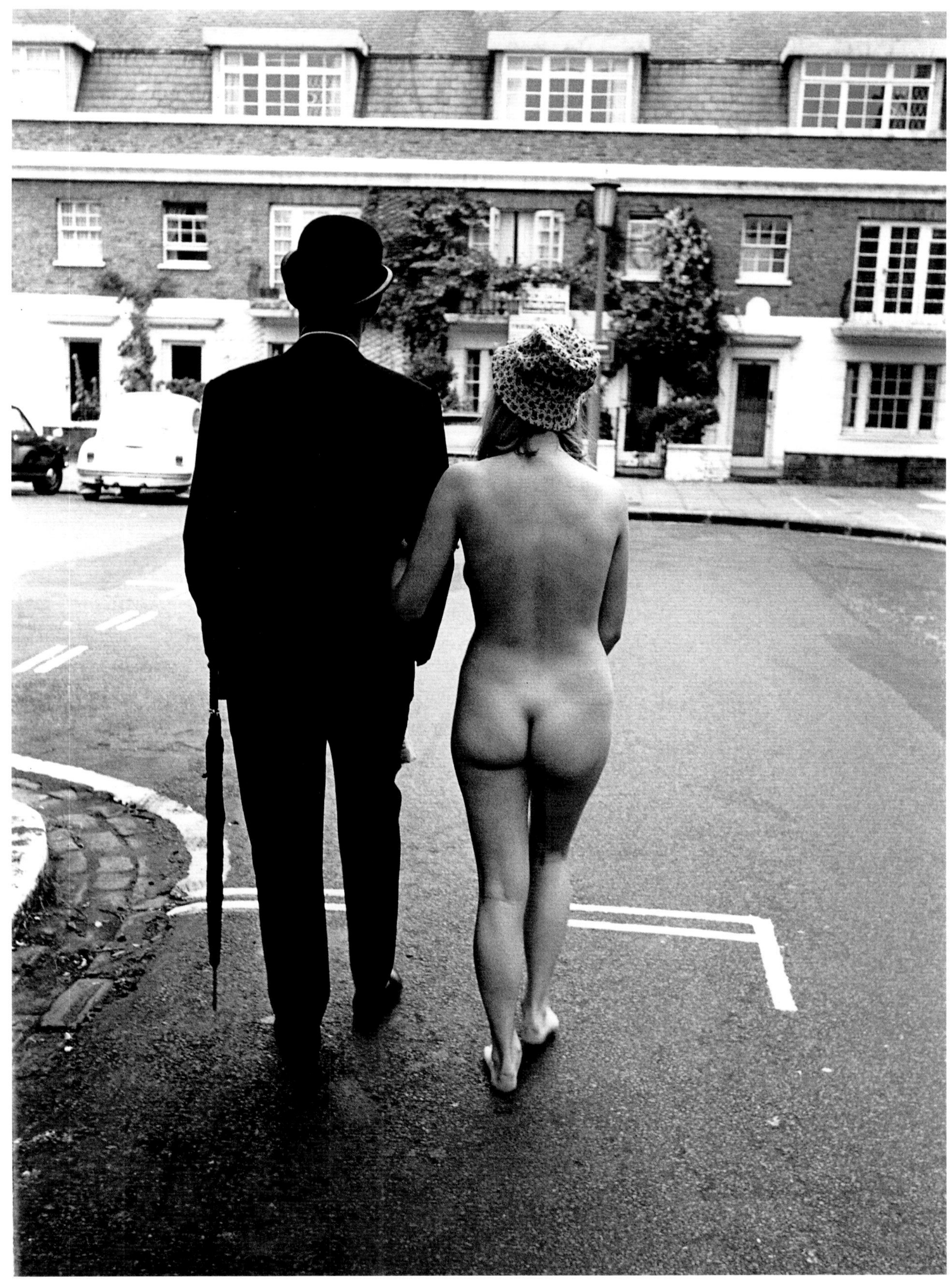

My gentle lady

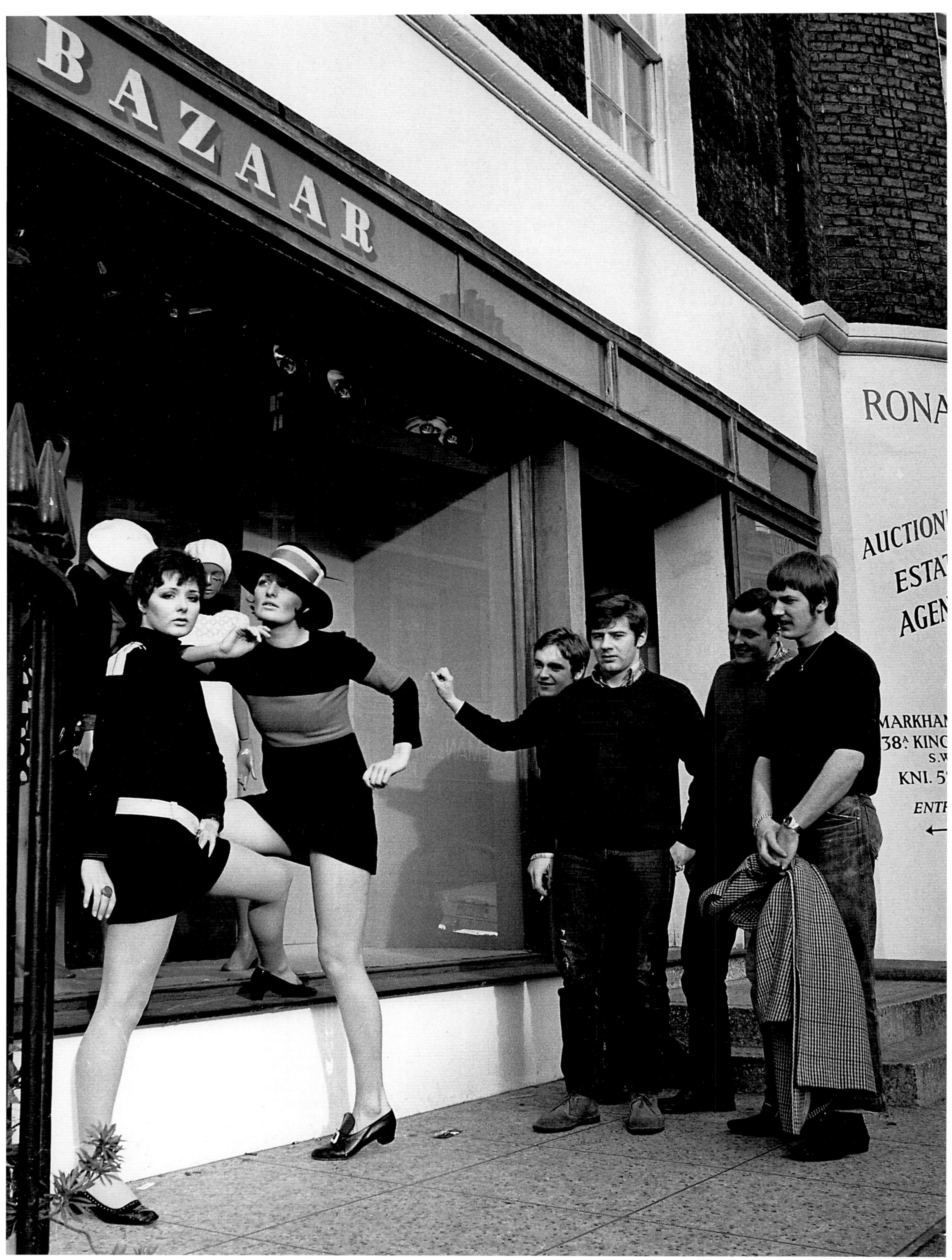
BAZAAR
RONA
AUCTION
ESTAT
AGEN

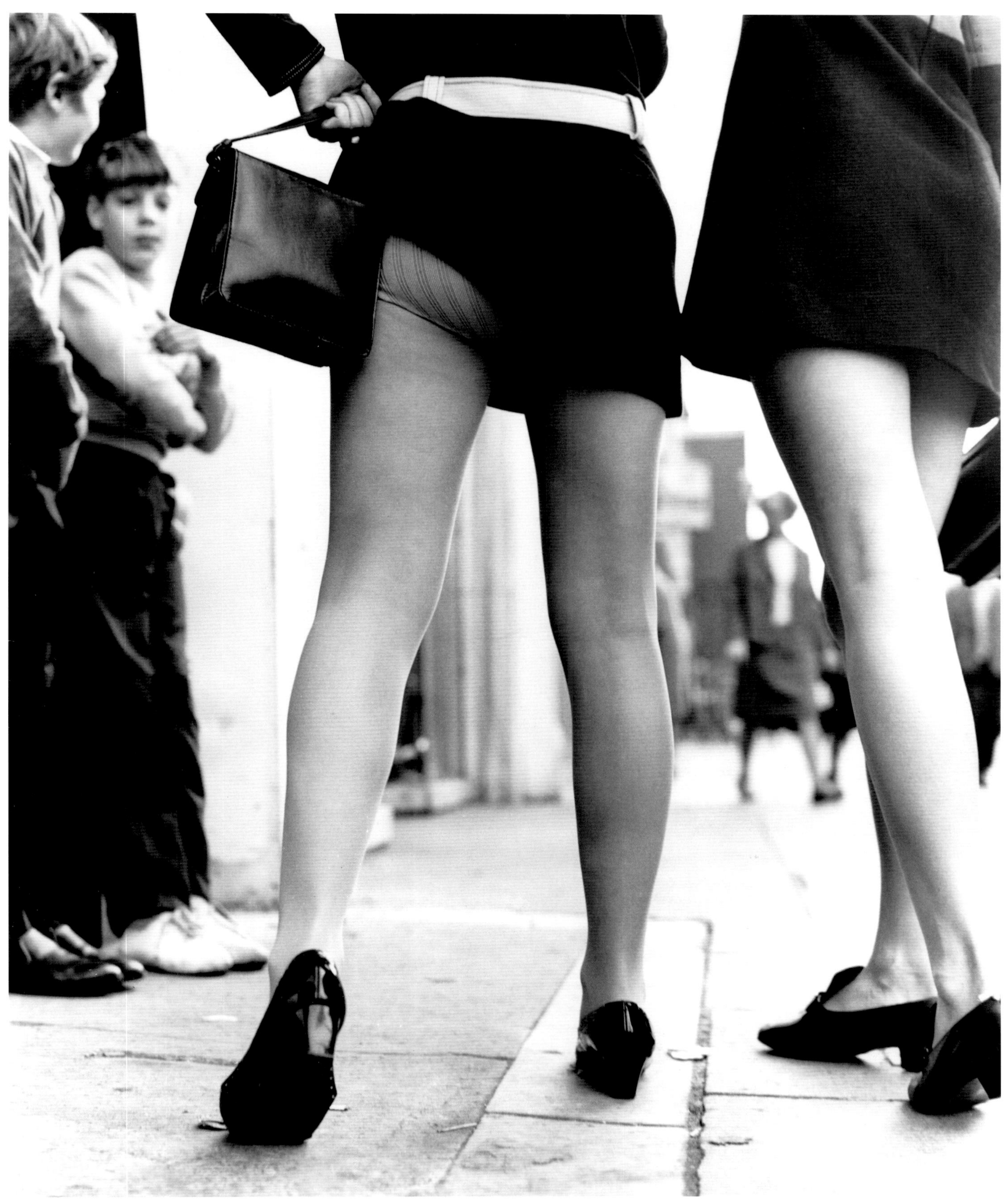

Reconnaissance – Bazaar Boutique, King's Road, 1967

My heart leaps up when I behold – King's Road

What do you think – Lincoln Street, Chelsea

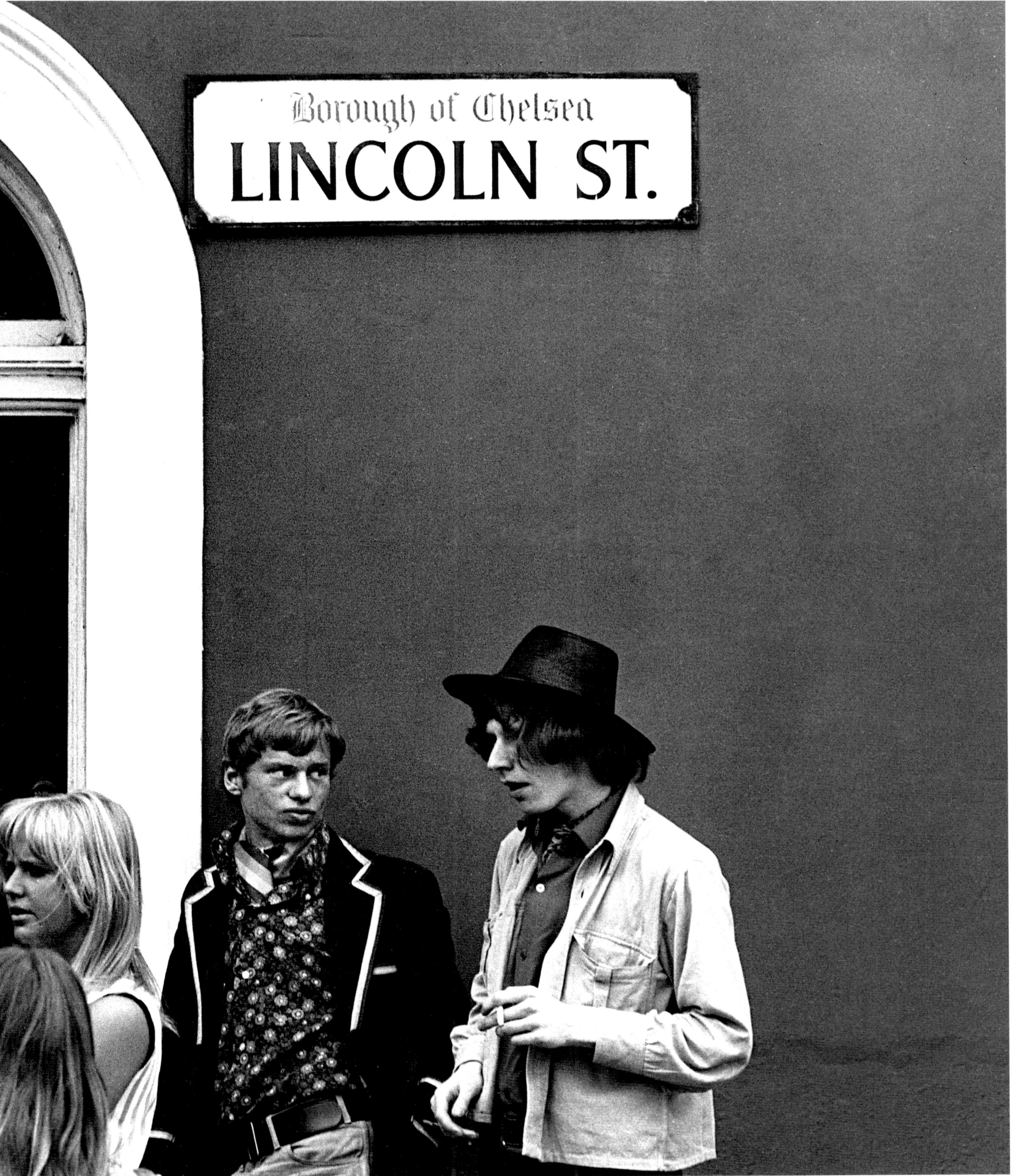
Borough of Chelsea
LINCOLN ST.

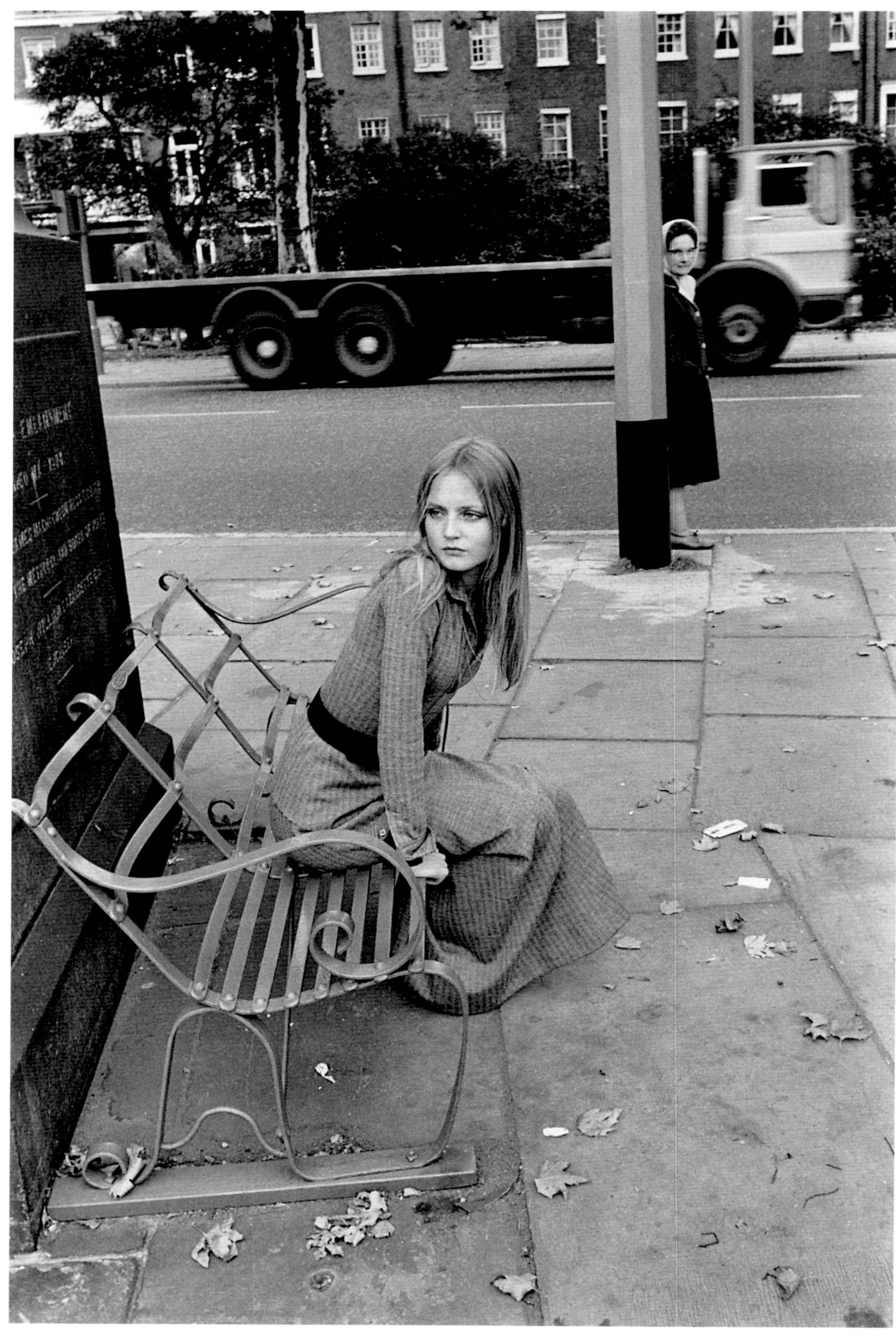

Beyond the yellow brick road – Ingrid Boulting, Biba Boutique model

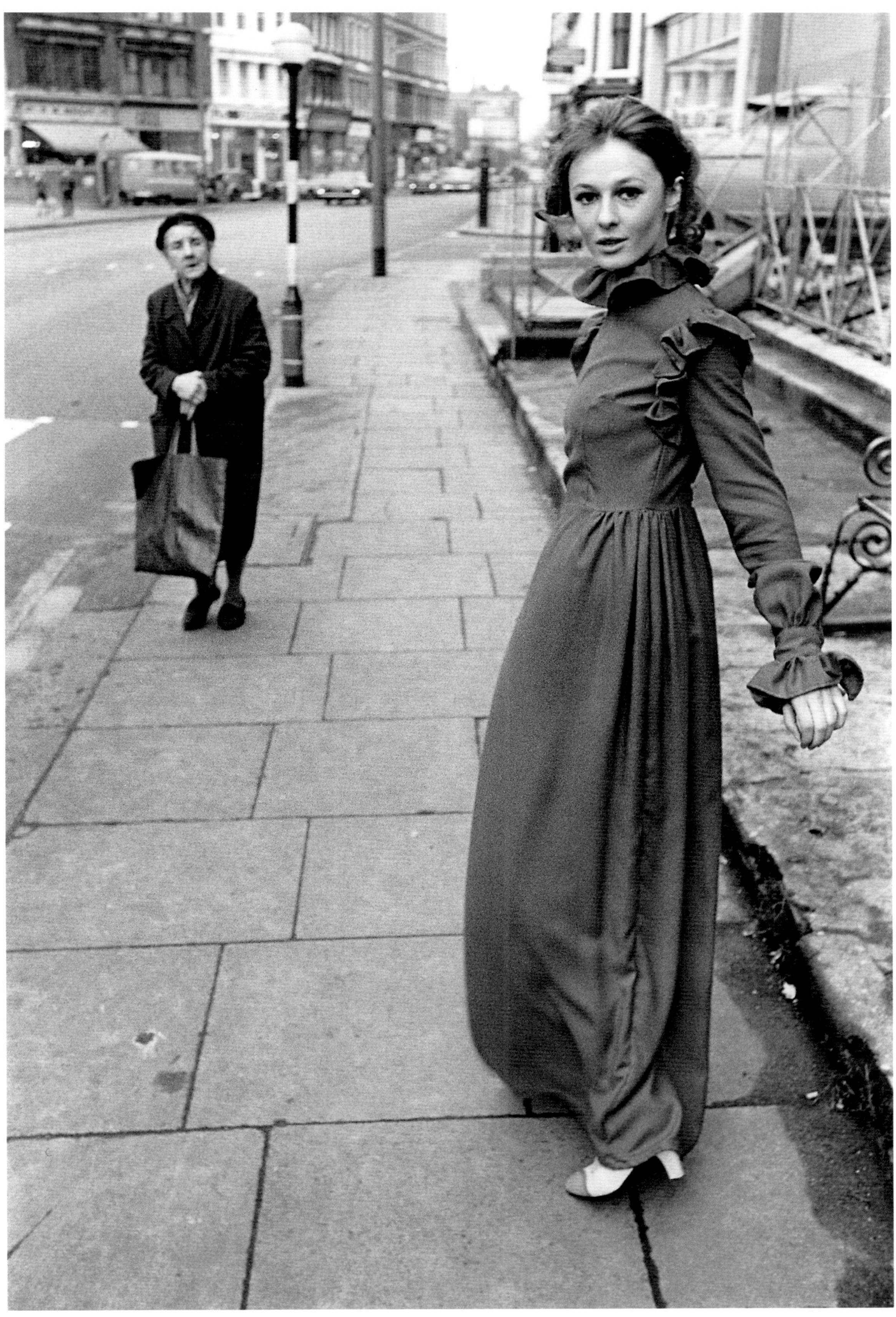

Generation gap – Jeanette Lang, Fulham Road

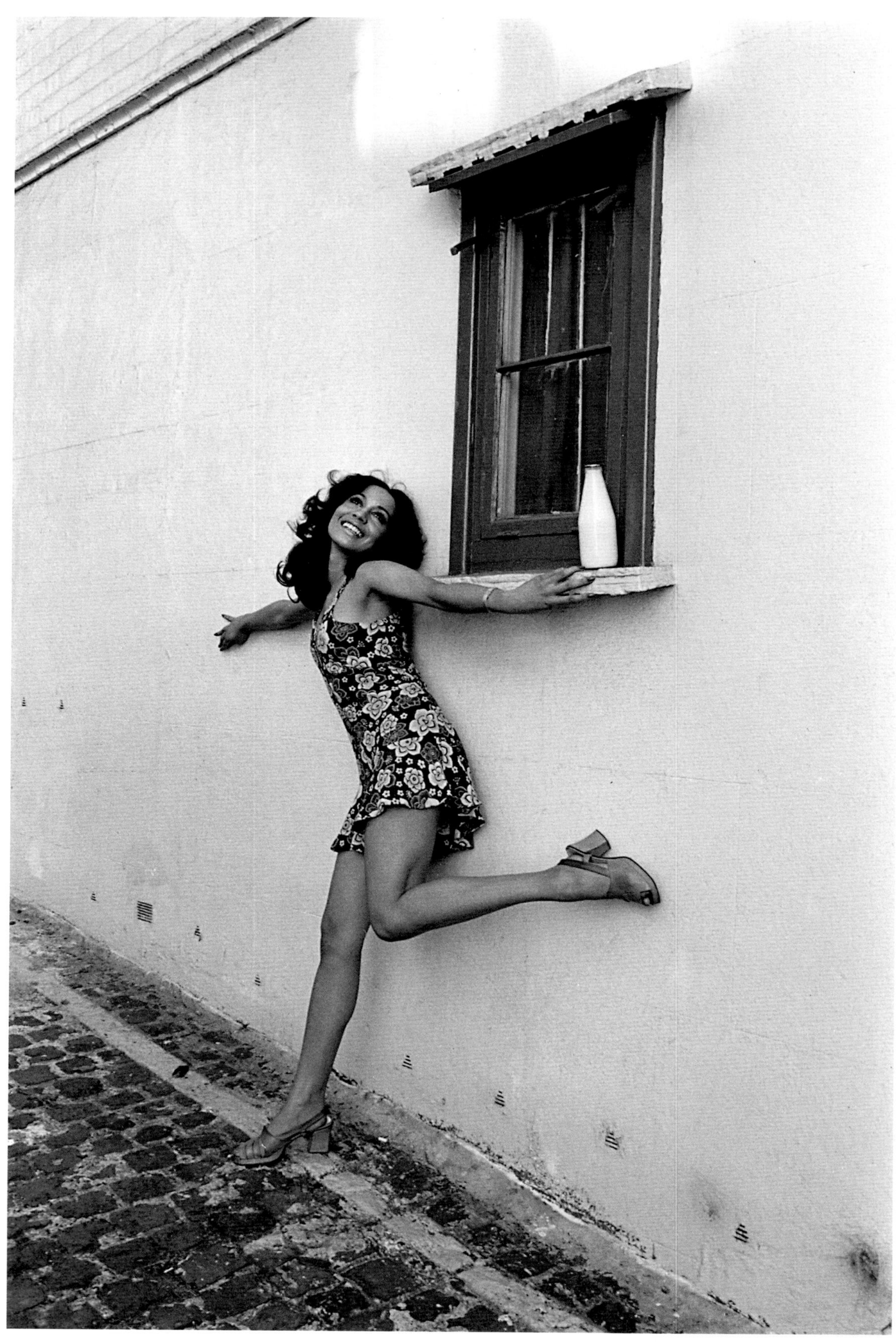

En Vogue – Hylette Adolphe, actress, Knightsbridge

A familiar face passing by – Ingrid Boulting

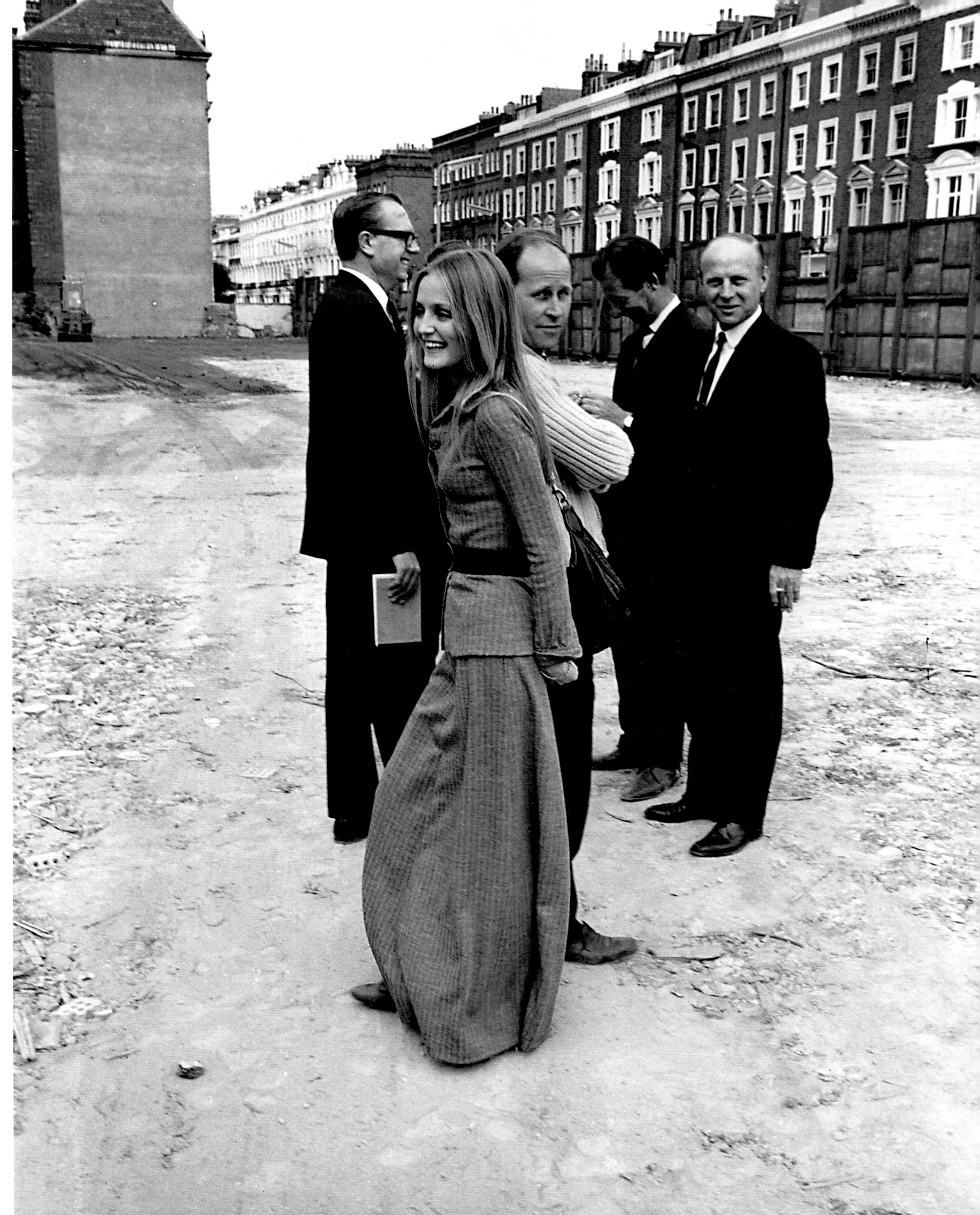

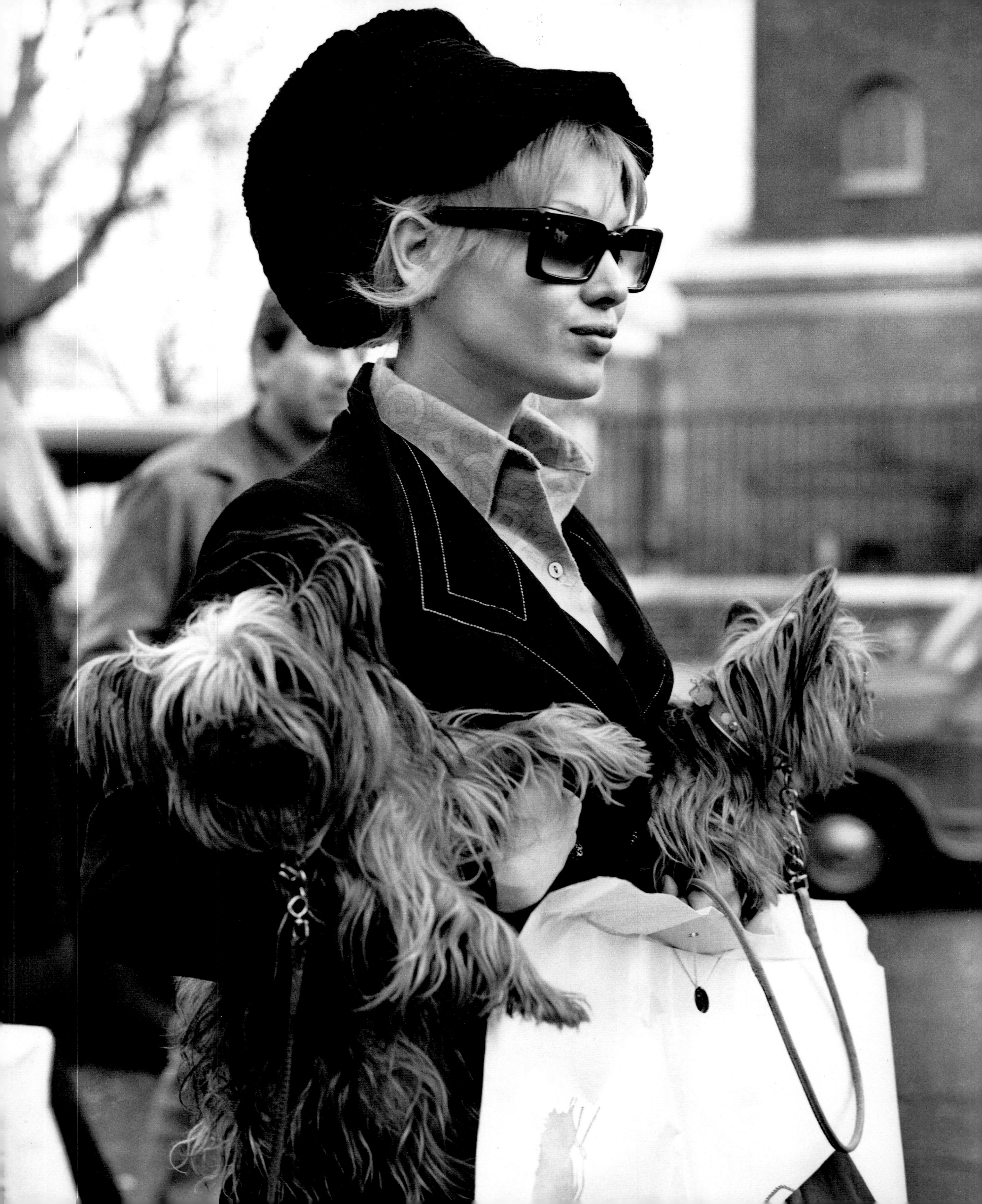

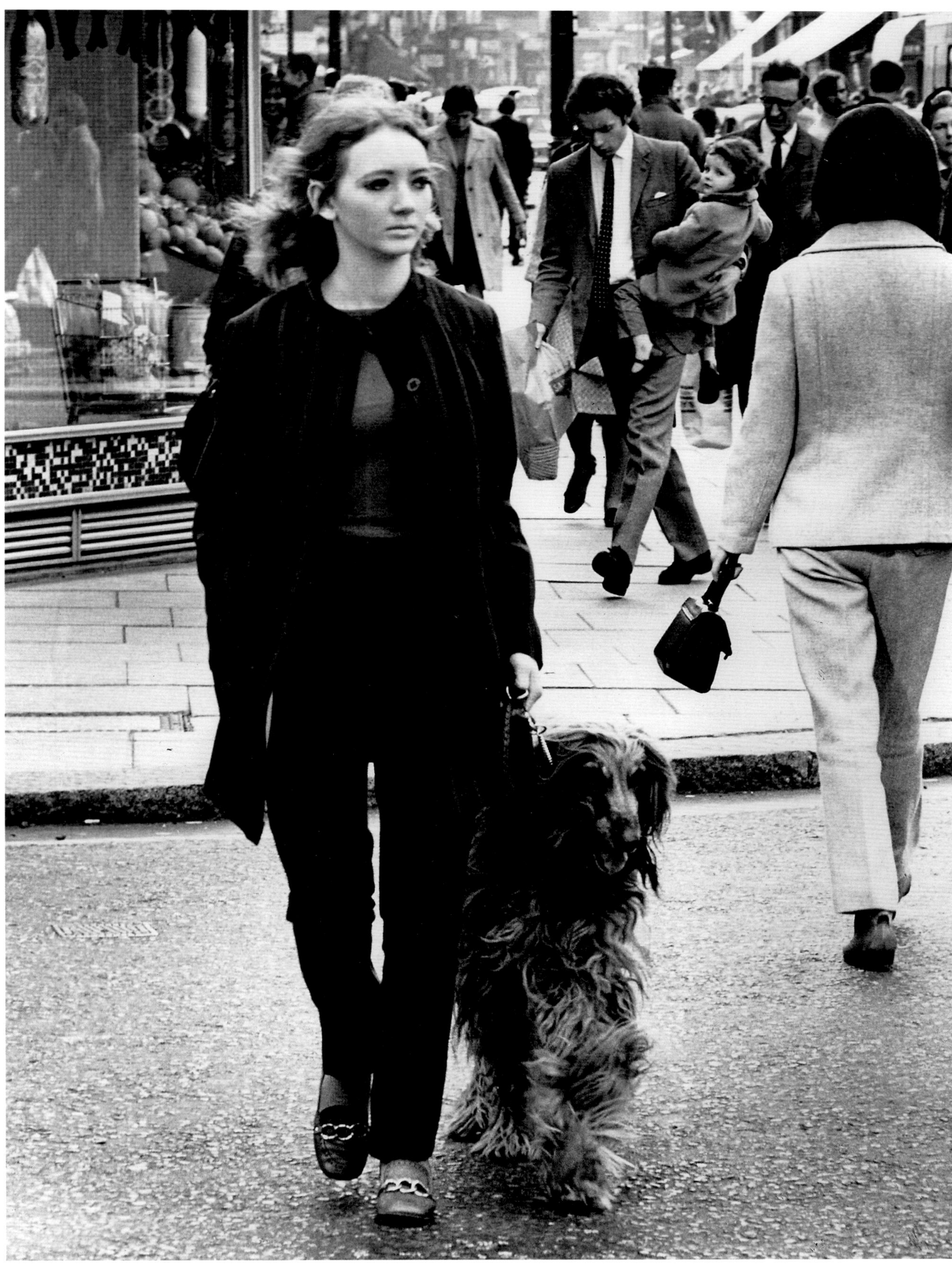

Puppy Love – King's Road, Chelsea, 1966

All you need is love (and a dog)

Fred Marshall, Entrepreneur and Friend

Fred Marshall, an American living in London, film director and generous supporter of the arts, was in his own way a controversial figure. He was certainly not living on a shoestring. He had a way about him and was able to experiment with money and life. Fred was often on the brink of success, determined to achieve his goals—yet in my eyes his projects were often lacking the professional touch. Ideas often remained ideas, seldom seeing the light of the day. We had our differences, particularly in the pursuit of personal paths, but we enjoyed a good friendship.

Prior to writing his own movie script "The Free Life," Fred founded his own production company Fremar Film Productions. He loved films and music, and enjoyed dating young starlets and models.

Fred supported many artists including young musicians and photographers. I was the director and photographer of what I thought was a shoddily compiled photographic album titled *Chelsea Birds,* brimming with pretty girls parading Chelsea's King's Road on a Saturday morning, which may well be a sought after publication today.

Fred was a gentle giant, always obliging and blessed with a black sense of humor. He enjoyed his Chelsea environment walking on the "sunny side" of the street accepting whatever the day had in store. Fred threw many parties, even at the posh Hilton Hotel, often inviting friends and actresses from Hammer Horror Film Productions. Young starlets were in demand, like Jane London, Veronica Carlson, or the presence of actor Milton Reed, the chubby exotic James Bond performer, adding to the atmosphere of the night.

Fred was full of mischief at times, an enfant terrible. I remember him once sitting in the London Tube greeting elderly ladies while removing his wig and bowing his head in obedience. He was open-minded with a taste for oddities and unusual happenings. One Saturday morning, he paraded through King's Road, dressed in black and flanked by a nude lady who was garnished with only a hat. On another occasion, I photographed Fred being firmly saddled on horseback in one of Knightsbridge's mews, wearing a city gents outfit and bowler hat, as he encountered a perfectly shaped angel without wings, in human form as nature intended. This bare encounter image gained global recognition. It was recently juxtaposed with Christine Keeler's immortal Sixties image in Taschen's historical volume: *London – Portrait of a City.*

Fred is now in heaven's arms, I think in company of angels.

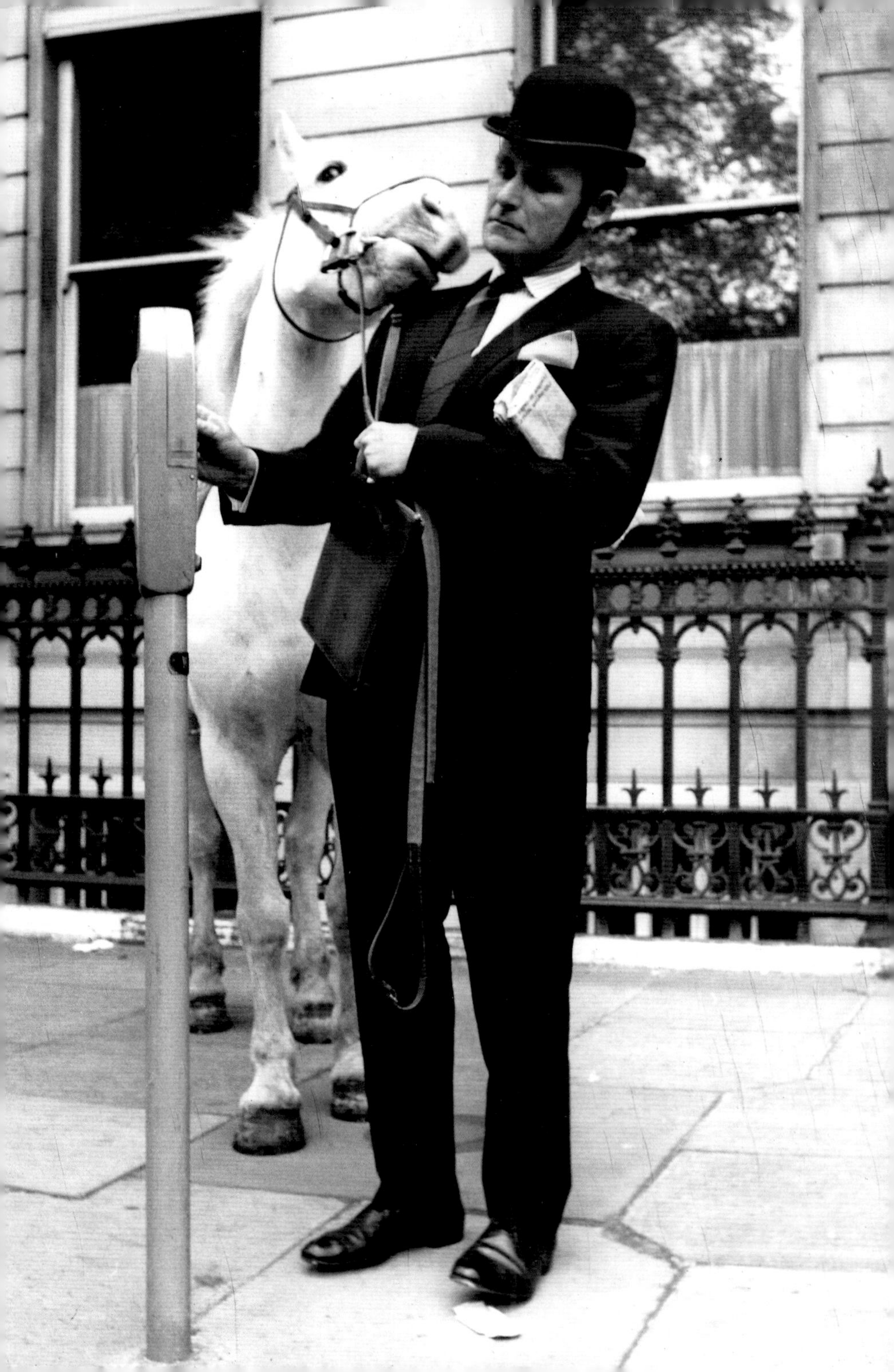

Bare encounter – near Knightsbridge, 1969

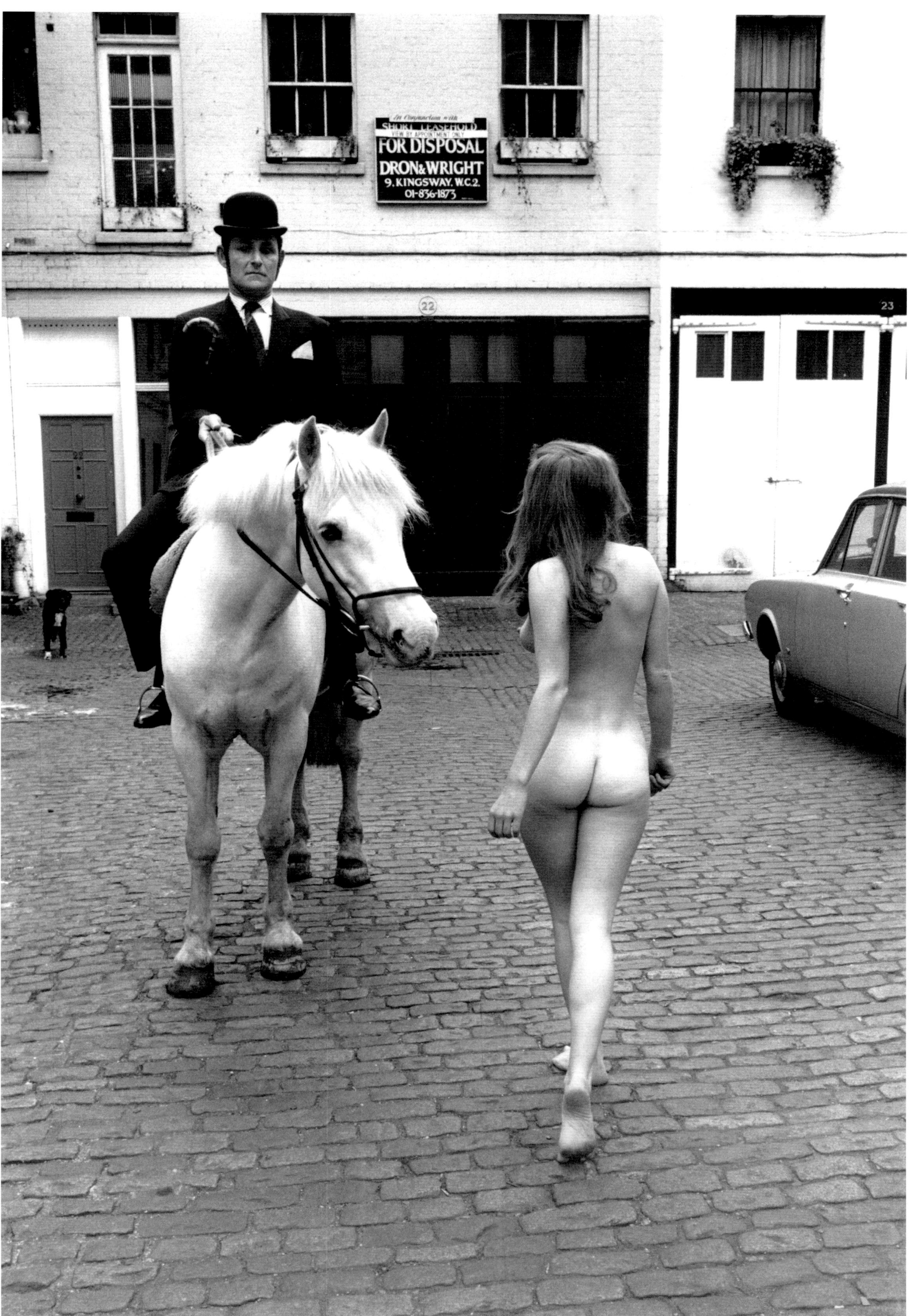
VIEW BY APPOINTMENT ONLY
FOR DISPOSAL
DRON&WRIGHT
9. KINGSWAY. W.C.2.
01-836-1873
22
23

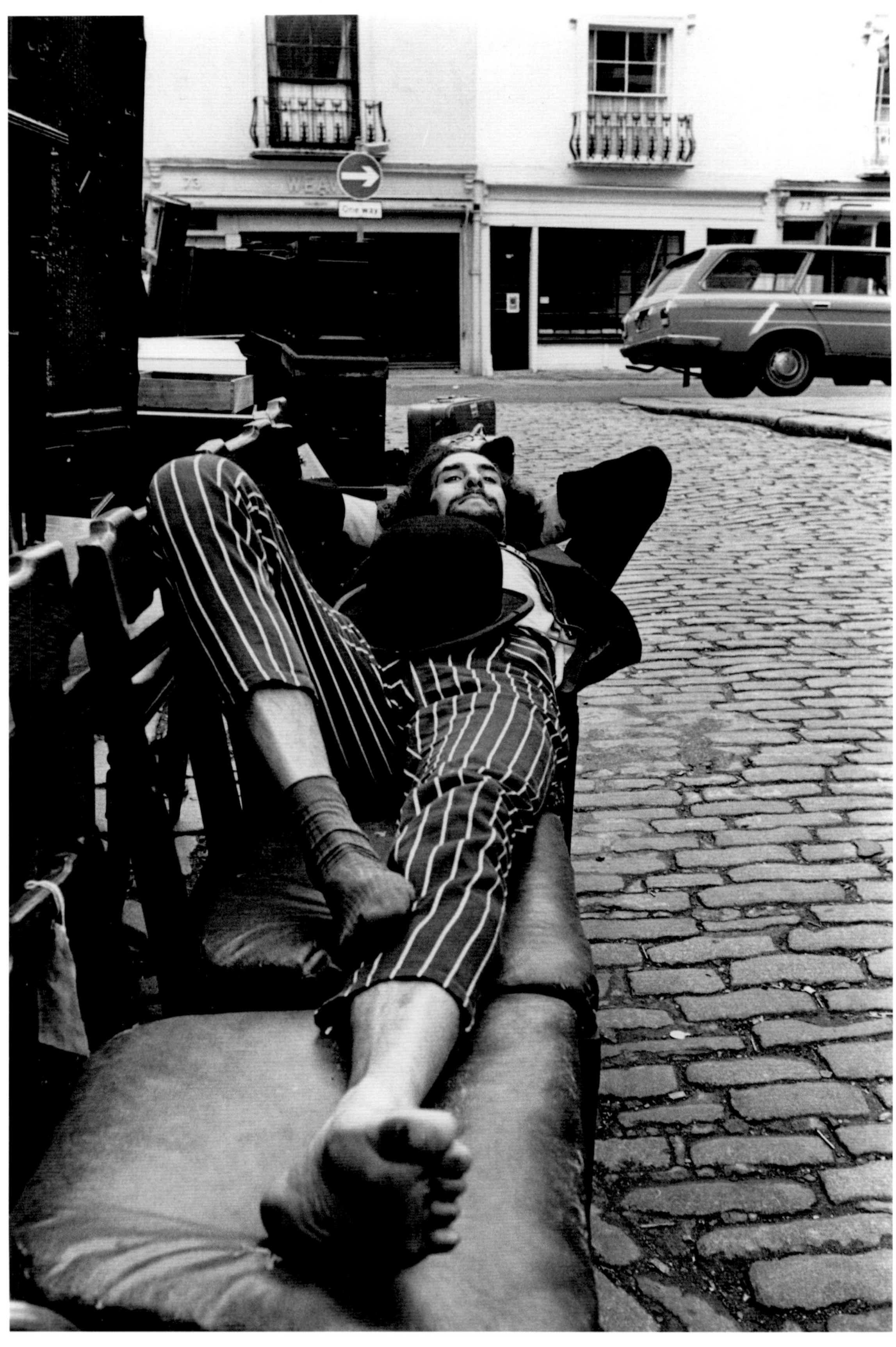

I'll stay a while – Ian Channel, street performer, Portobello Markets

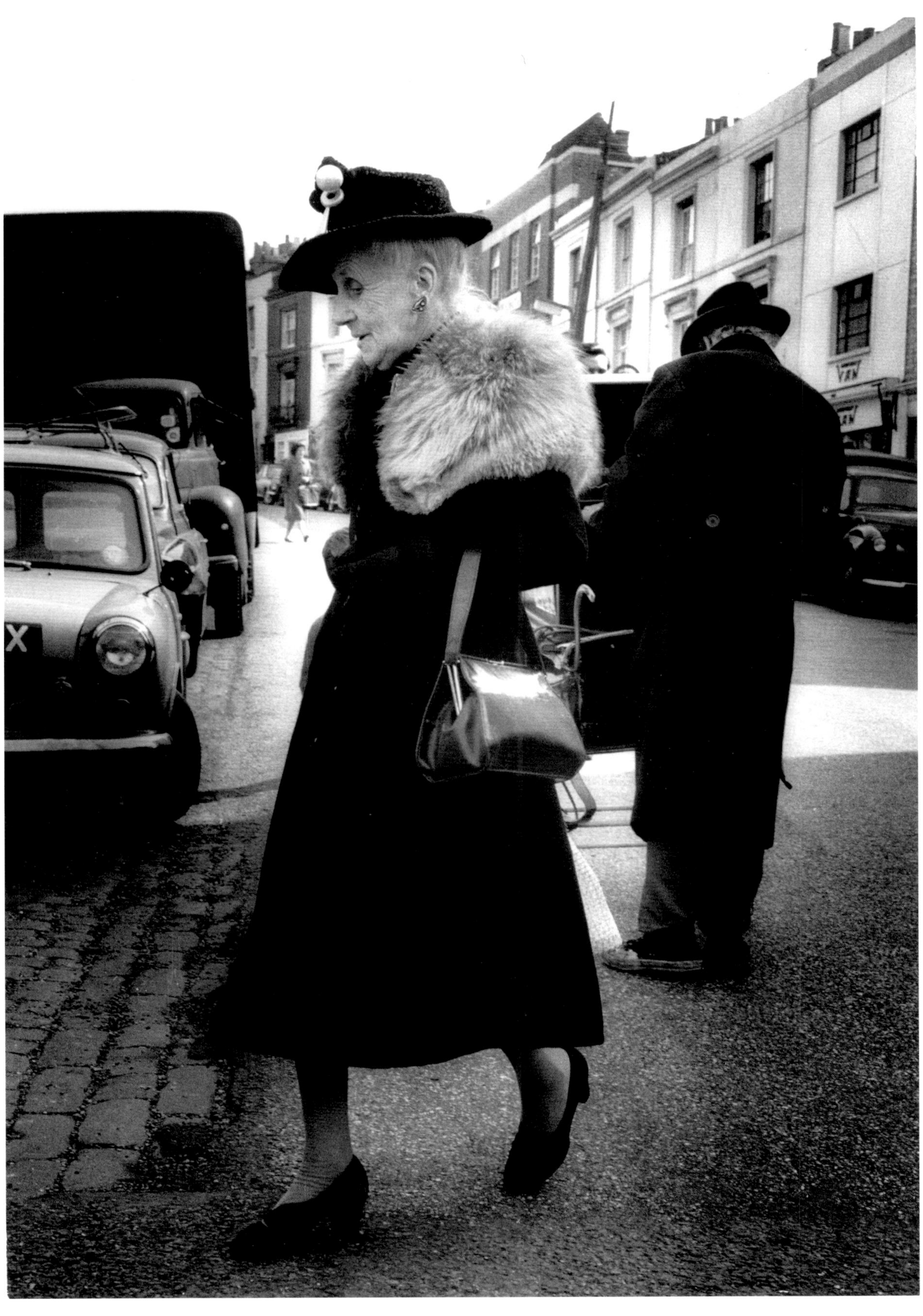

Loving life and becoming wise – Mrs. Black, Portobello Markets

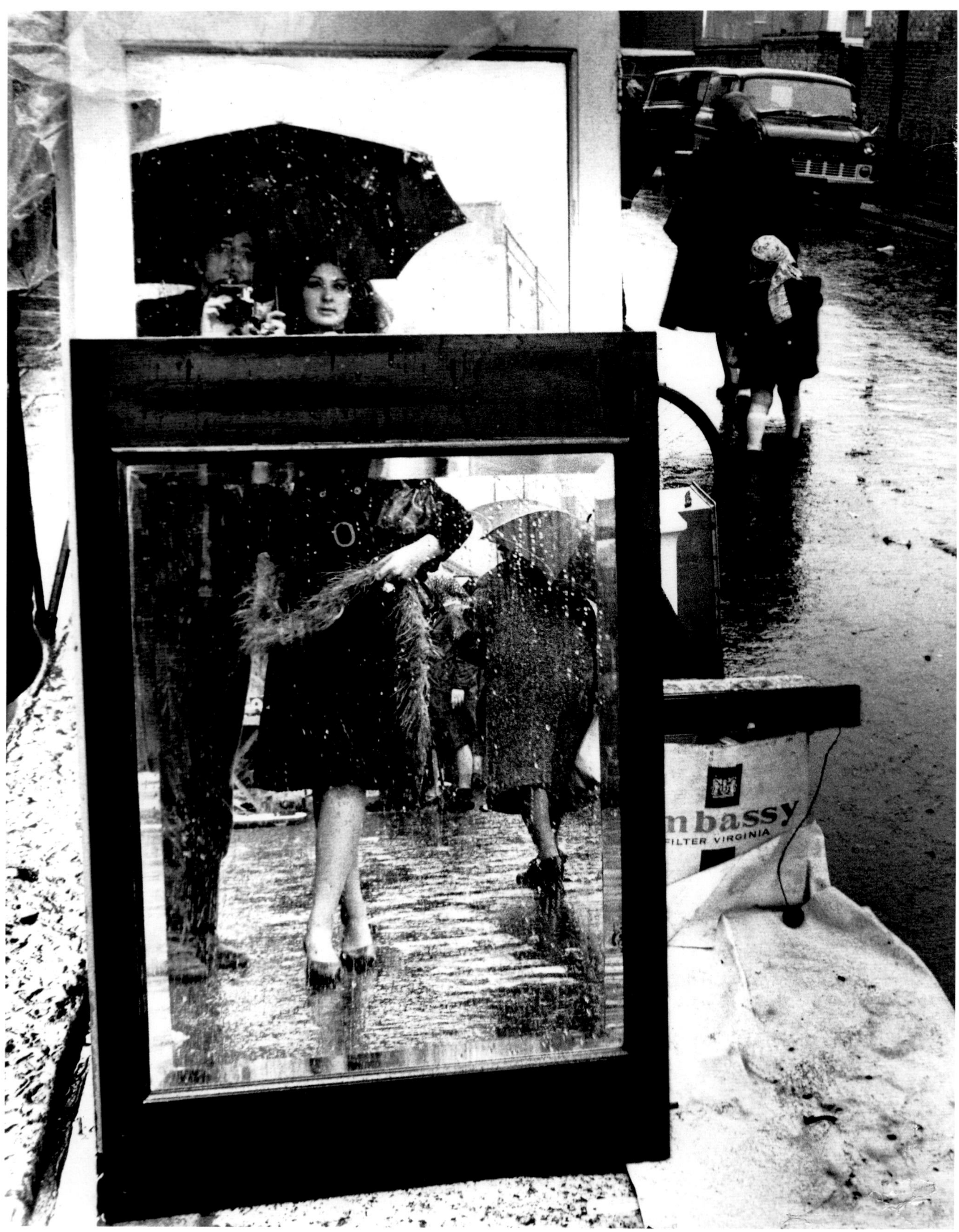

Mirror, mirror on the street – Oxford Gardens W10

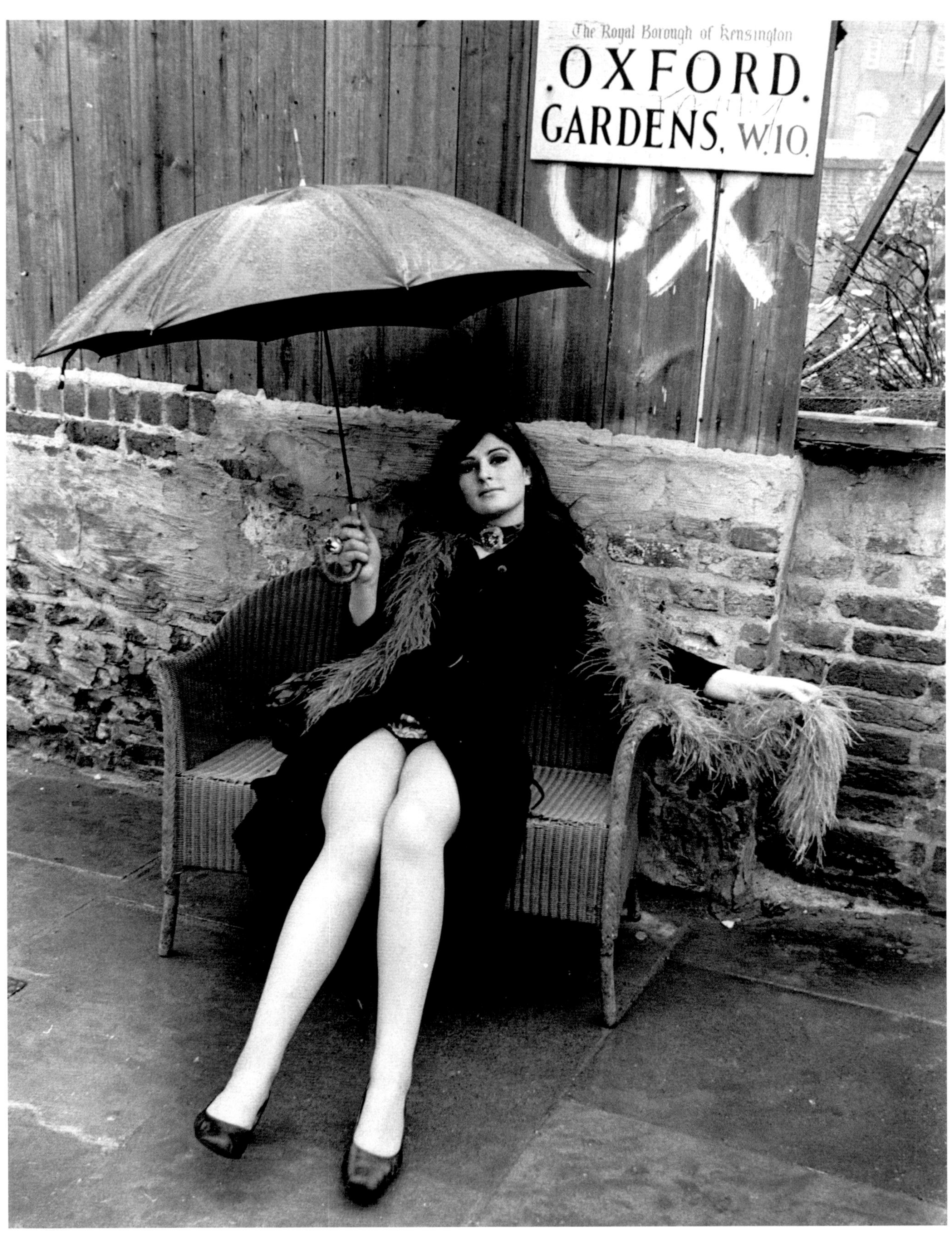

Four seasons in one day – Paula, Oxford Gardens

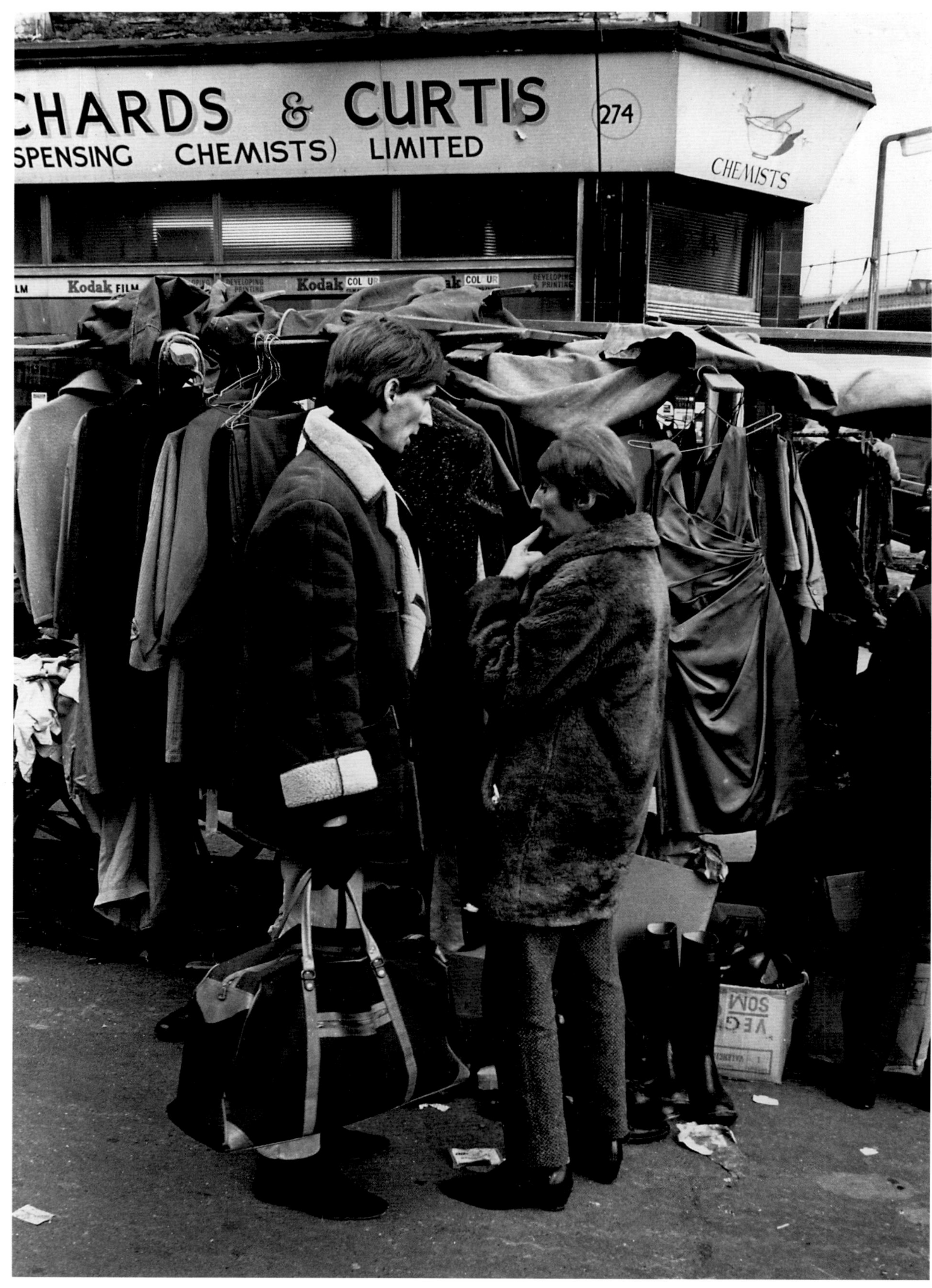

Who was the previous owner? – Portobello Road

Careful how you touch it – Portobello Markets, 1964

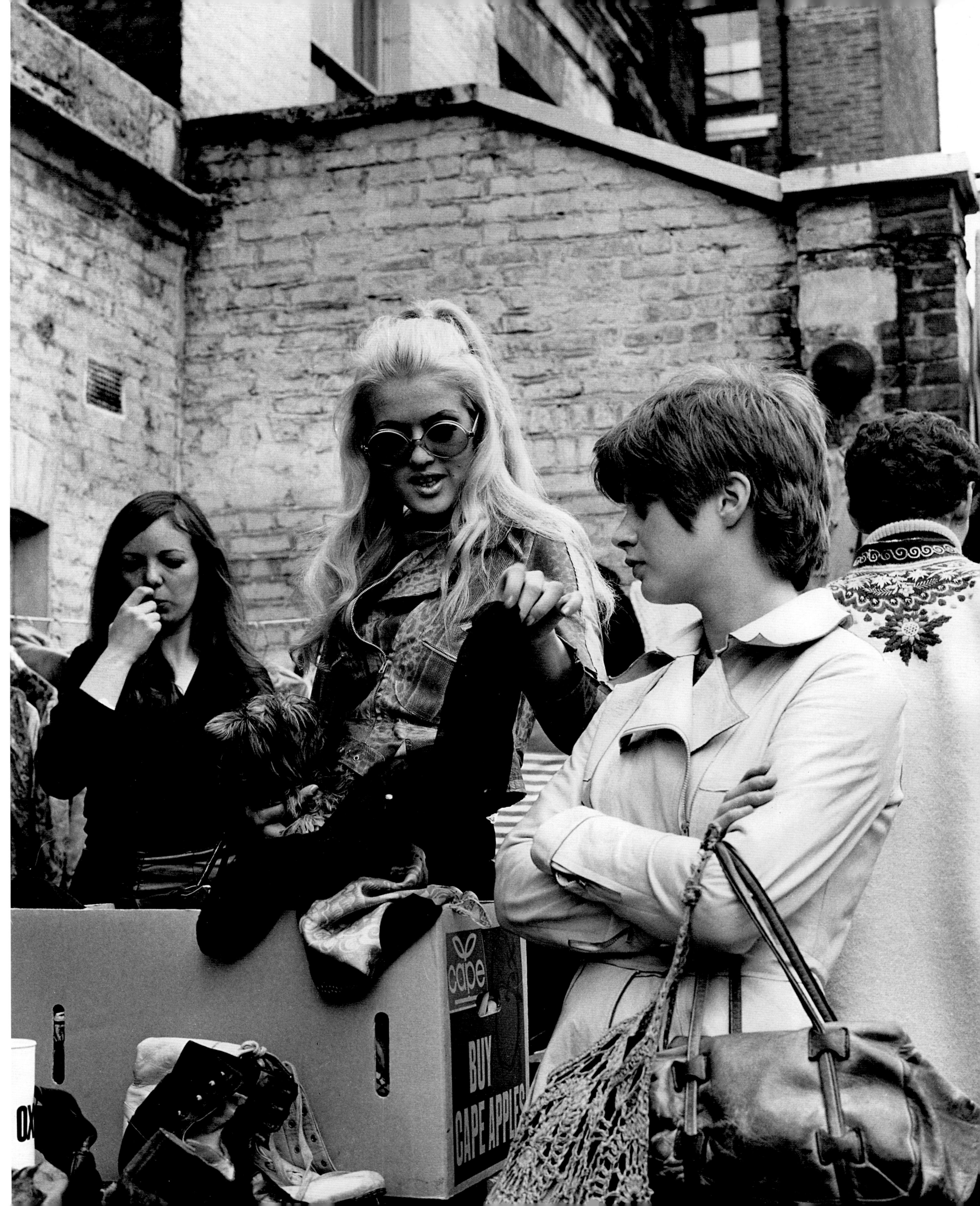
cape
BUY
CAPE APPLES

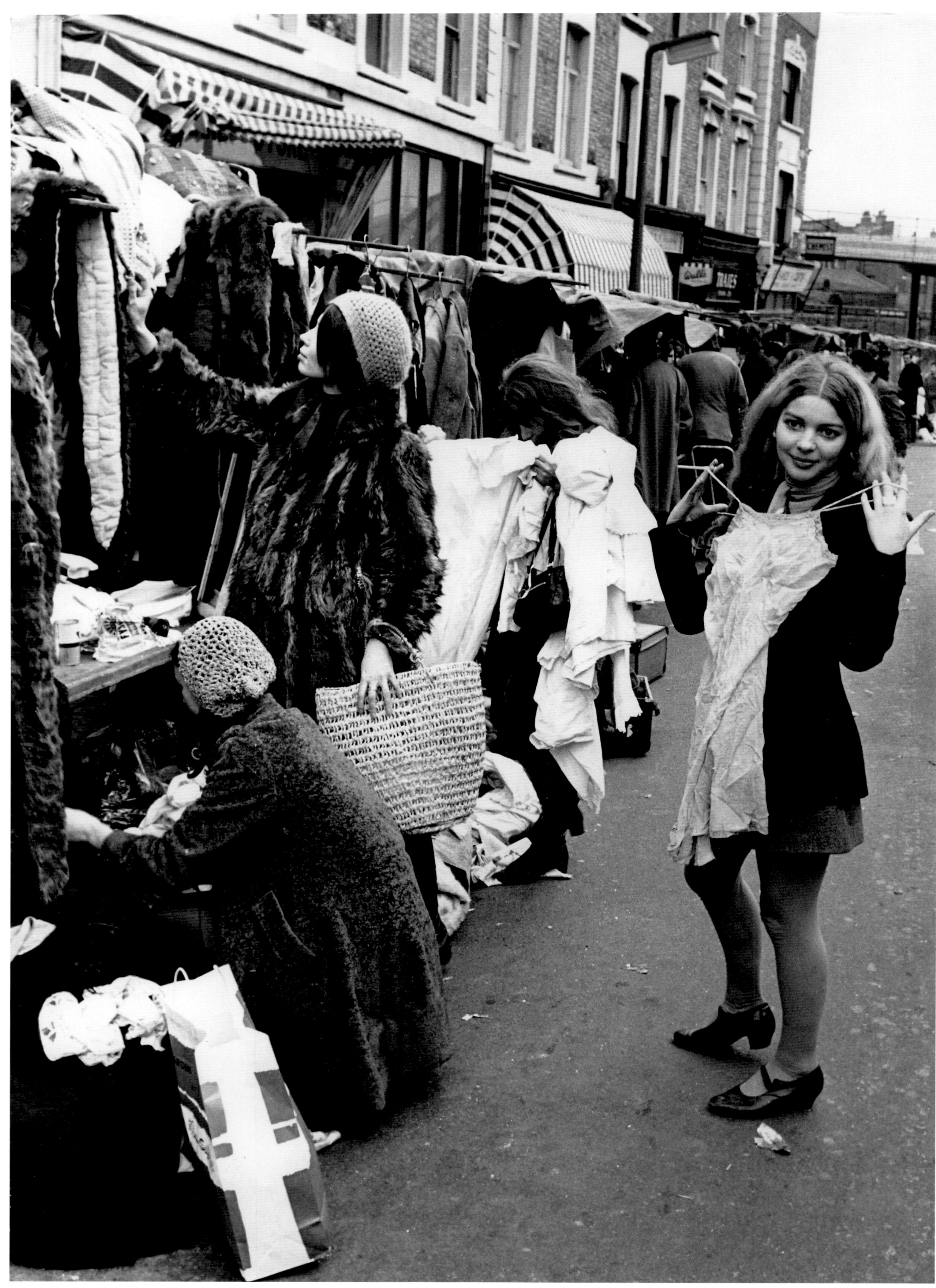

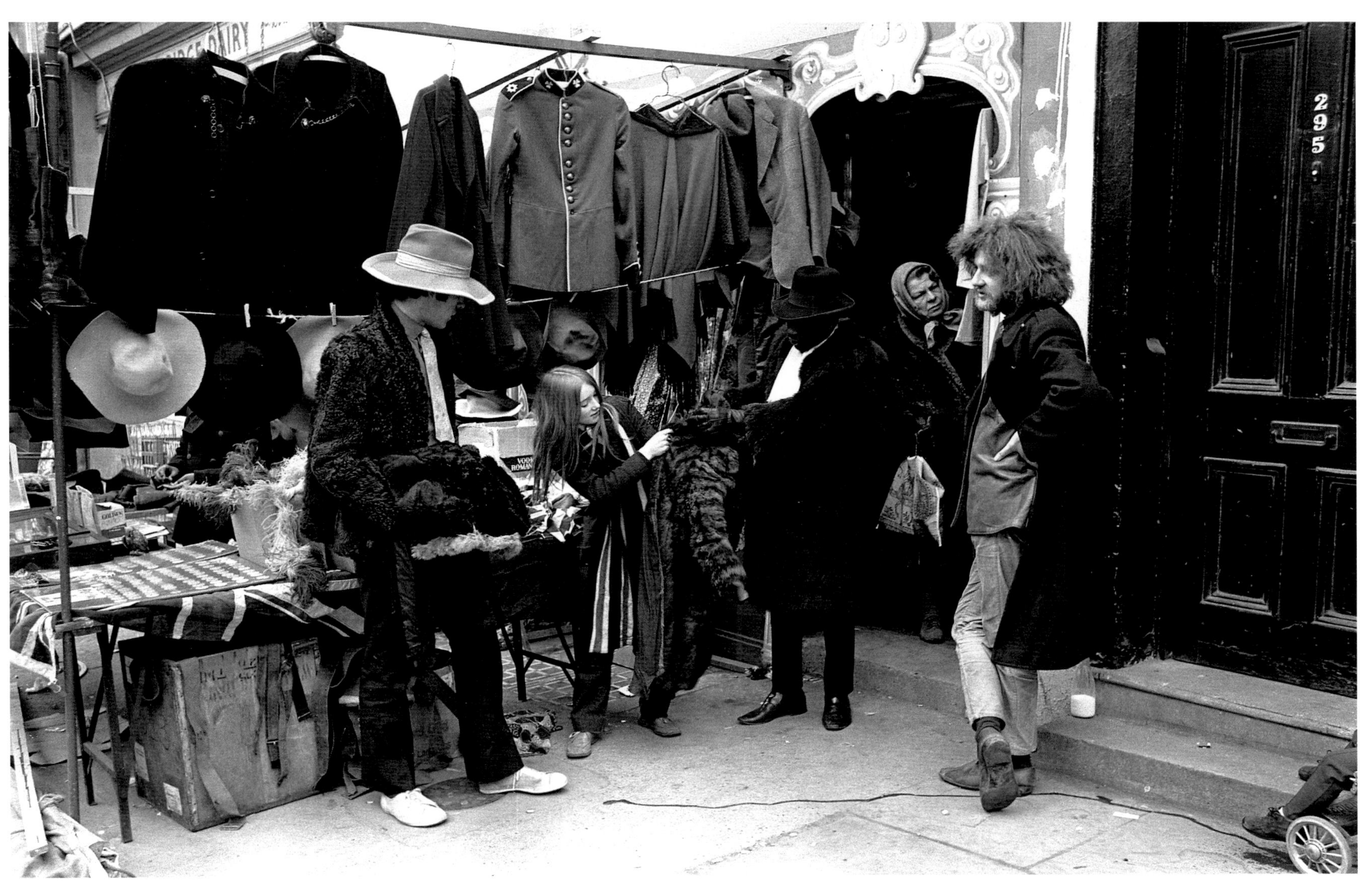

If it fits – Portobello Road

Cloak and dagger – Portobello Road

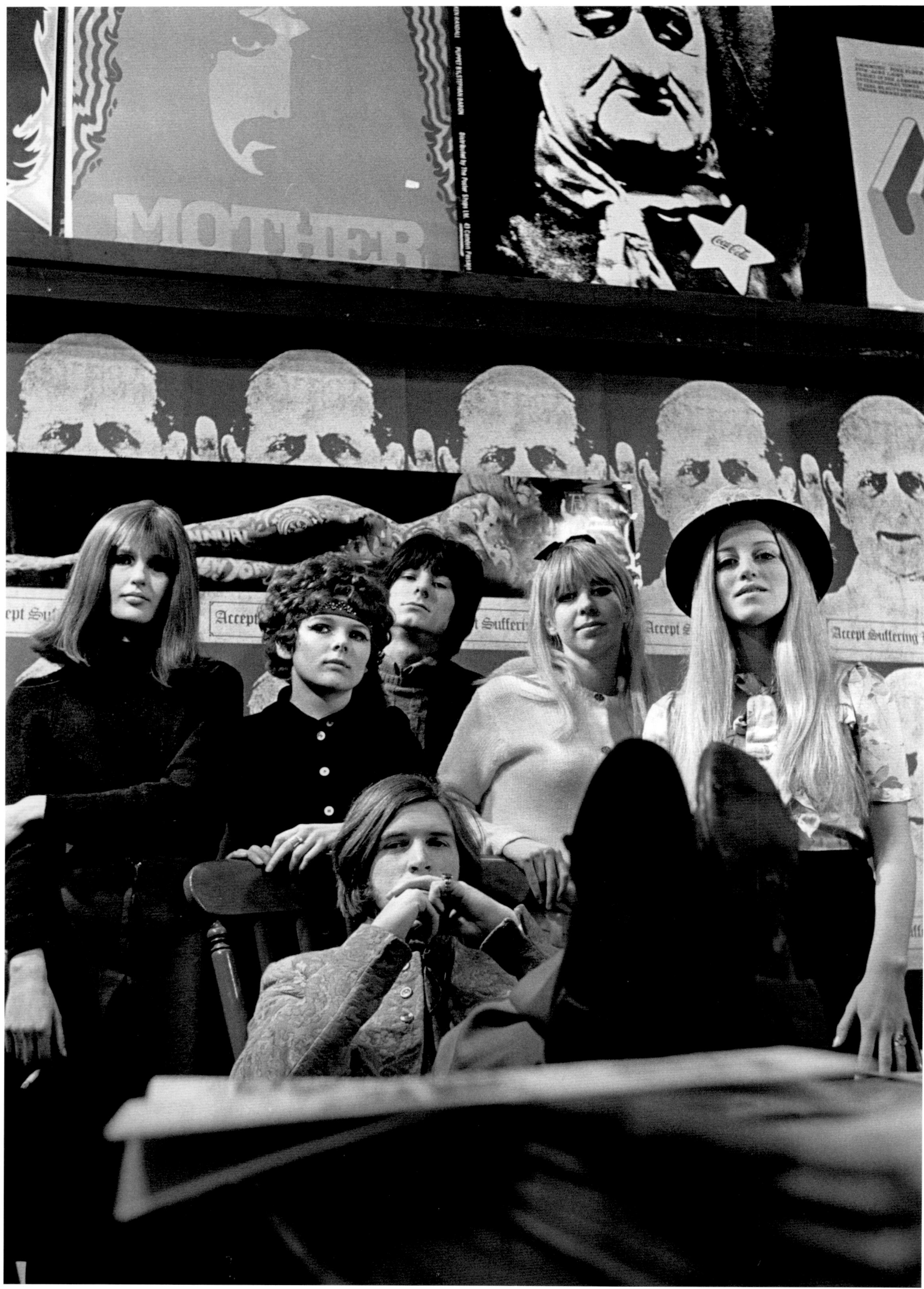

Last judgement – Kensington Markets

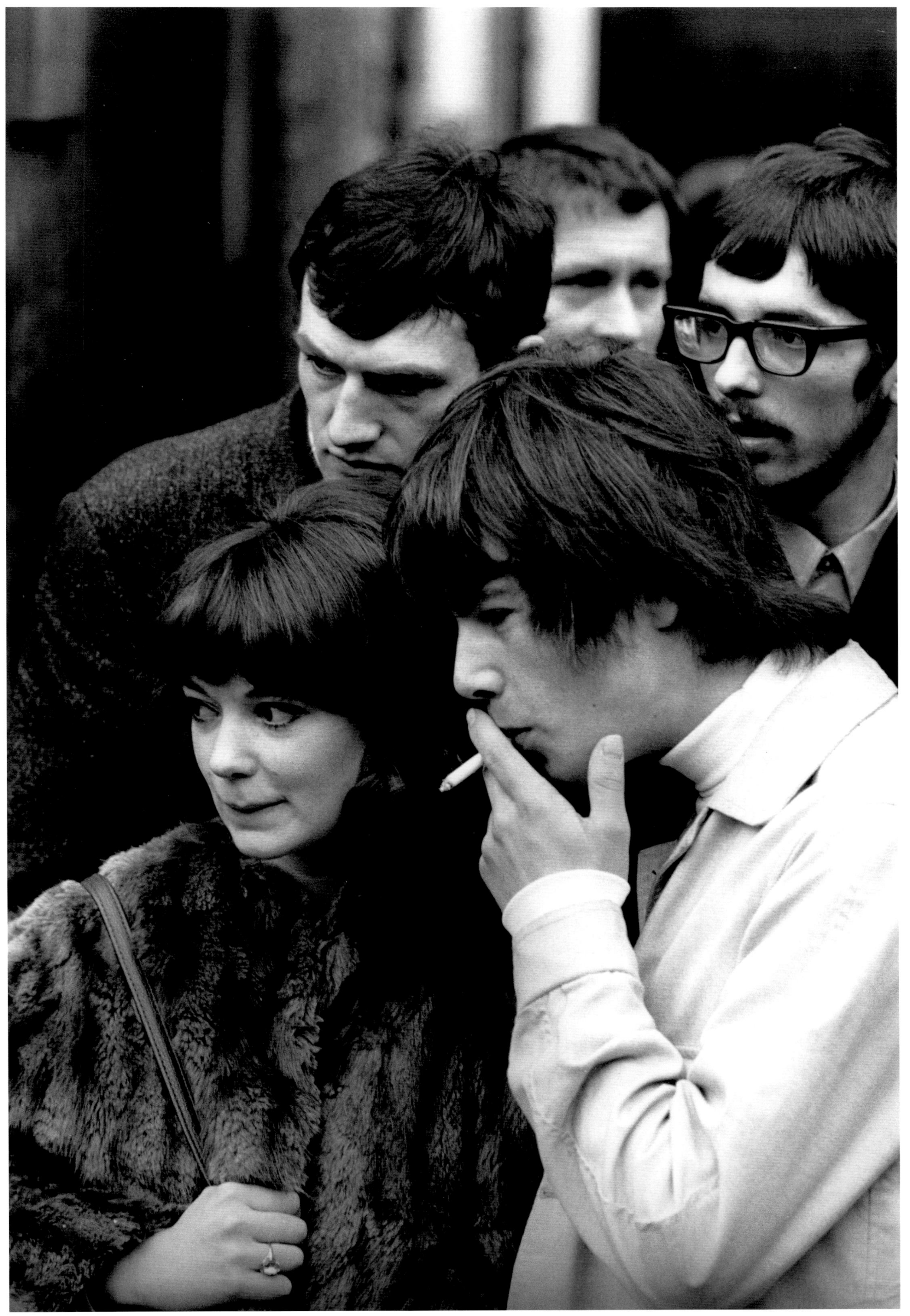

What do we do once we unite? – King's Road

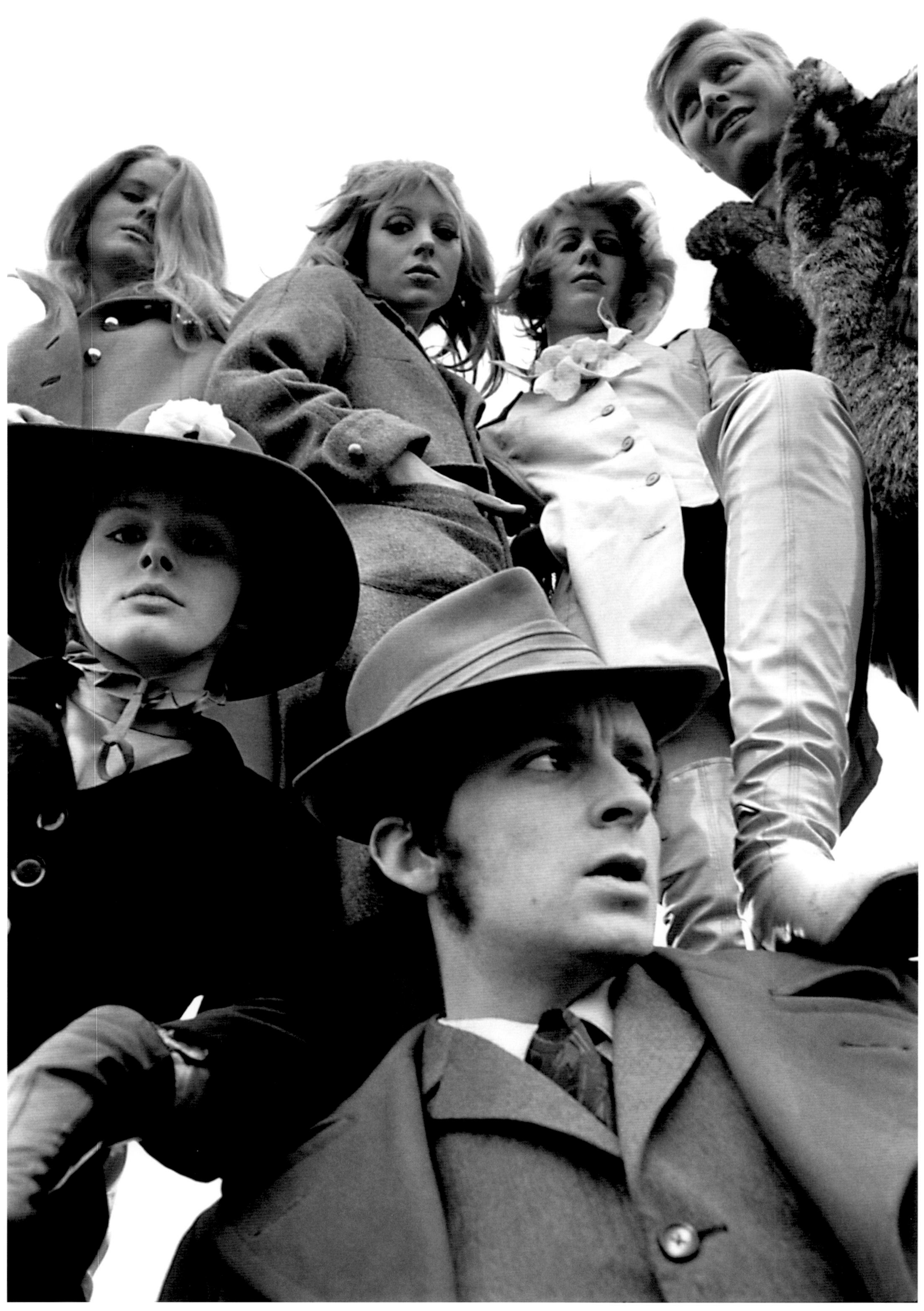

Pile up of friends – Courtfield Gardens SW5, 1968

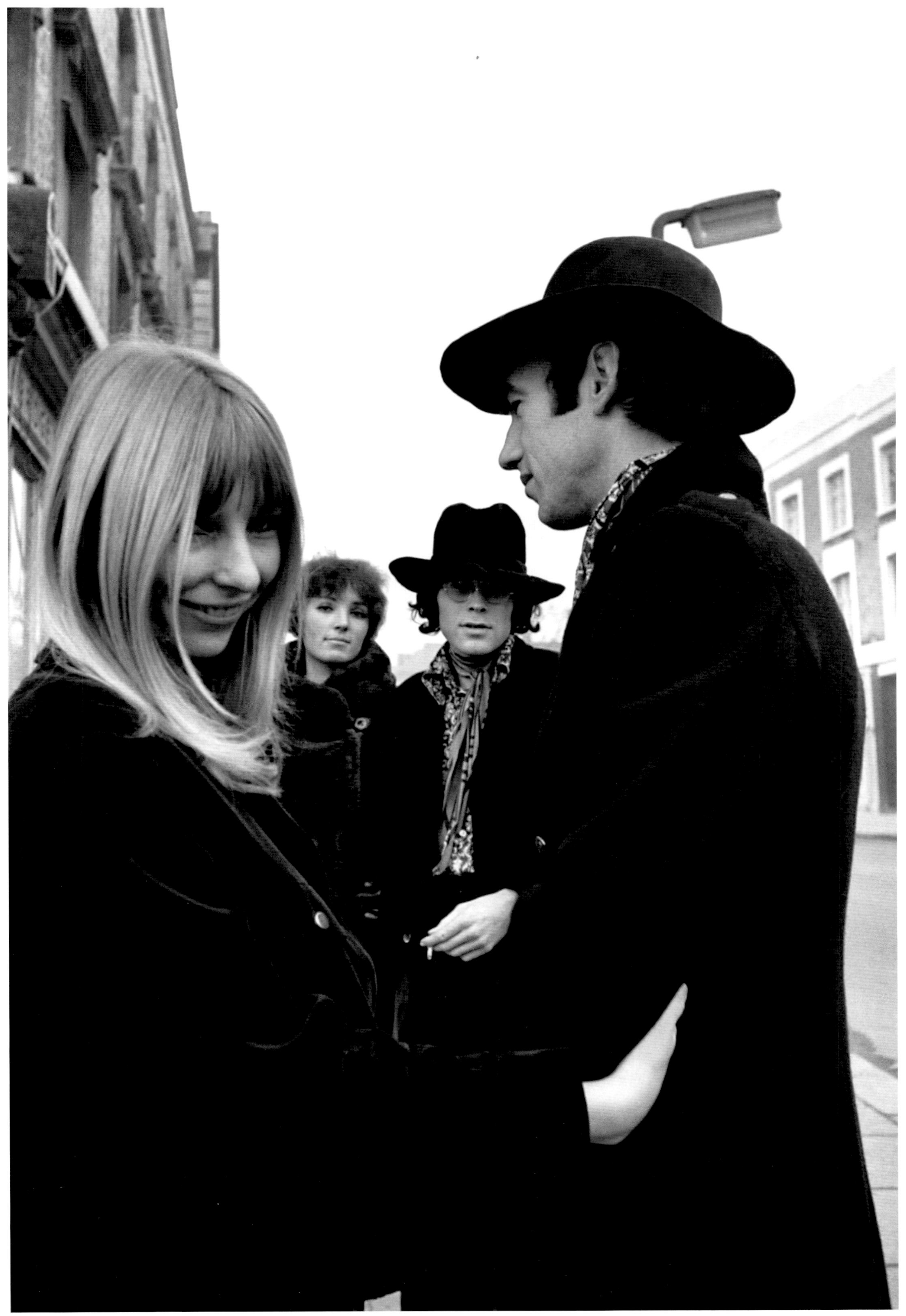

He's my beau – near Waterloo Station

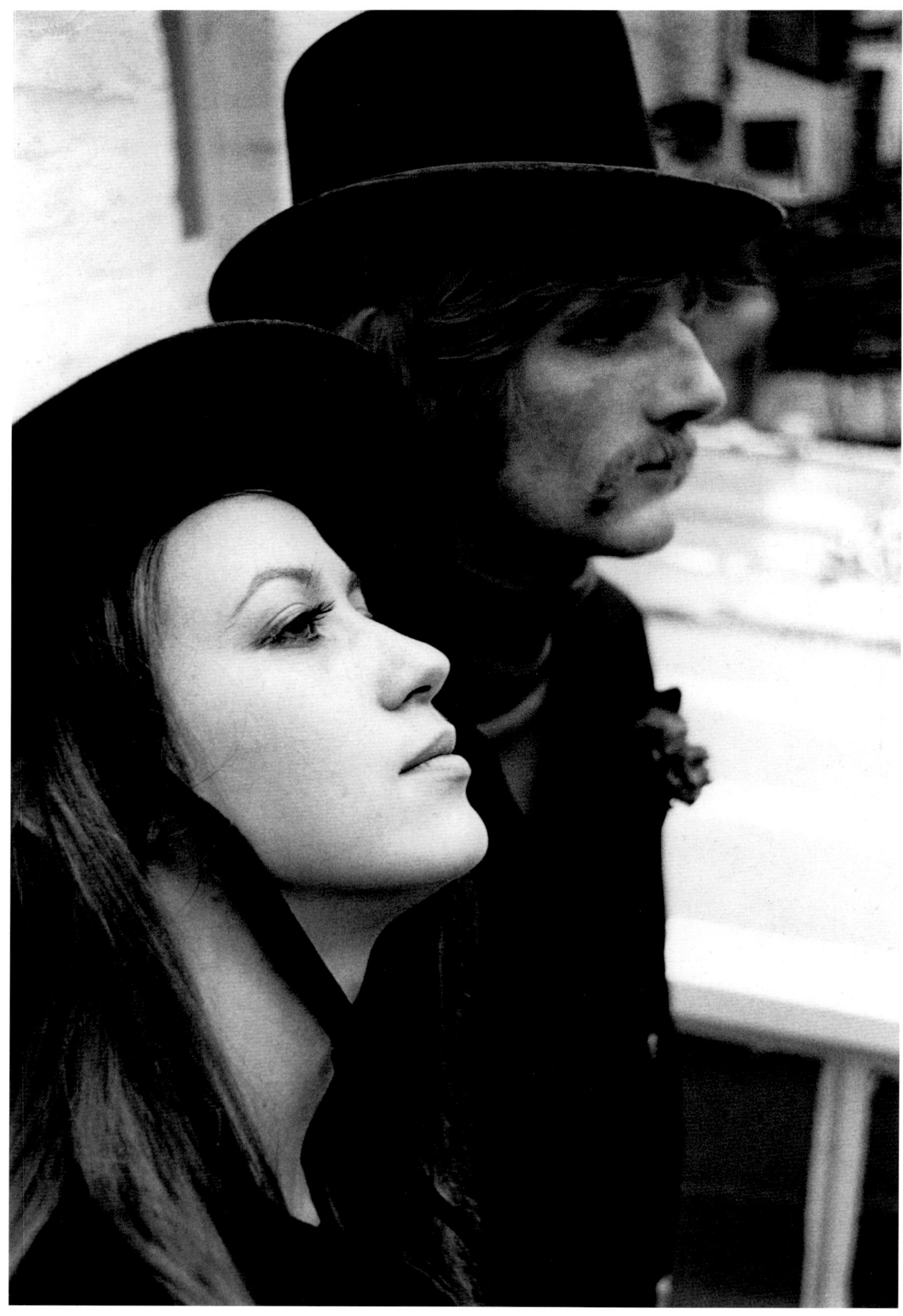

Towards a new Horizon – Wimbledon

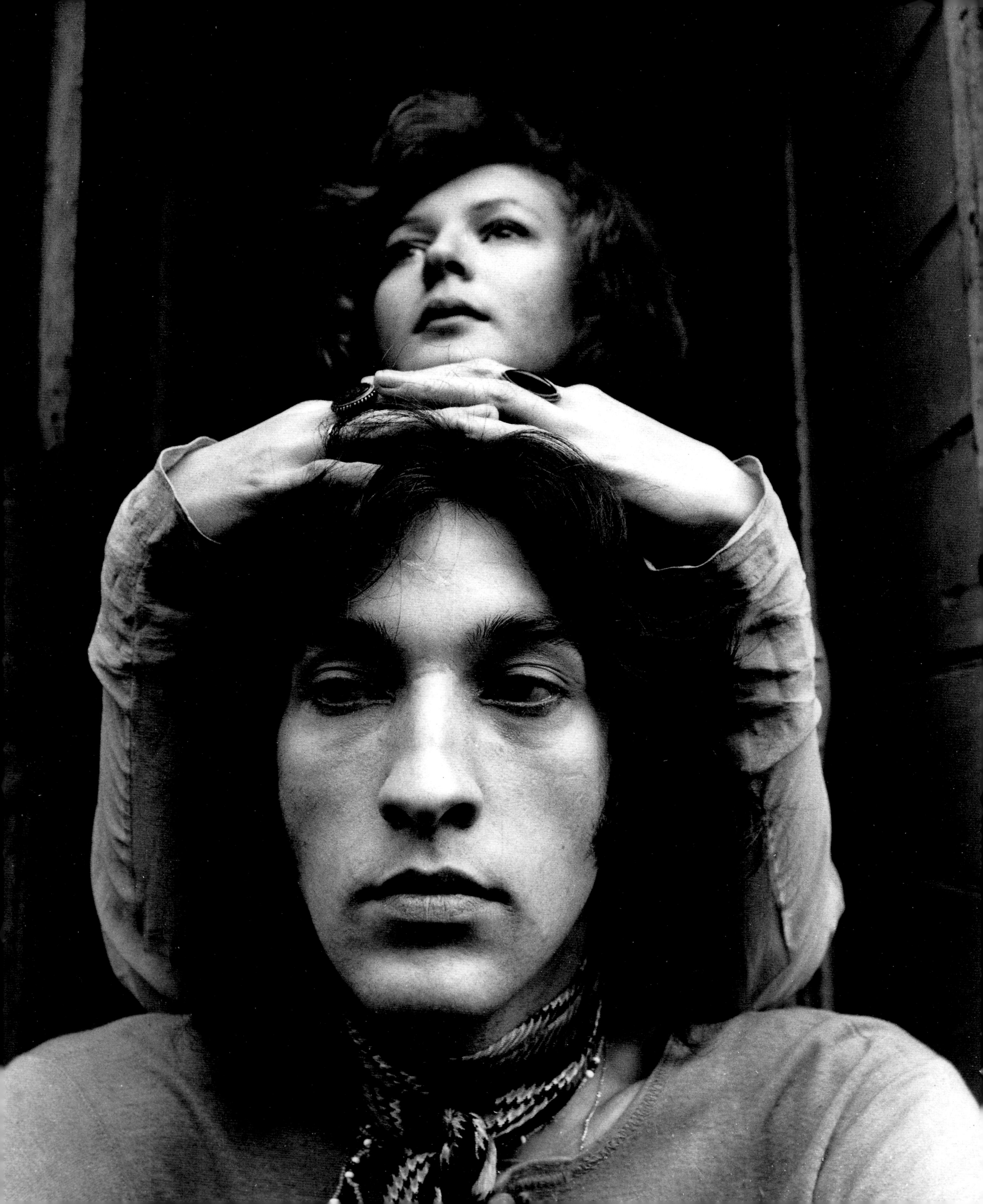

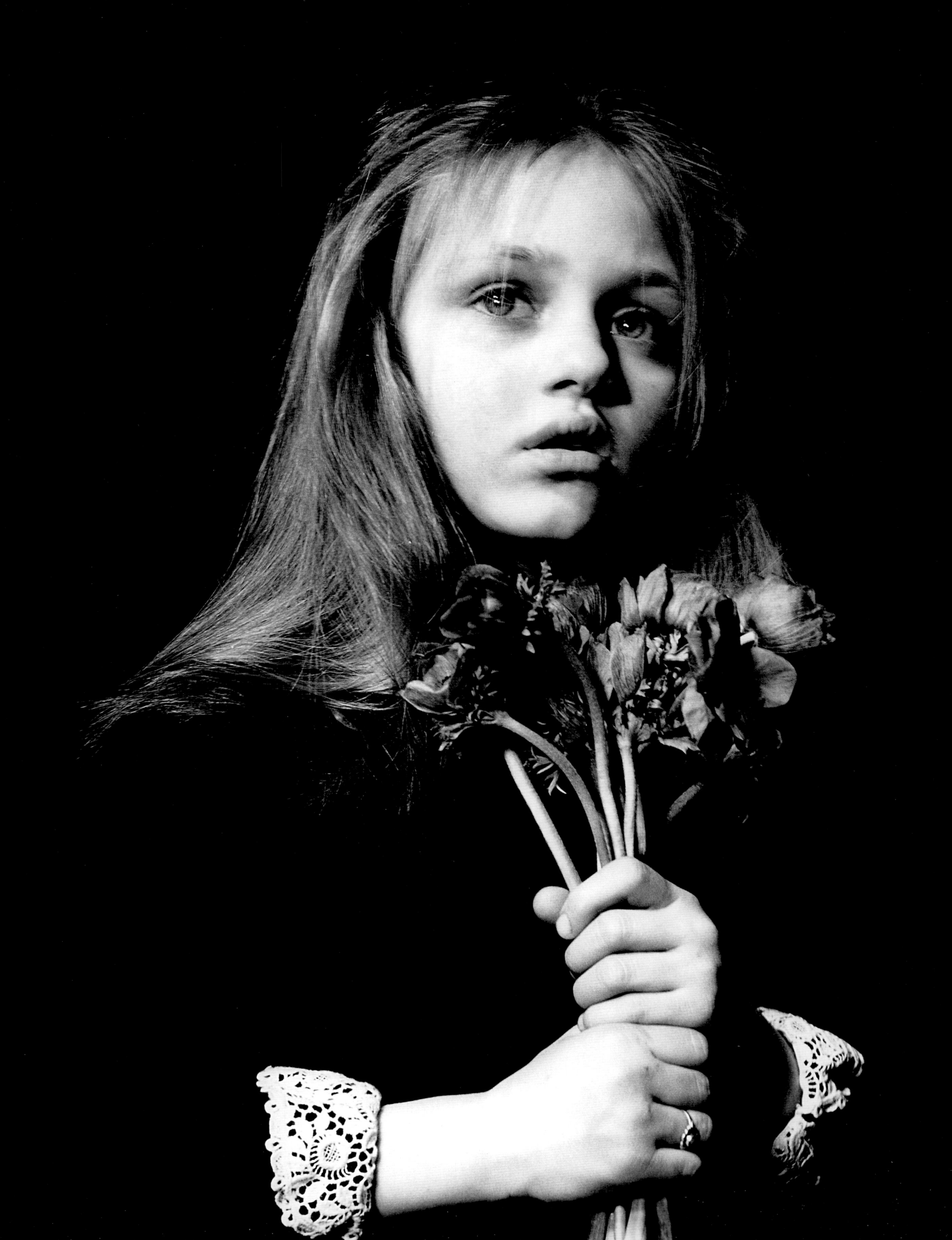

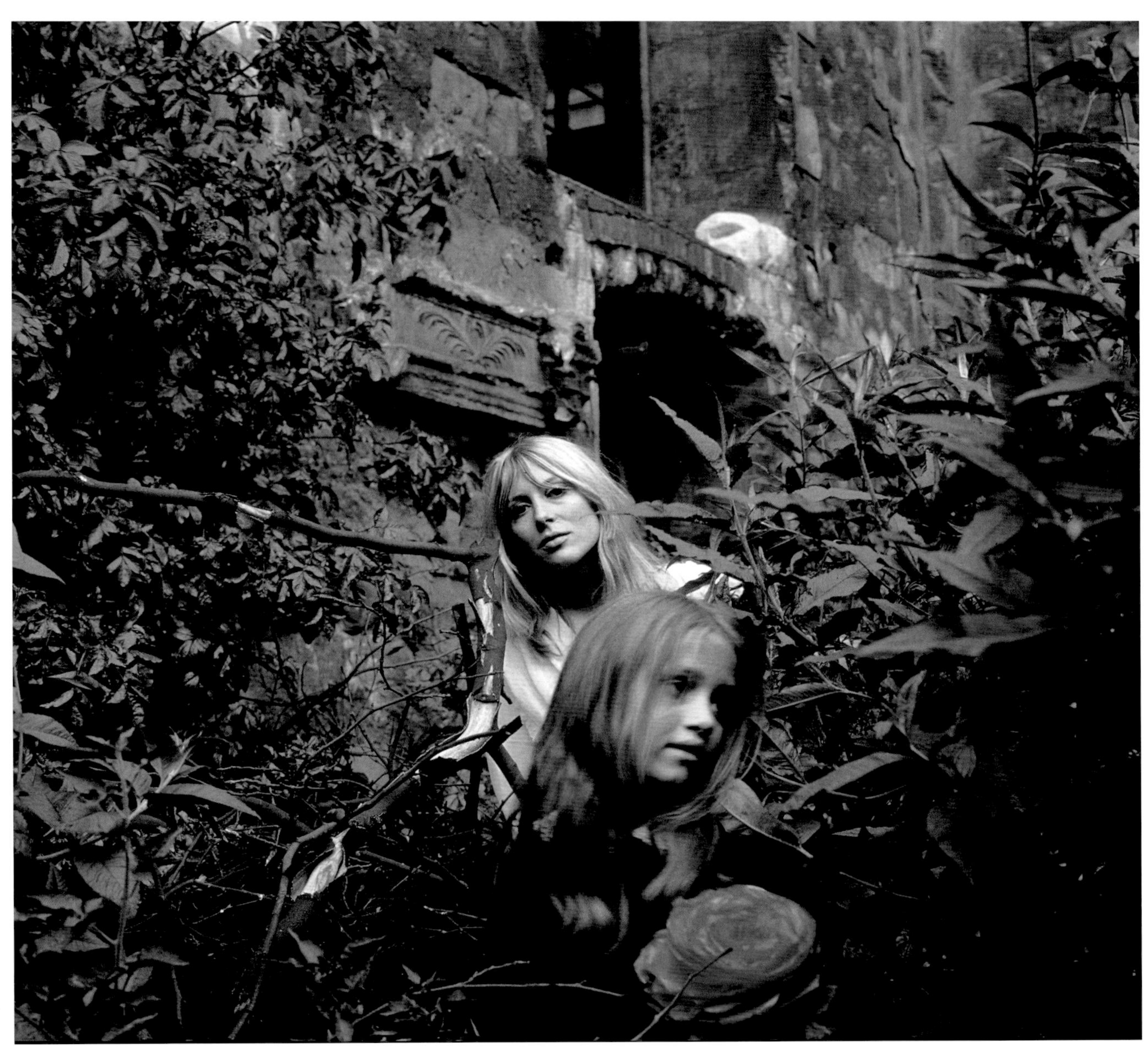

Someone to watch over me – Tina, 1969

Carol

I always enjoyed photographing Carol, a woman with inner and visual beauty. She was natural, calm, and carried an air of innocence. She lived and was brought up in London's East End. Carol was a modest, giving person. She posed for me with friends from all walks of life in London's environment. Most photos I took were fantasy shots, generally taken in the East End, where I mingled Carol among street kids in street markets and outside memorable derelict buildings.

Carol and I became good friends. She became a stallholder in the now famed Kensington Markets (when they opened their doors in Kensington High Street). The markets were catering to bohemian and hippie culture. Carol was offering vintage clothes and homemade jewelry. Before the mid-seventies, Freddie Mercury and other prominent people of those years had stalls there.

In 2001 the prominent building (a former warehouse) was pulled down. When looking through the murky glass of some of the market's leftovers, one can see a wooden sign left by the builders:

THE PAST. IN THANKS TO ALL ITS CUSTOMERS FROM PAST GLORY.

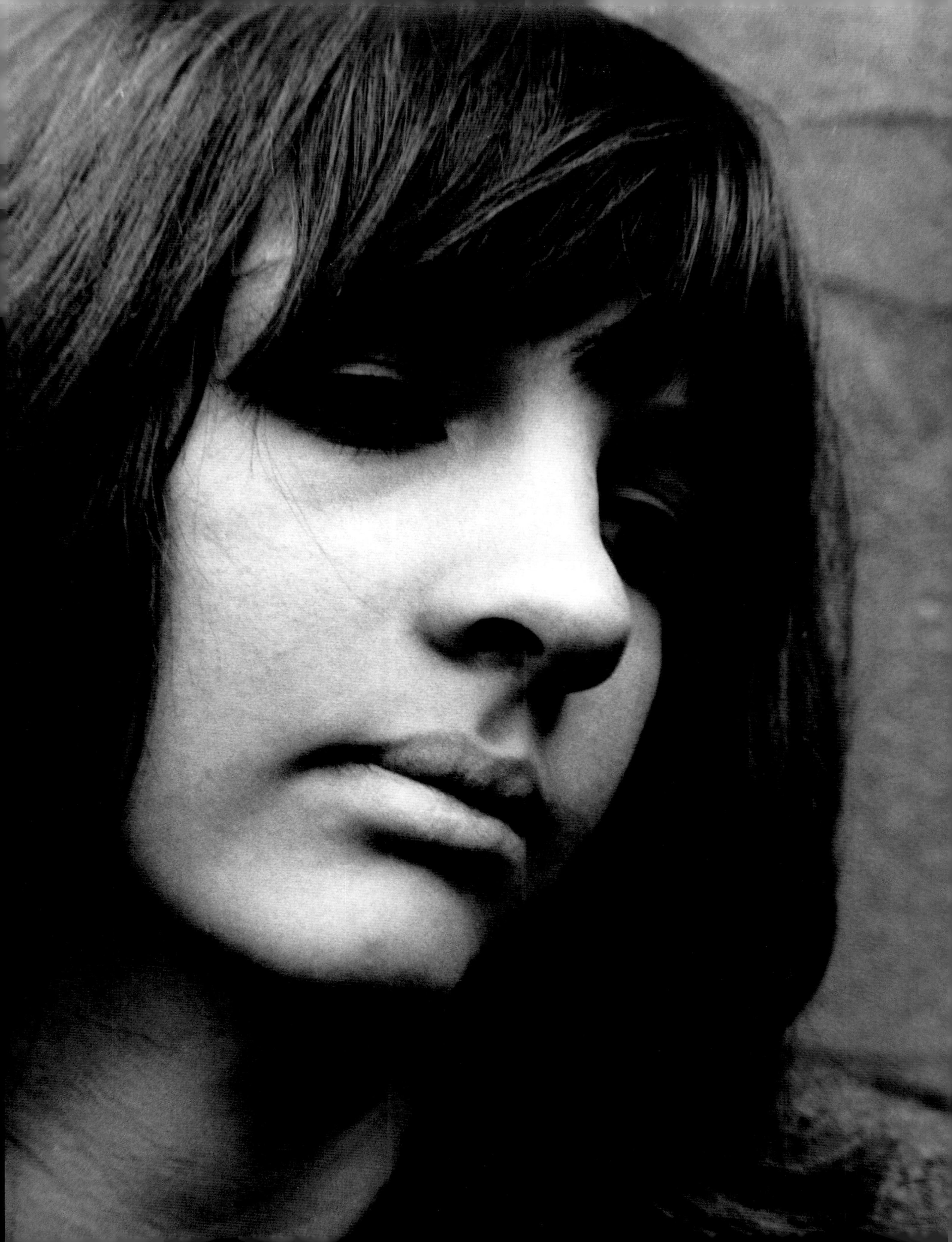

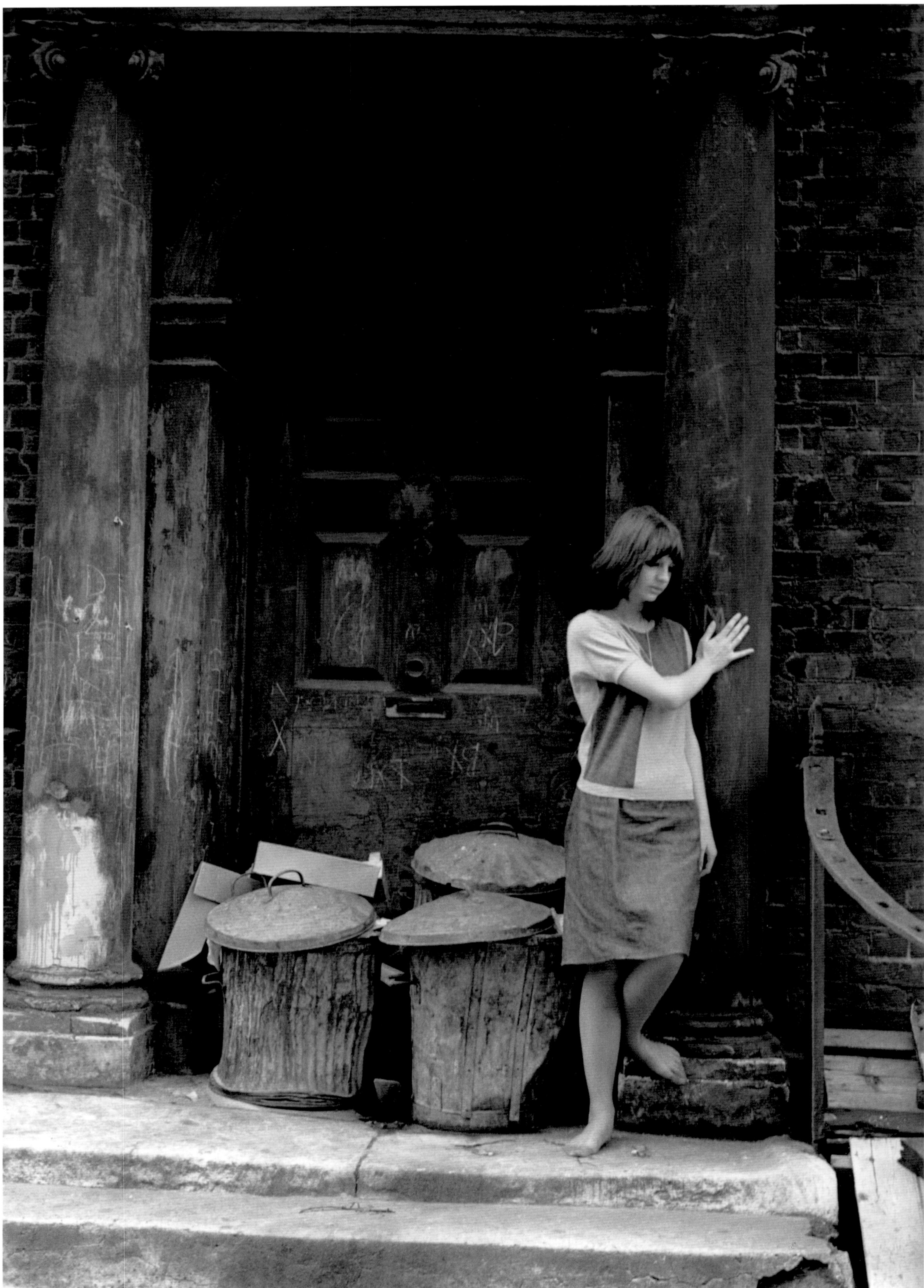

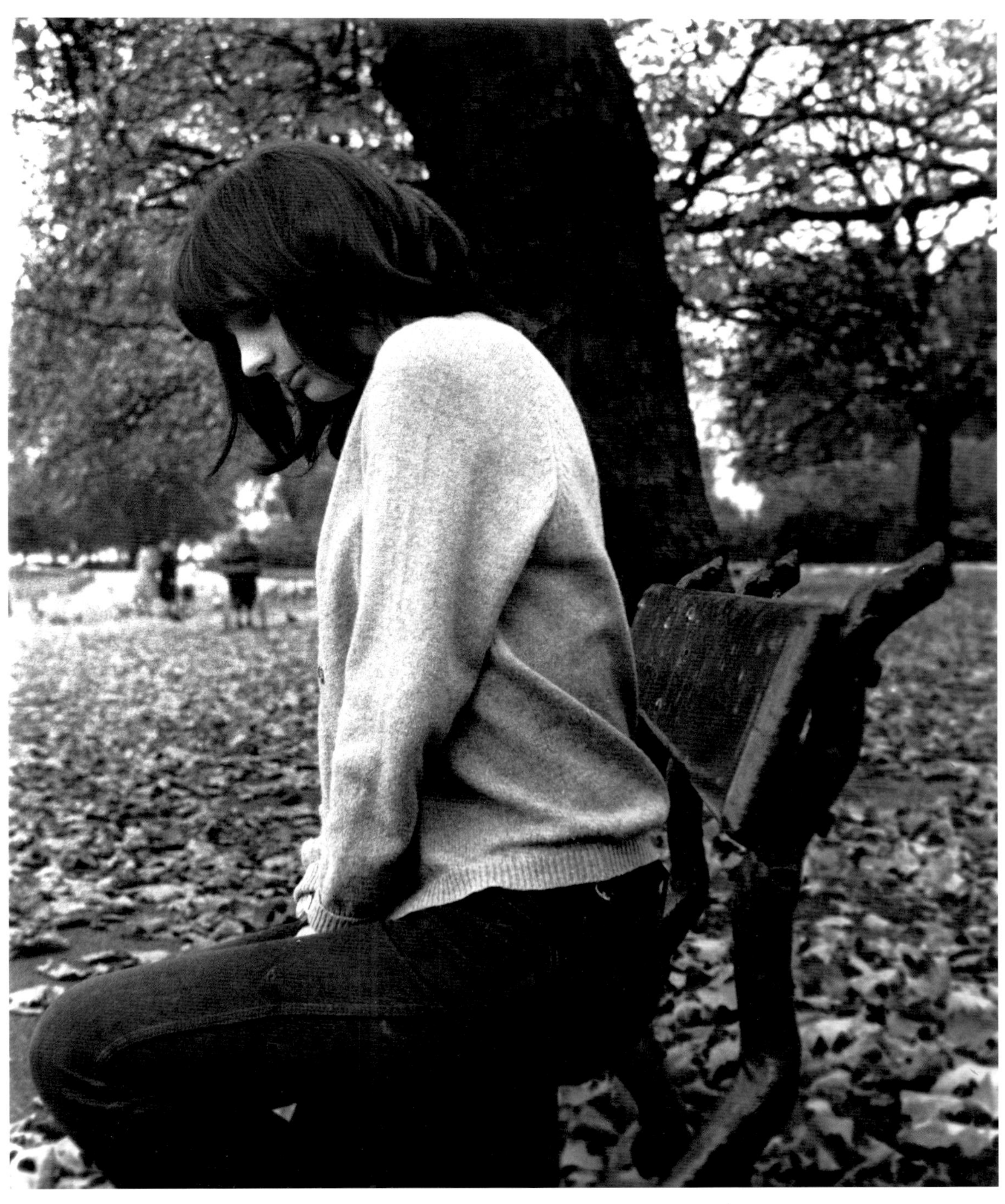

Carol, Hyde Park

34 Courtfield Gardens

"A home away from home." No doubt, this address shaped my Sixties and cemented my future.

The typically terraced house, with its colorful and constantly moving bedsitter occupants from all walks of life, was in London's SW5 district. It was located between Earl's Court and Gloucester Road. My weekly eight Pounds rent secured the building's highest one-off apartment on the fifth floor.

I enjoyed thirty-two square meters of living space. A bedsitting type room with a coin operated gas heater eager to be fed in the winter. Through the push-up bathroom window, I could reach the small terrace decorated with flowerpots and at times empty wine bottles. A few winding steps led up to my "iconic" rooftop. The views of a parallel running street also revealed a never-ending roofline. The adjoining Earl's Court district was known as Kangaroo Valley with its numerous Australian and New Zealand inhabitants.

My favorite open-air studio was my fifth floor rooftop. Hundreds of chimney pots dotted the continuous roofing of my street. It was a melting place for exuberant parties on mild summer nights. As an outdoor studio, it was a perfect environment for aspiring models wanting fashion images and portraits to enhance their portfolios. A number of my models ended up with television contracts as well as fashion or advertising assignments.

At one end of the rooftop, across the street towards Earl's Court, was an old age pensioner's home. Distinguished gentlemen of advanced ages rarely missed out on observing any of my rooftop shoots. As on some occasions, my models contributed to the cinematic scenery in nature's outfit. None of my elderly neighbors ever raised an eyebrow.

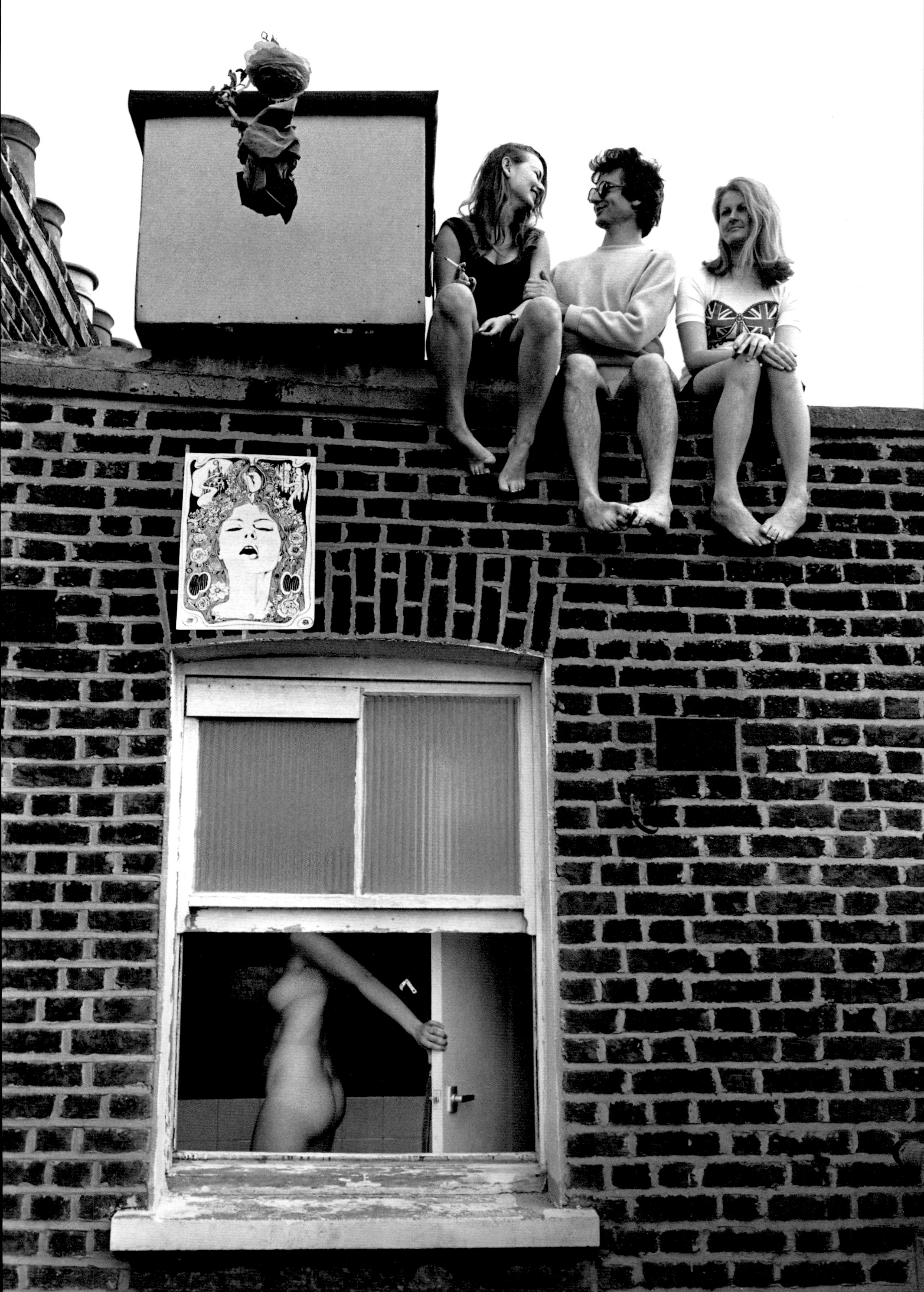

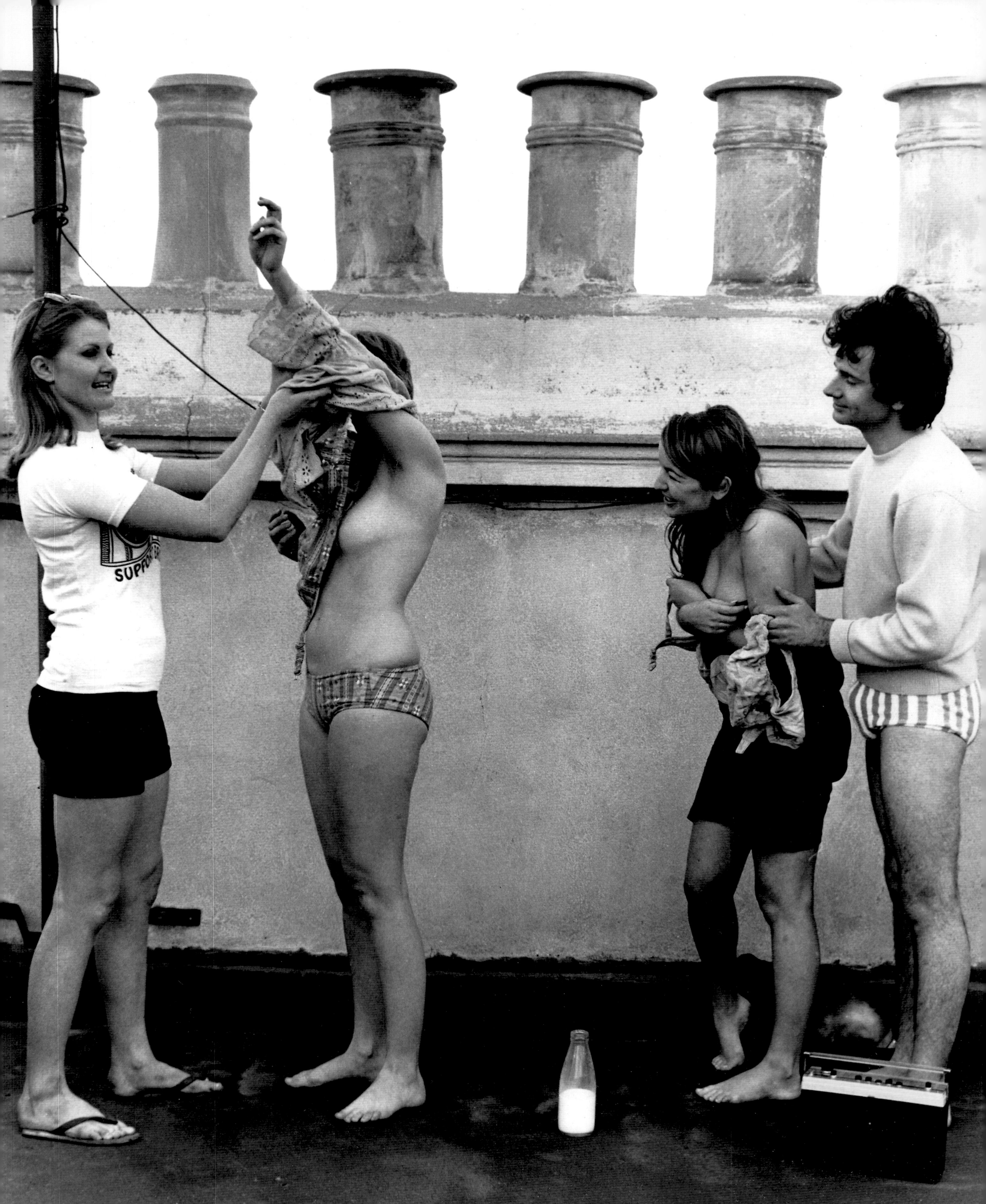

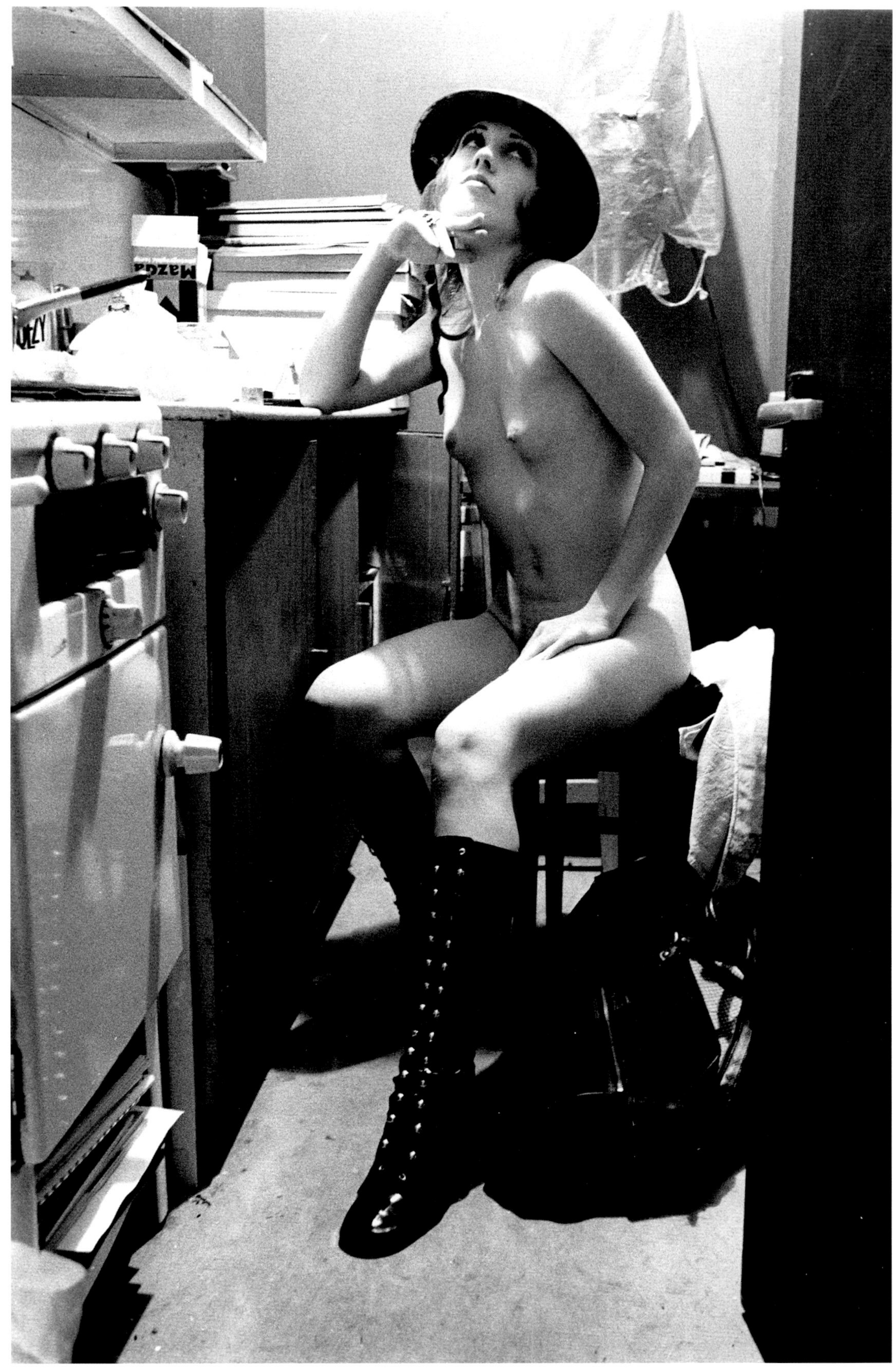

A bottle half empty, or a bottle half full?

A humble beginning – Photographer's first darkroom, Courtfield Gardens

Mirror, mirror on the roof – Courtfield Gardens

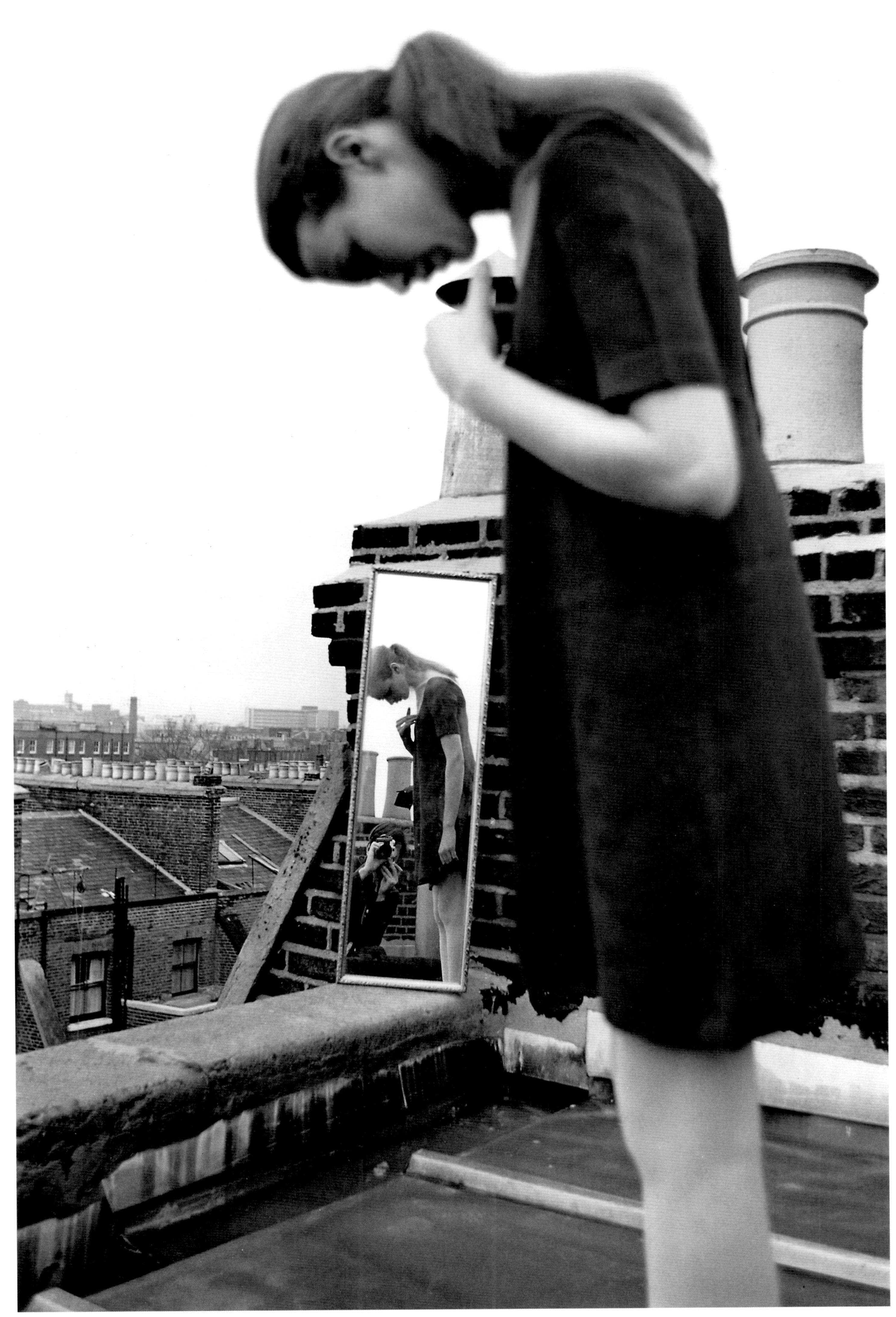

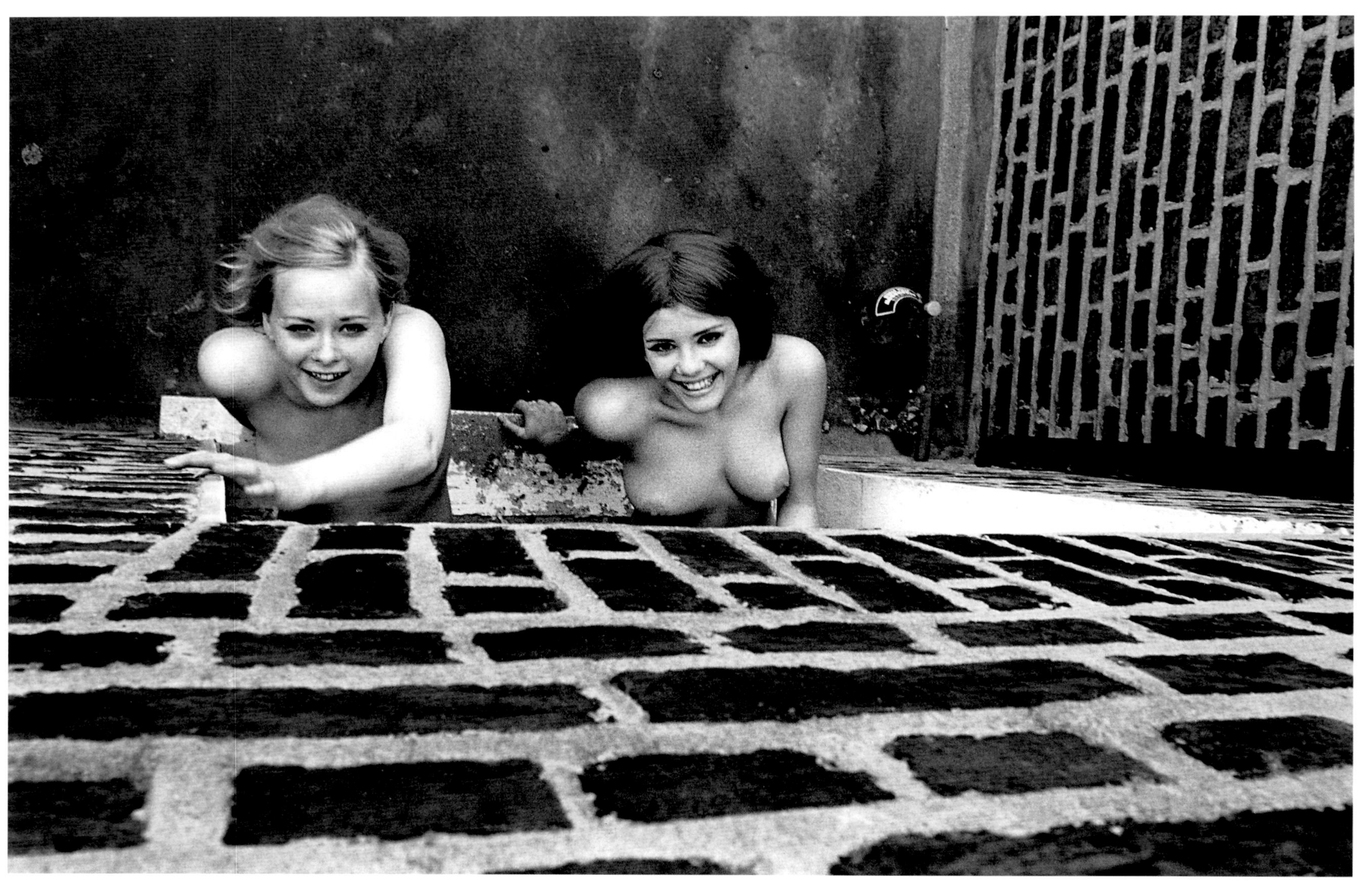

Good morning Sunshine

Rooftop – 34 Courtfield Gardens

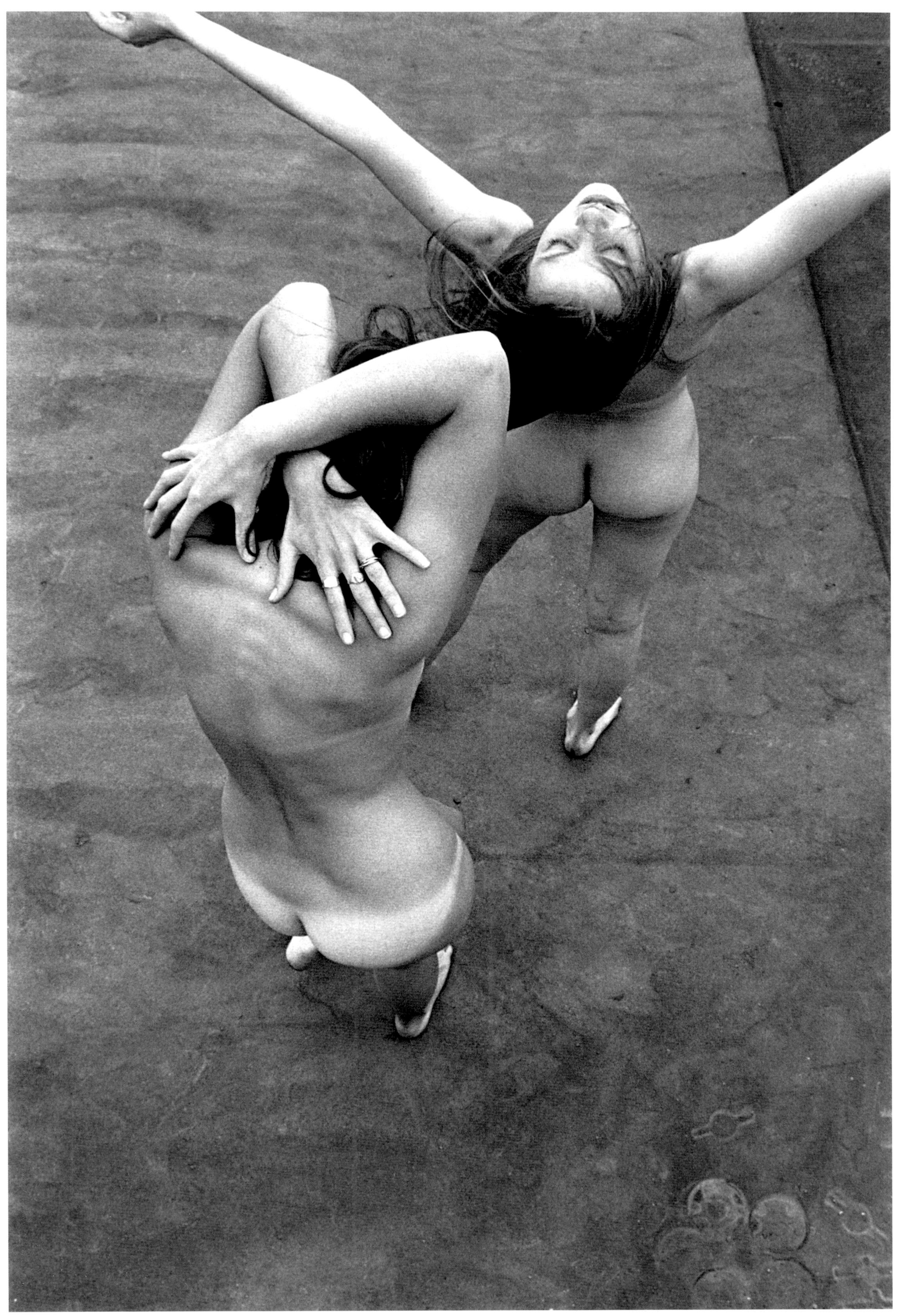

Meeting Christine

1969 was a year to be remembered and sealed with an affirmative tick in history. It was the year when the Americans first landed on the moon. The Beatles released what would be their last album *Abbey Road*. A succession of good fortunes happened to me that memorable year.

It was the year in which my first photographic book *Young London: Permissive Paradise* was published, lifting my profile in the publishing world. But for me, the highlight was my encounter with Christine, at a friend's New Year's party in Putney, where it became clear to me that "she's the one." I thank fate for having ended up at this party.

I had been looking forward to jumping into the New Year with Jane that night, my young starlet friend from Knightsbridge, a young woman who earned herself a name acting in creative horror movies, part of the Hammerstein Film Productions. I captured Jane on film, prior to the year's end on my Courtfield Gardens rooftop. Her husband David, apparently not aware of the shoot, cancelled the New Year's party on grounds of a flu attack after he saw the photographs. Later on that last day of the year, Fritz, a Carlton Tower receptionist friend from Austria with whom I had once worked, invited me to his party instead. He told me that I would not be disappointed. I accepted the invitation to join his crowd.

That night my eyes fell on a tall Austrian girl sipping from a glass of bubbly. We danced the night away, to then meet up the following day. Christine was different to my previous relationships. I had to take things slowly, to prove my sincerity towards her. Christine was a young woman with both feet on the ground. We lived in the Sixties, in the midst of the sexual revolution where the first commandment was "Make Love not War." But for me, it was now time to take a step back from casual encounters. For the first time, I felt I could engage in a lasting relationship.

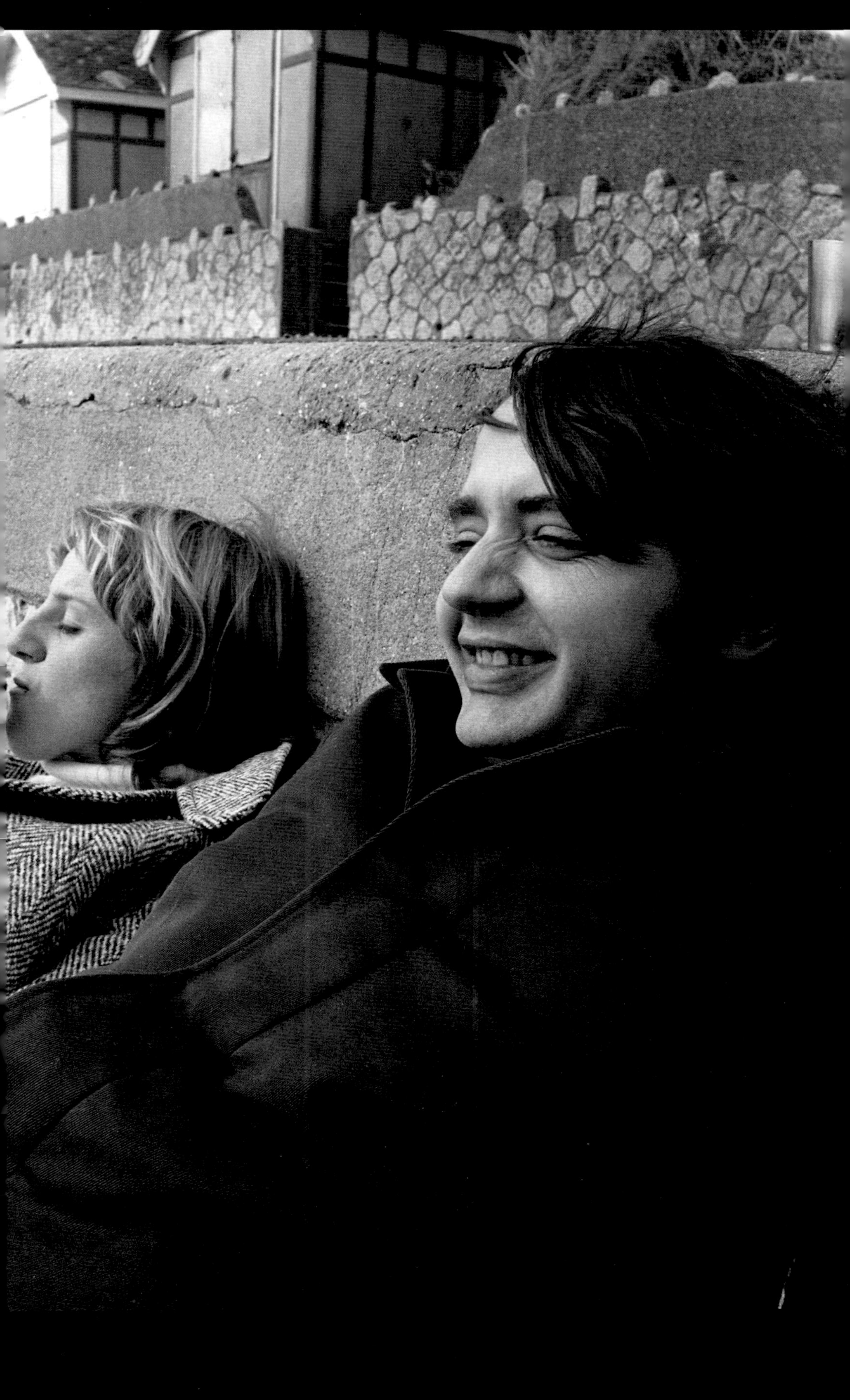

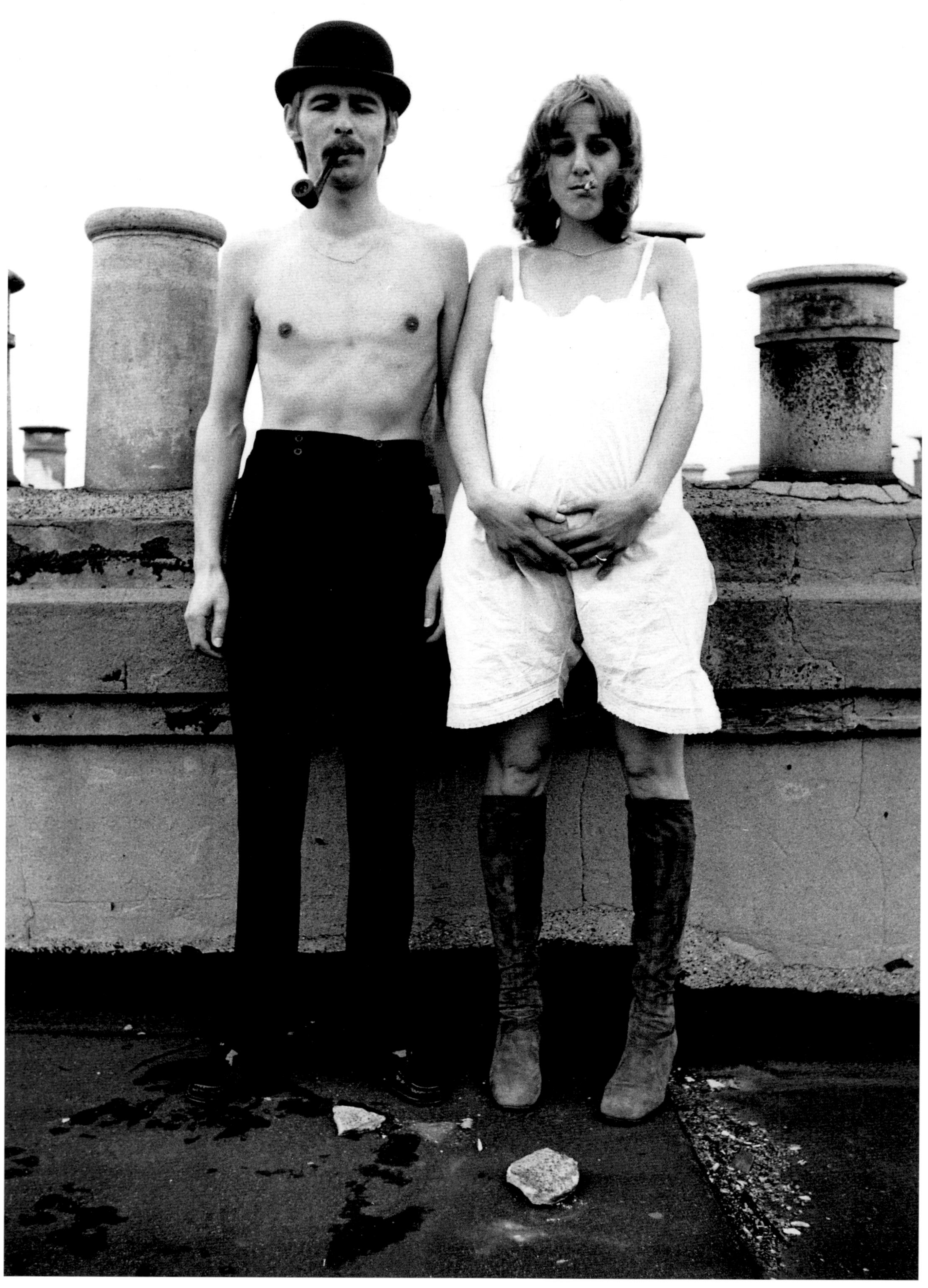

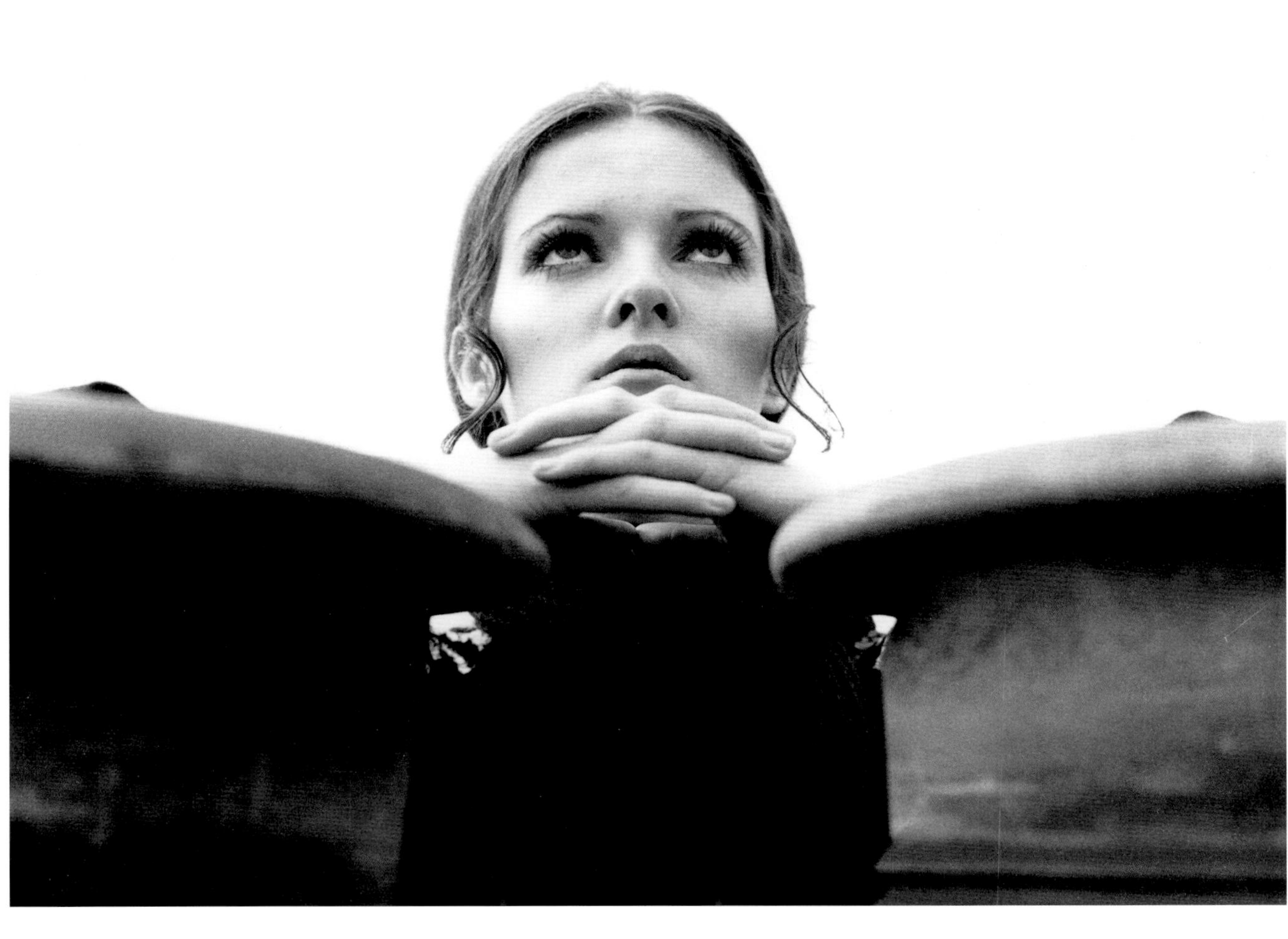

Till death do us part – Christine and friend Ditmar, 1969

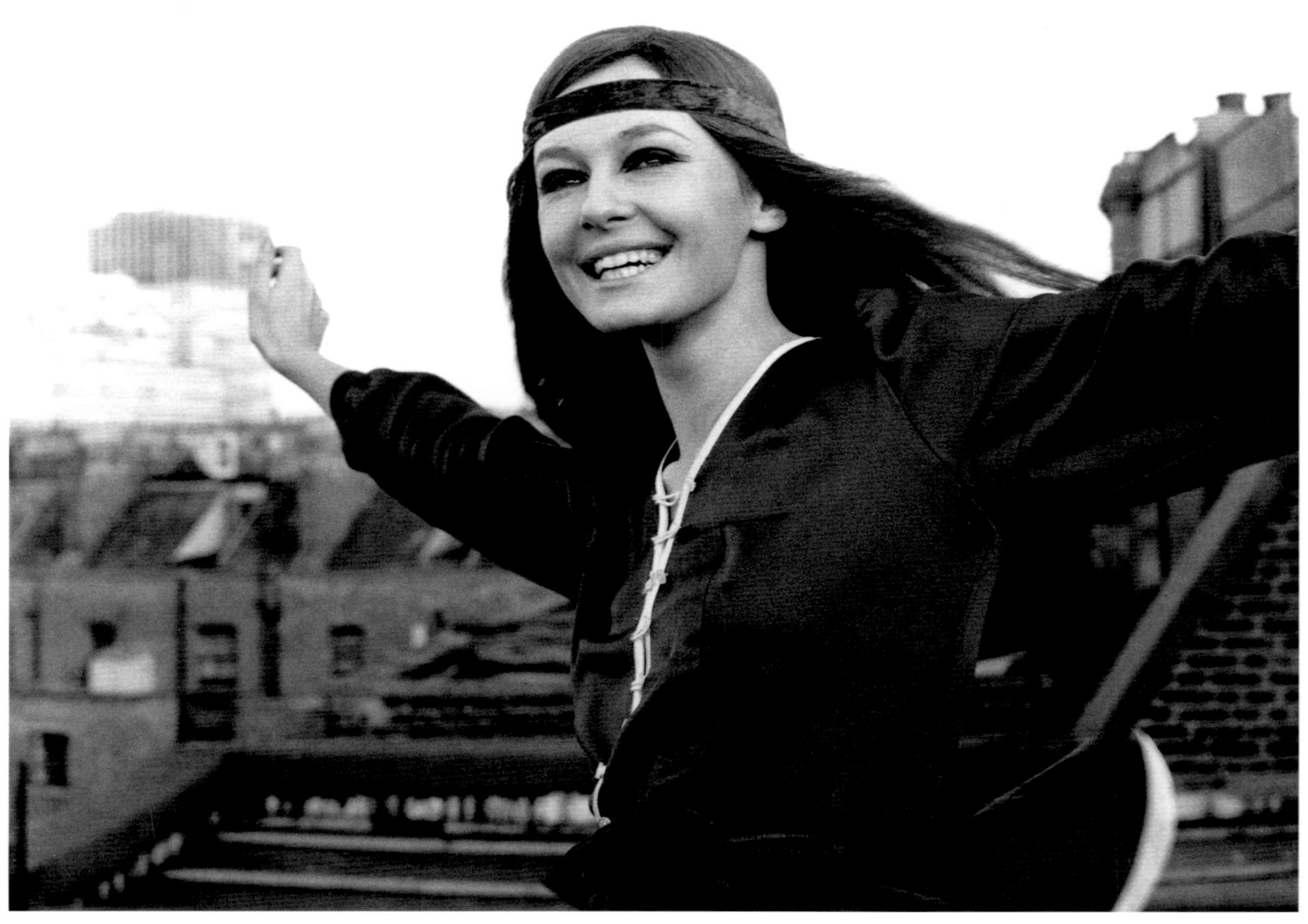

Above it all – Jeanette, photographer's rooftop, Courtfield Gardens

Joan, 1967

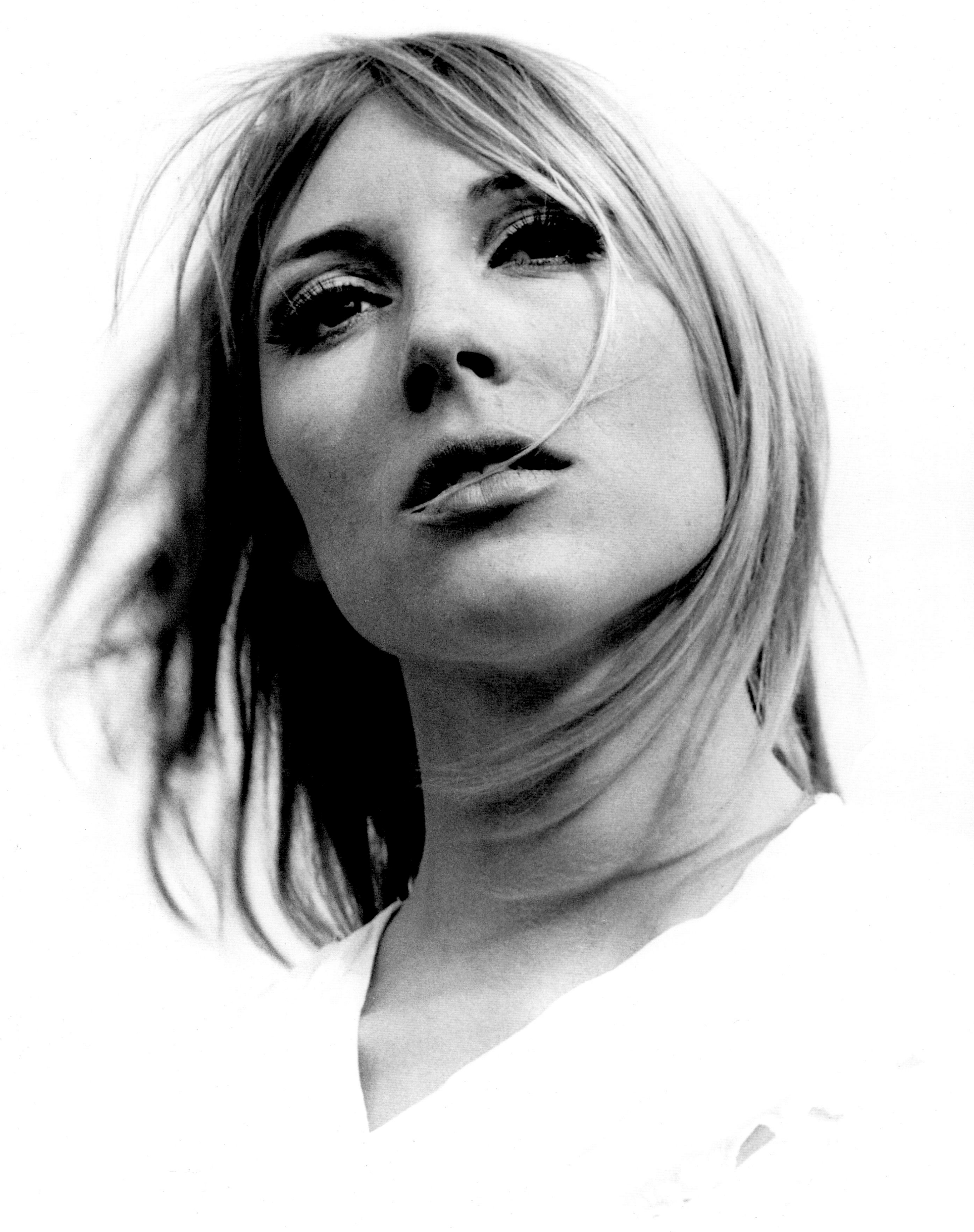

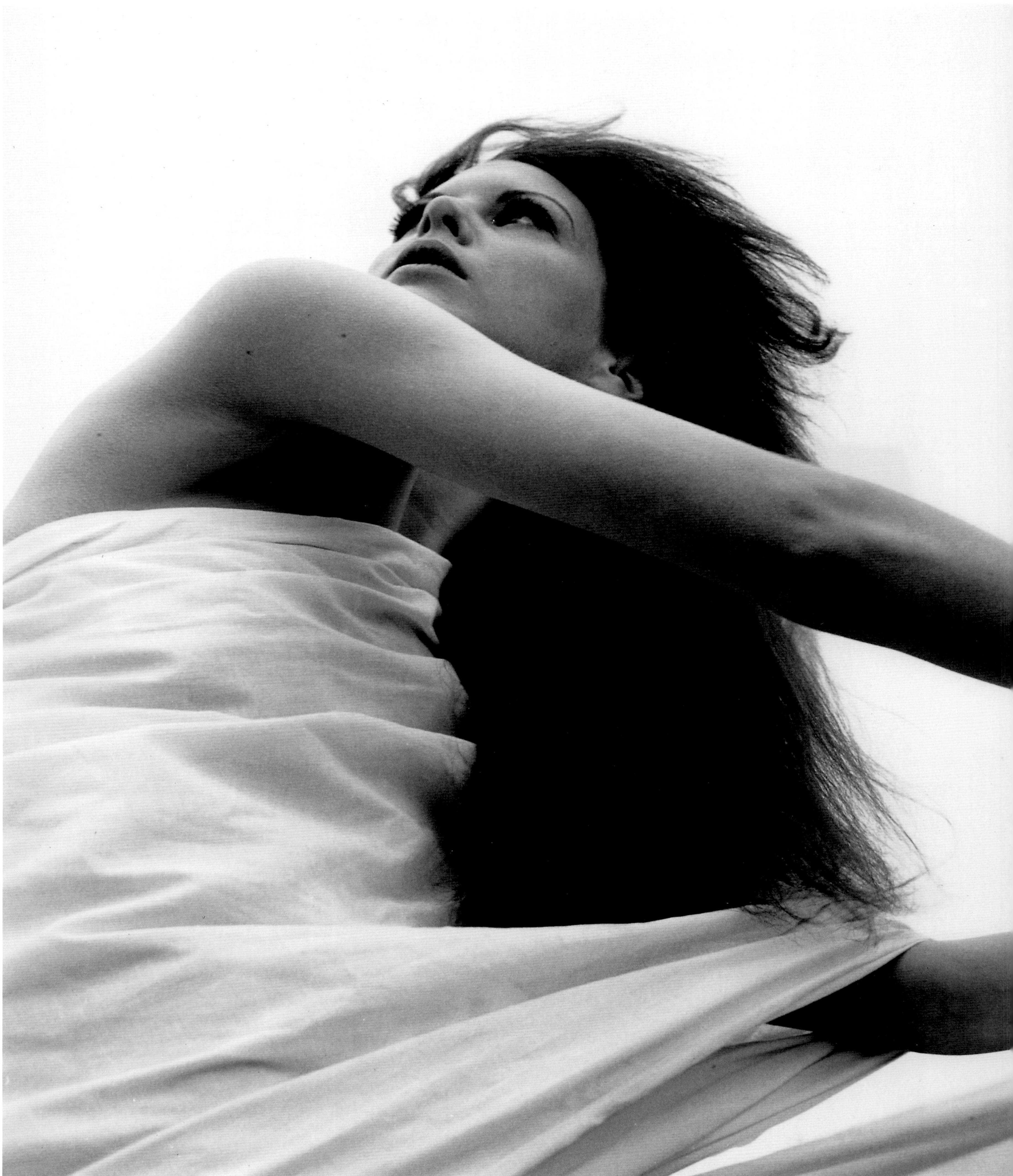

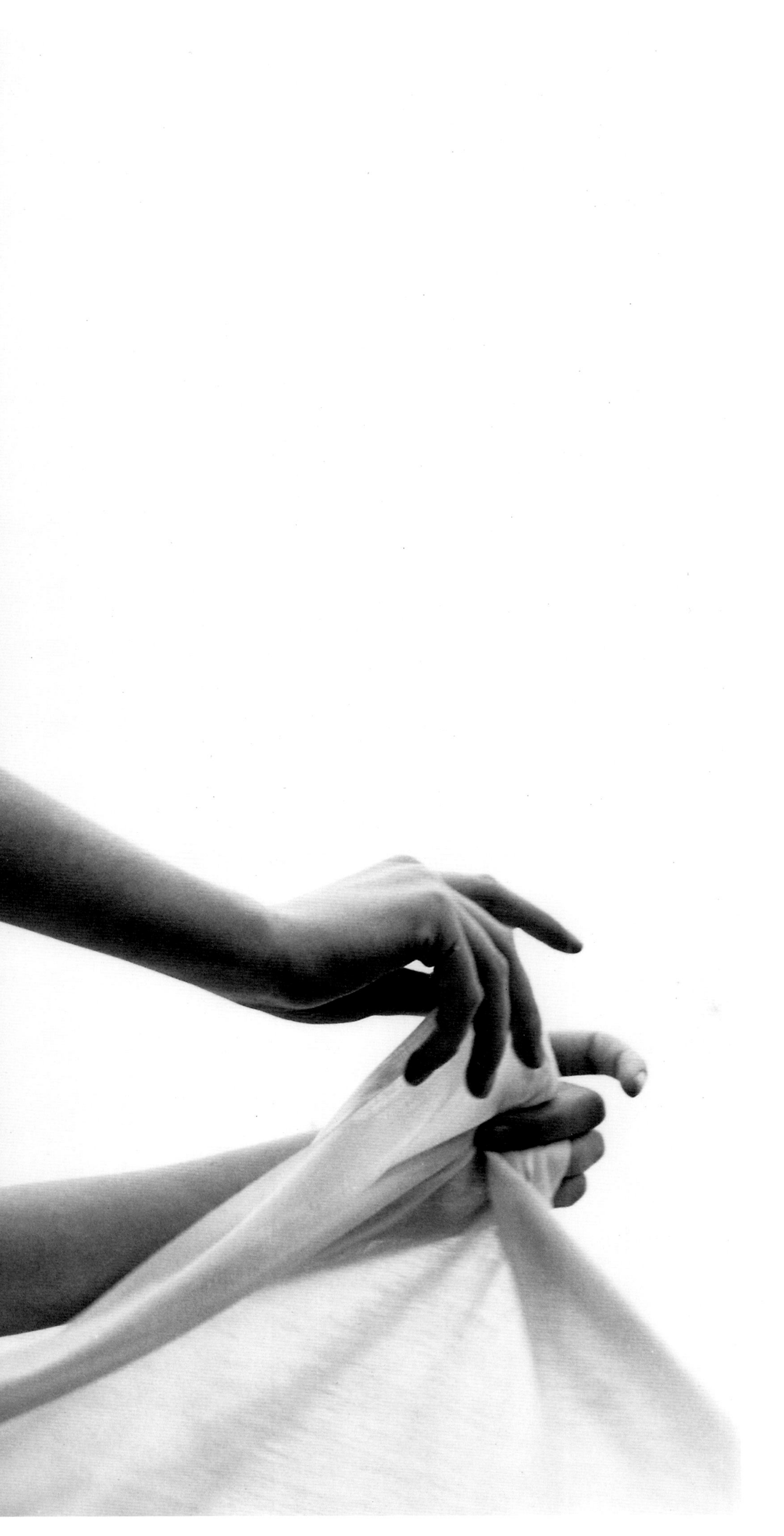

Celia, photographer's rooftop

Next pages:
On a day like no other – Rachel, Cork Film Festival, 1970

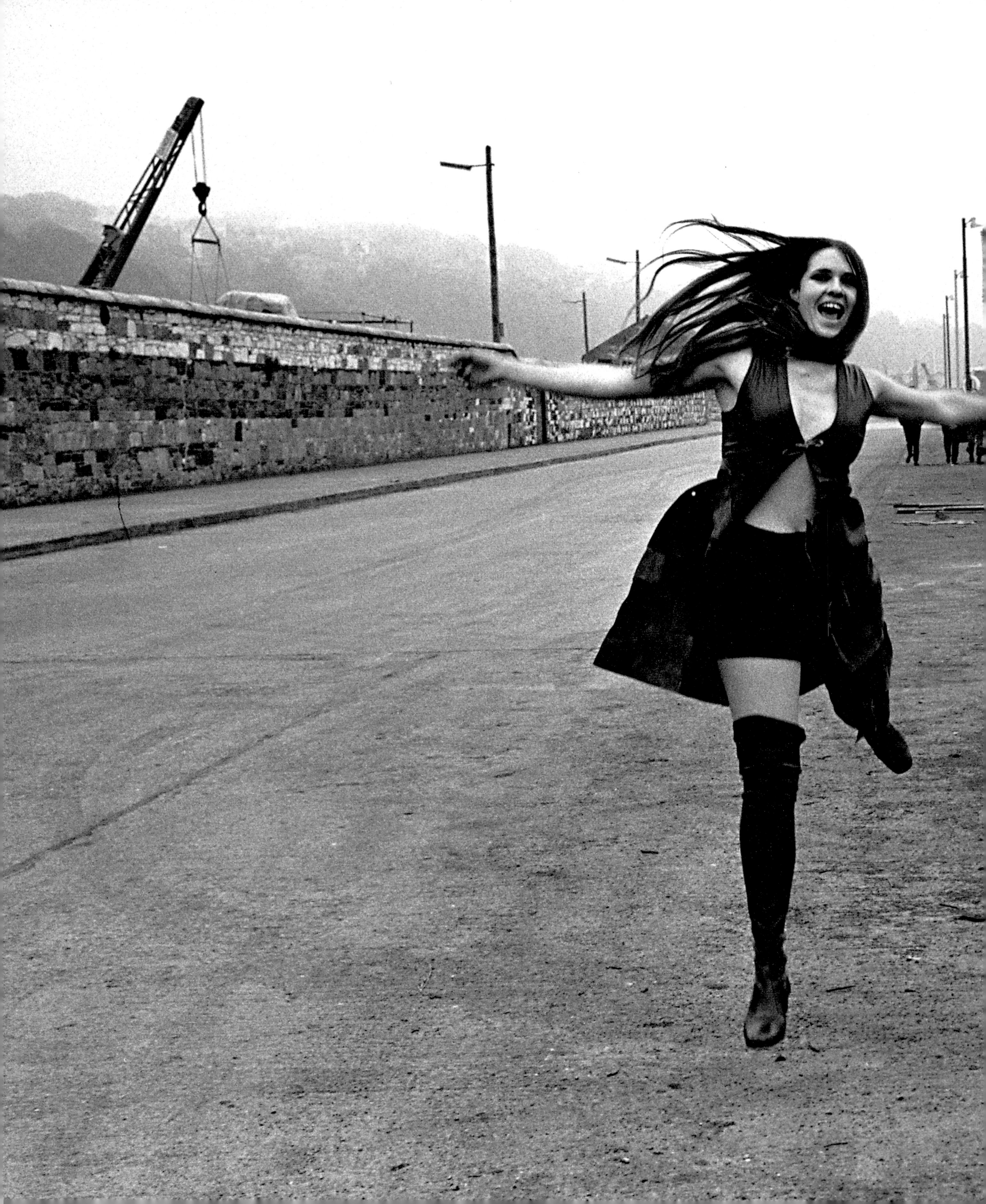

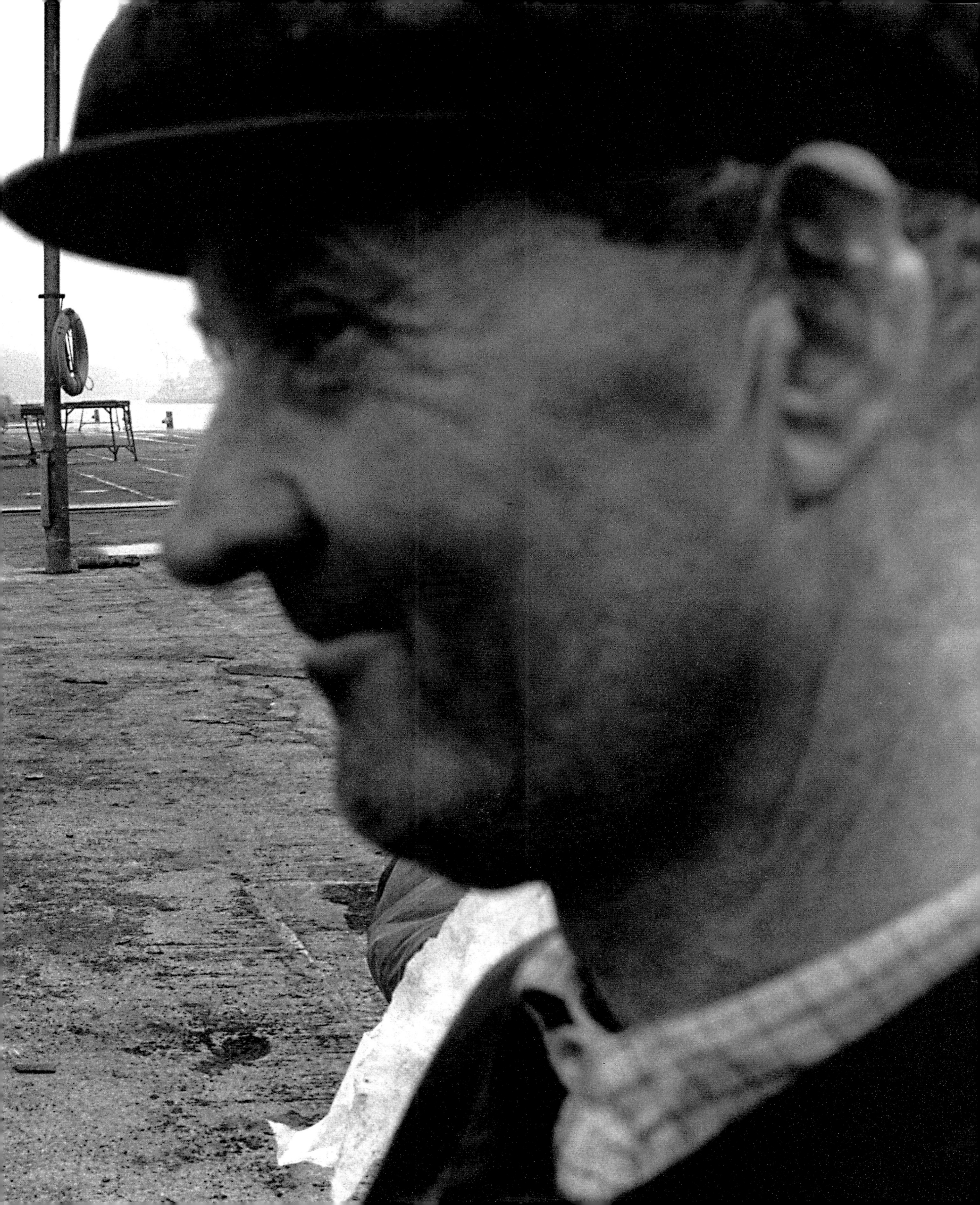

Rachel Williams, modelling for photographer

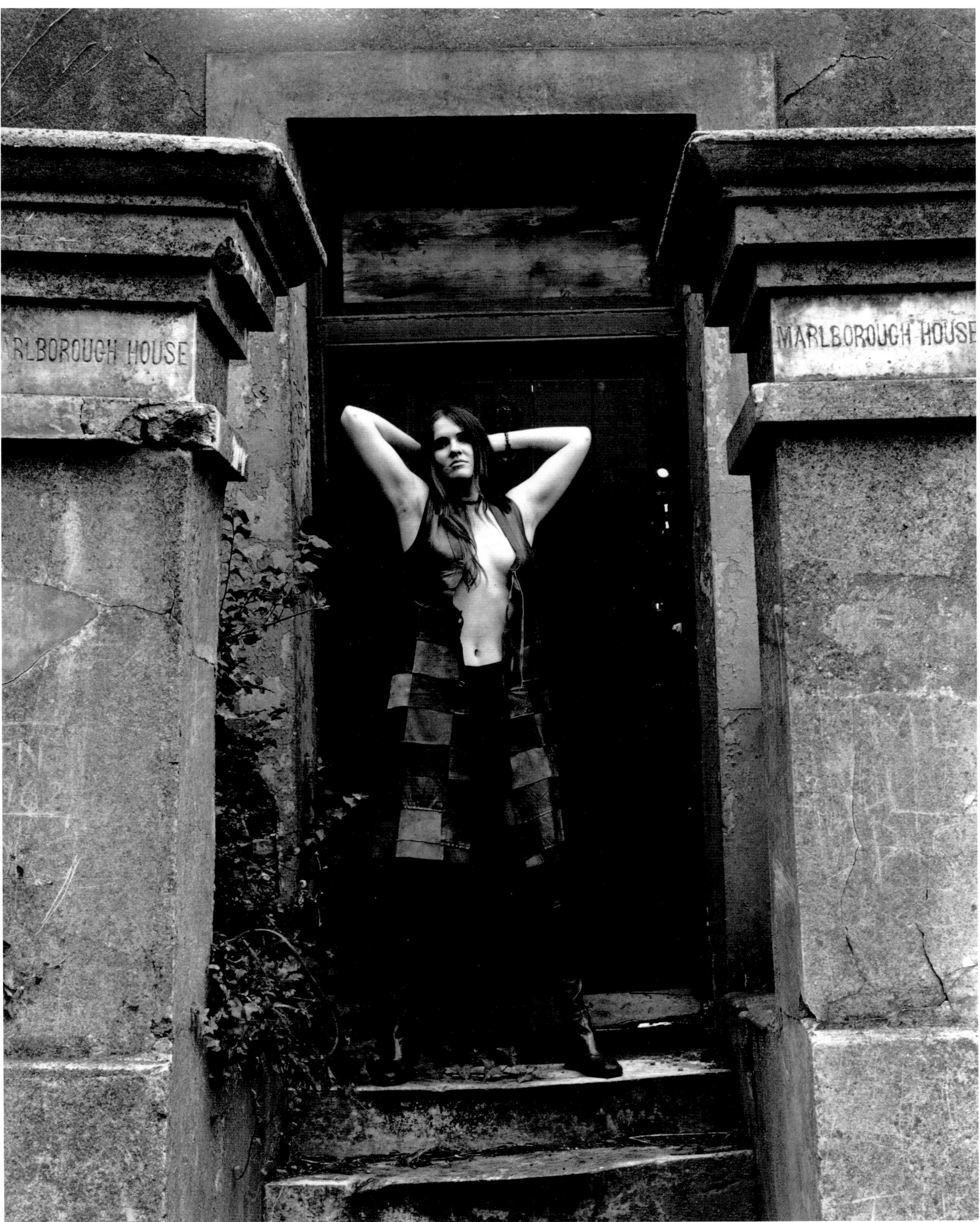
ARLBOROUGH HOUSE
MARLBOROUGH HOUSE

Bombed Church Rescue

Right next to St. Paul's Cathedral was a bombed church with Roman columns that reached far into the air. Lush ferns were growing in her yard, giving new life to scattered ruins. These were fragments of history where once church bells rang.

There was no public access and on that Sunday morning that I will never forget I had to reveal its location and entrance to the authorities.

Susan, my sporty girlfriend at the time, courageously climbed up the church wall, so I could take the most unusual photos ever. Susan was in God's costume, revealing her full beauty. To reach the church tower she balanced her way over a plank that tumbled down as soon as she made it to the other side. The plank plummeted into the ferns below, almost giving me a heart attack. There was no safe way for Susan to get down!

After losing my courage and nerves, I resorted to calling the fire brigade from a nearby phone booth, despite being aware that there might be a hefty fine coming my way. I clearly remember my words after dialing the number for the emergency services on that Sunday morning: "nude girl trapped on church tower" close to St. Paul's.

To my absolute amazement, only minutes later, the air was filled with sirens and other repelling sounds. There were policemen on motor cycles rushing to the scene and God only knows how many fire engines came racing to the church, trying to find their way through hidden and overgrown pathways. And not to mention the ambulances, even one carrying a stretcher!

I concealed myself among the ferns, hiding from the big dreaded monster fine. The simply mind-blowing entertainment from the rescue operation of a trapped nudist played out before my eyes. Susan was not unattractive and this was of good fortune as to my utter surprise, the mission was not sealed with a fine.

No fine for me was fine by me.

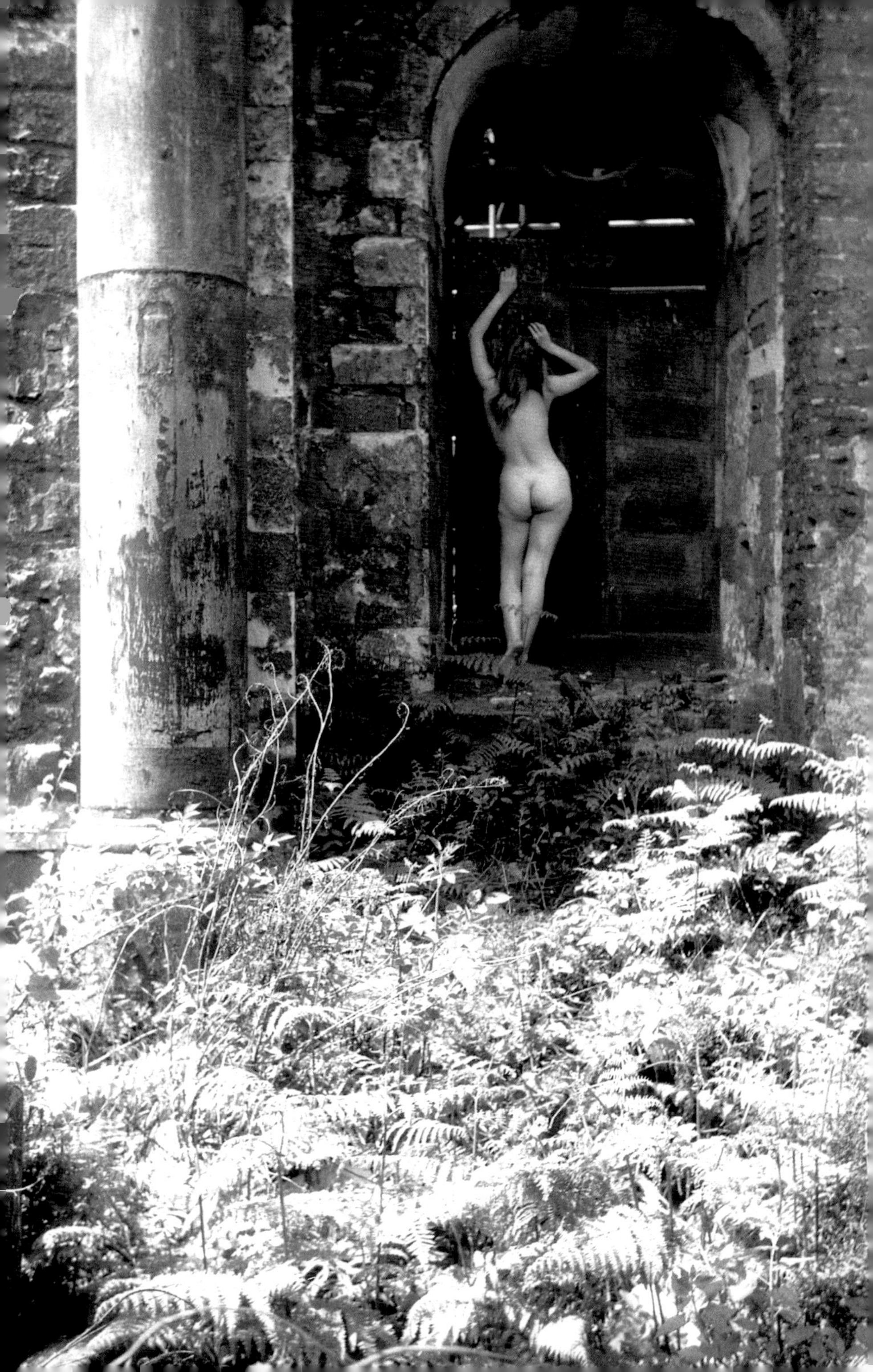

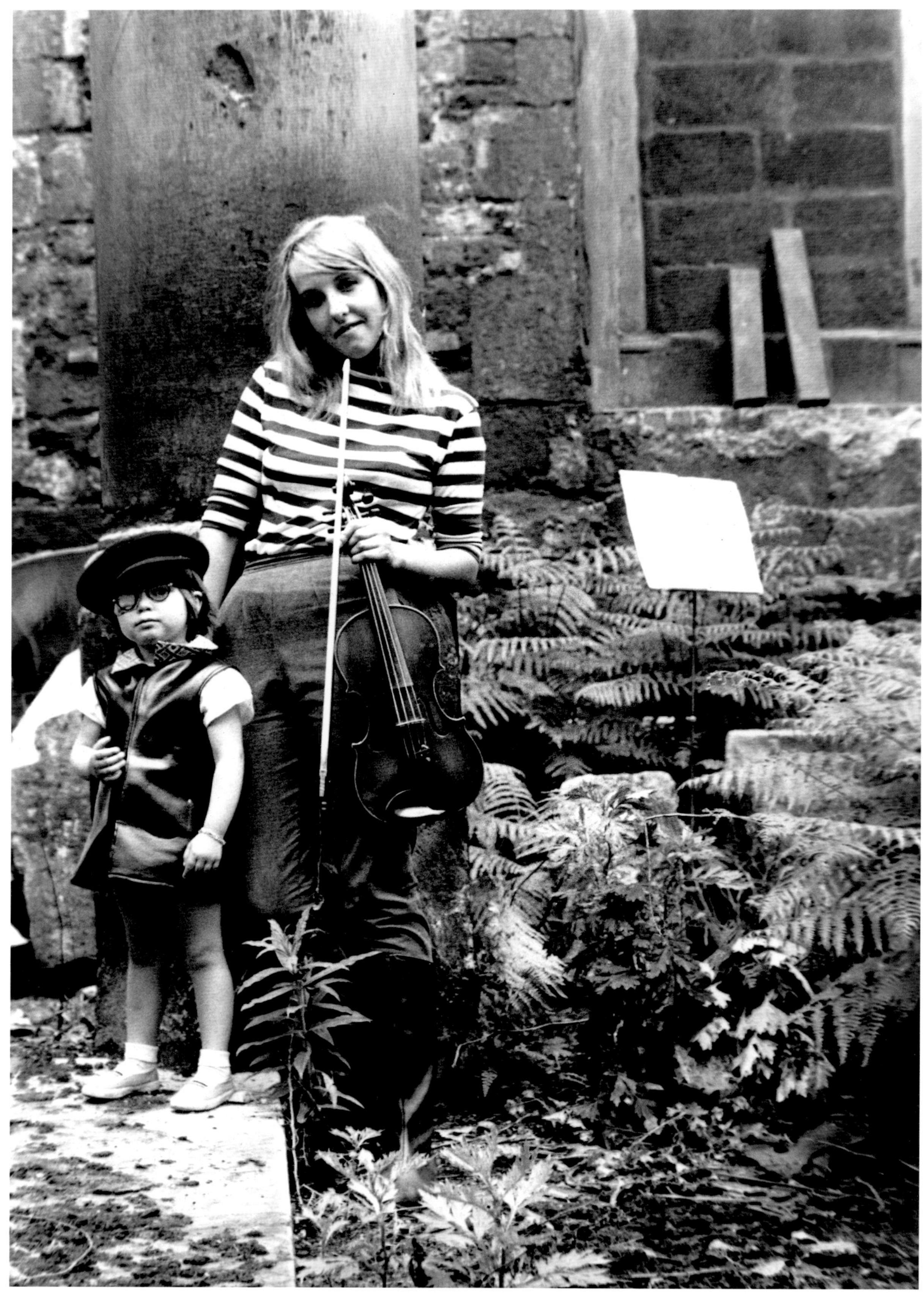

Susan and child, St. Paul's, 1968

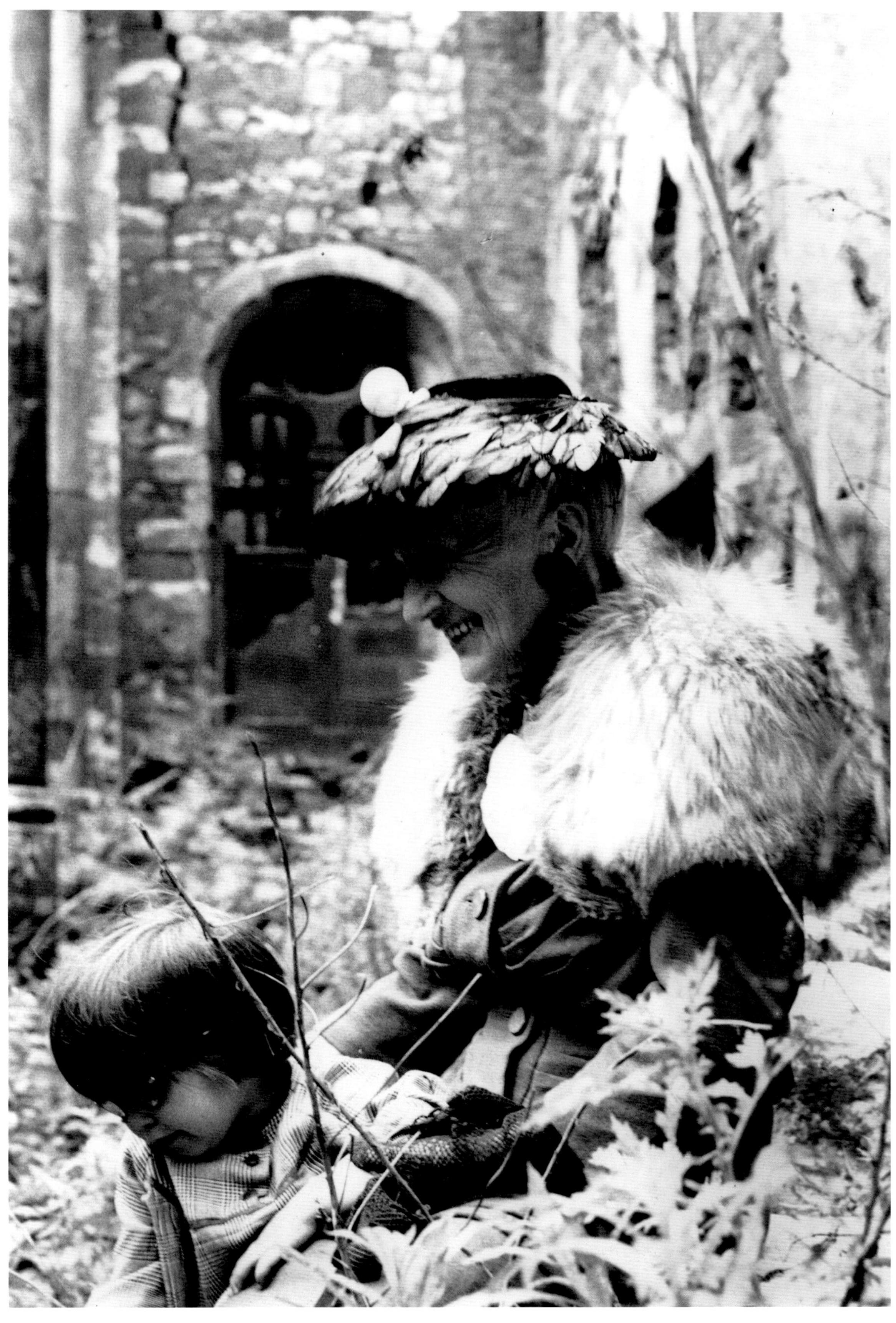

Mrs. Black, socialite and child

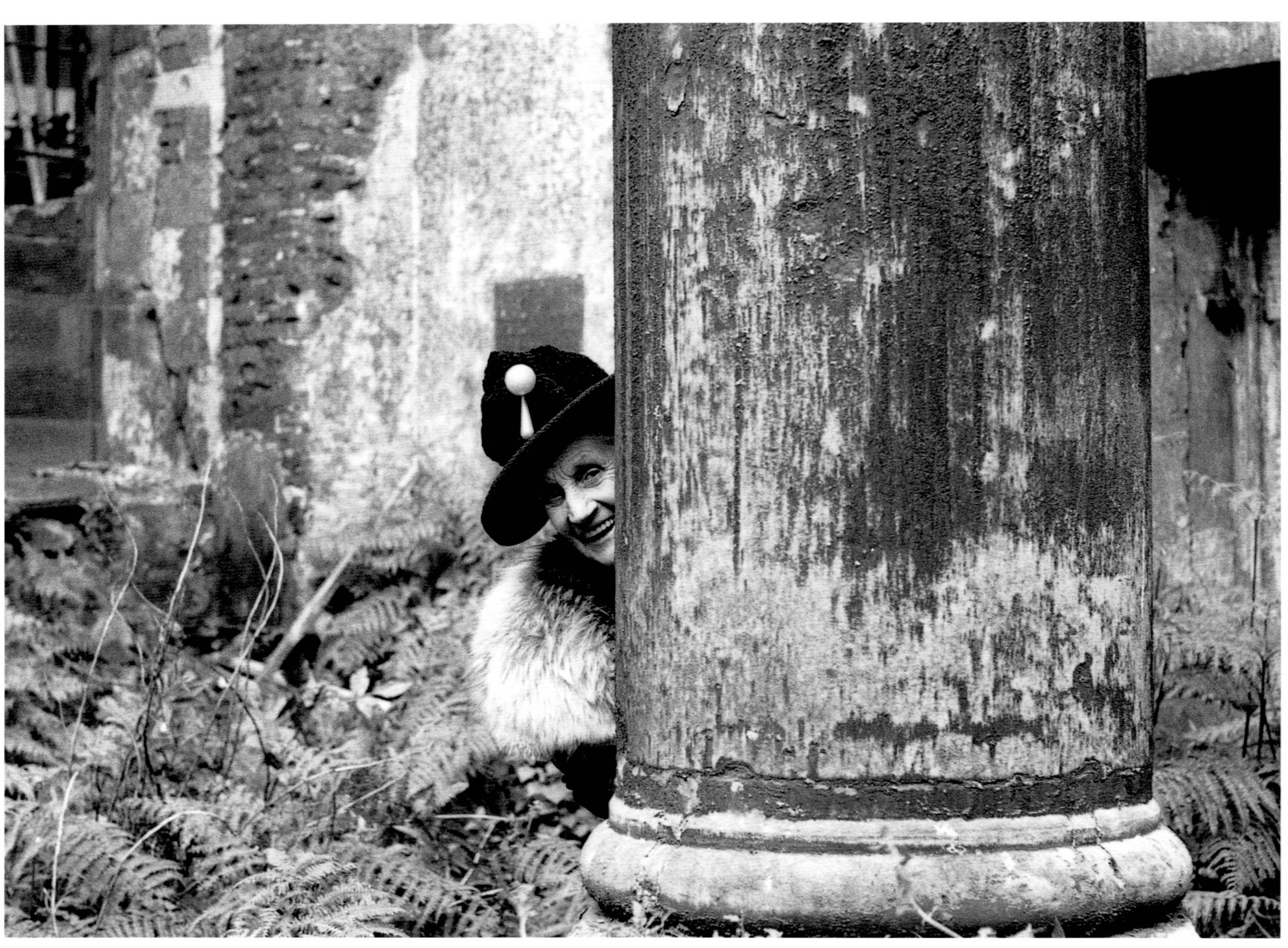

Out of sight, out of mind

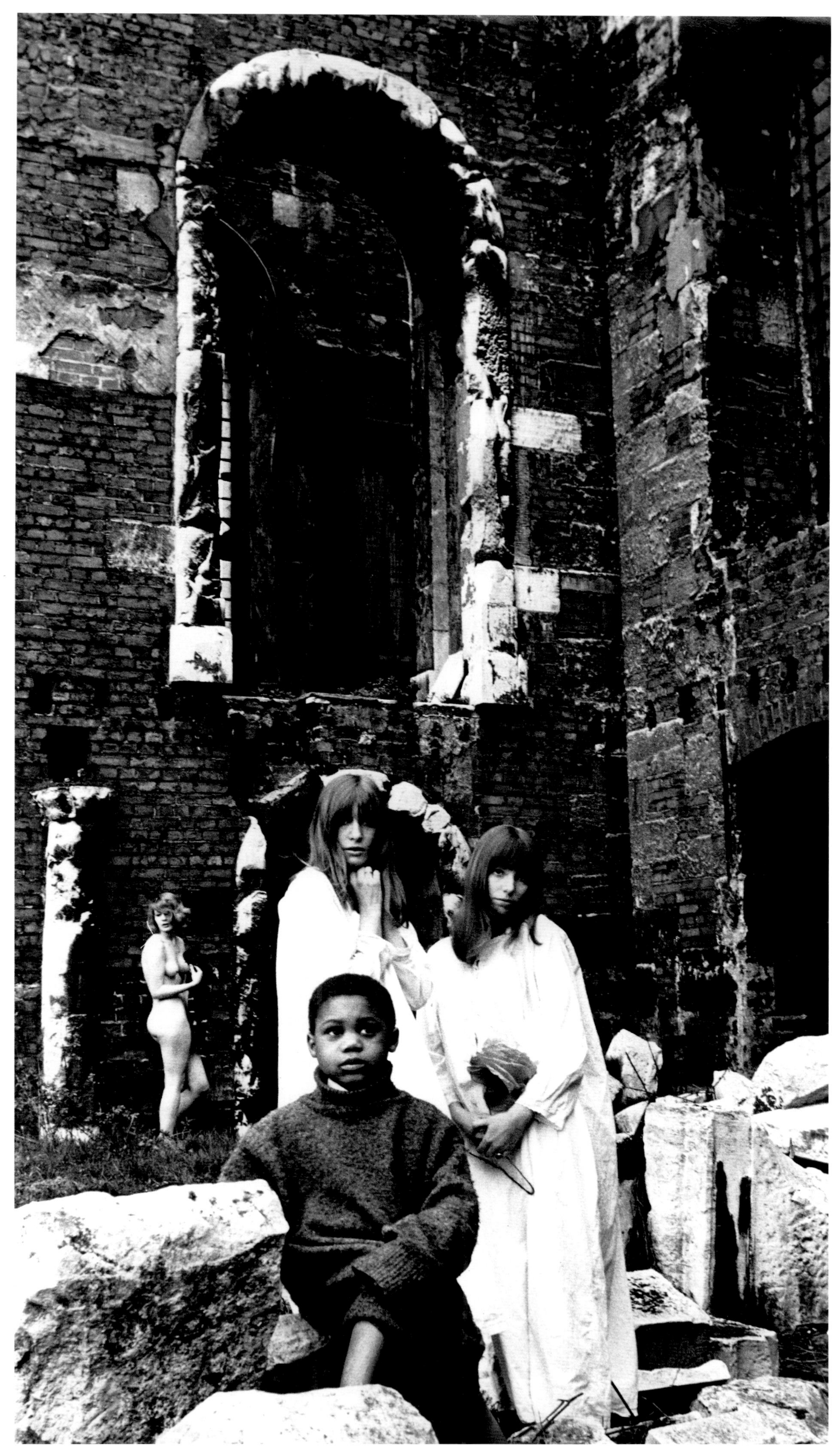

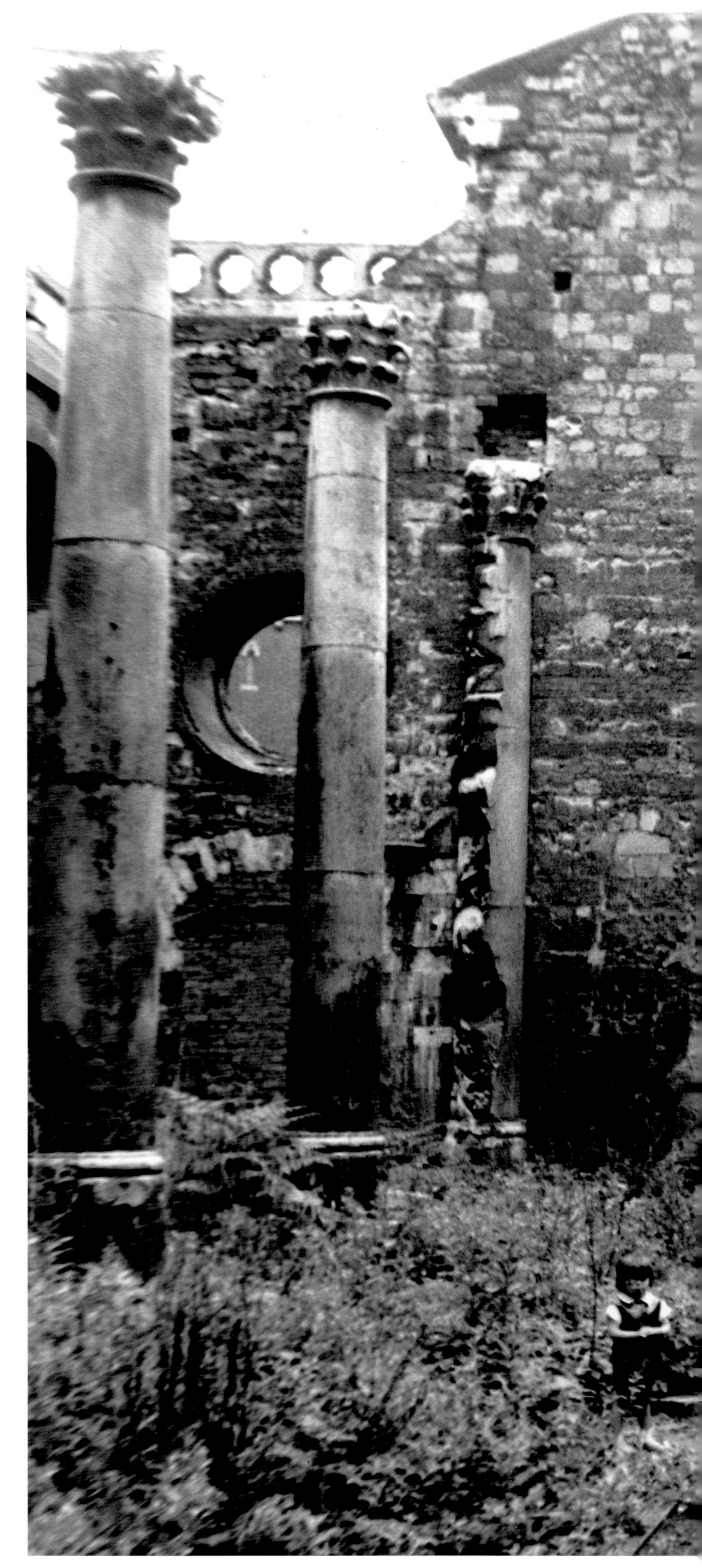

Once upon a time in the Sixties

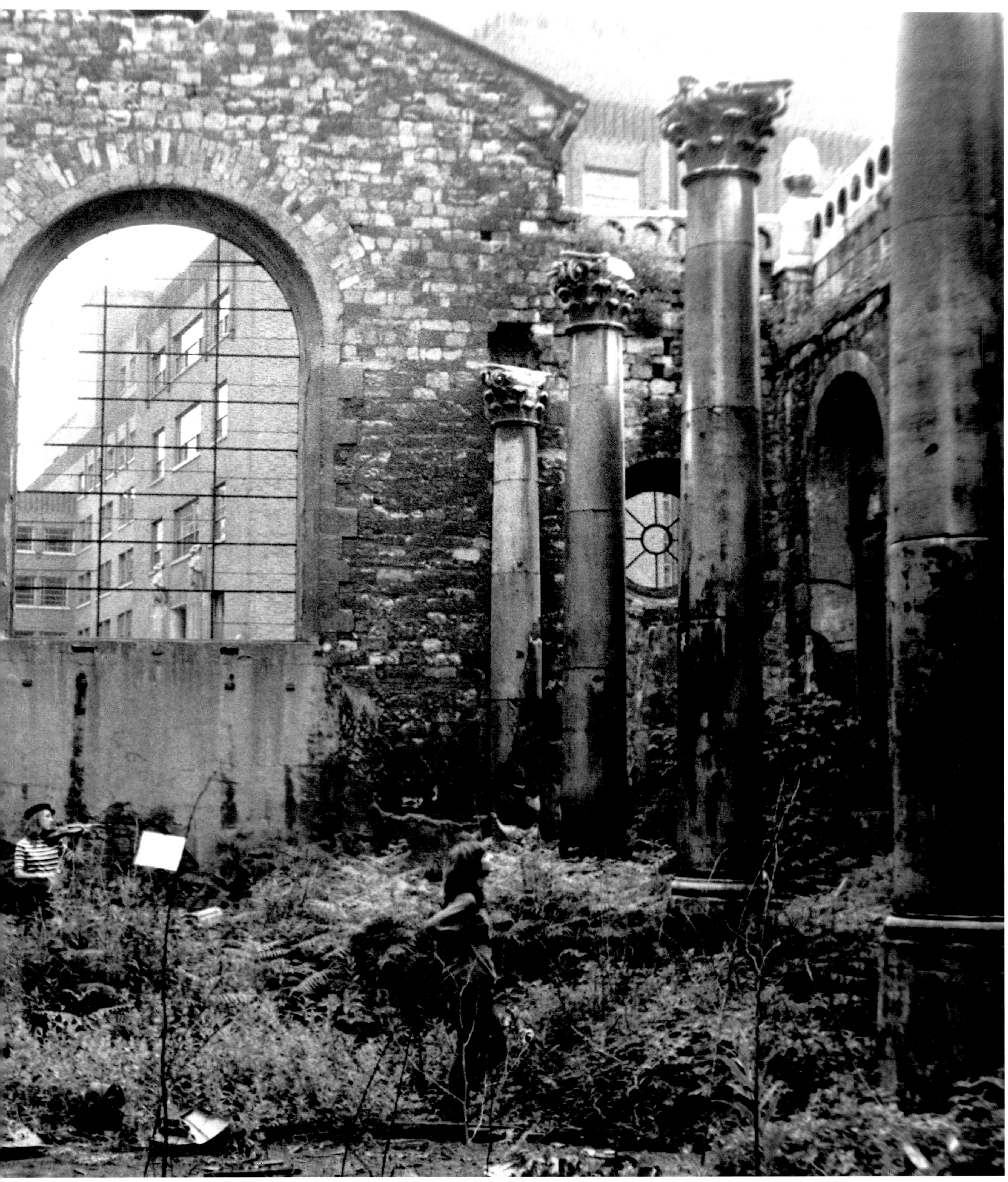

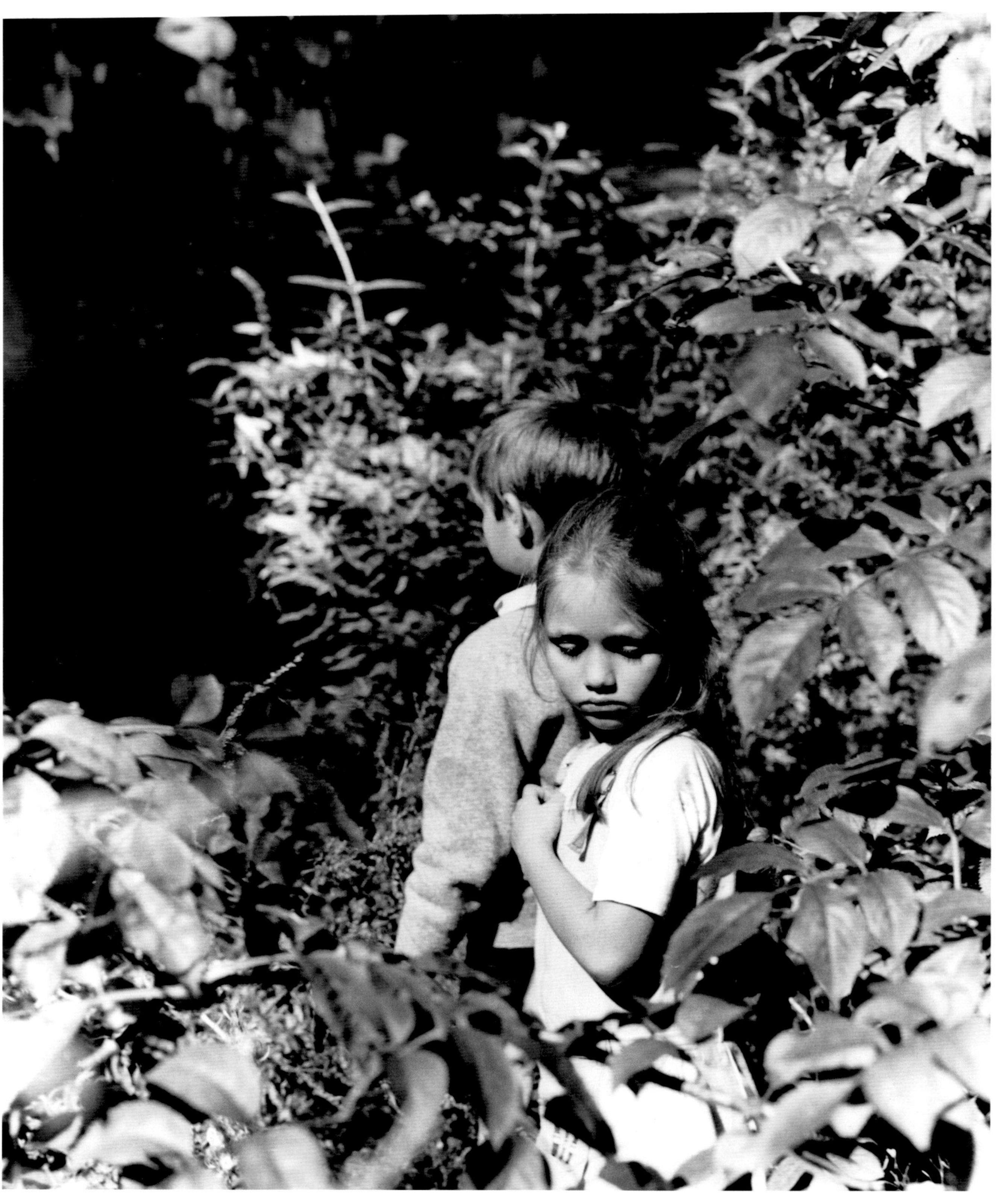

And live happily ever after – Little Tina and companion

Where the minds meet – Pimlico district, 1969

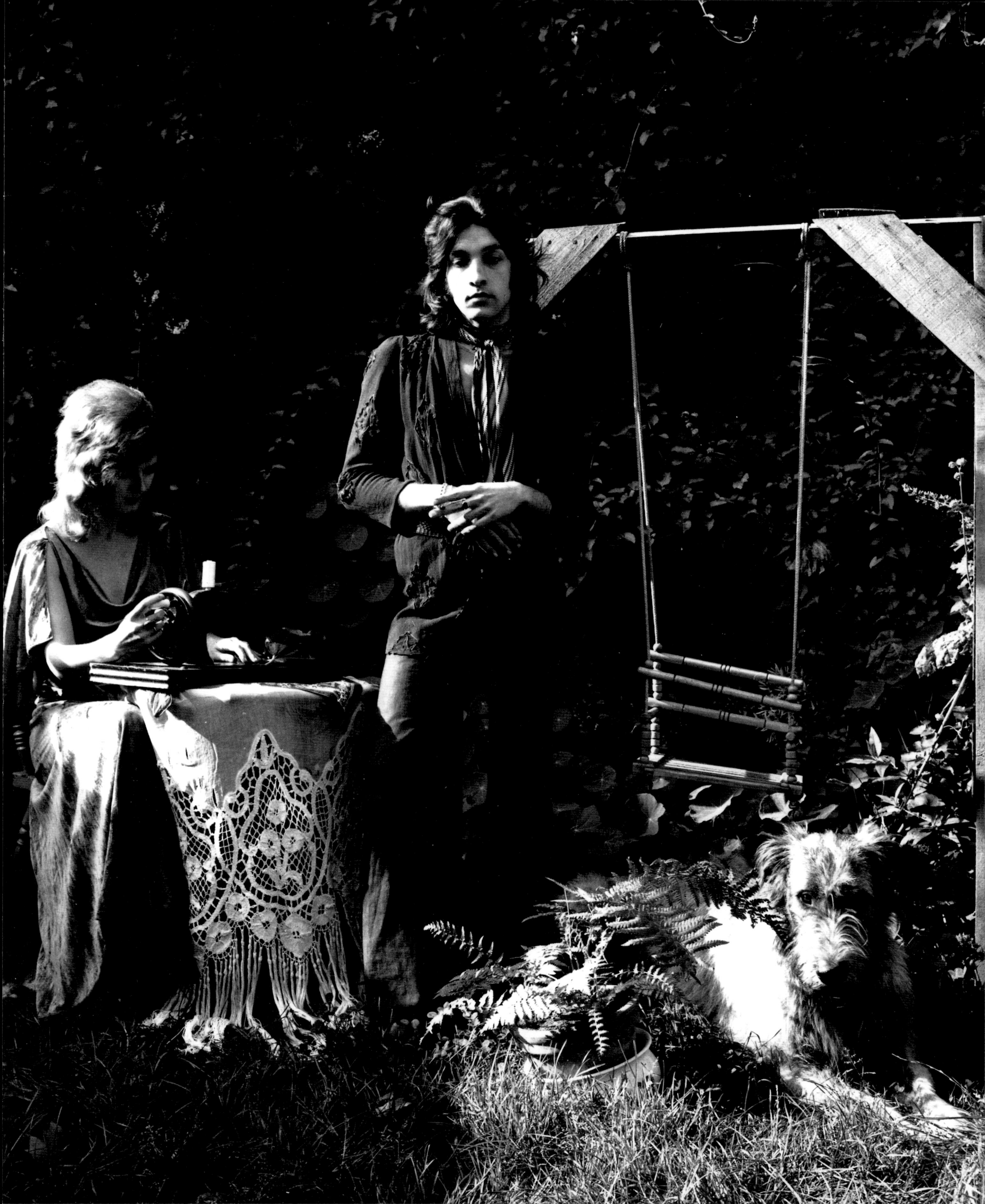

Connie Kreski

In the early seventies when my portfolio gained momentum, I began to work on a freelance basis for the Playboy Club in London's Park Lane. I enjoyed taking photographs of attractive girls who were applying to be Bunnies. In 1968, I had an eye on *Playboy* magazine's future Playmate of the Month Connie Kreski, who ended up as Playmate of the Year in 1969. I was taken by Connie's charm and good looks. At that time she was romantically engaged with Playboy executive Victor Lowndes, and they lived in a luxury mansion in Mayfair.

I was trusted and had access to Victor's house at any time of the day, where I took a wide range of alluring images of Connie. Photographing her in such an environment meant everything to me. She was so playful, feminine, humble, and always cheerful. Lowndes's luxurious home exceeded by far any studio setting. It was overflowing with art, creative pornography, and artifacts that I had never experienced before. I was blown away.

Connie glided through all departments of life, starting at a young age as cheerleader, then an usherette in a Michigan theater, and upon graduation at the Mercy College in Detroit she enrolled in a nursing program. After cheerleading for a university football team in Michigan, she was discovered by *Playboy*. Connie moved into sophisticated circles, mixing with the likes of Tina Sinatra and Jacqueline Bisset, and enjoying parties with Roman Polanski, while climbing the ladder of success.

Connie lived her life to the hilt for the next ten years, also performing as a TV and film actress. For years to come conquering all "in" places of our world. Once coming back to London and wanting to stay for only a week, Connie decided to stay for a year. Swinging London fascinated her so much. She loved the vibrating Sixties. The fashion, the scene, and the rhythm of the city, yet she also was an outdoor girl, enjoying sports and horse riding. Sadly Connie died of a blocked artery in 1995 in Beverly Hills, California.

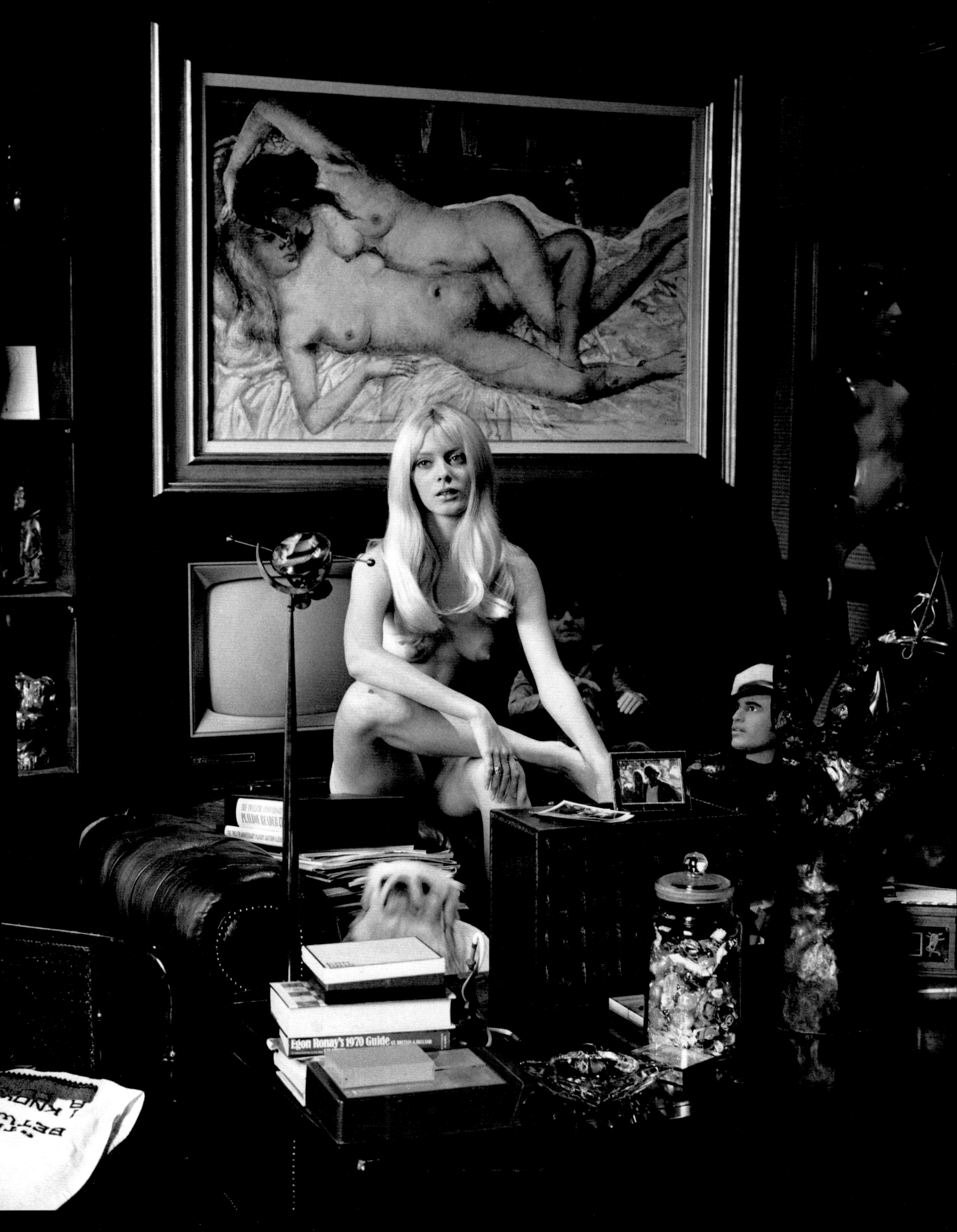
Egon Ronay's 1970 Guide

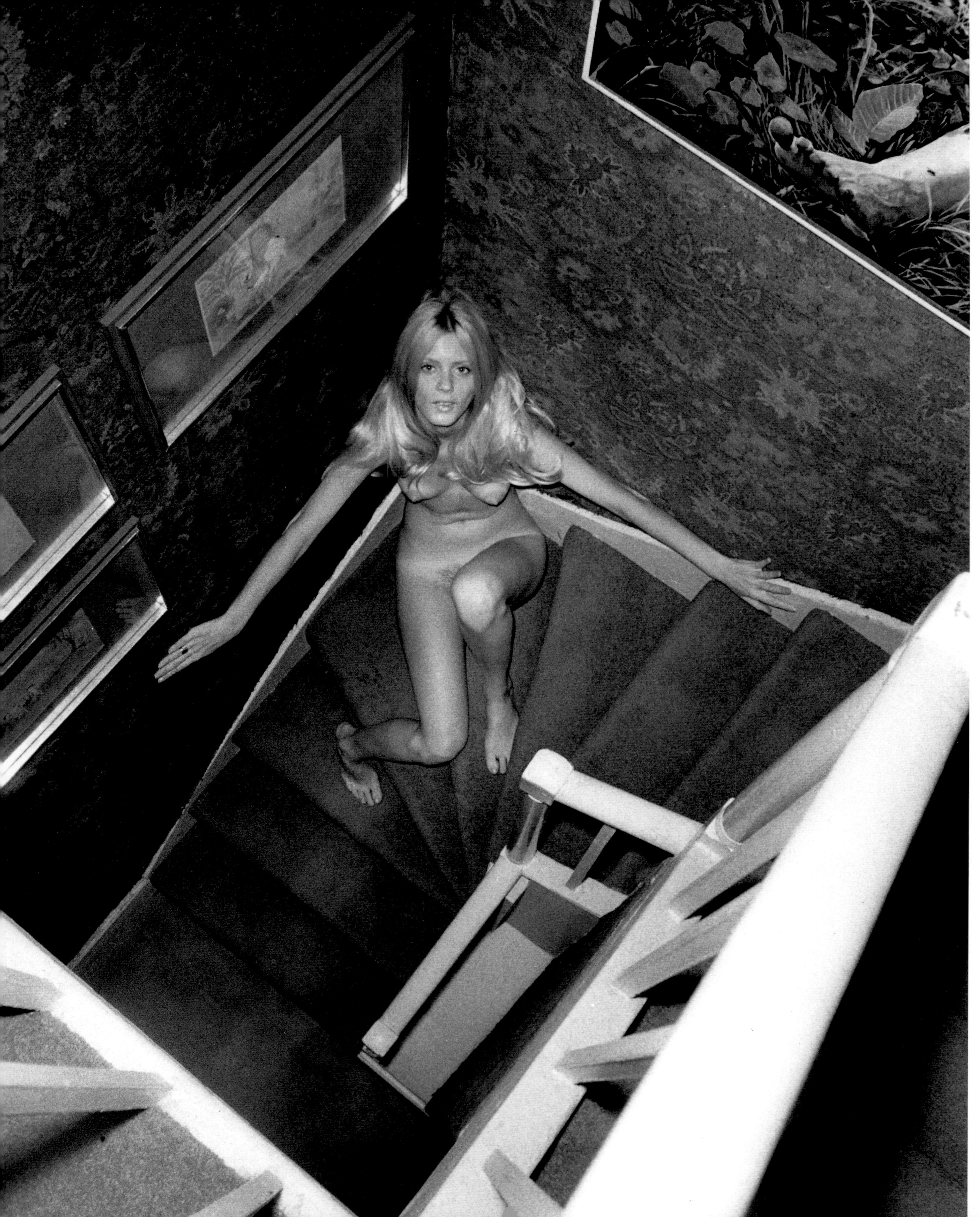

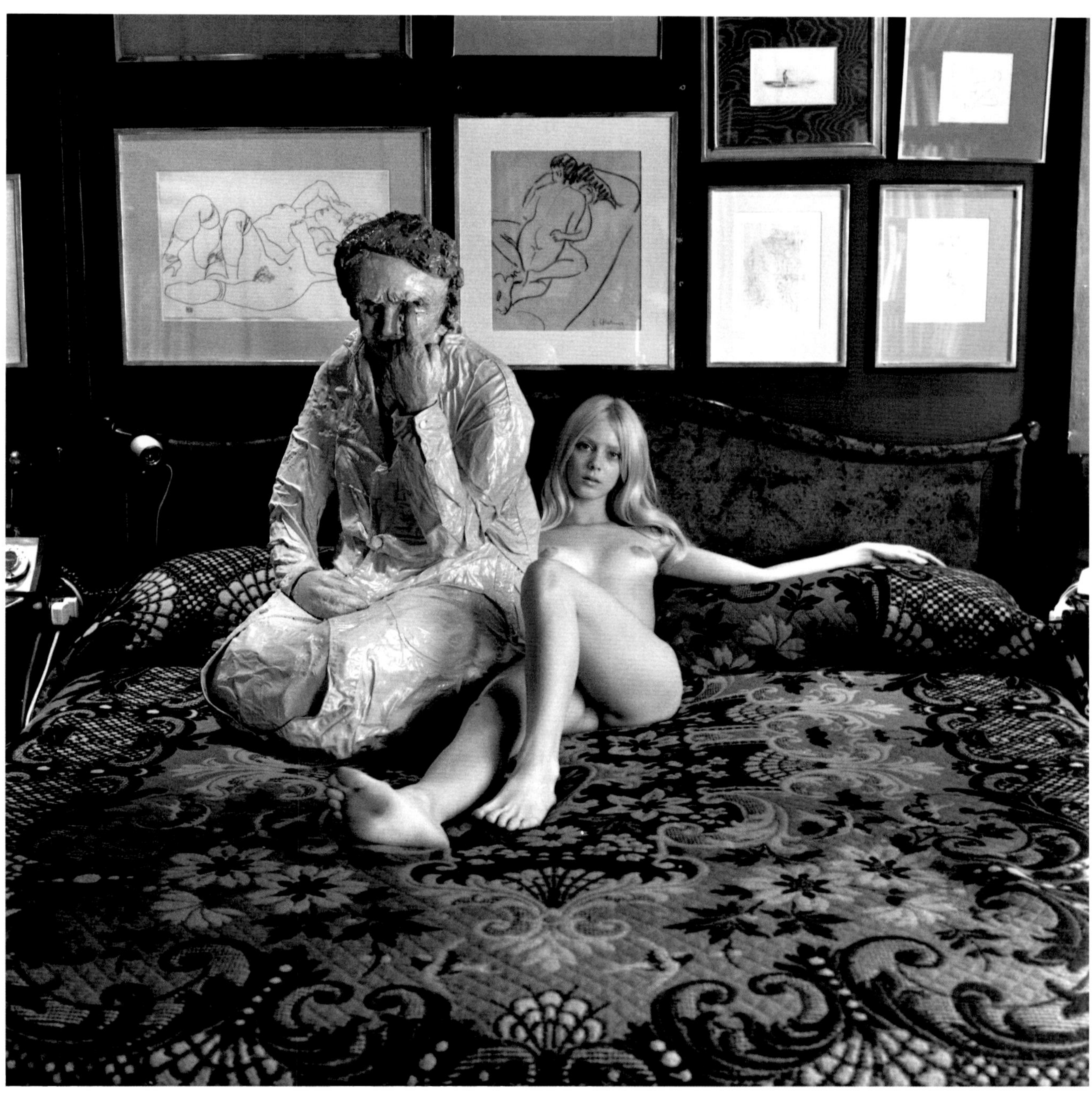

Nurse, Actress, and Playboy Playmate Connie Kreski, London

Connie Kreski, Playboy Playmate of the year, 1969

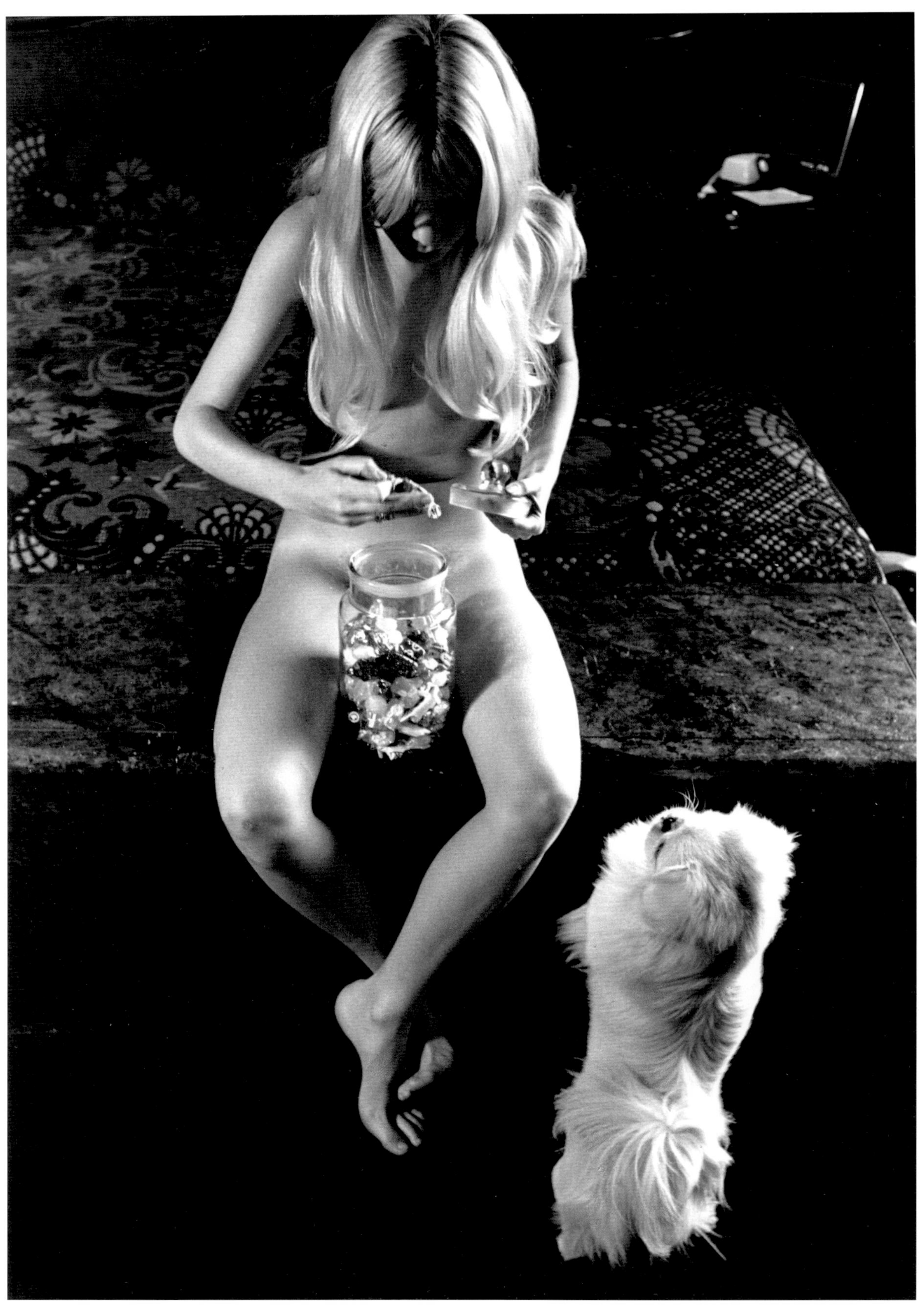

Sweets for my sweet – Connie, 1968

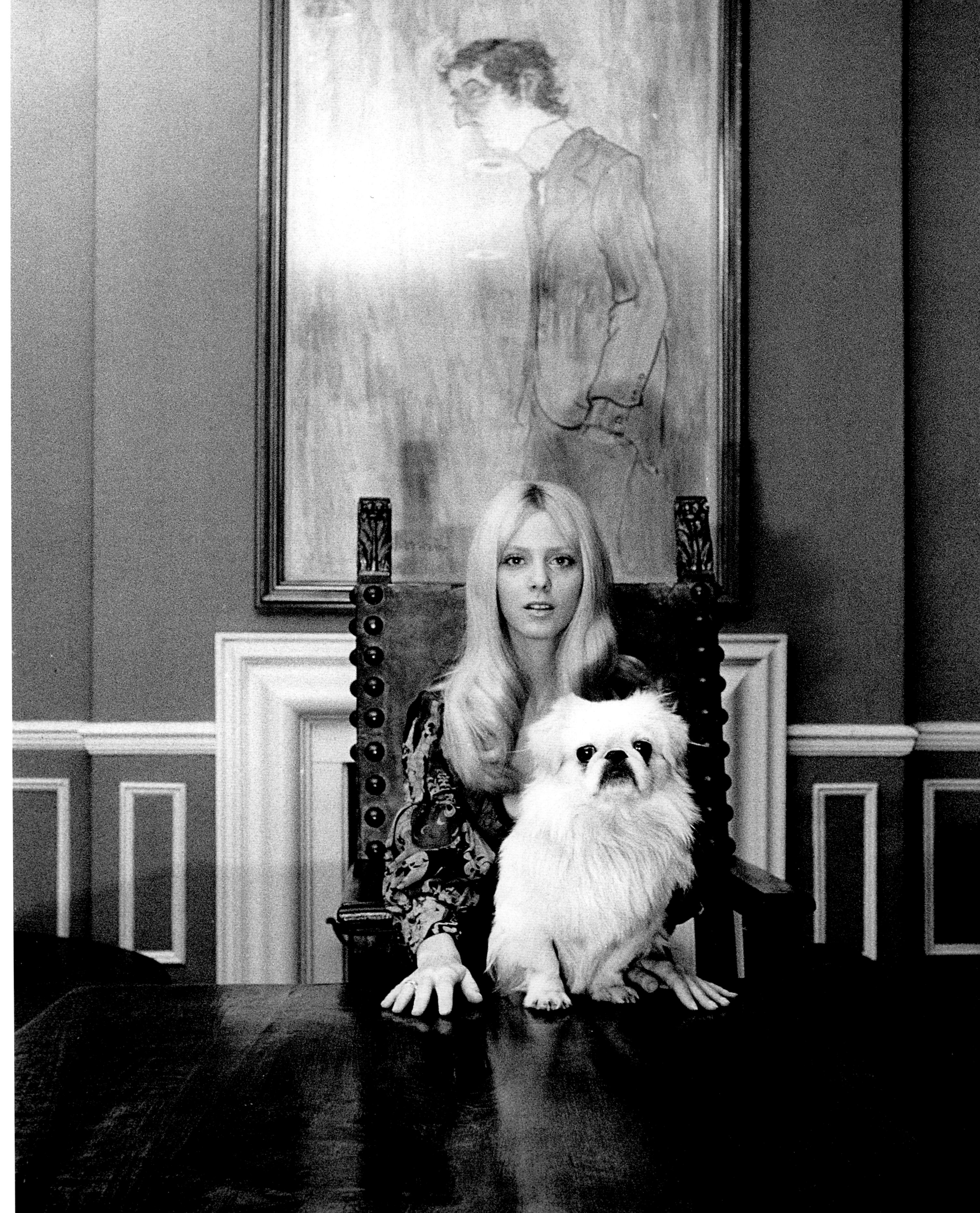

Ulla, Swedish model, photographer's studio

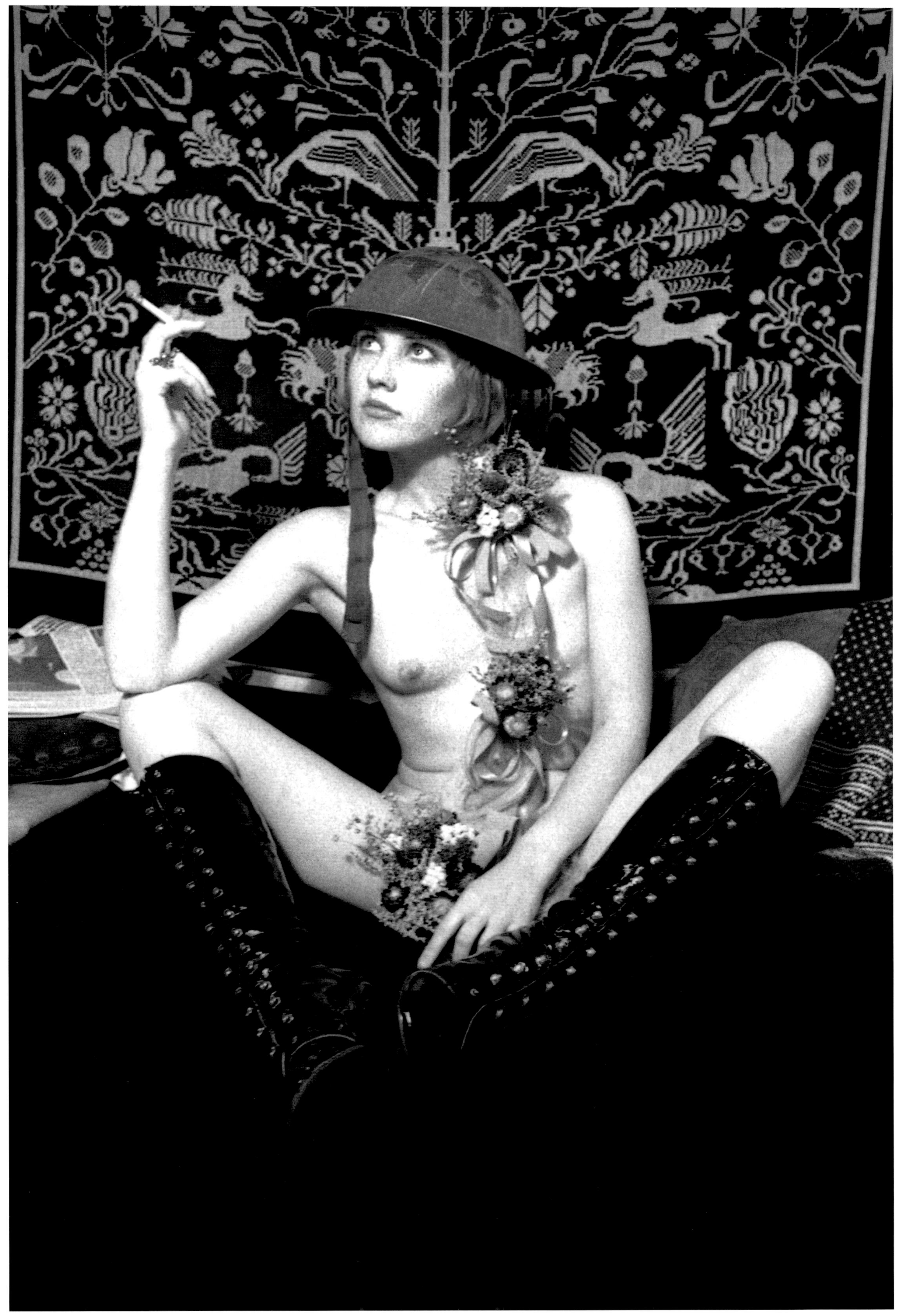

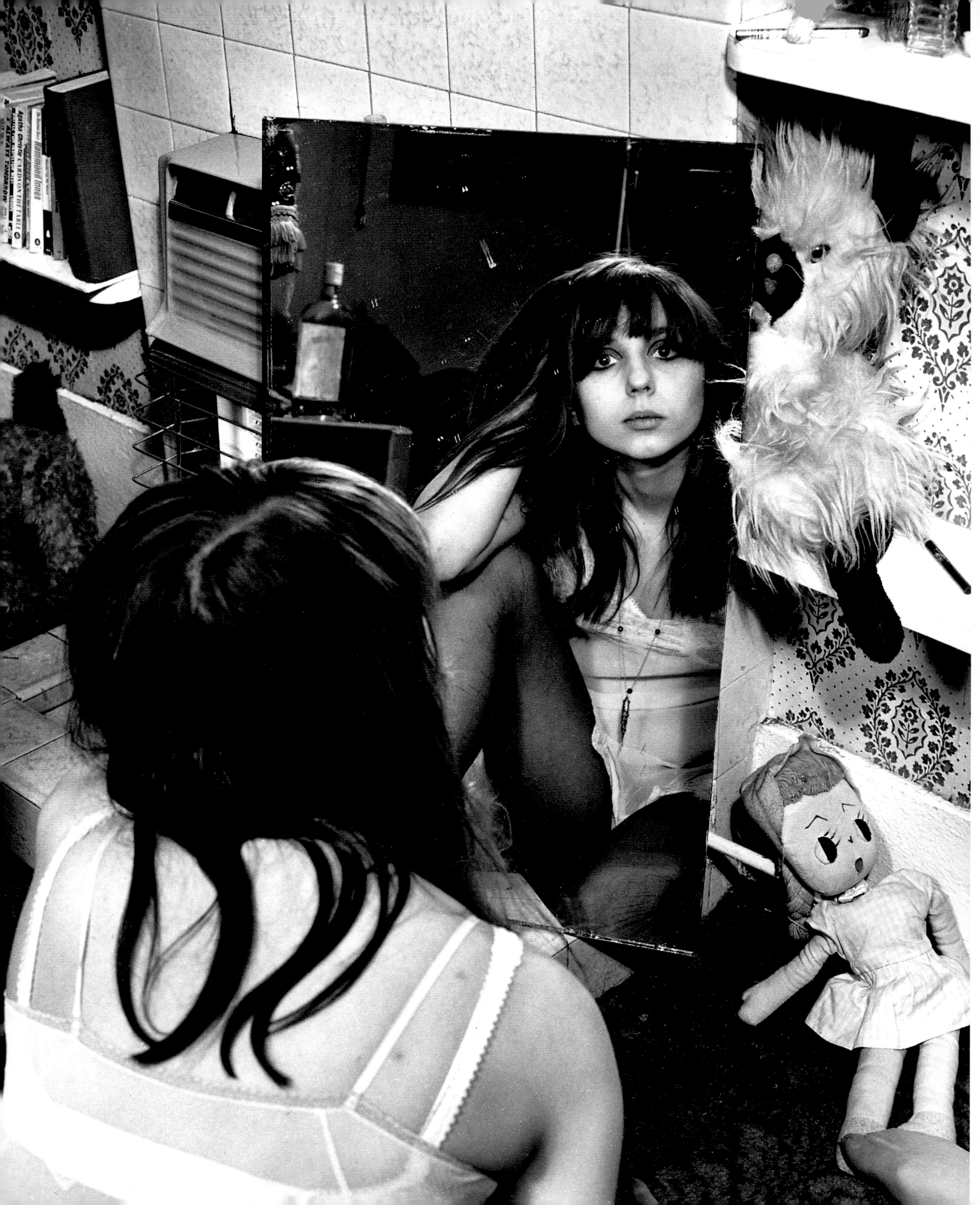
ALWAYS TOMORROW
Agatha Christie CARDS ON THE TABLE
Hammond Innes

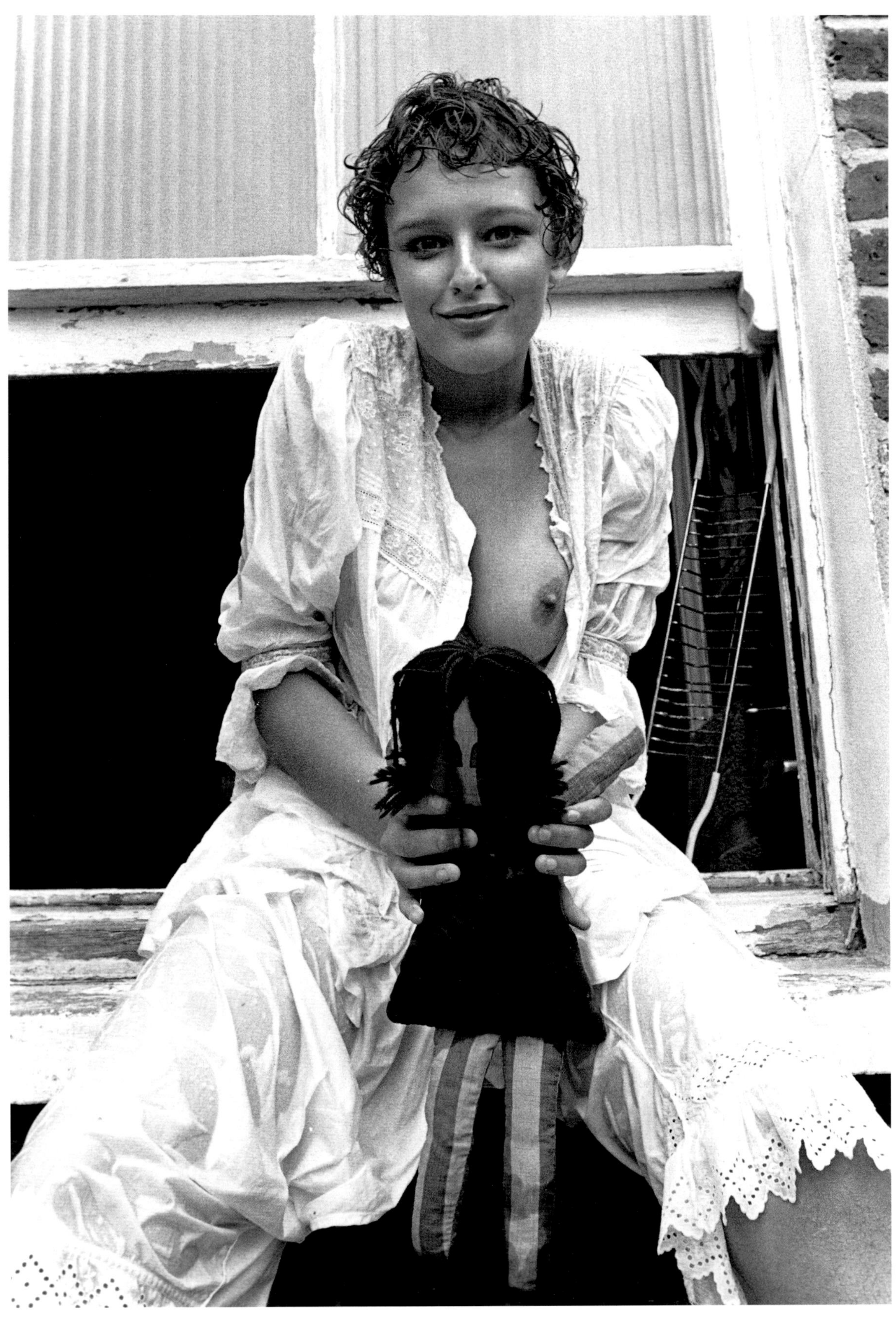

Do you think it's all right? – Earl's Court, 1967

Always tomorrow – bedsit girl, Earl's Court

Next pages: Marriage à la mode – rejected image for beer advertising campaign, 1969

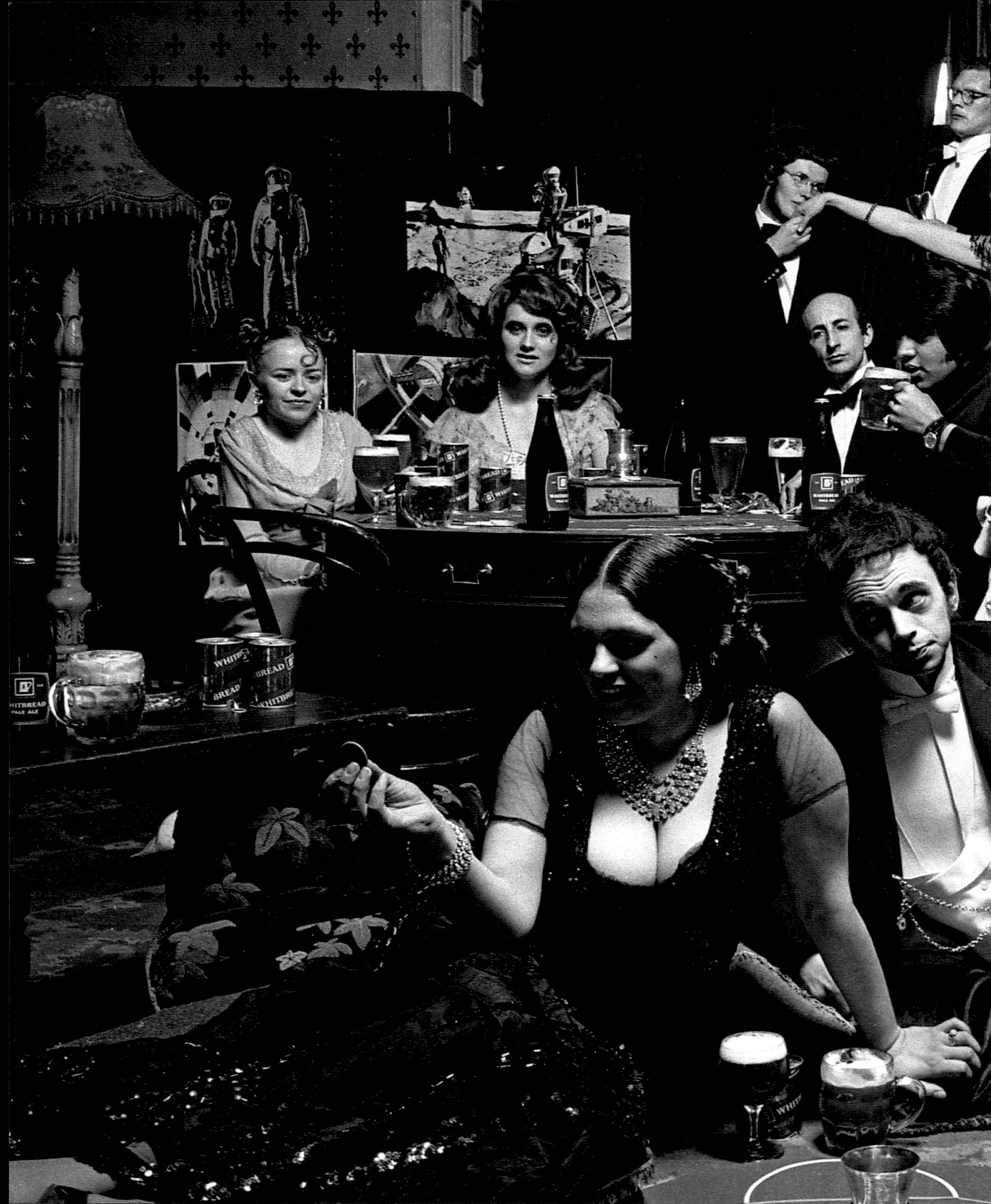
WHITBREAD
PALE ALE

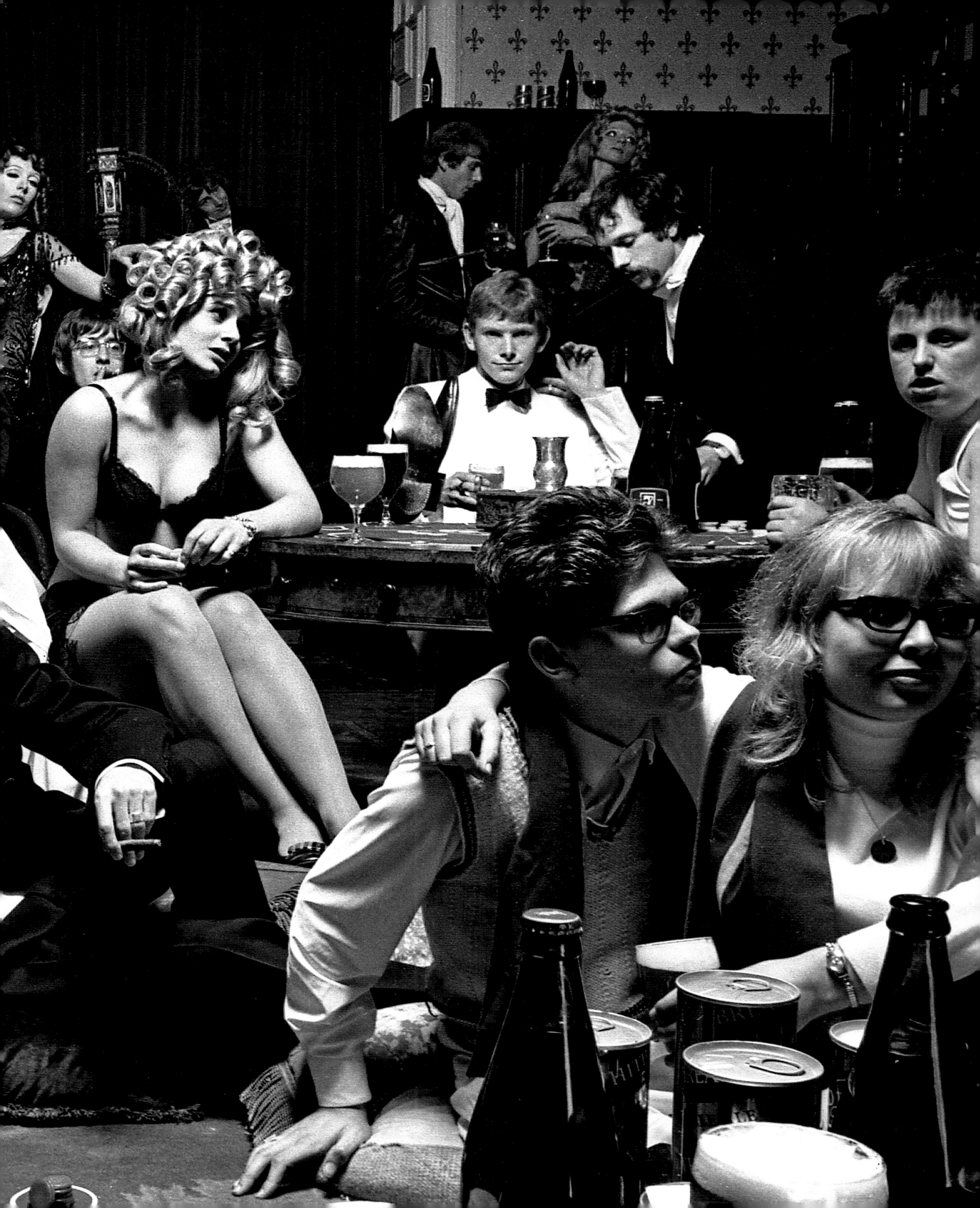

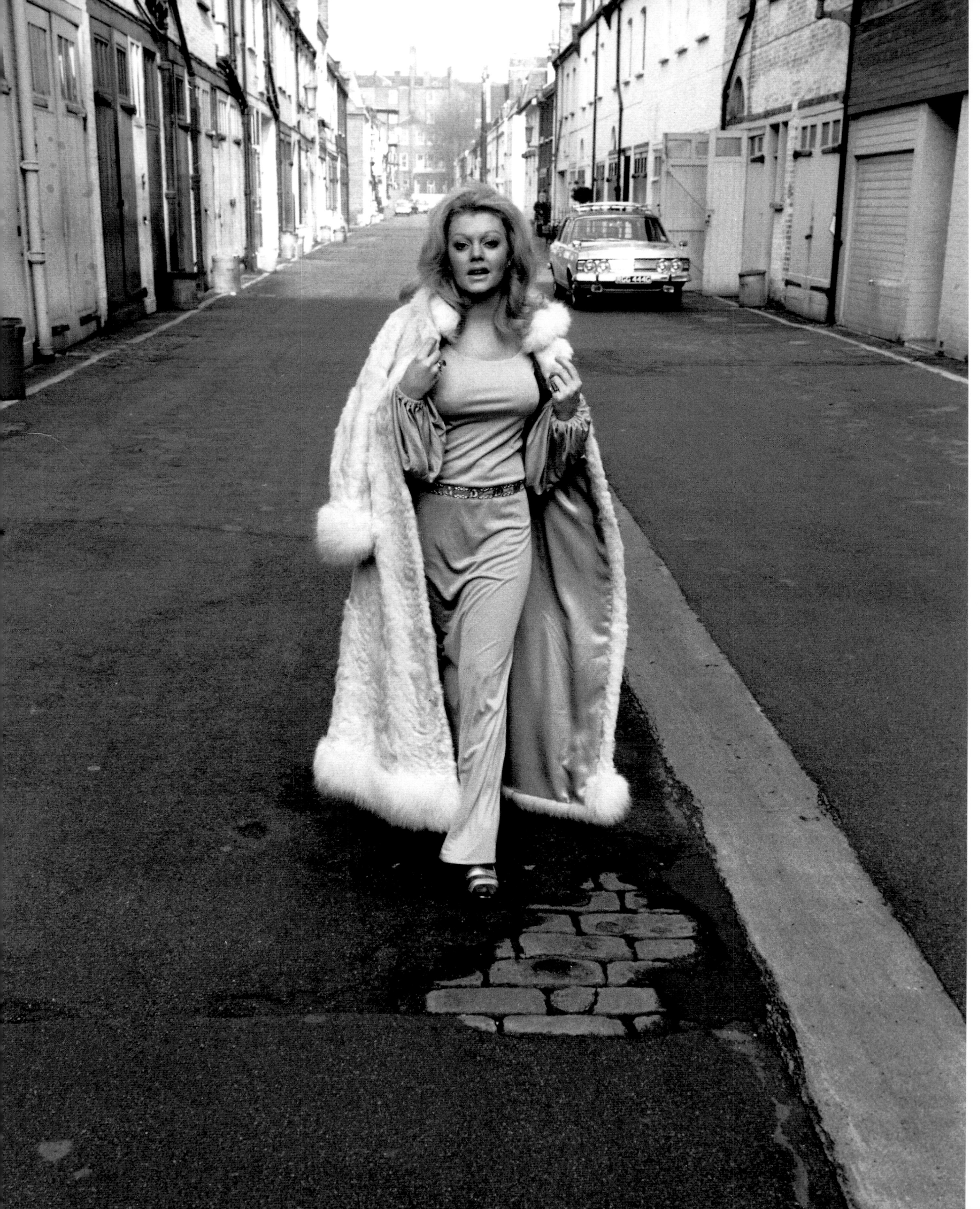

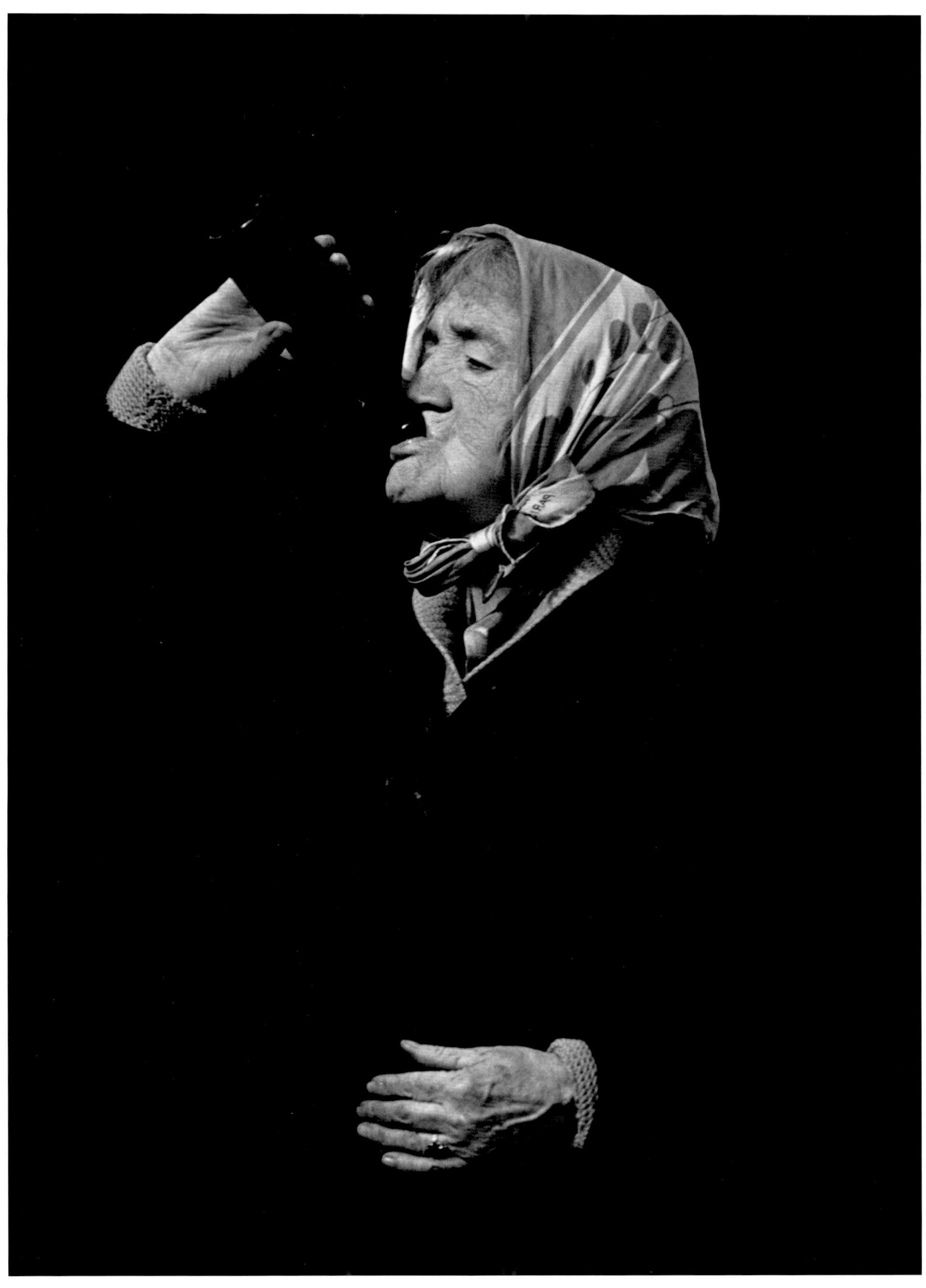

The morning after – Liz Romanoff, film actress, Knightsbridge Mews, 1969

Accepting one's fate – London's East End, 1969

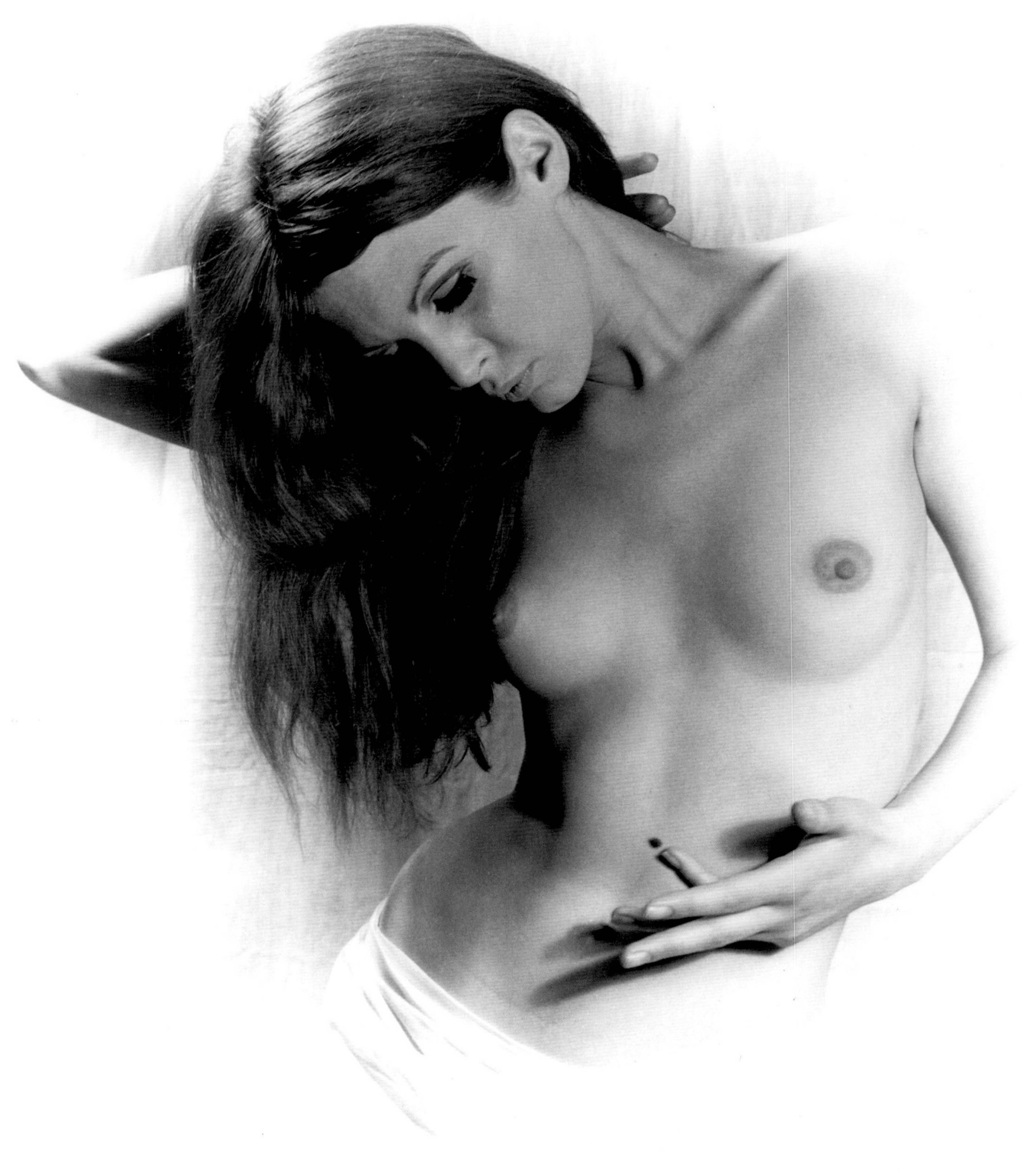

Celia

The two of us – Penny Spencer, actress star of Sixties TV series "Please Sir"

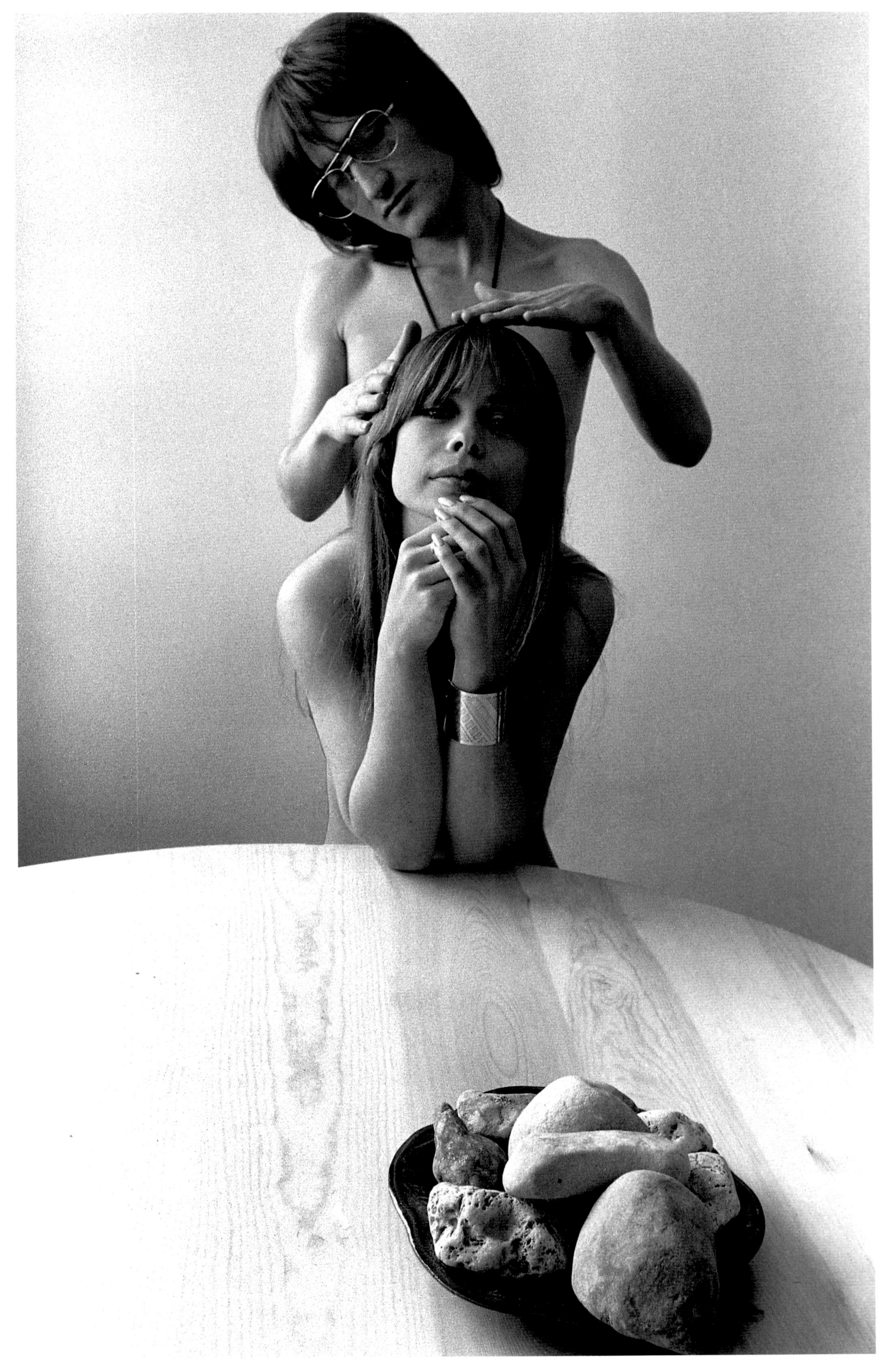

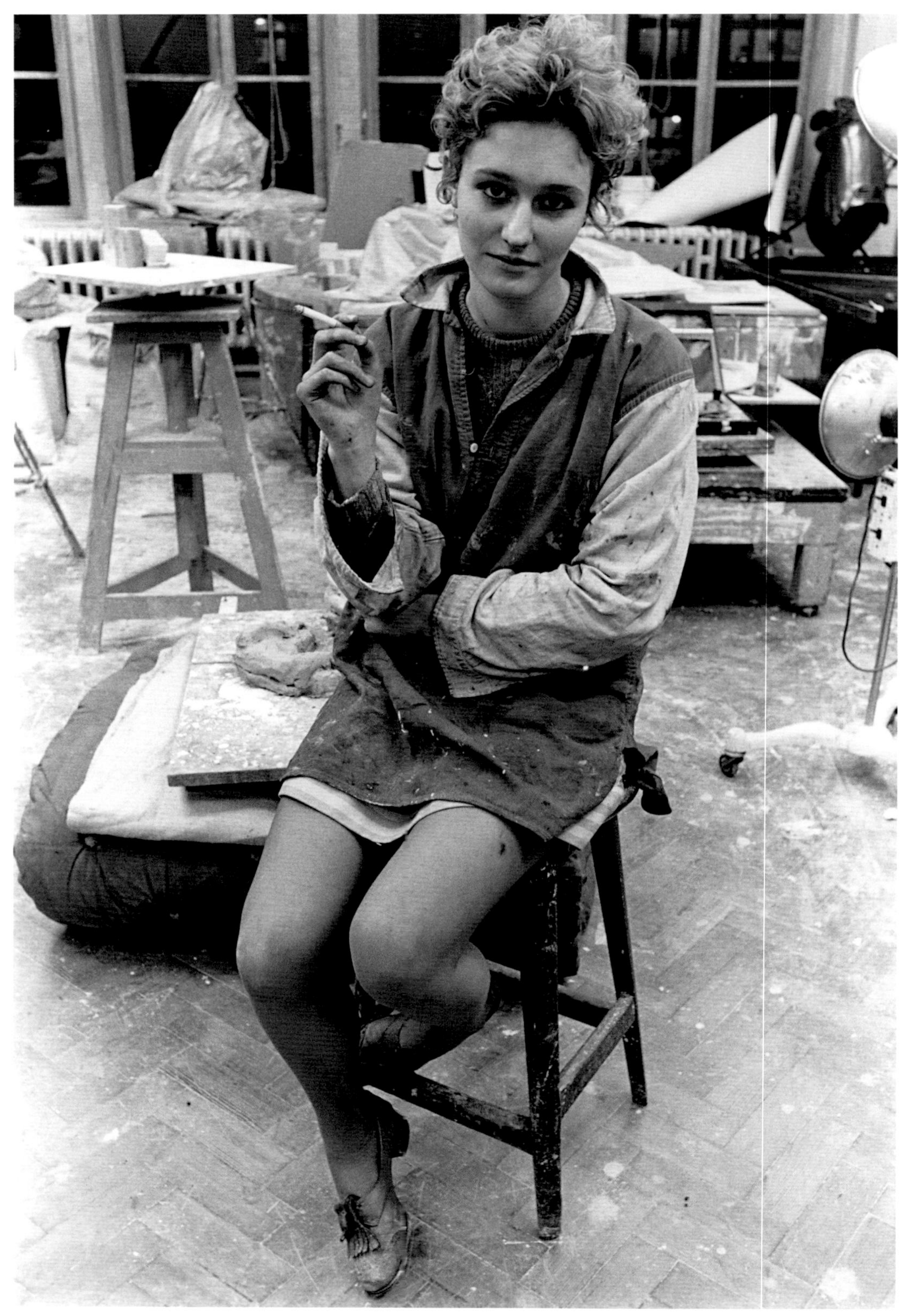

Fine arts student, St. Martin's College, Holborn

Tate Gallery, 1967

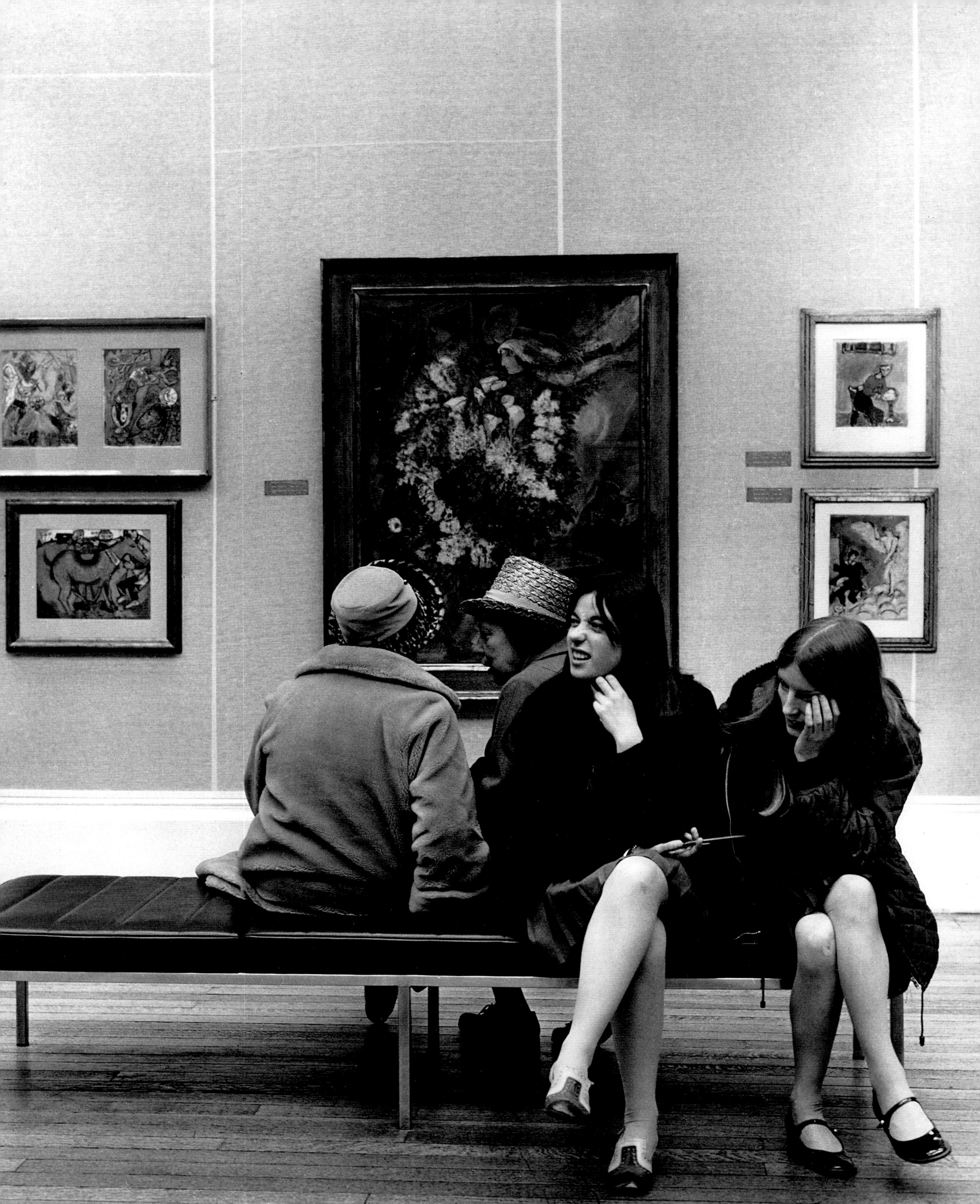

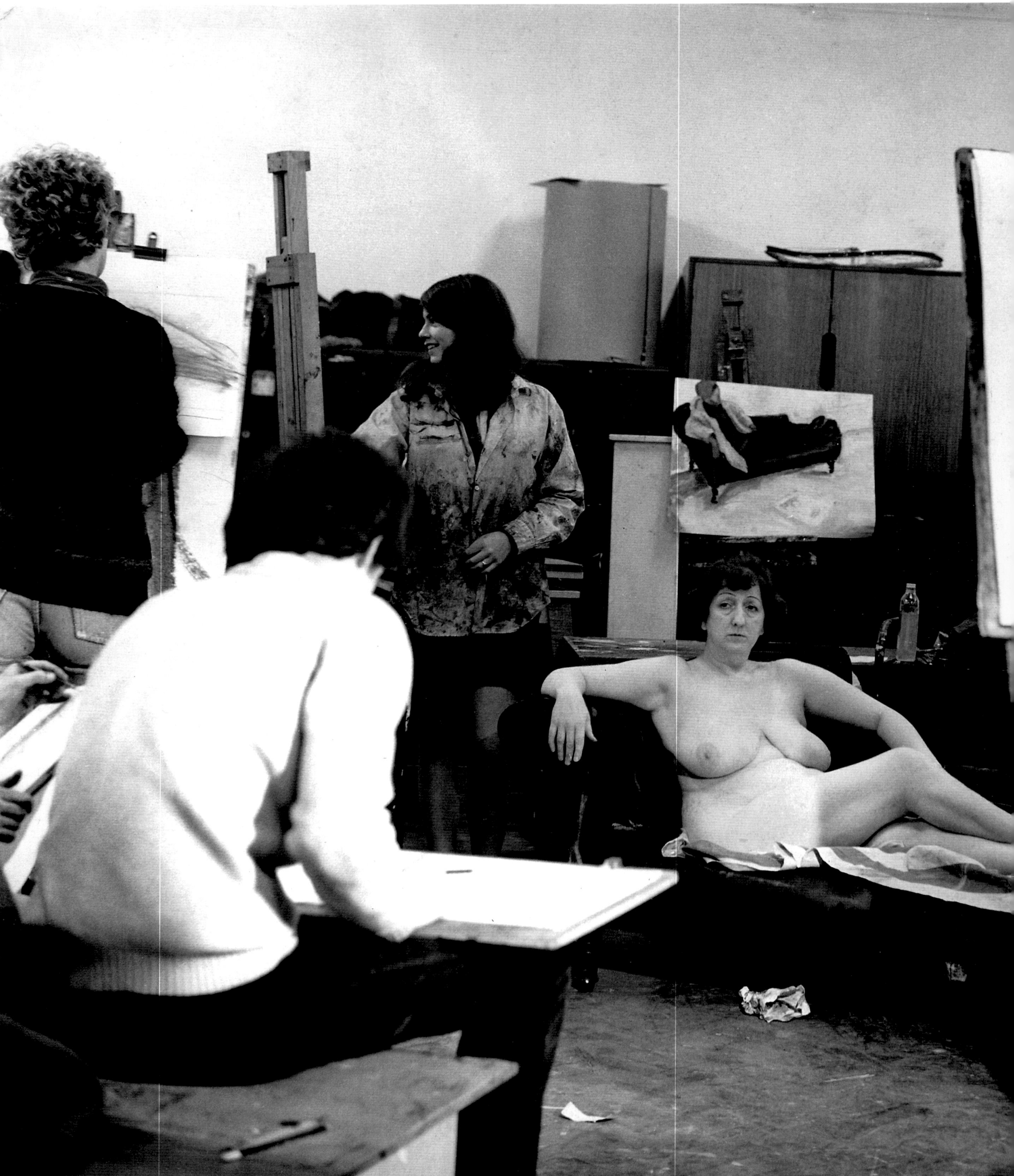

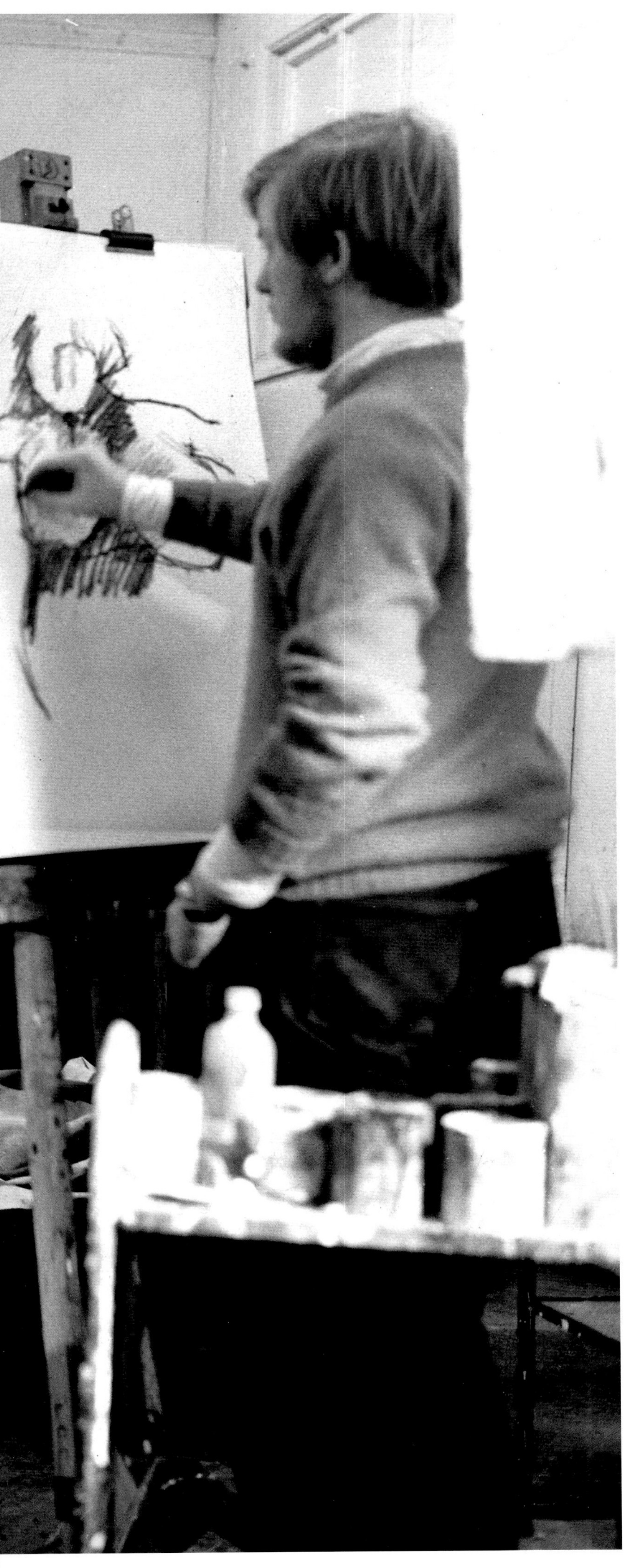

Life drawing, St. Martins College, 1967

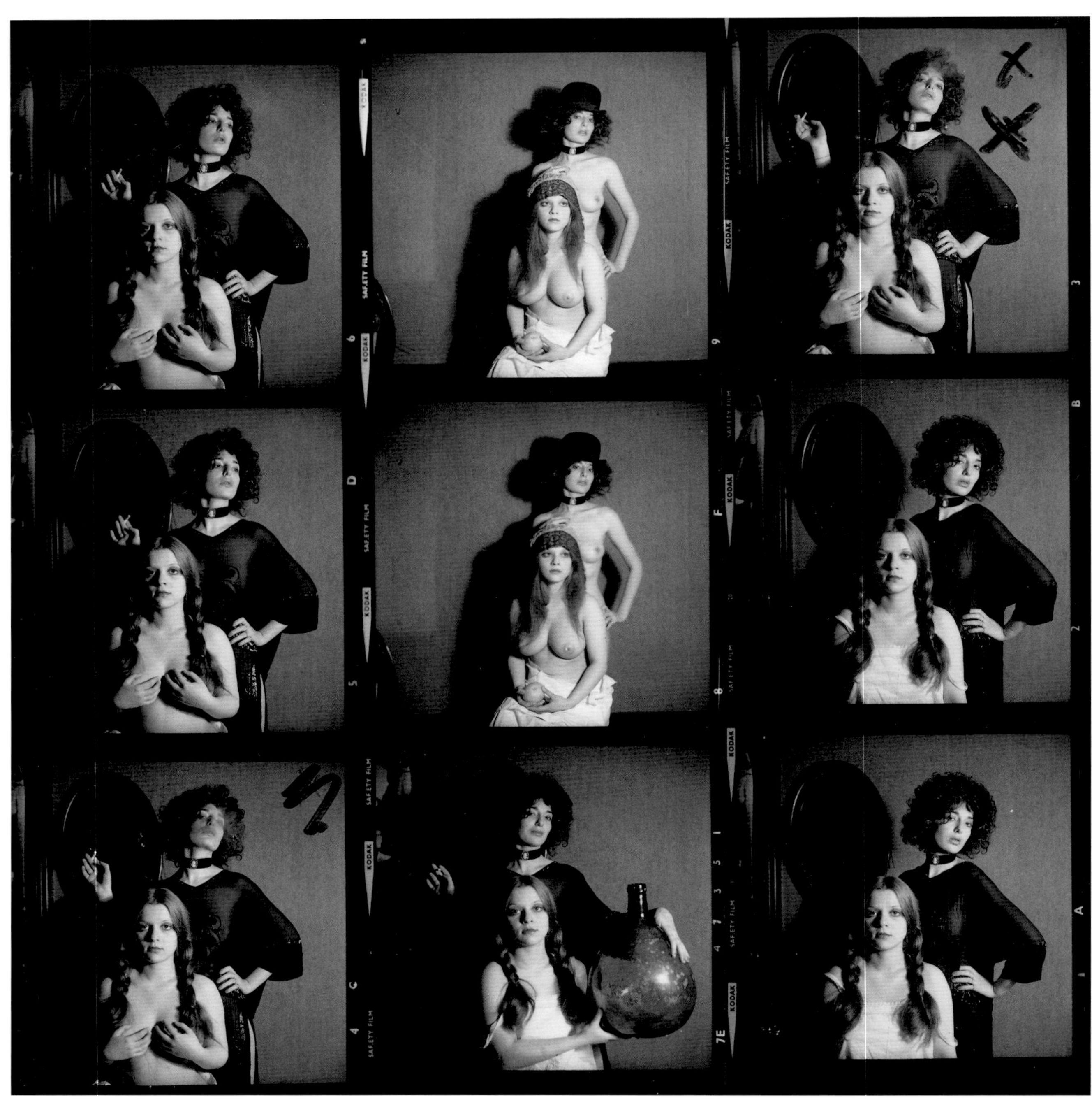

Les Mademoiselles – photographer's studio Courtfield Gardens, 1966

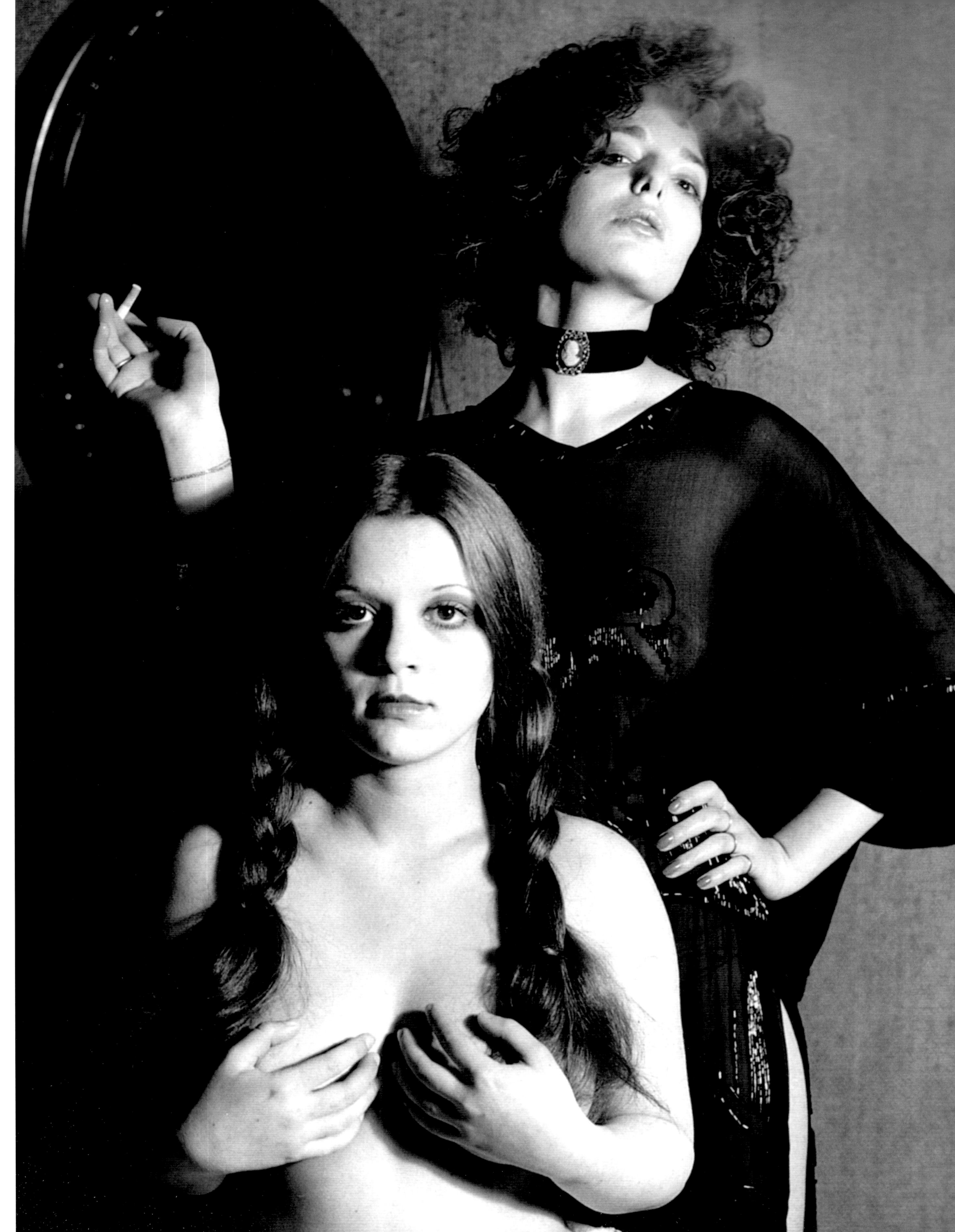

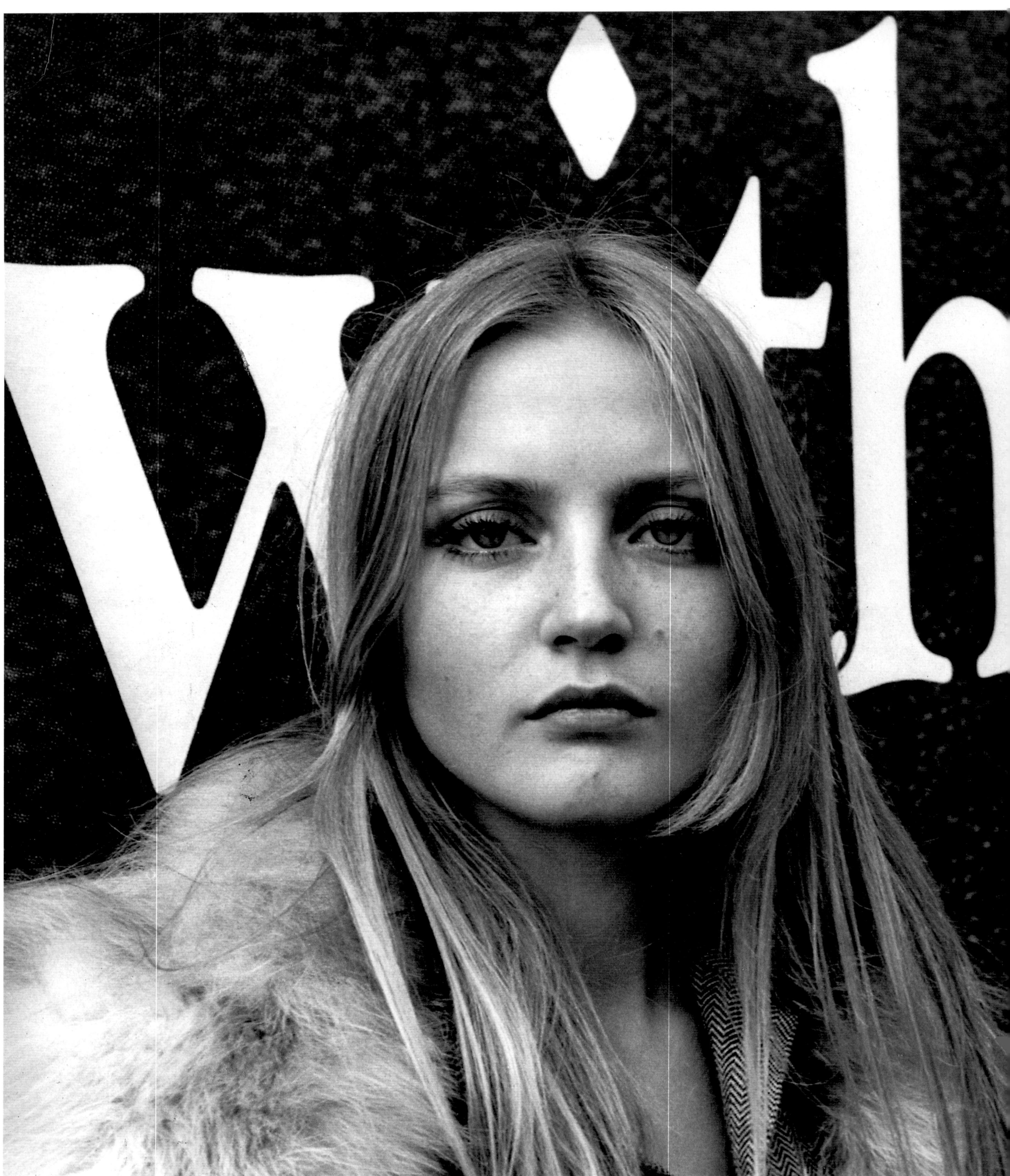

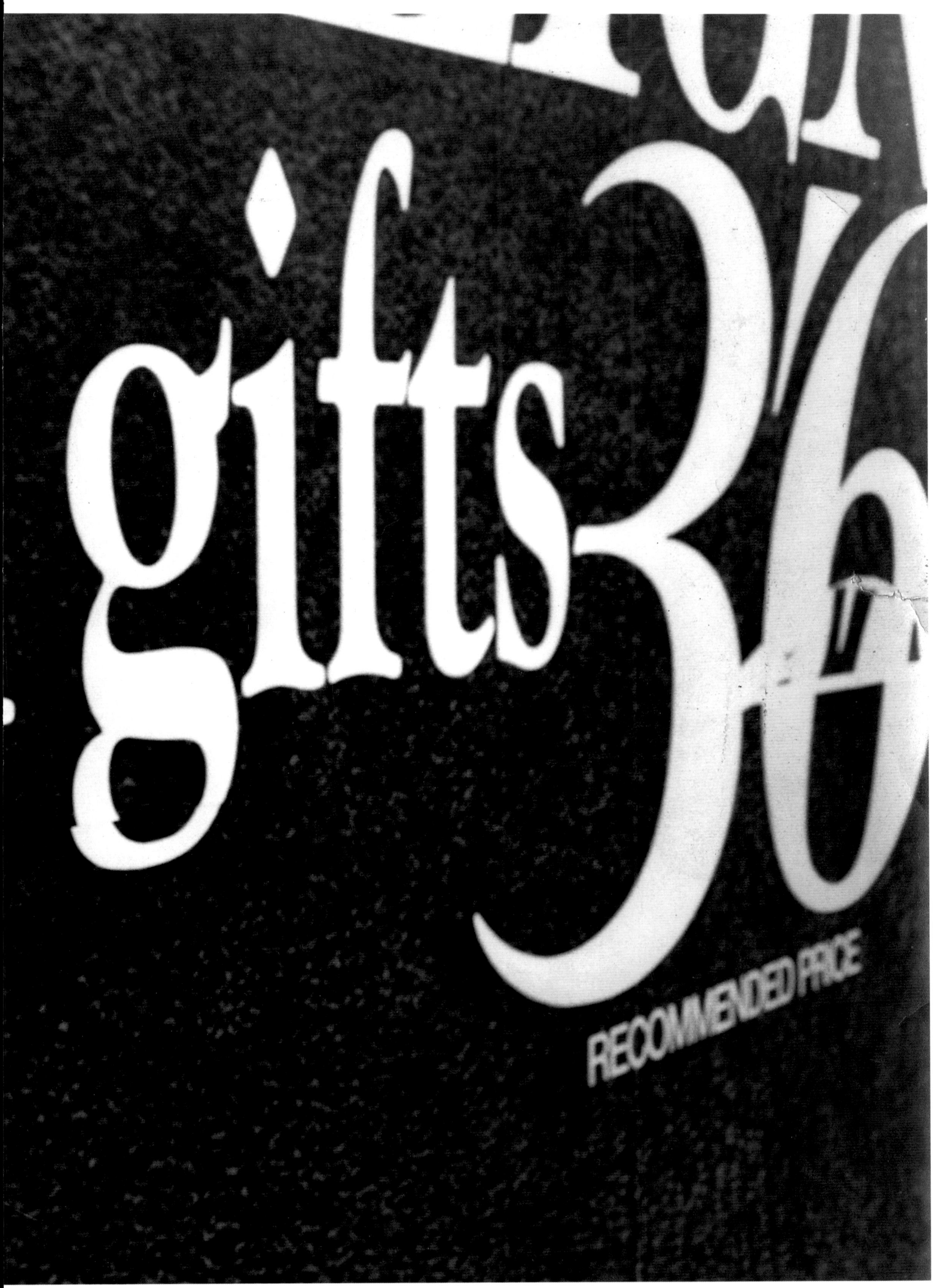

Ingrid Boulting,
Biba poster model,
King's Road

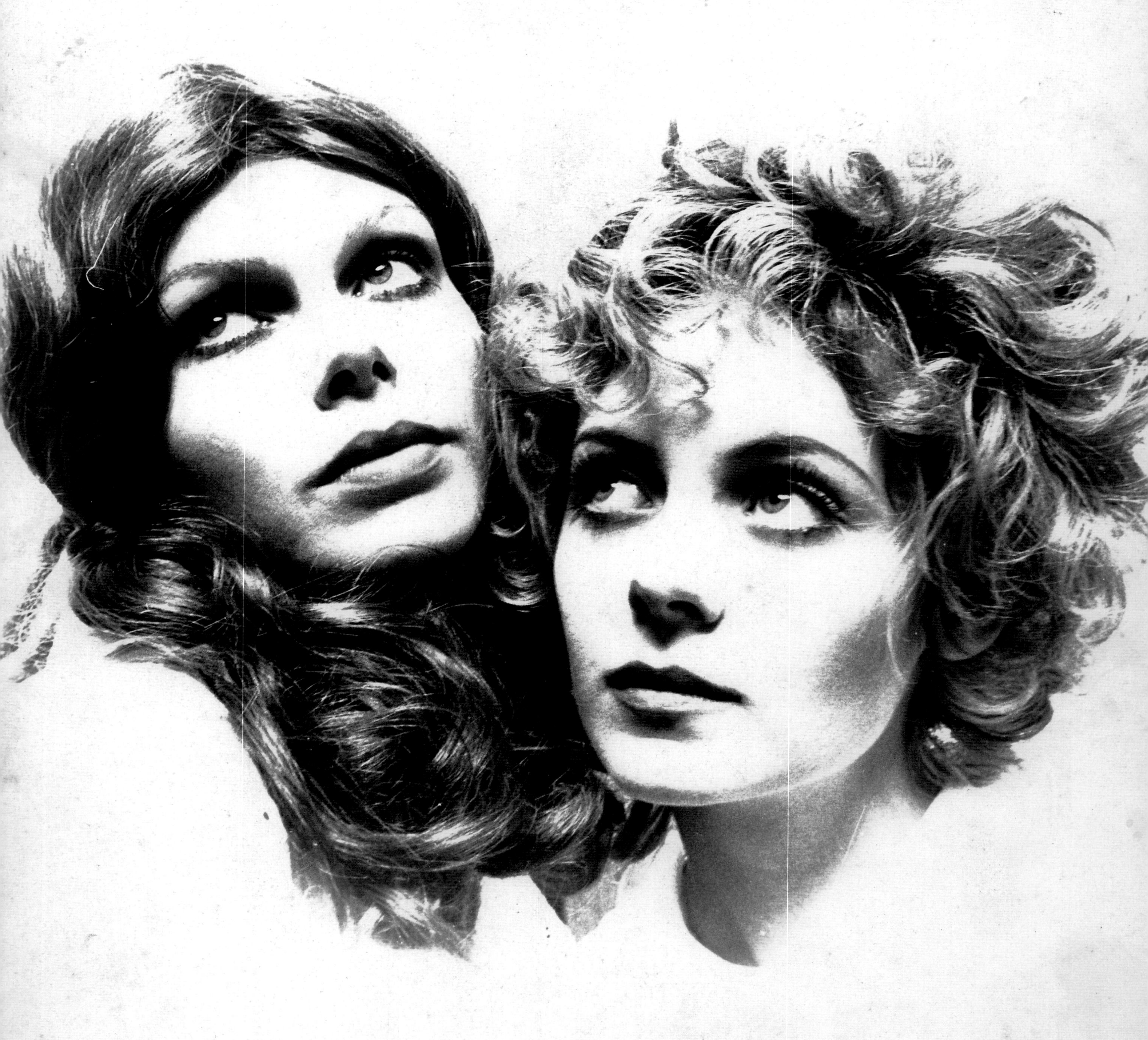

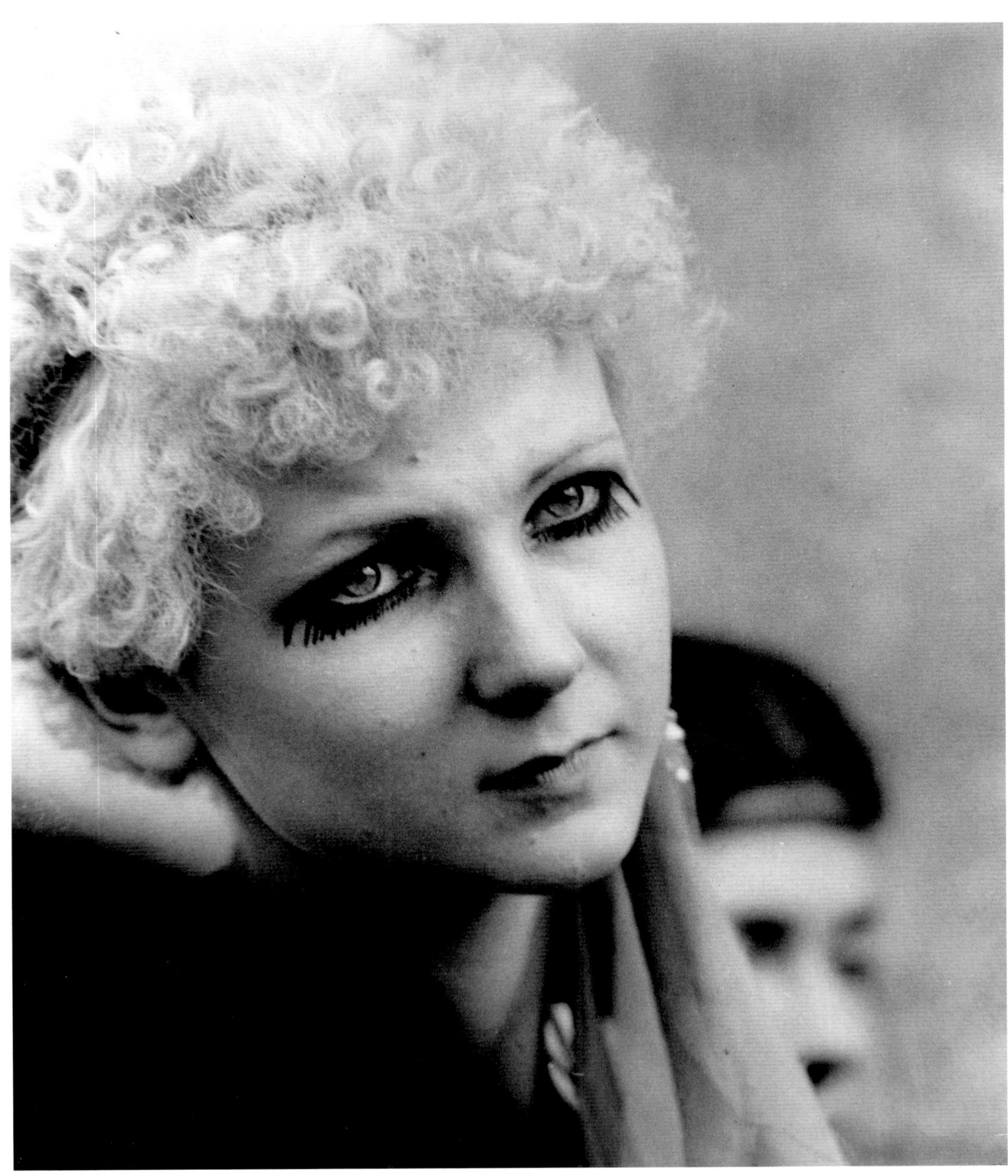

Linda & Paula, photographed for Peter Lumley Model Agency

Flower Power – King's Road, 1967

Virginia, Golders Green

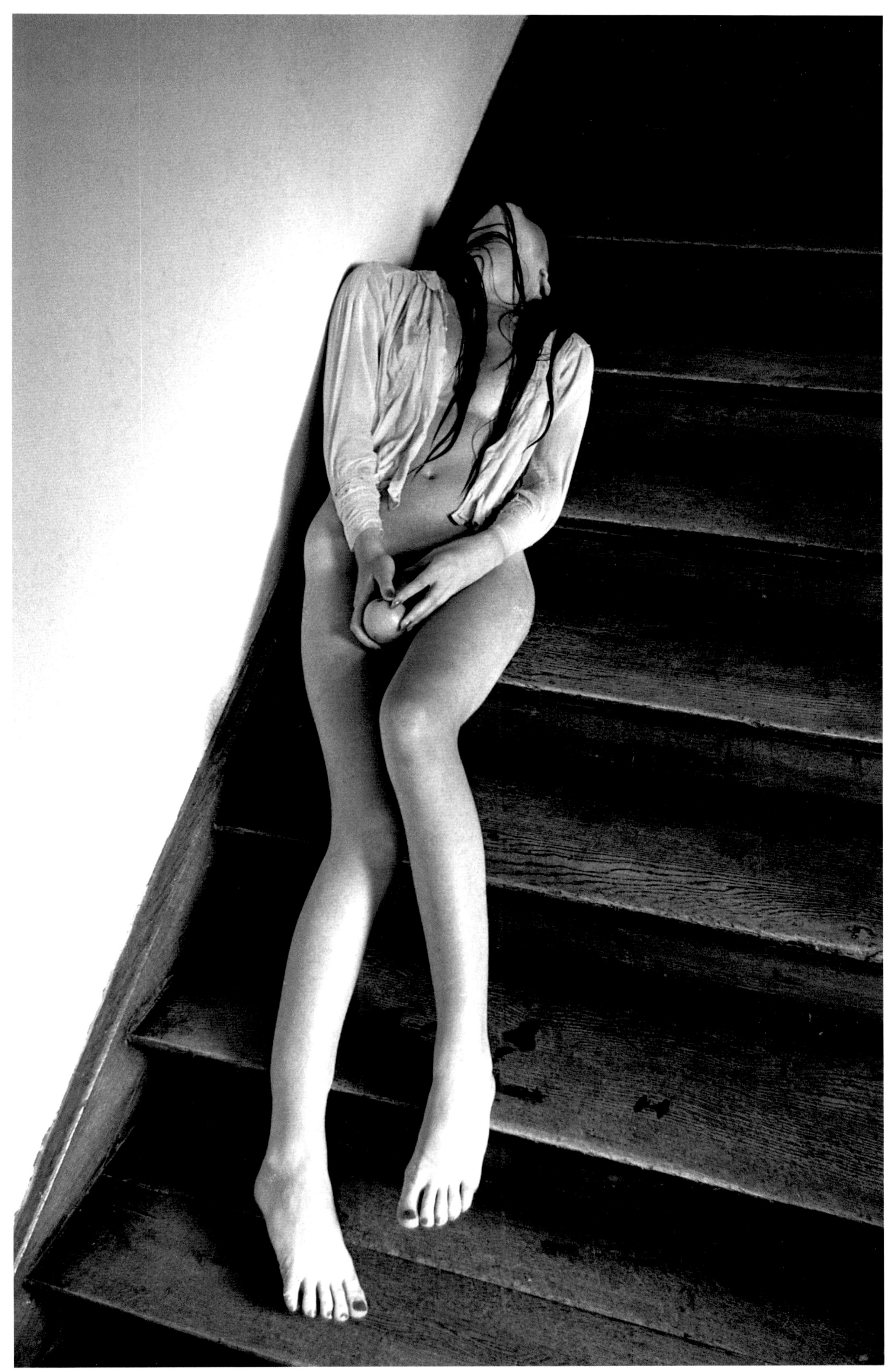

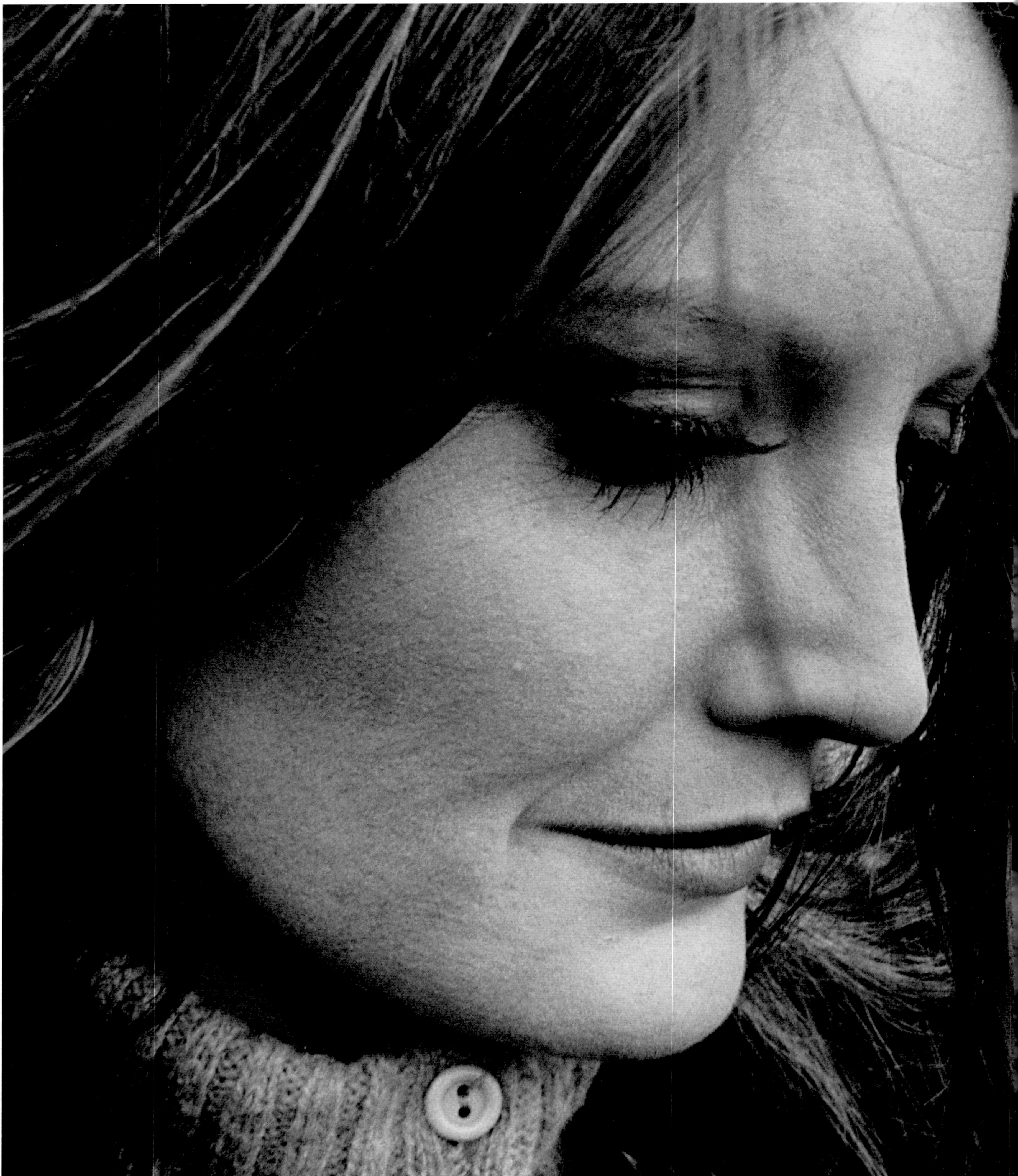

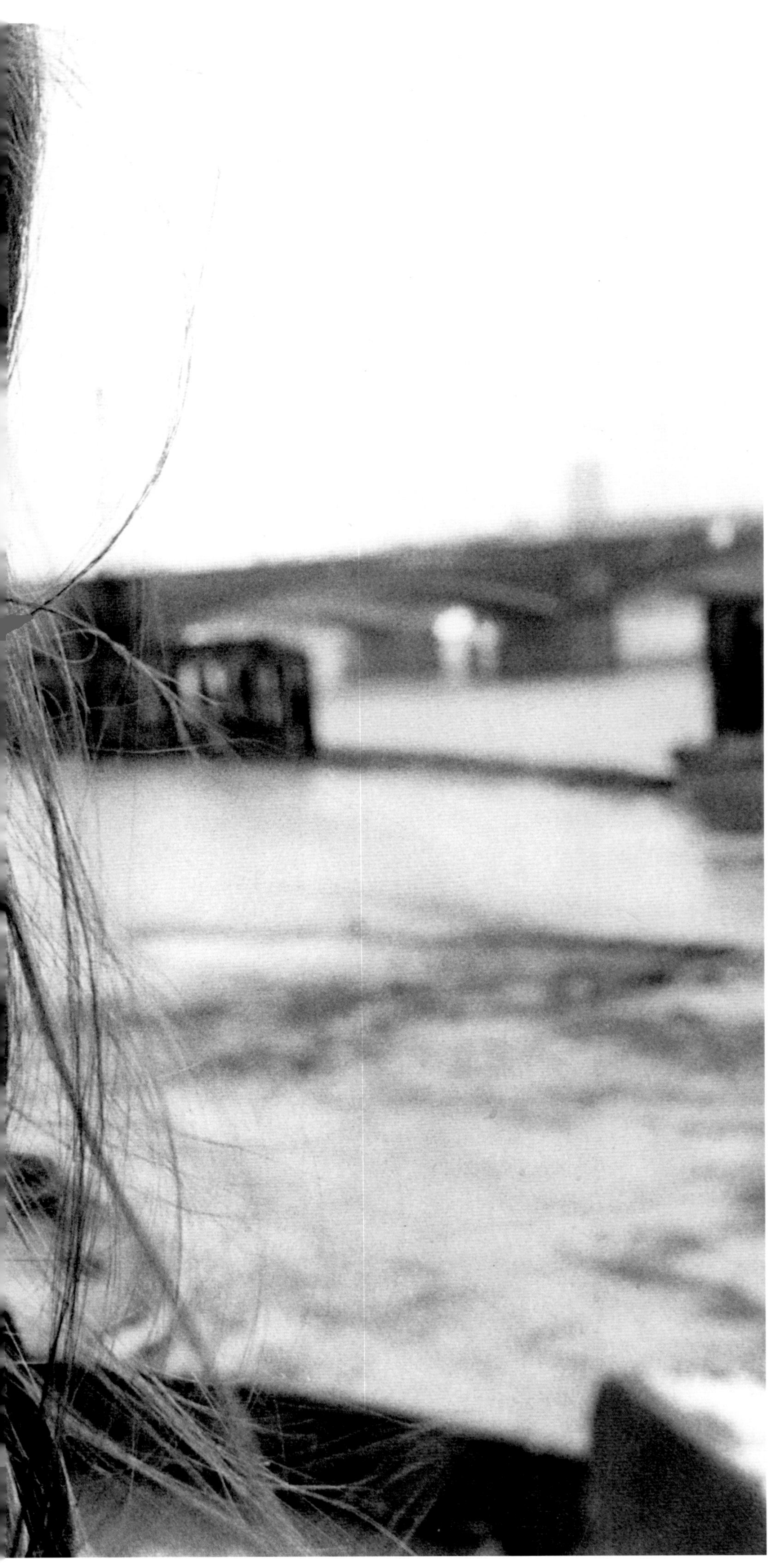

“Puppet on a String” – Eurovision singer, Sandy Shaw, 1967

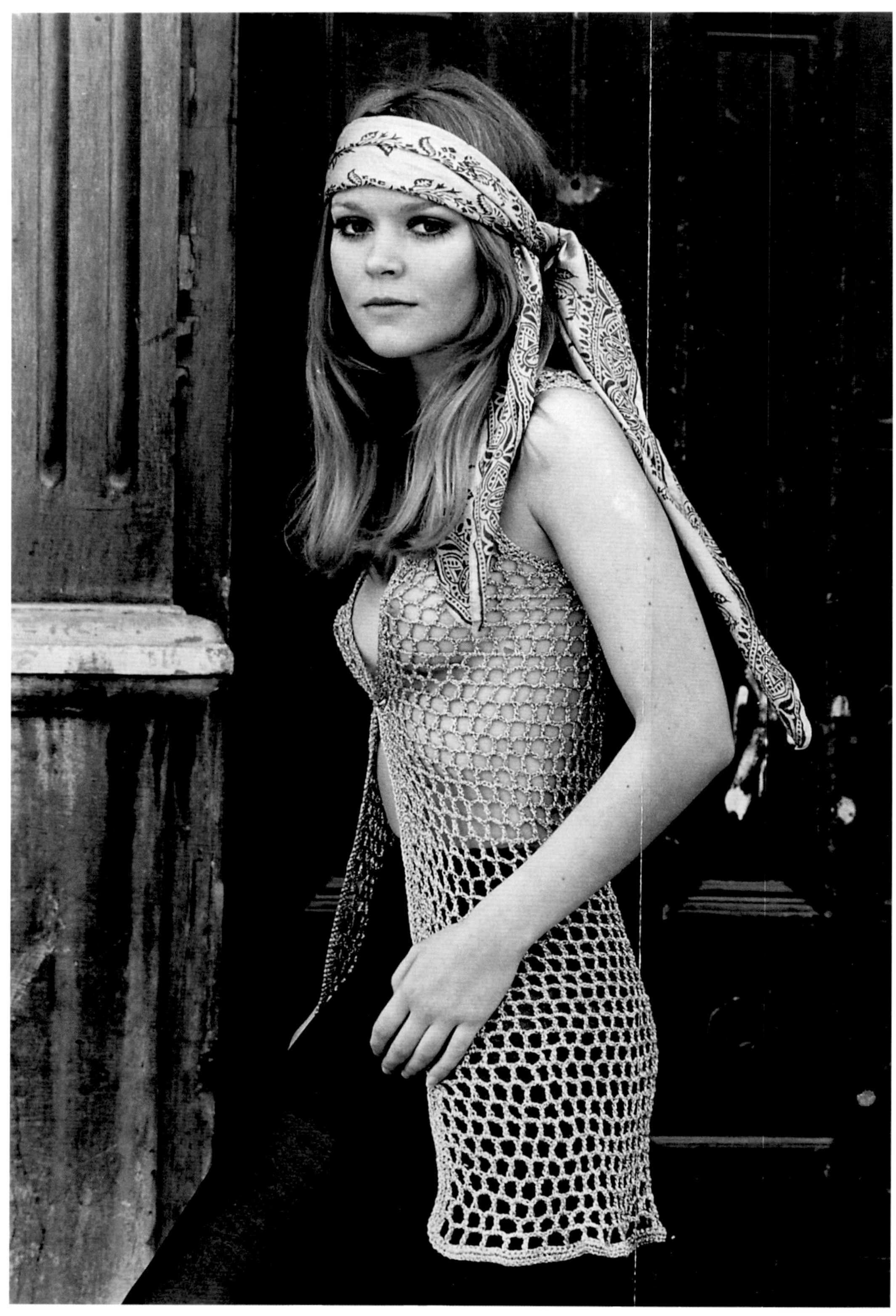

Janet Stevens, model and actress, Fulham Road, 1967

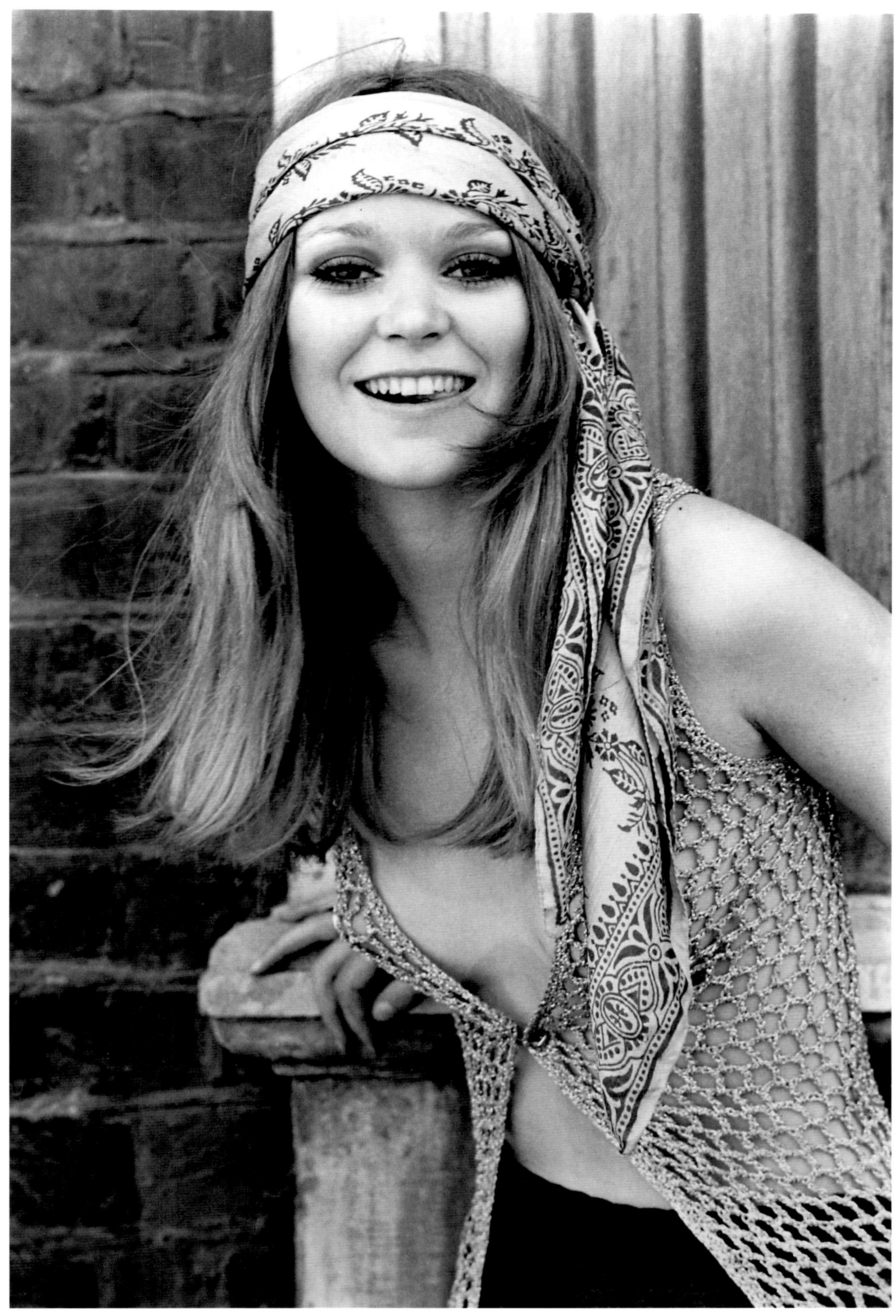

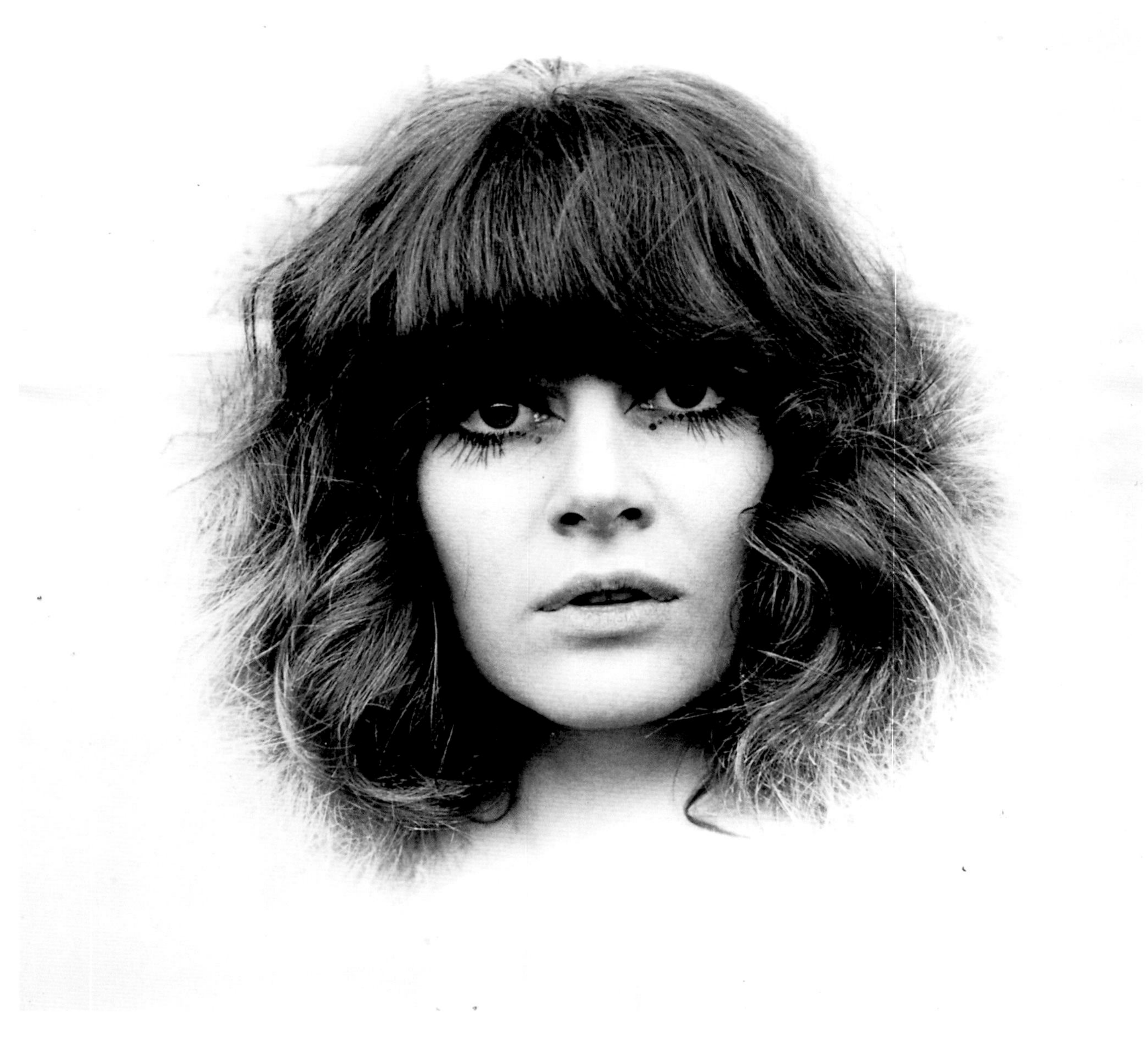

Caroline Coon, author and advocate for addicts

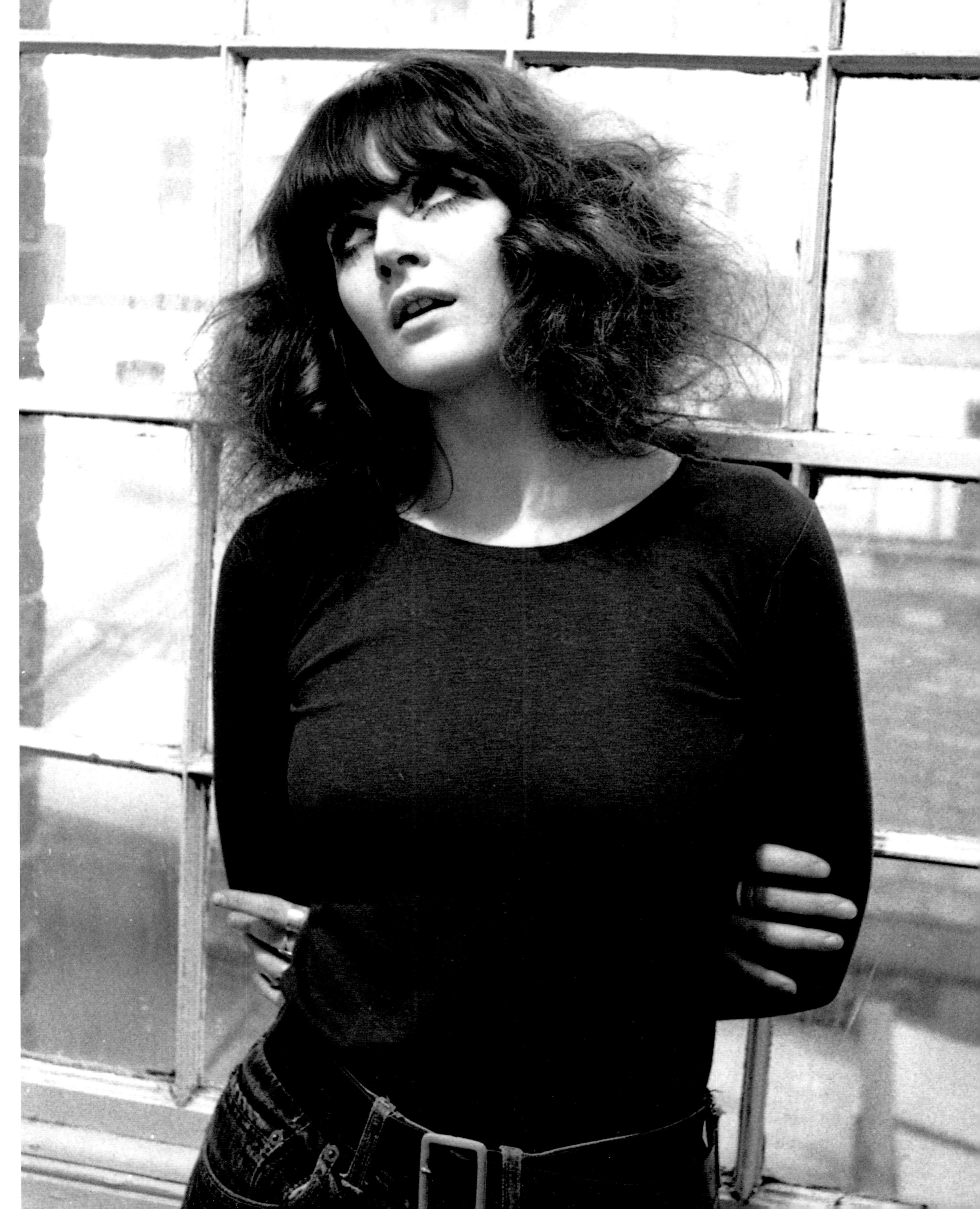

Jane and Serge

Jane and Serge still linger on in my mind. Their talents emerged in the Swinging London scene. Serge Gainsbourg was a successful singer, songwriter, and actor of the time. Jane Birkin was a celebrated actress and singer. Together they created the iconic hit "Je t'aime . . . moi non plus." I had an unforgettable encounter in Oxford in 1969 when I photographed the two with Jane's daughter Kate Barry, born in April 1967. Kate was a gifted and renowned fashion photographer, working for *Vogue* and *The Sunday Times Magazine*. Her father was the songwriter John Barry. The day I photographed the three was guided by the spur of the moment, seemingly tailor made, in which I immortalized their charm and seductiveness. Sadly, Kate took her life in Paris on December 11, 2013.

Jane Birkin is also a caregiver with impeccable human qualities and humanitarian concerns. She worked with Amnesty International on immigrant welfare and aid issues. She has visited troubled countries like Bosnia, Rwanda, Palestine, and Israel. In mid 1968 she fell in love with Gainsbourg and their relationship lasted over a decade. In 1971 Jane gave birth to the talented actress and singer Charlotte Gainsbourg. Jane left Serge in 1980. Above all, Jane kept her youthfulness and charm until today.

Serge was regarded as one of the most important figures in French popular music. He was renowned for his often provocative songs as well as his diverse "artistic" output from jazz, chanson, pop, and rock. He was battling alcoholism and was hardly ever seen without a cigarette in his hands. Serge was known for controversial outbursts in public, television, and on stage.

In 1991 he died of a heart attack. His funeral brought Paris to a stand still. His music reached legendary stature in France and Europe.

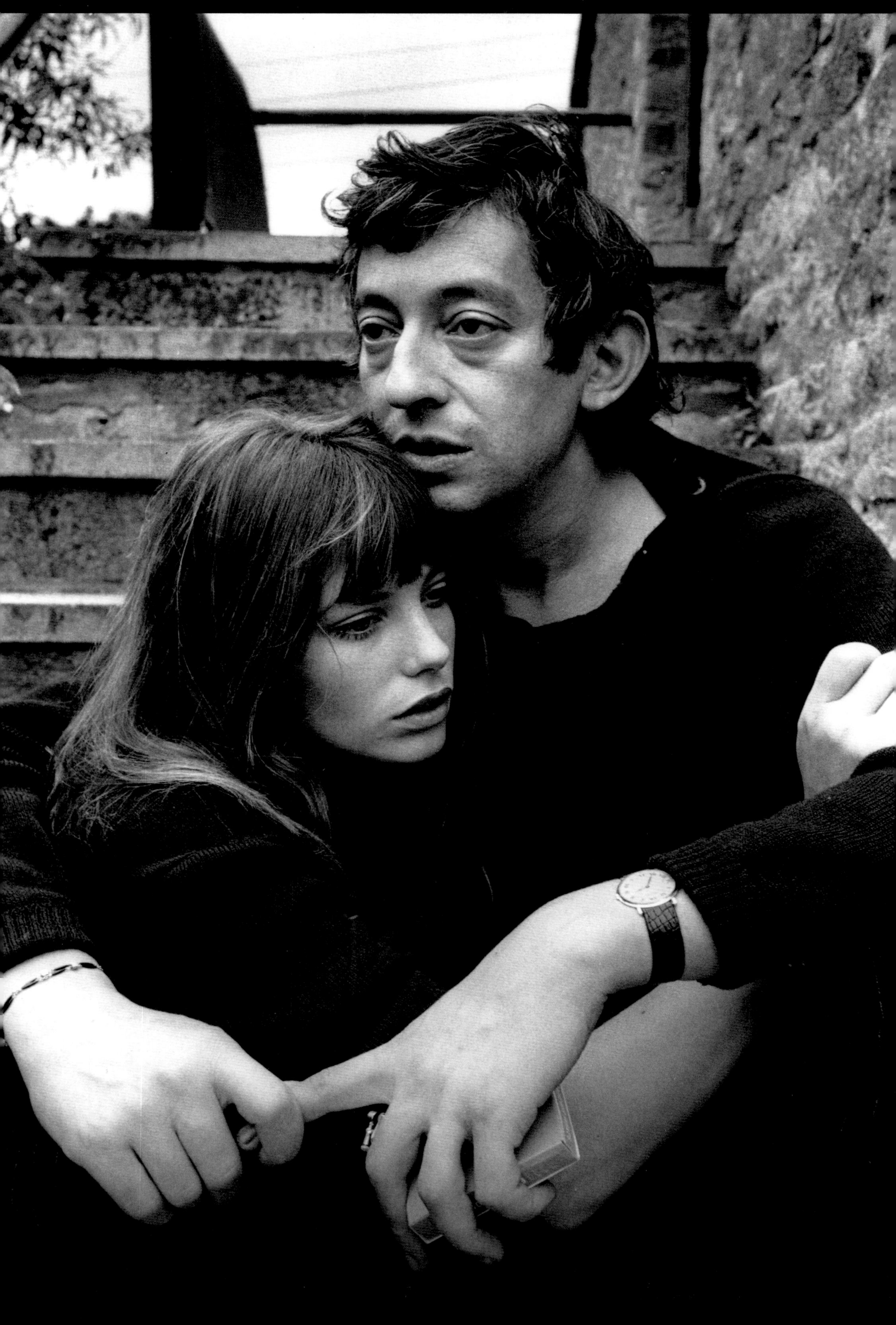

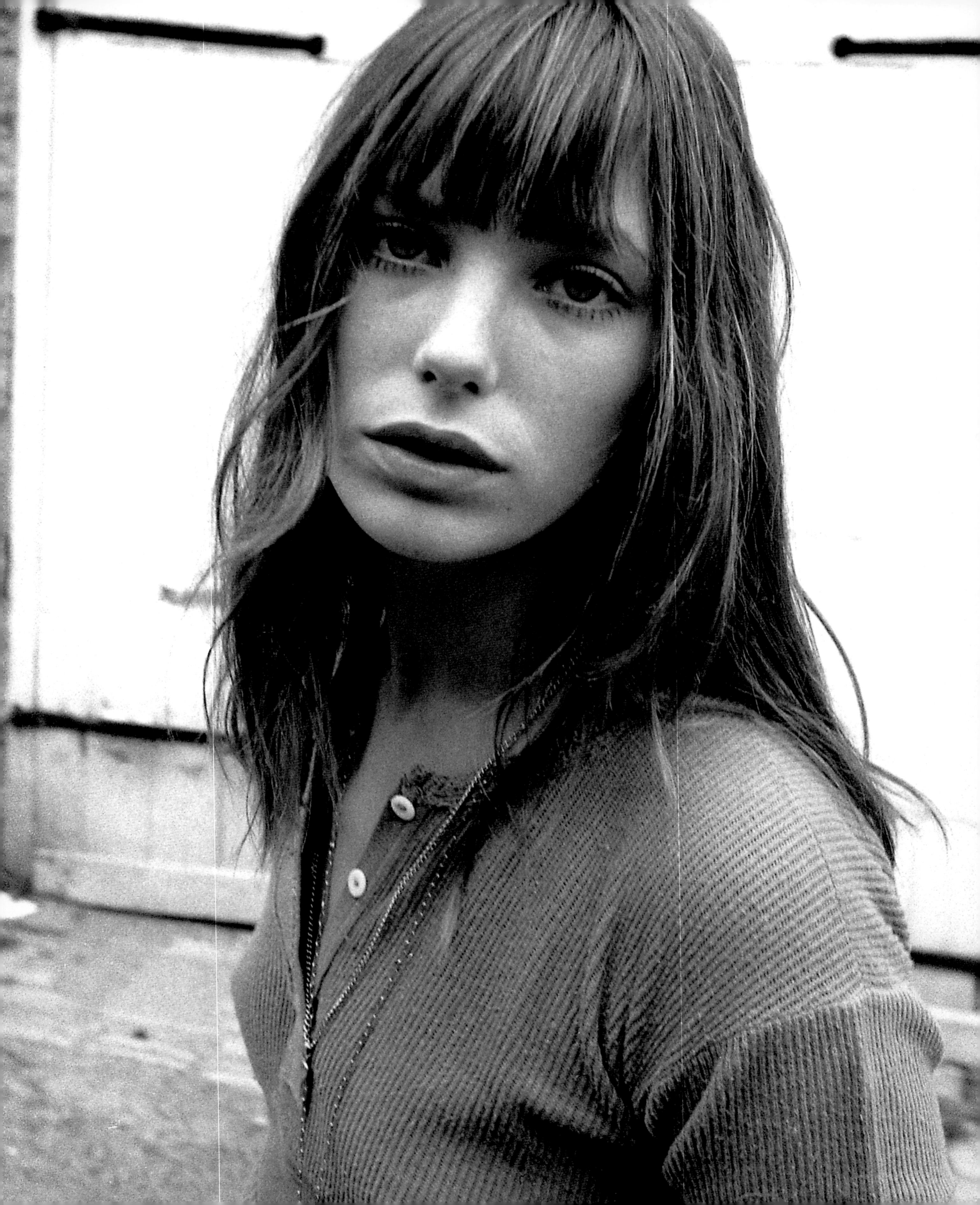

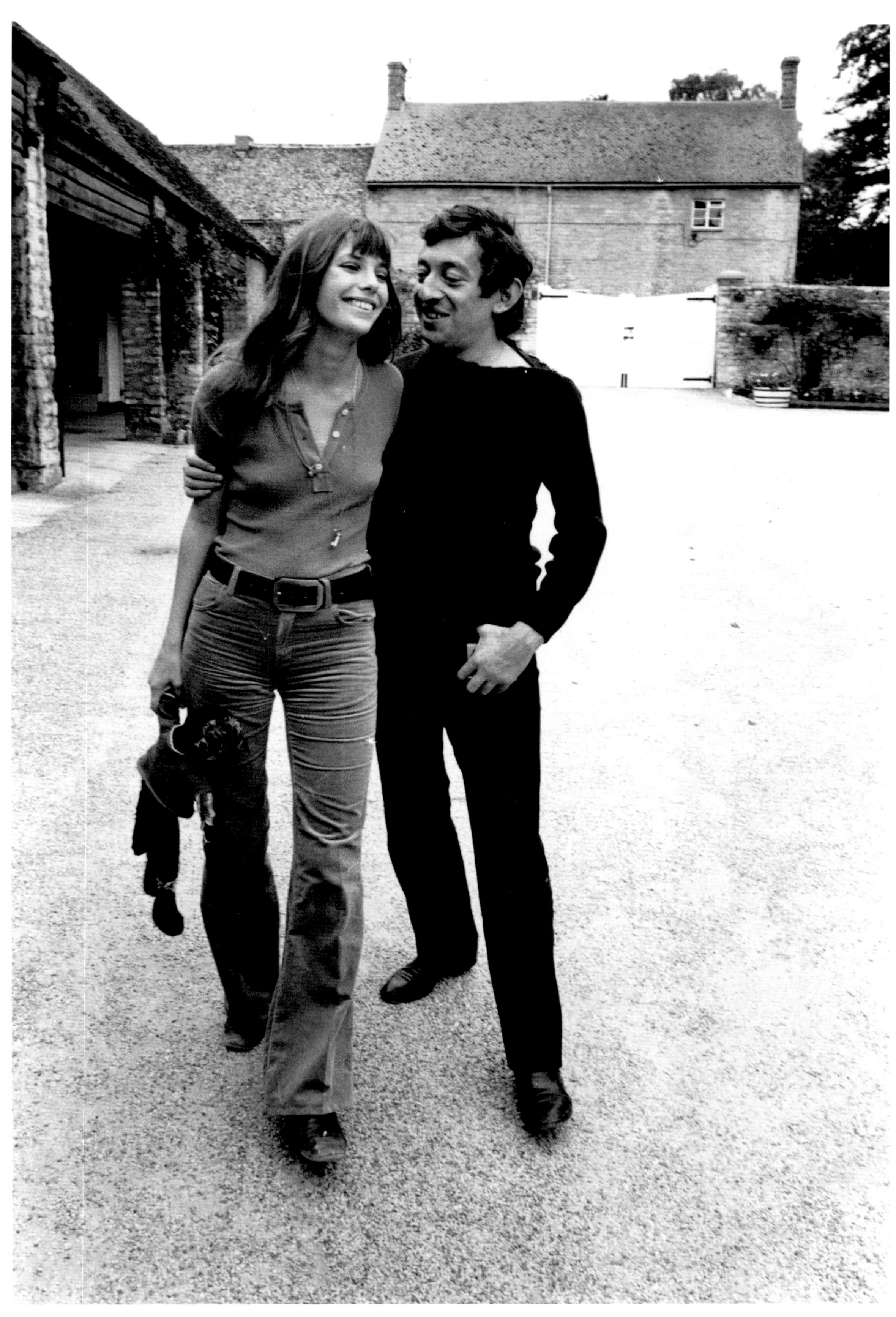

Jane and Serge Gainsbourg, singing duo, Oxford, 1969

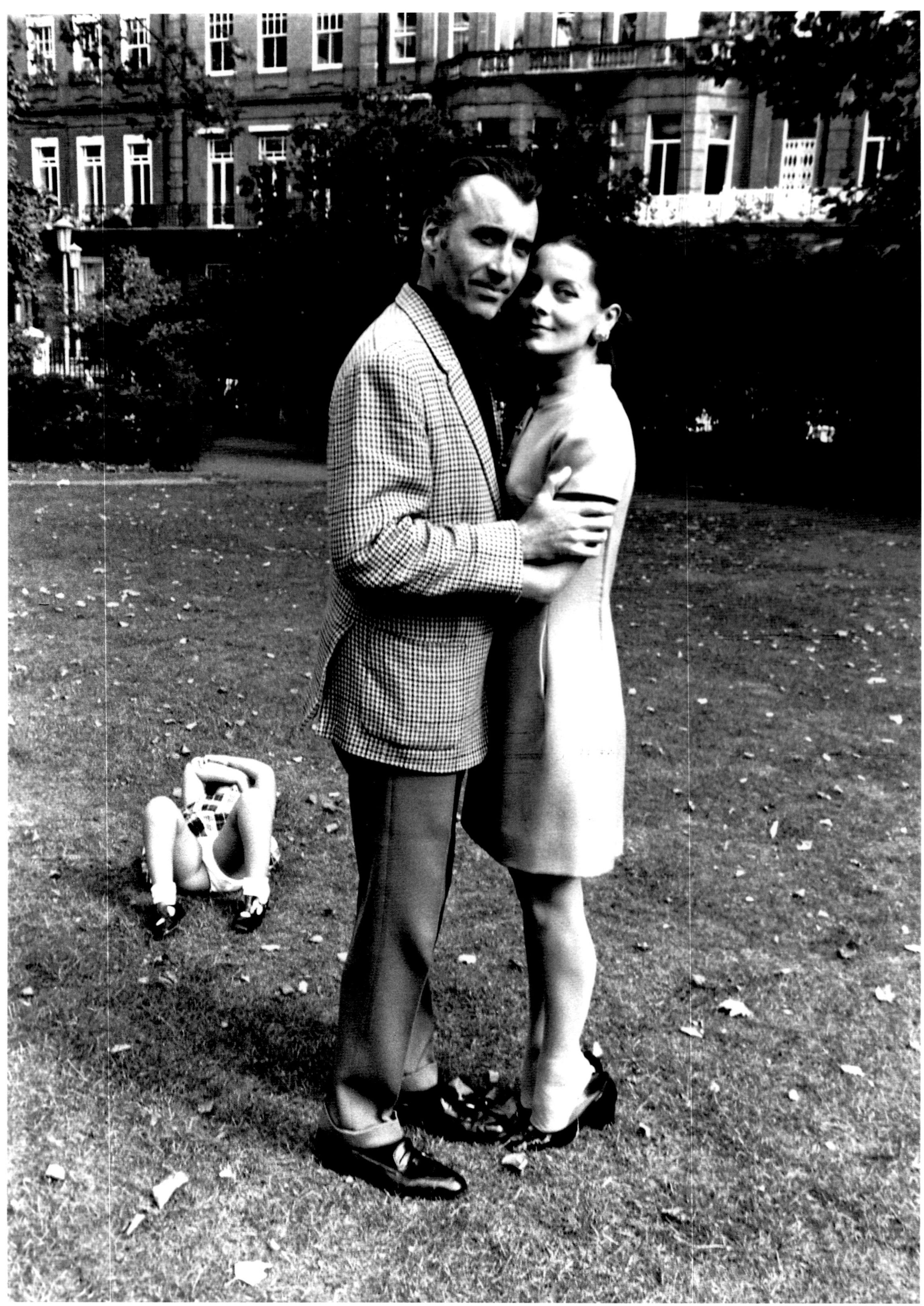

Christopher Lee, Dracula performer, and family, Belgravia

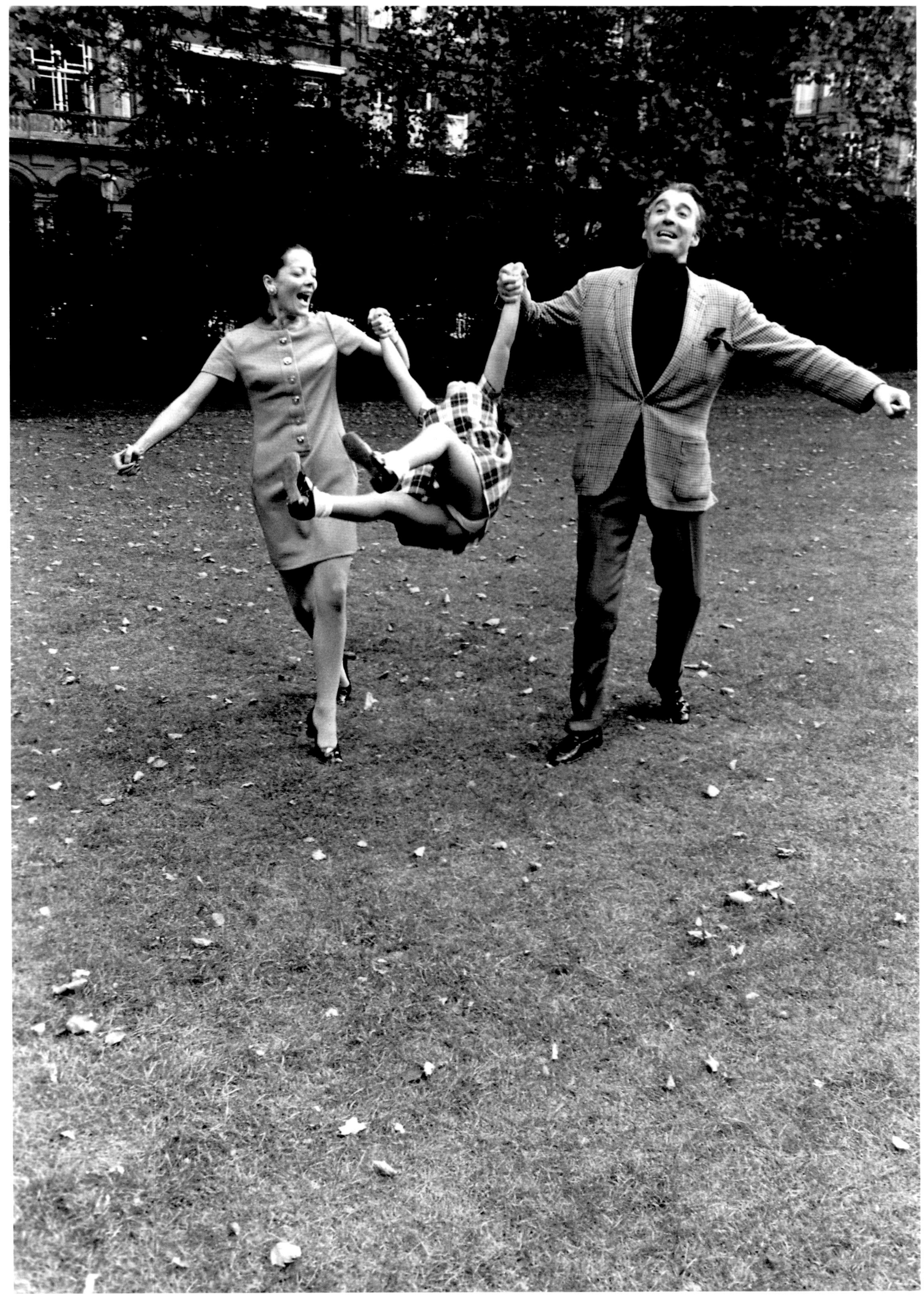

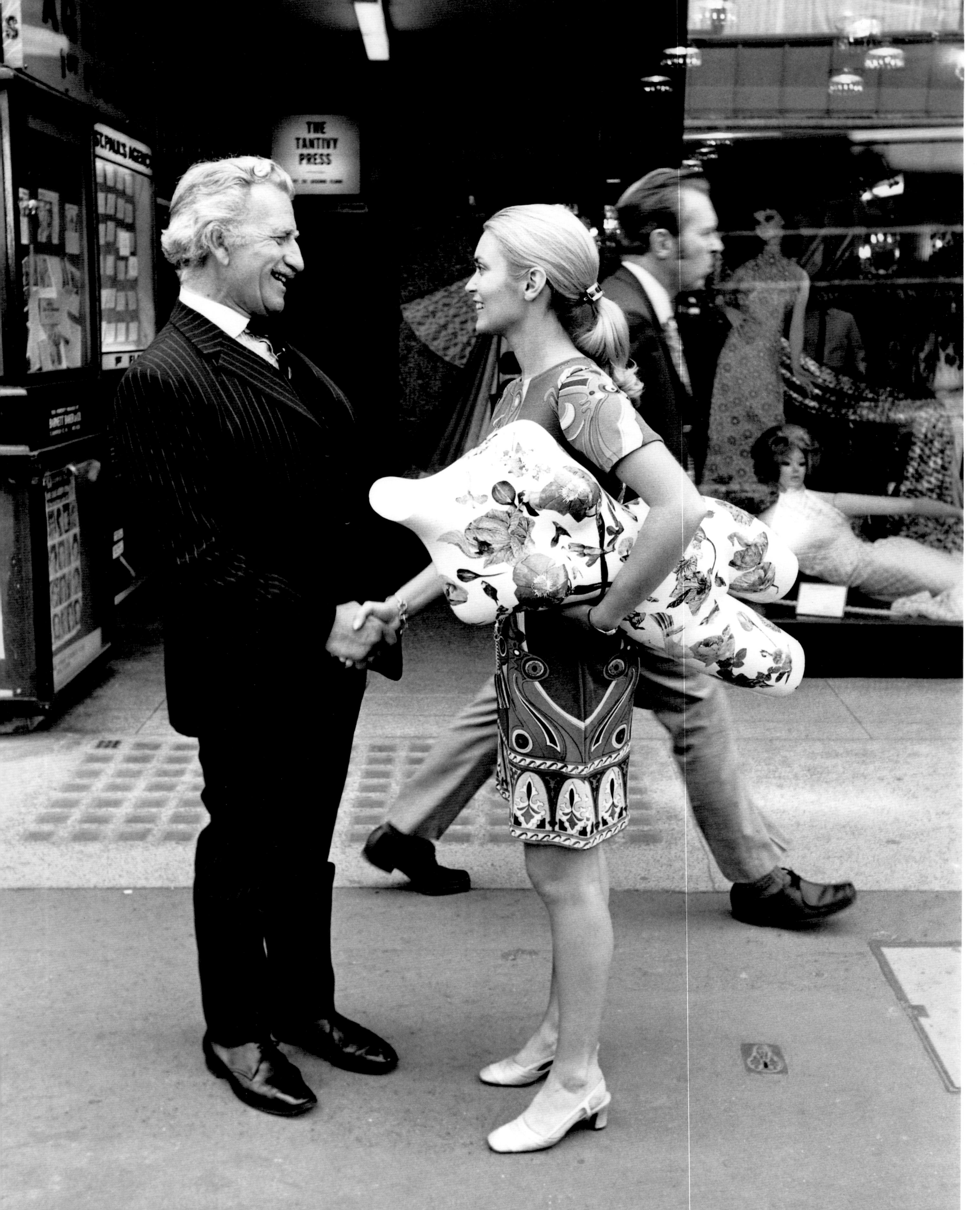
THE
TANTIVY
PRESS

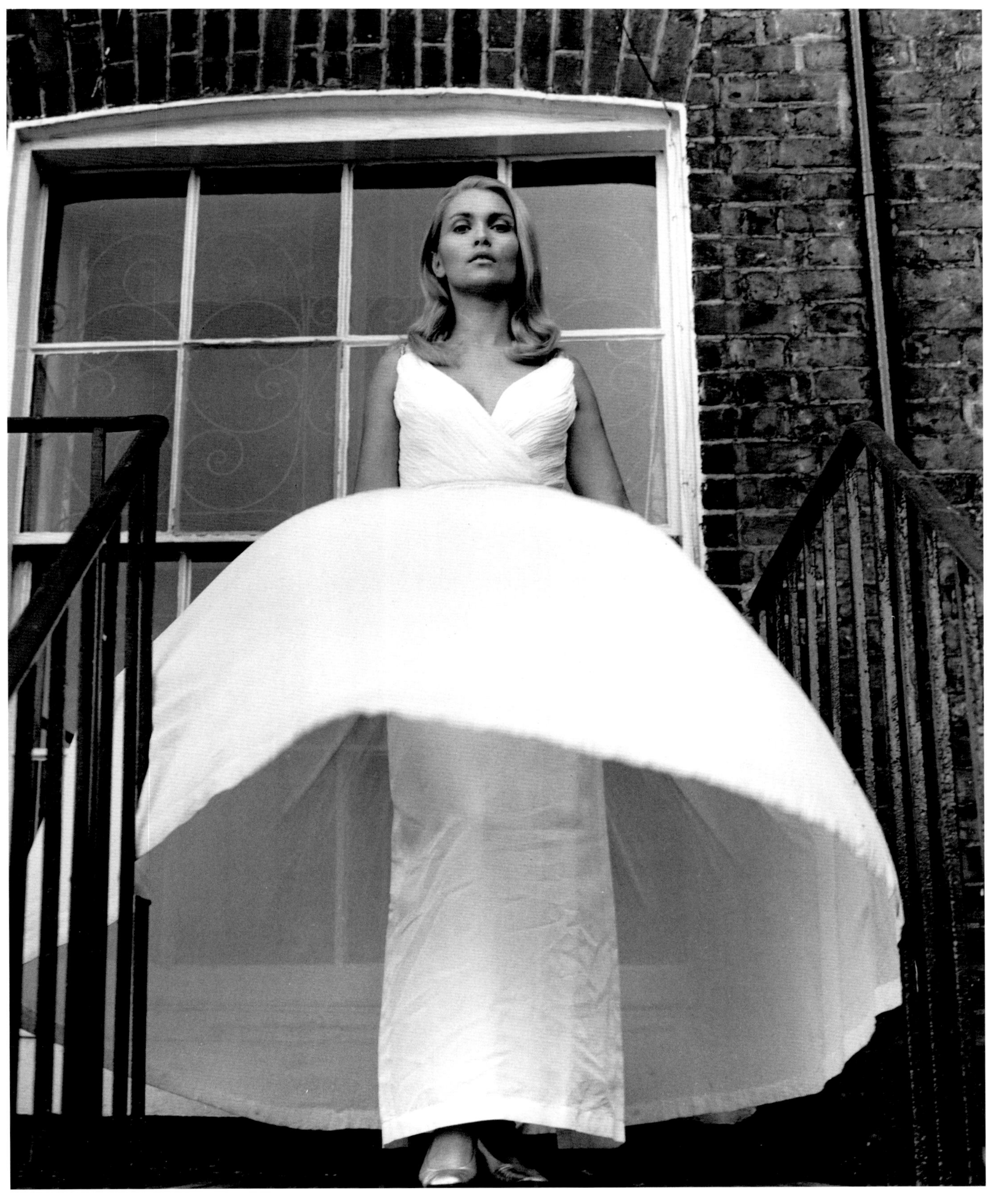

Voulez vous un rendez-vous? – Alexandra Bastedo, actress, Bond Street

Alexandra Bastedo, “The Champions” TV series, mid-Sixties

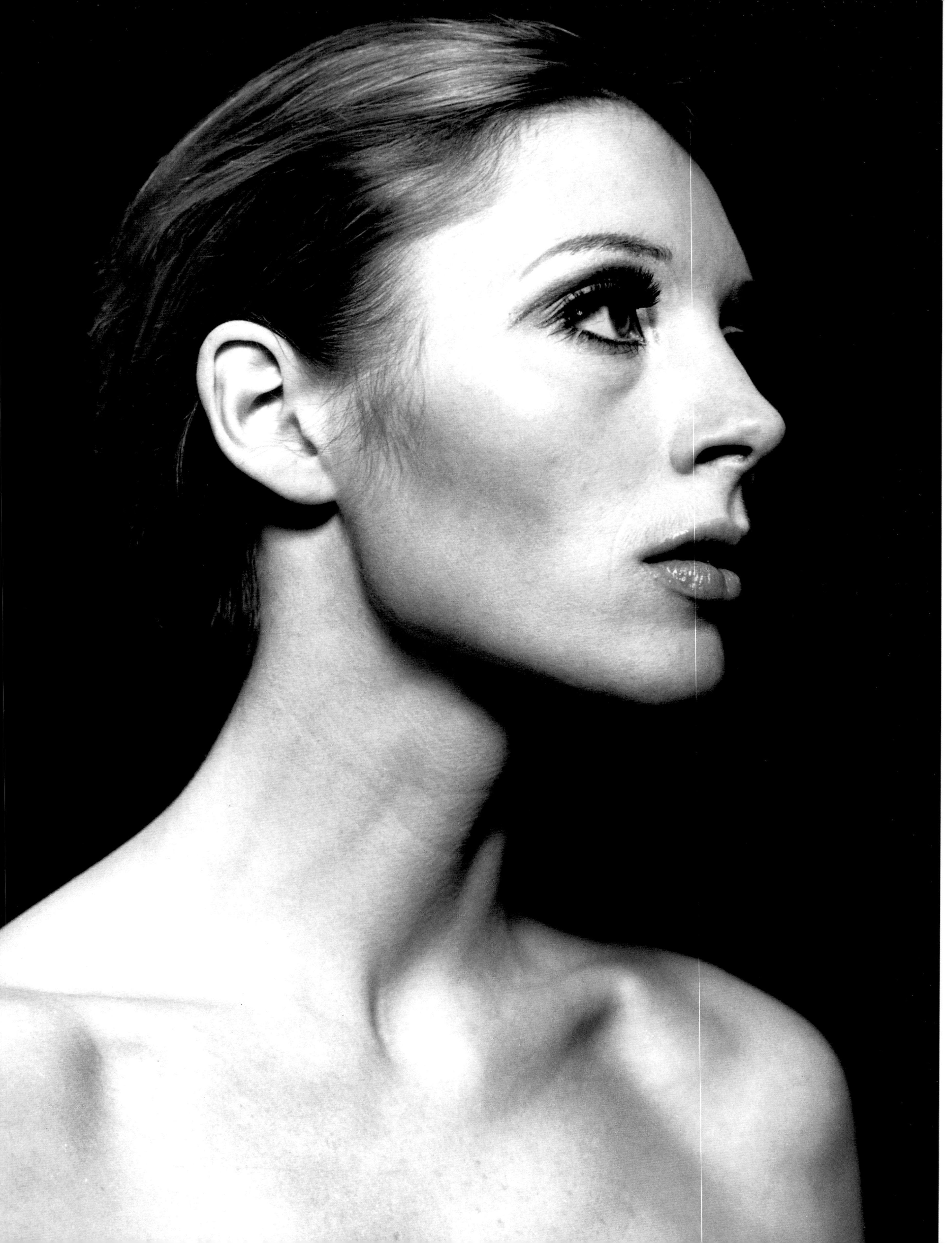

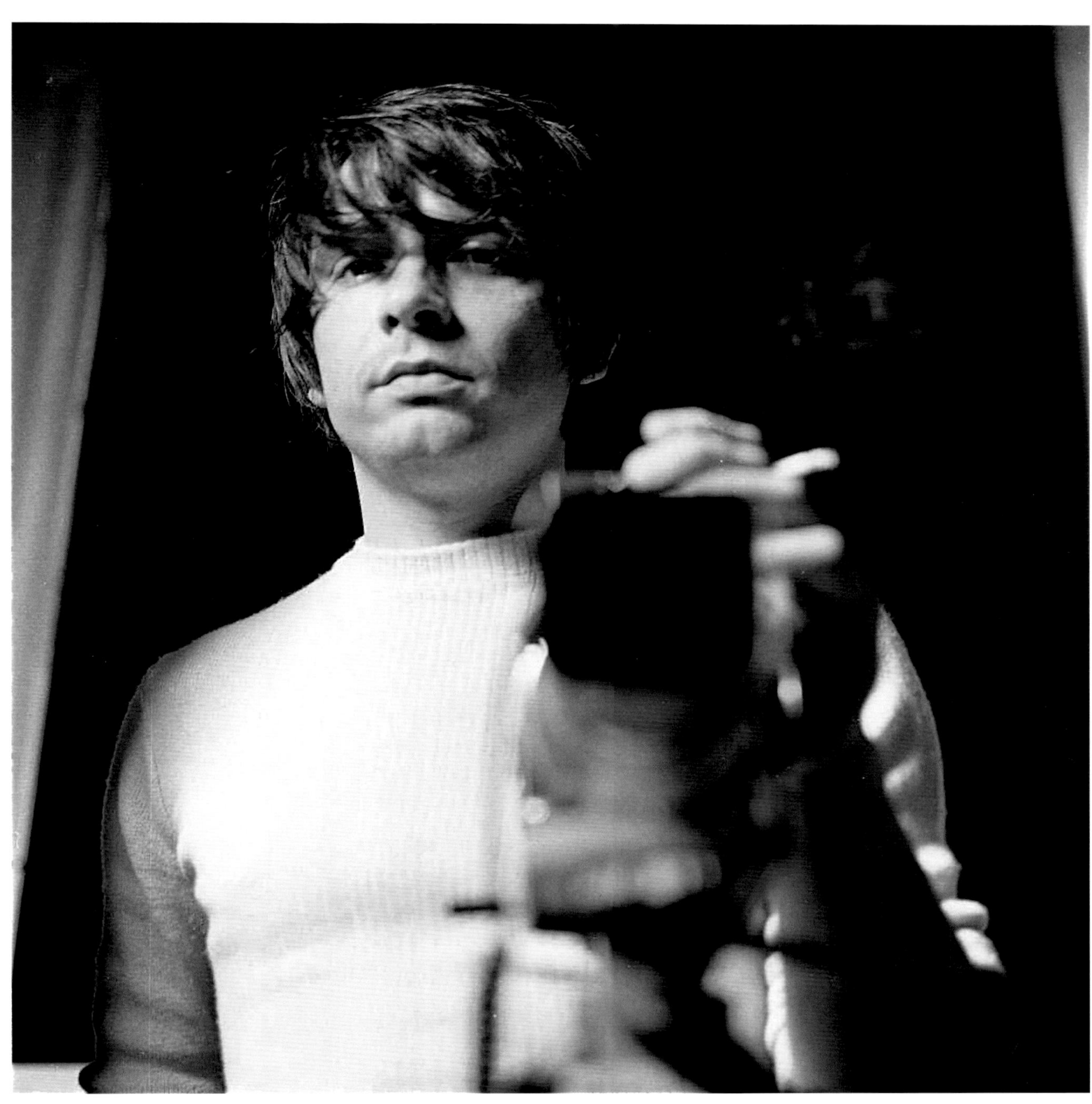

Joan Ferguson, fashion designer, Kensington Markets

David Bailey, fashion and portrait photographer, West End

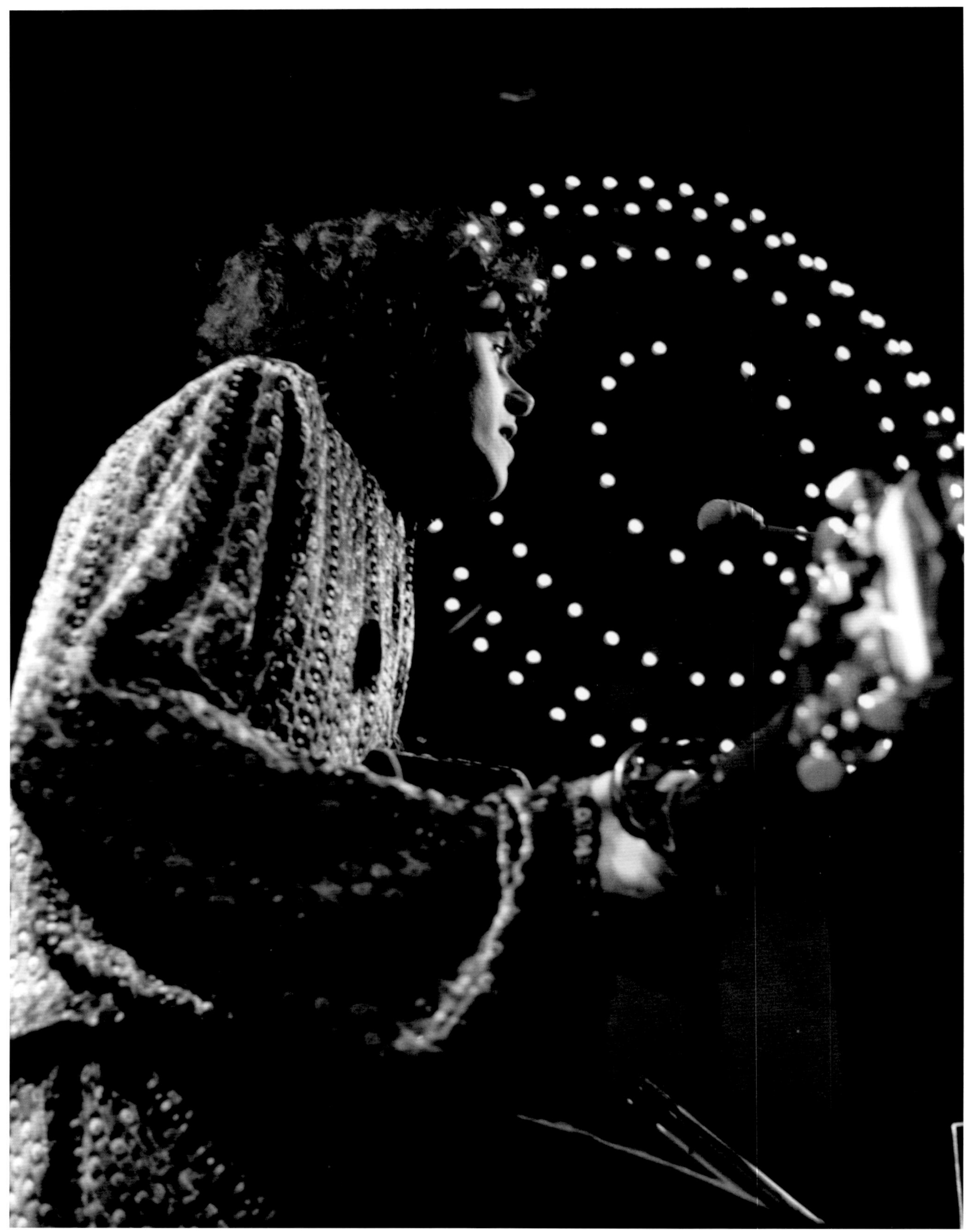

“Mellow Yellow,” Pop icon Donovan, Top of the Pops, BBC Studios, London, 1968

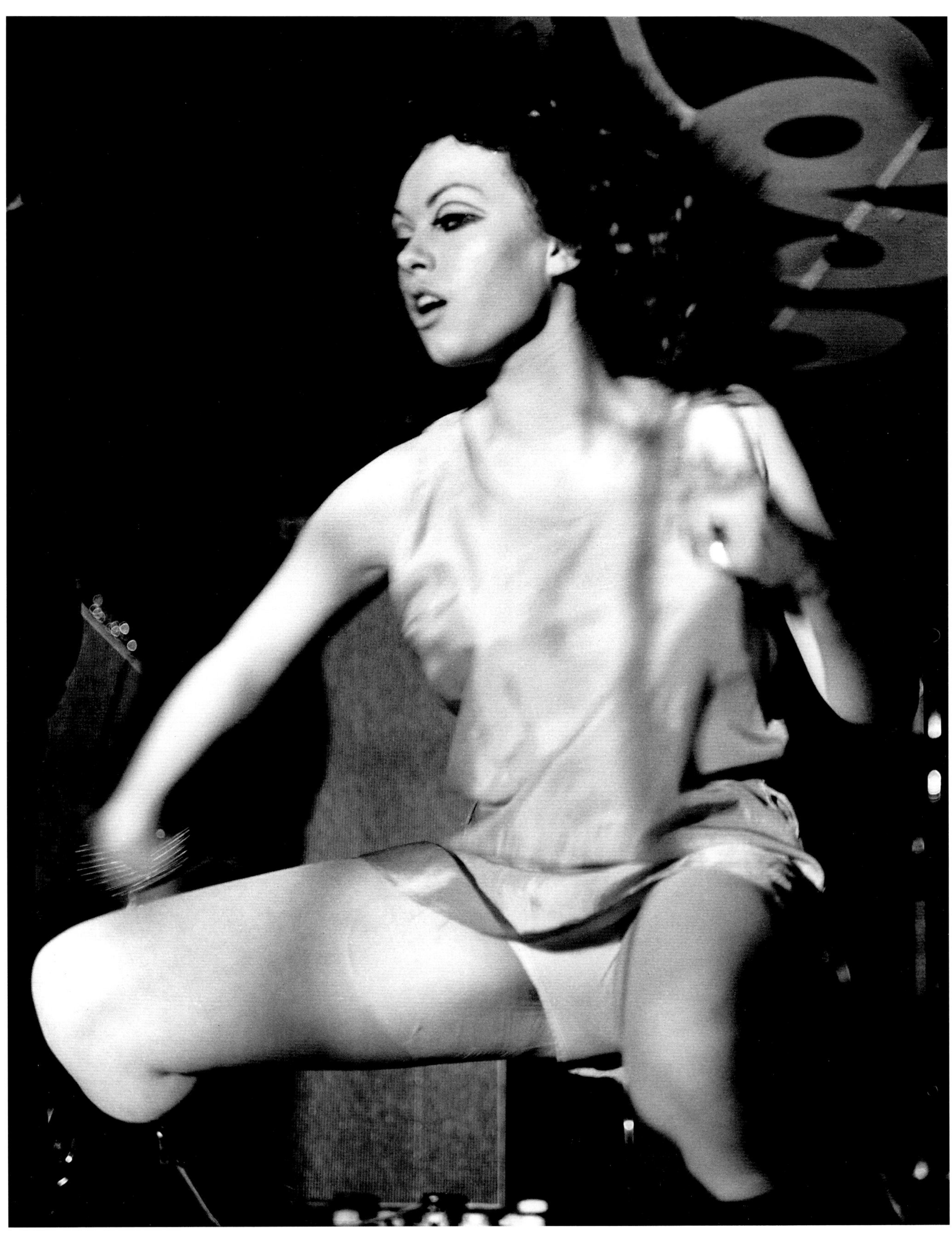

We could have danced all night – Middle Earth club, mid-Sixties

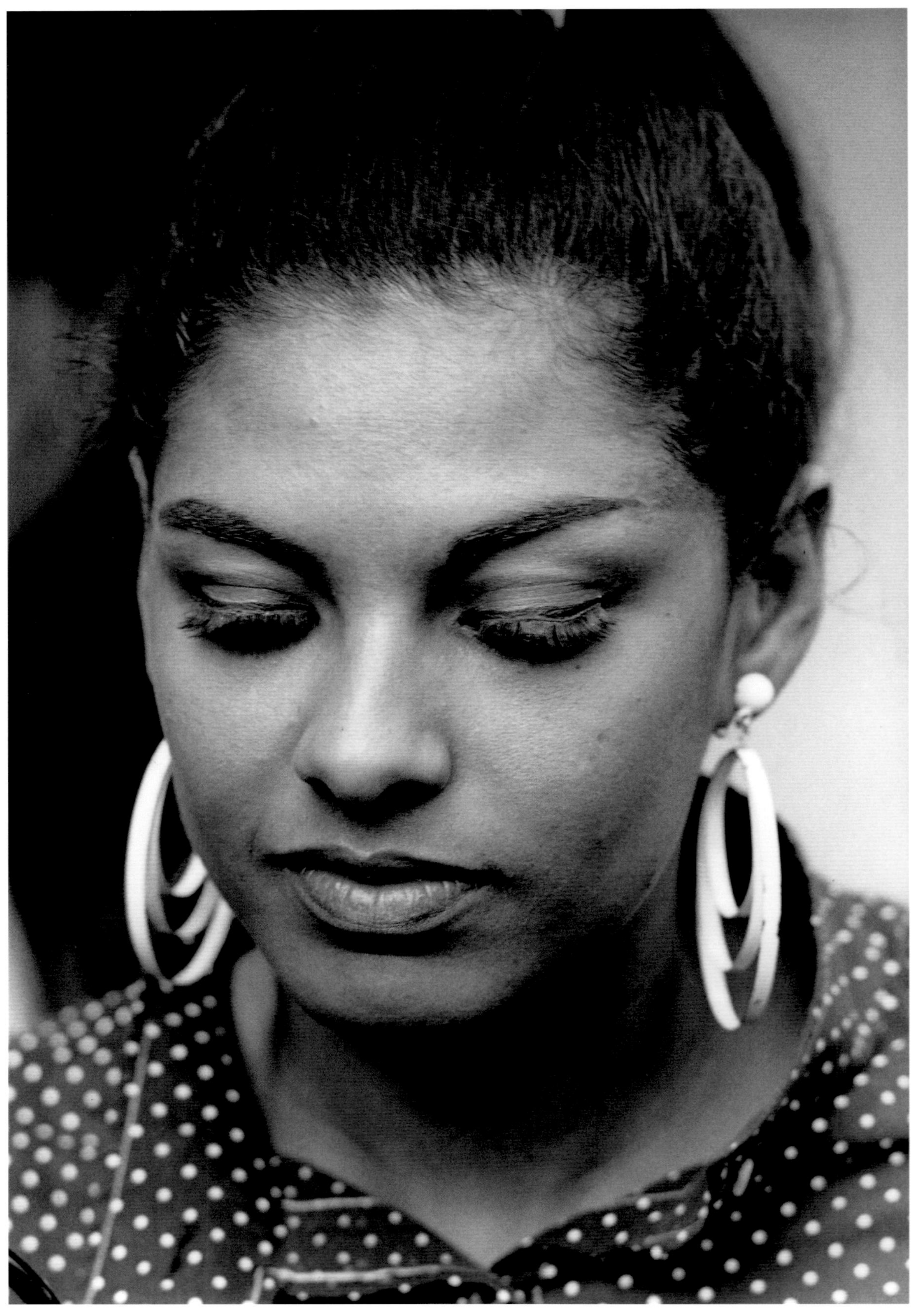

On the sunny side of the Street – friend of Sammy Davis Jr.

Sammy Davis Jr., singer and entertainer, King's Road, 1966

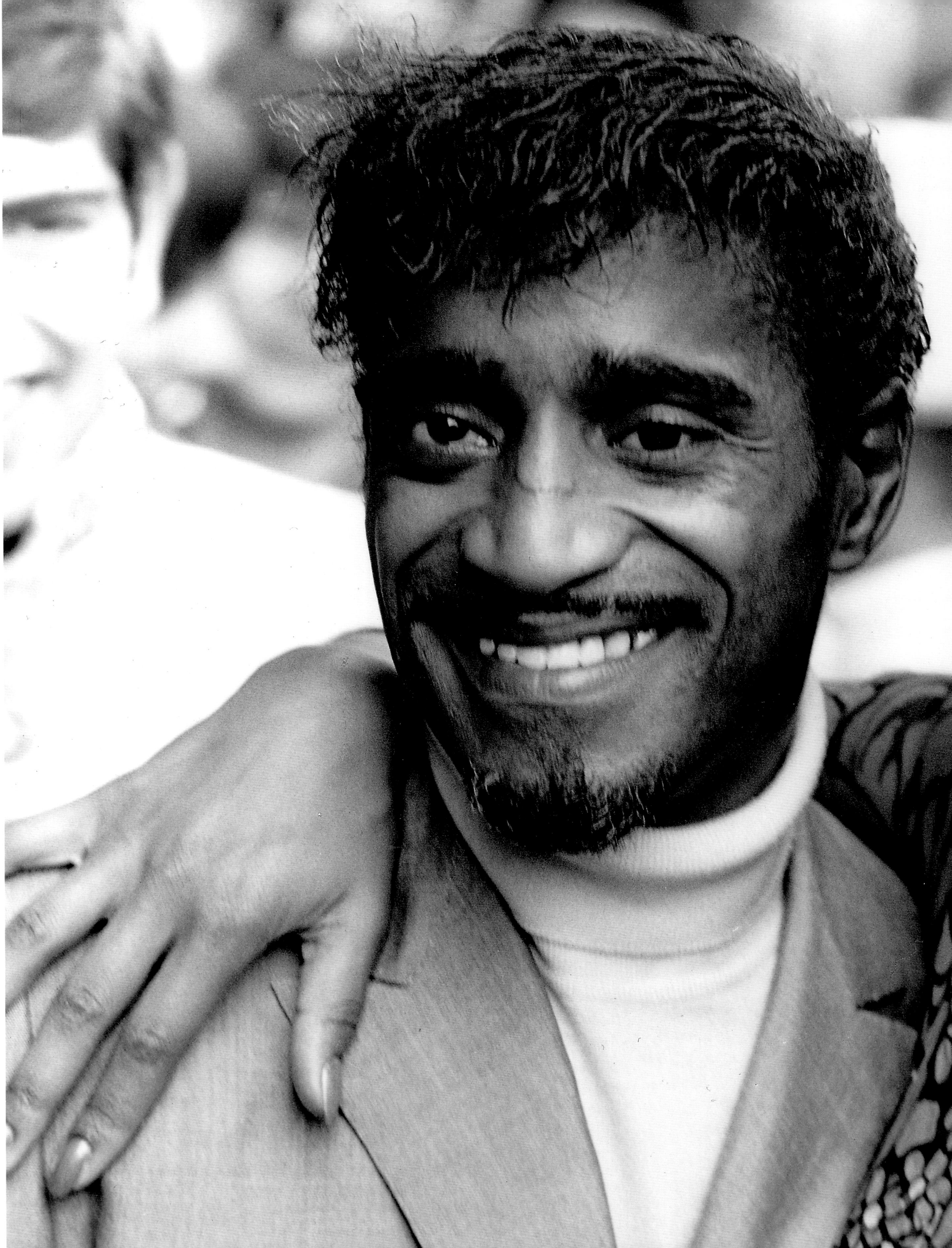

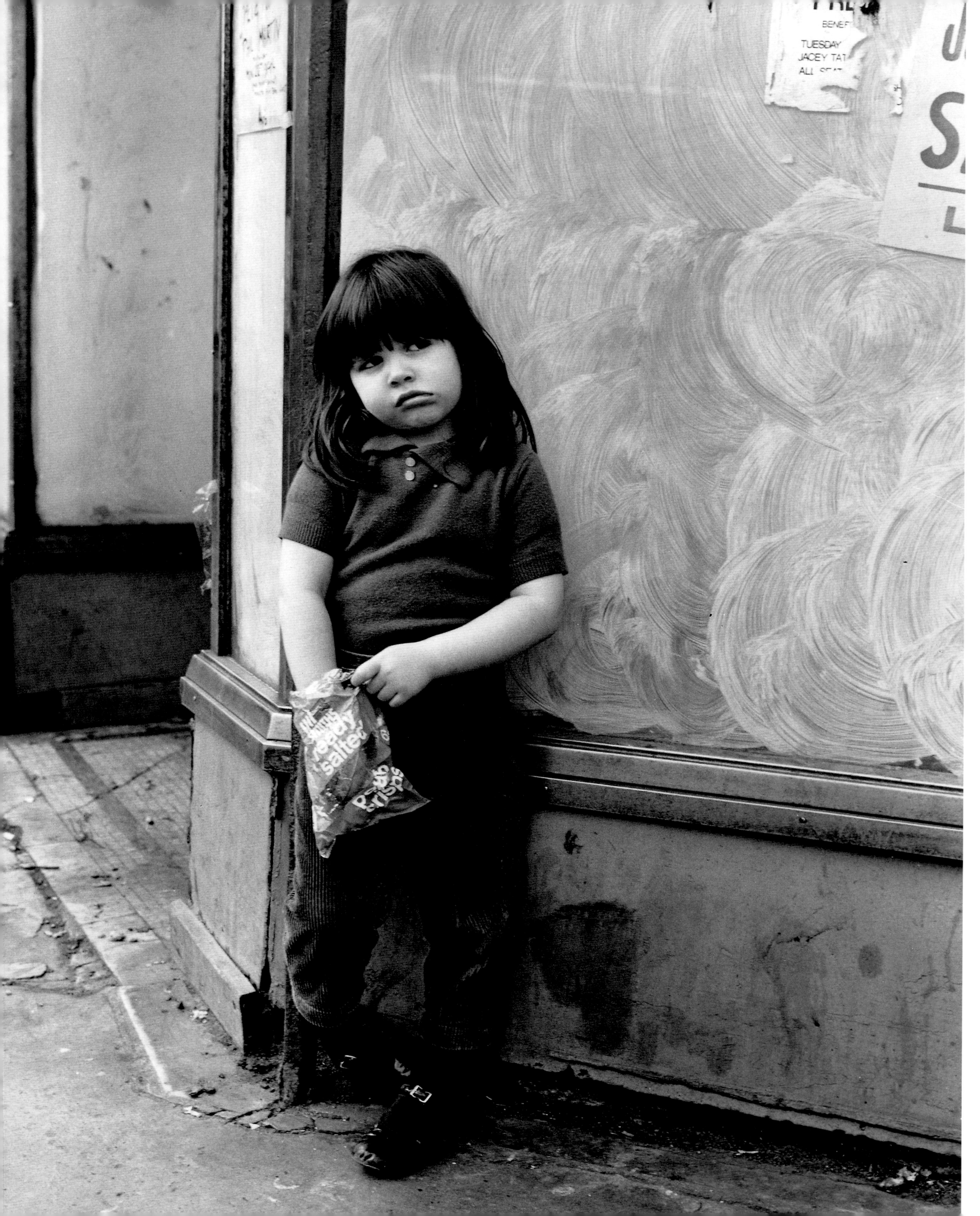
TUESDAY
JACEY
ready
crisps

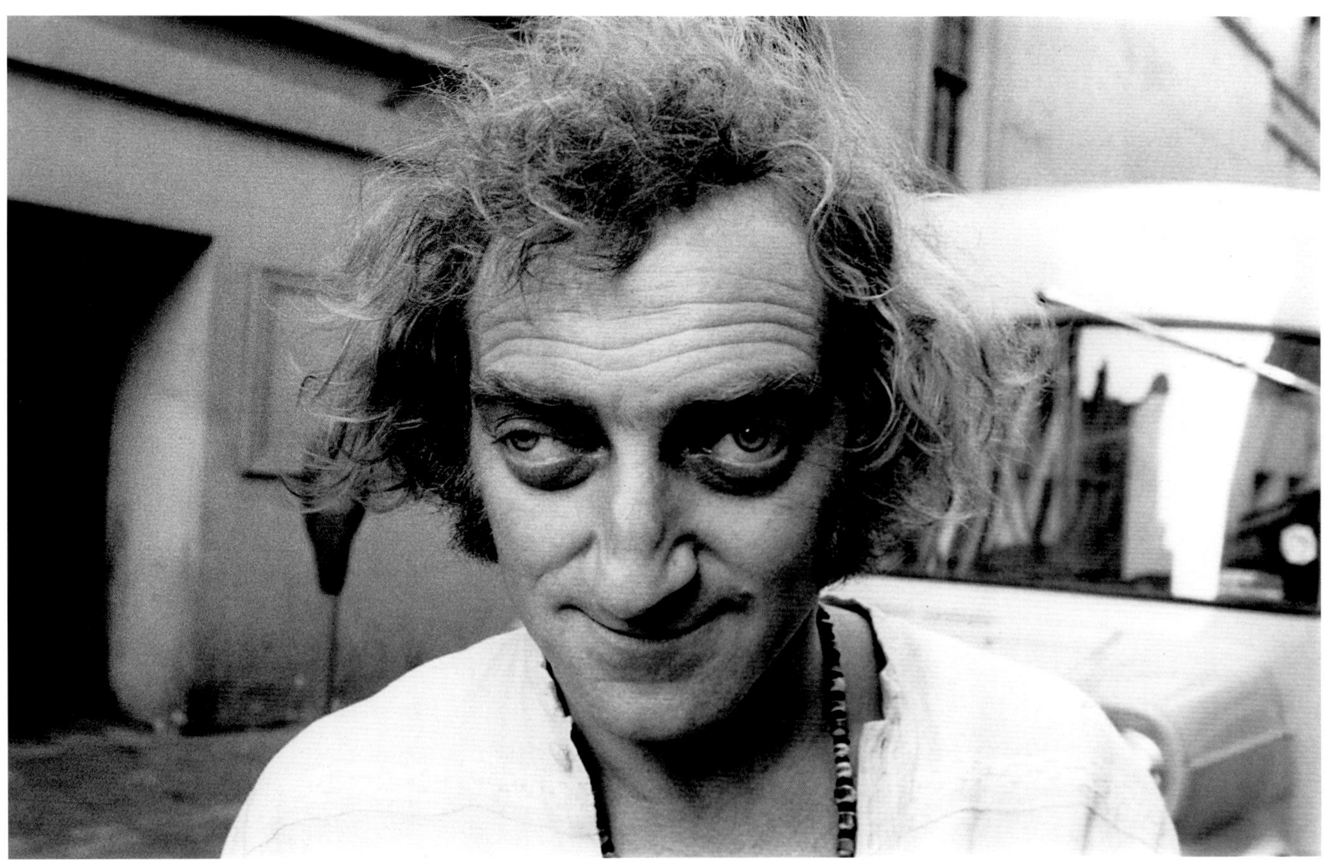

Scepticism – King's Road, 1967

Marty Feldman, film actor and comedy writer, Pimlico

Franco Nero "The Virgin and the Gypsy" film, 1970

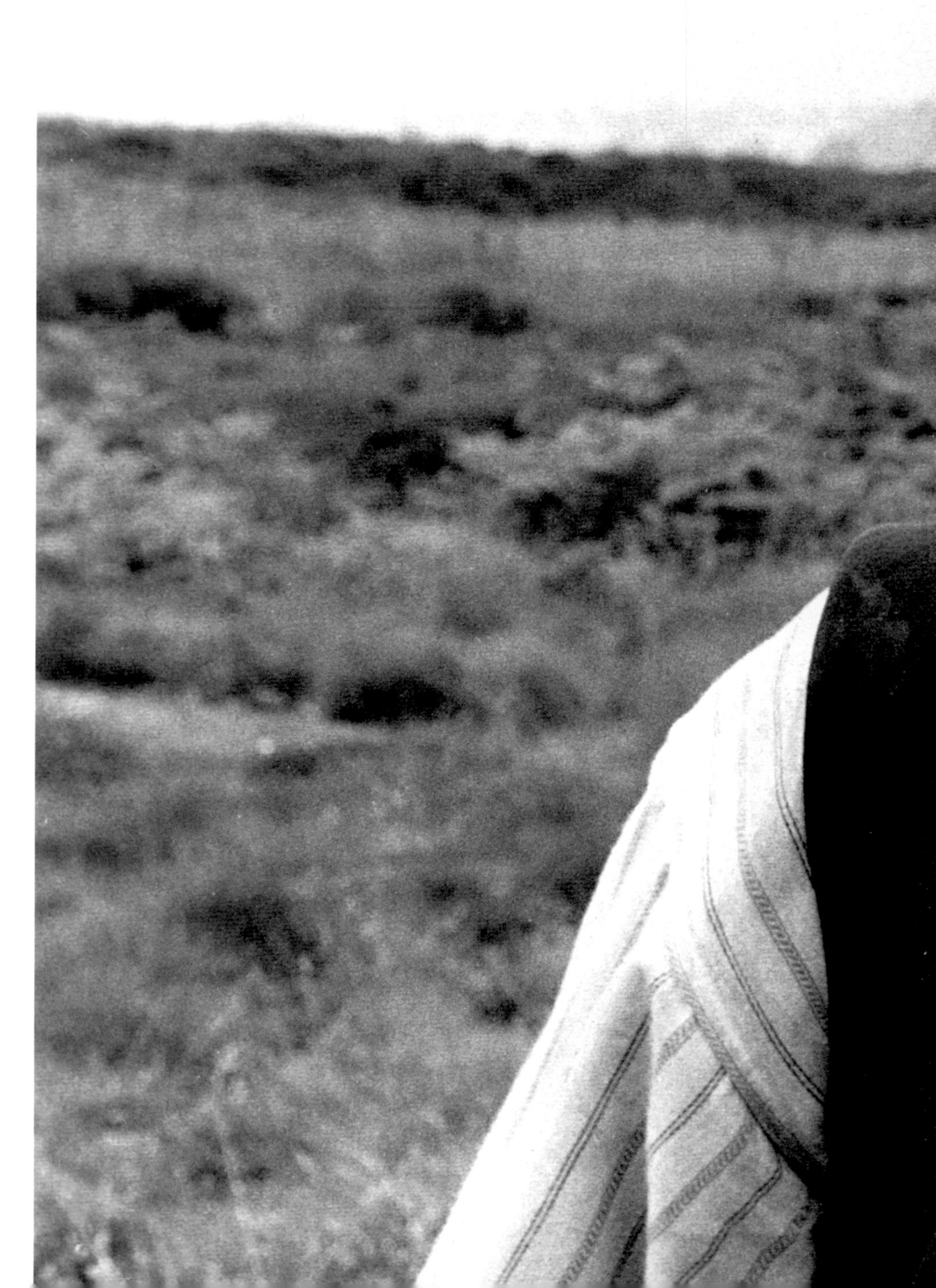

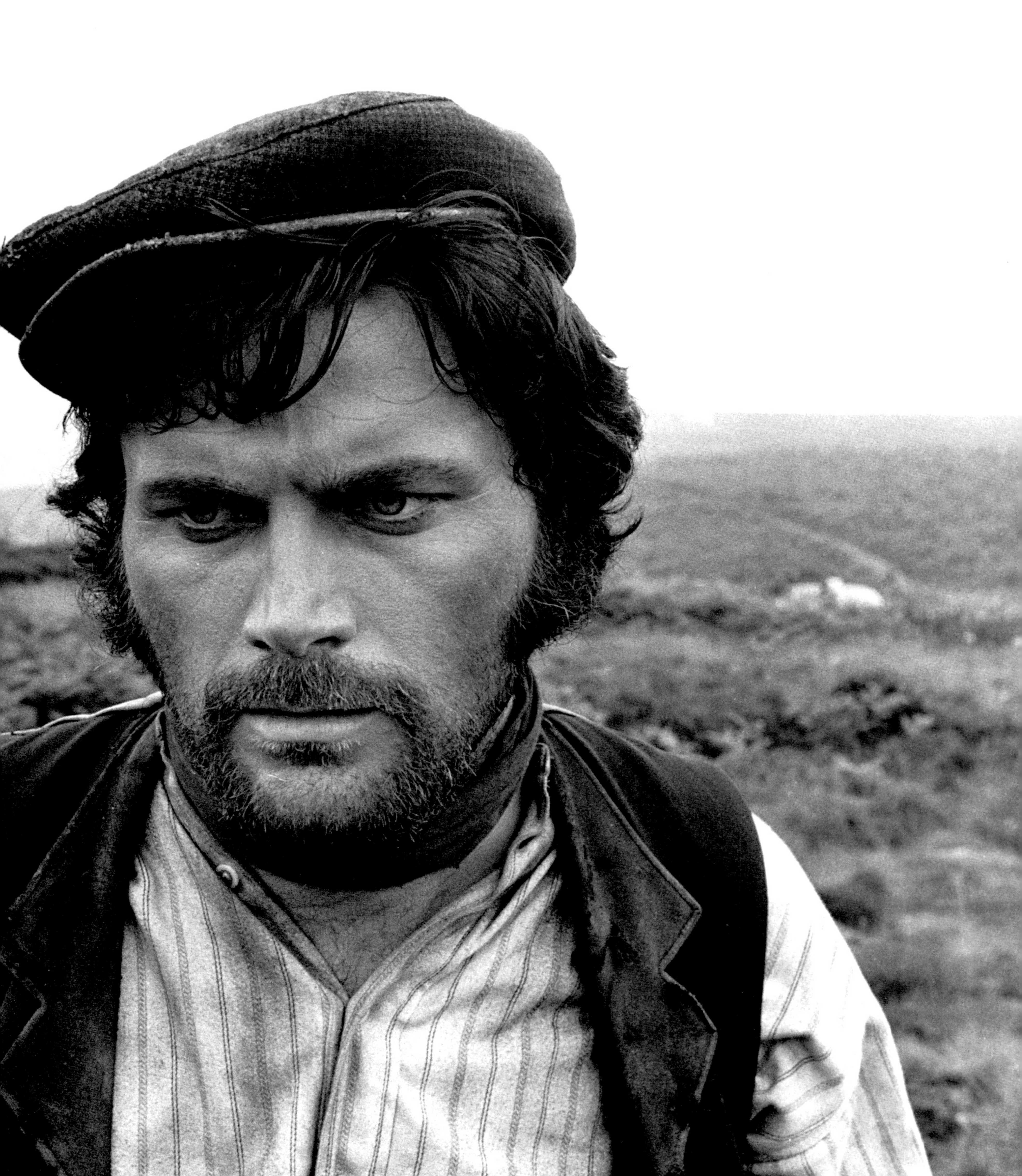

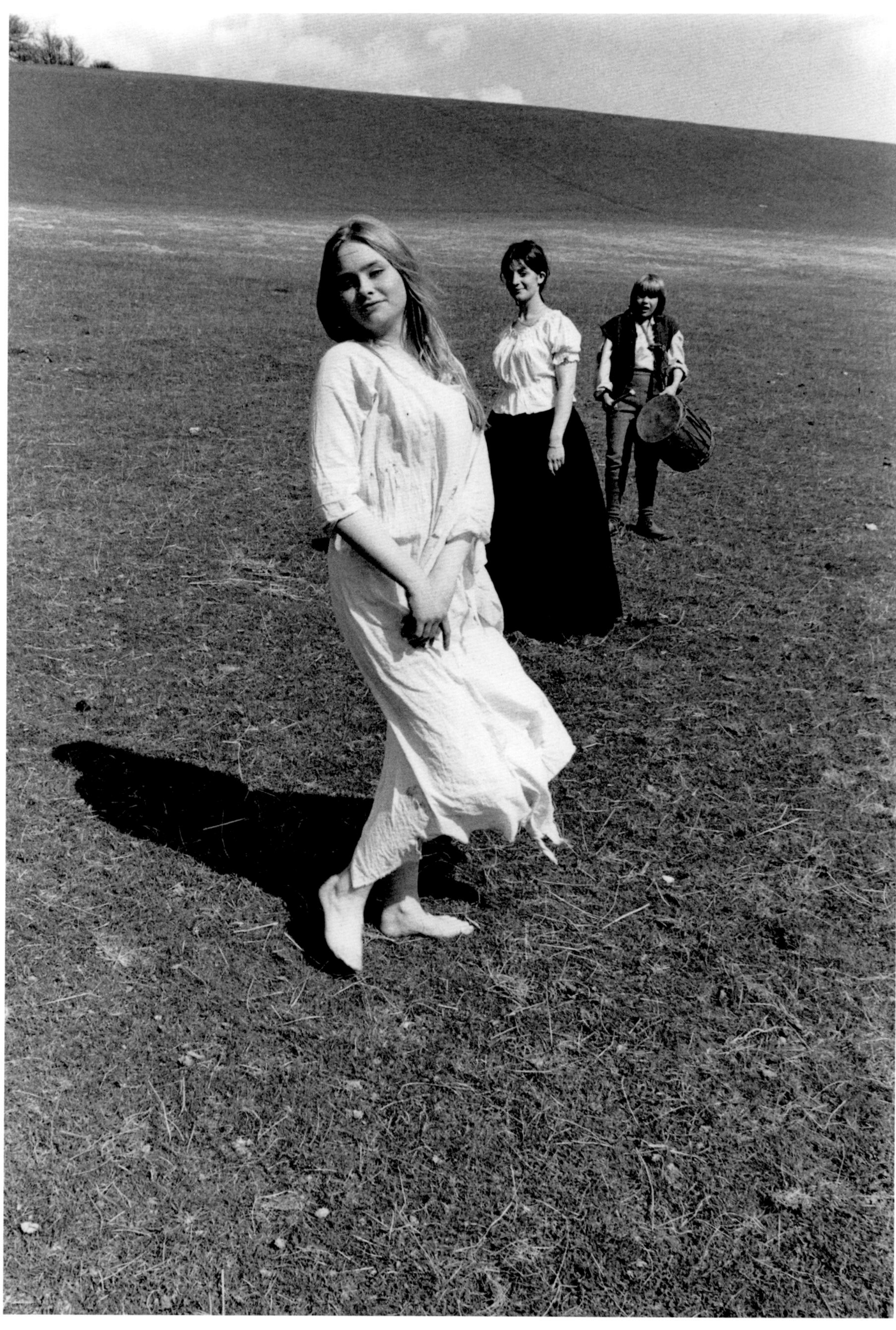

Linda Hayden "Blood on Satan's Claw" film, 1971

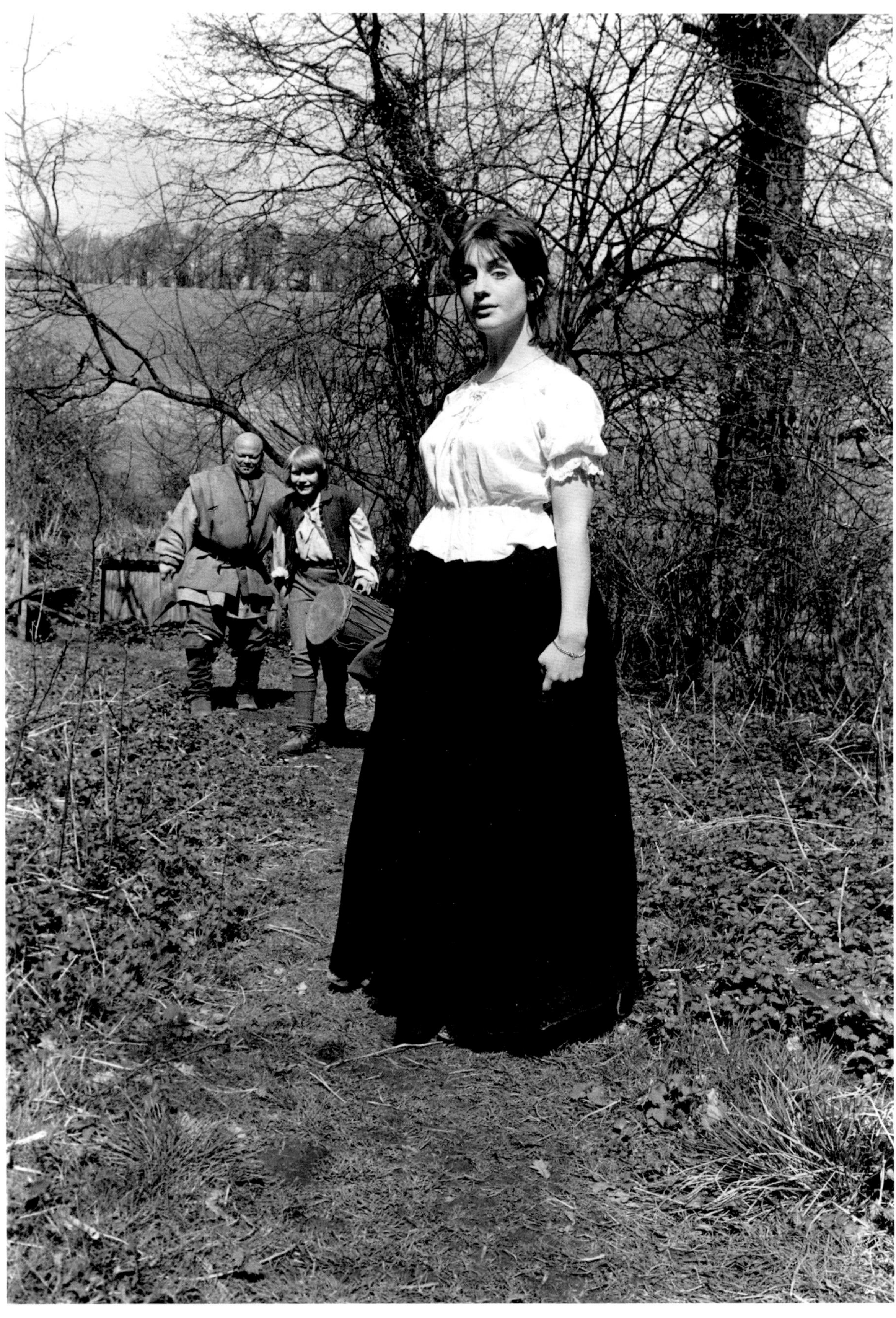

Yvonne Paul, Milton Reid and film extra, “Blood on Satan’s Claw”

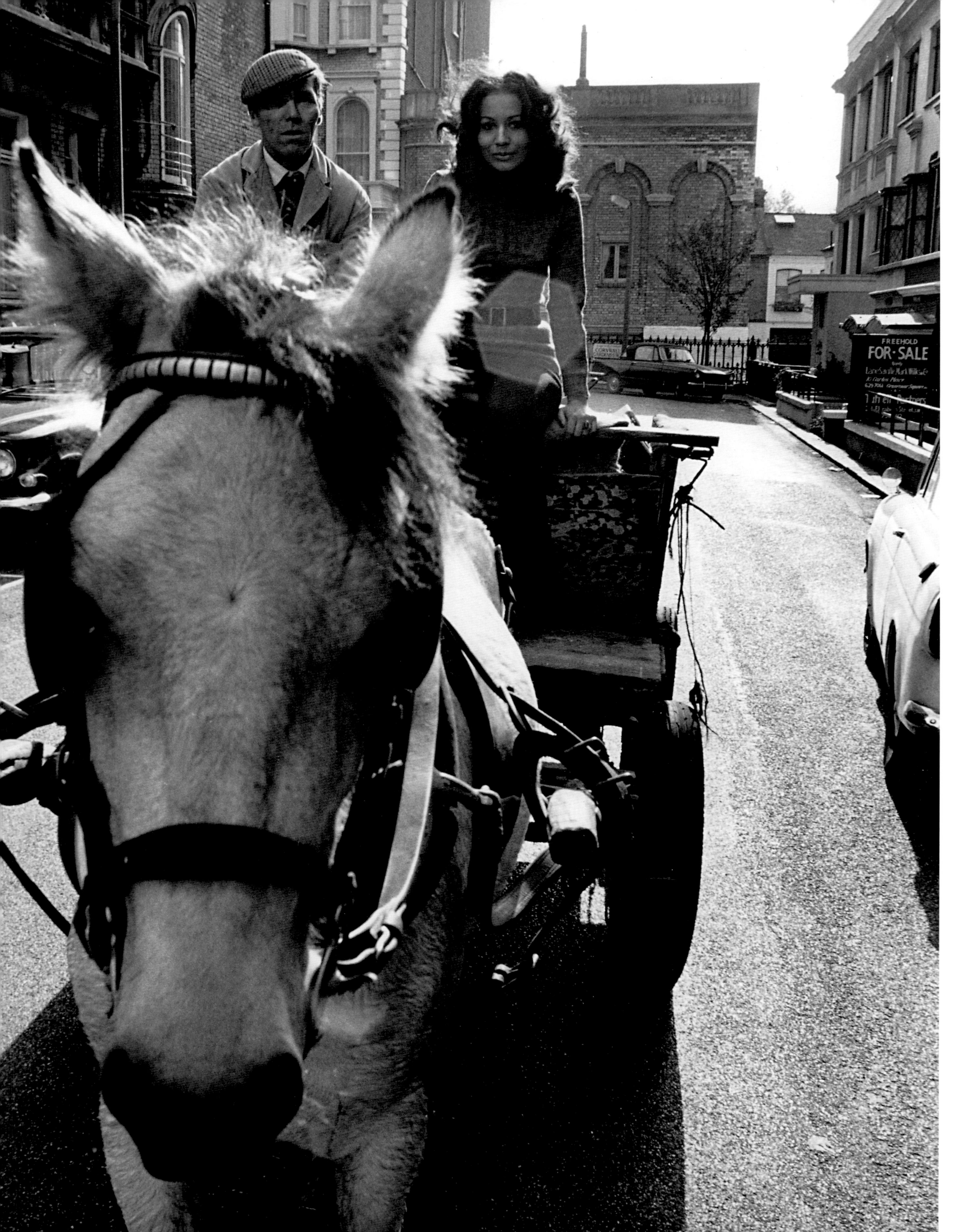
FREEHOLD
FOR·SALE

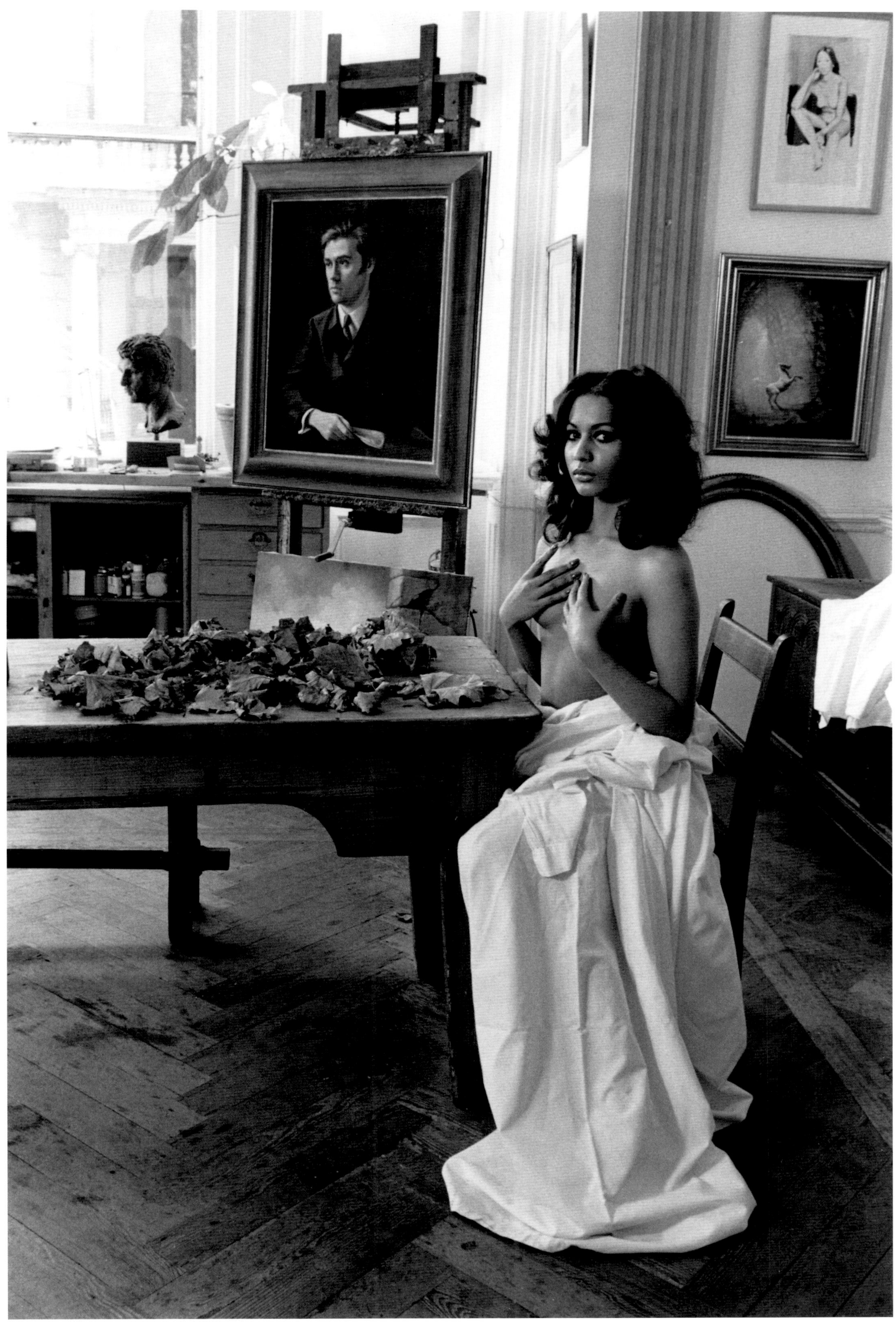

Hylette Adolphe, actress and mysterious beauty, Kensington

Hylette Adolphe, star in Fellini's "Satyricon," 1969

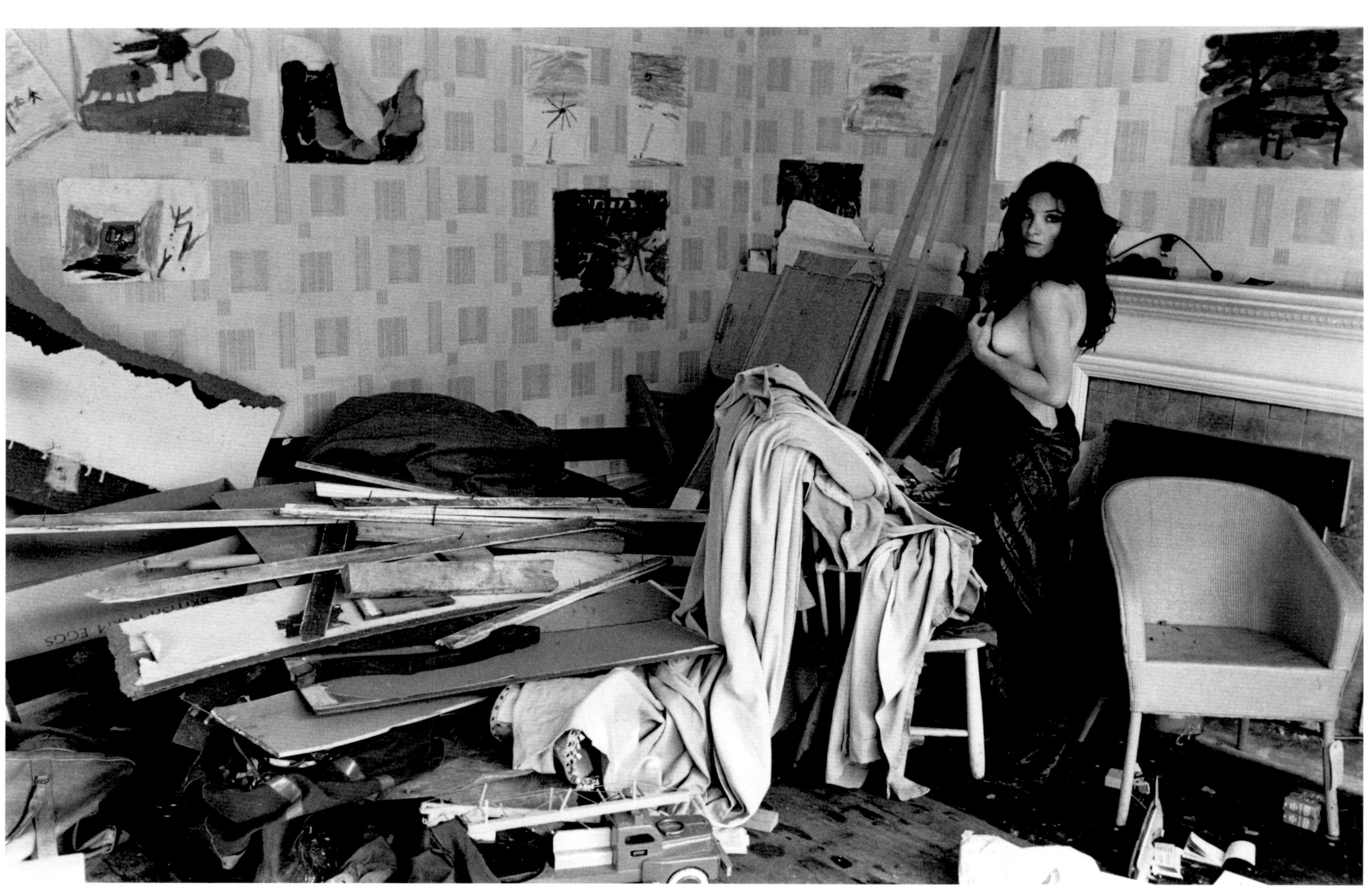

Femme Fatale – Kate O'Mara, star in "Vampire Lovers," 1970

Model Vicky Hodge, famous for wearing first see-through T-shirt

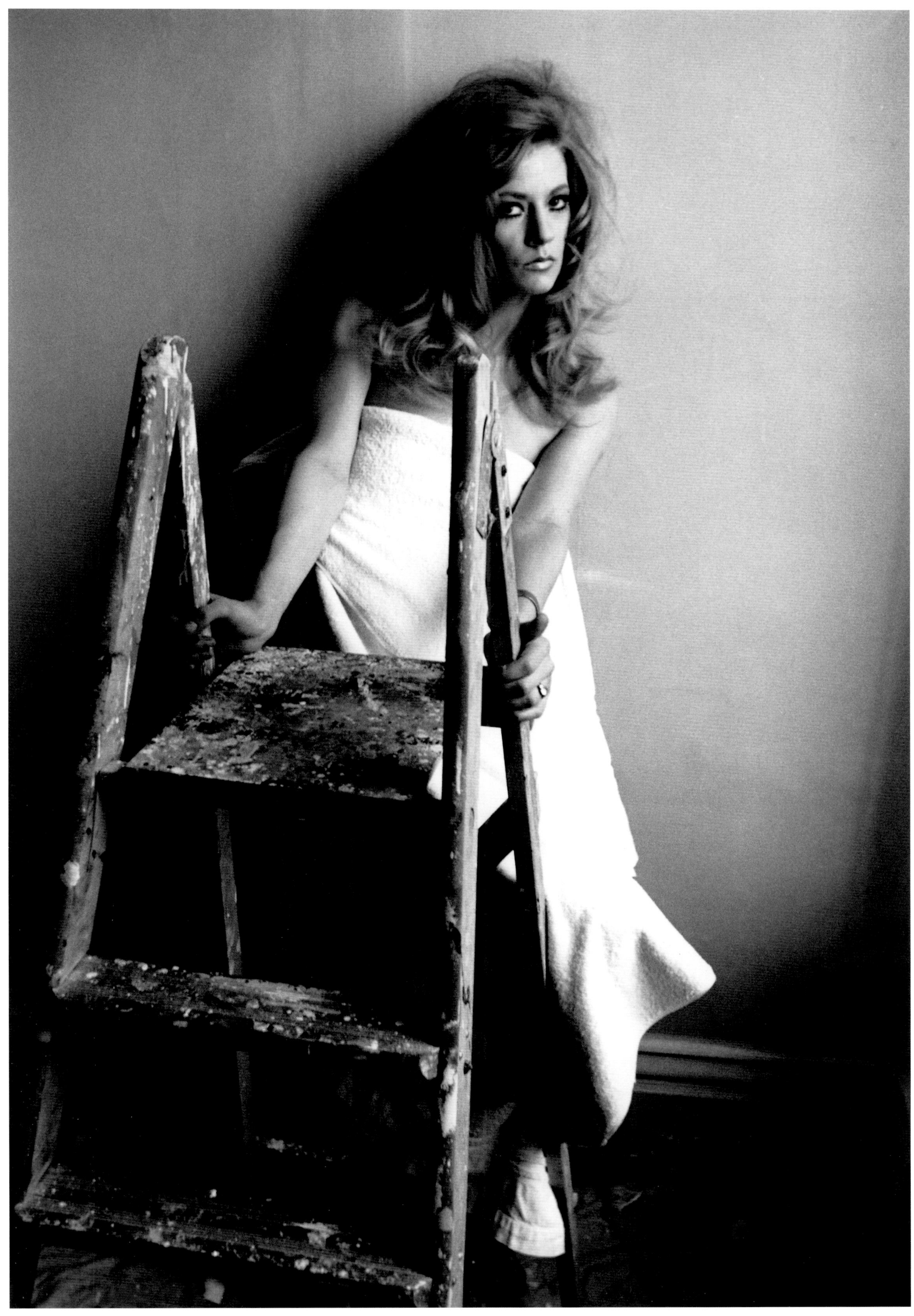

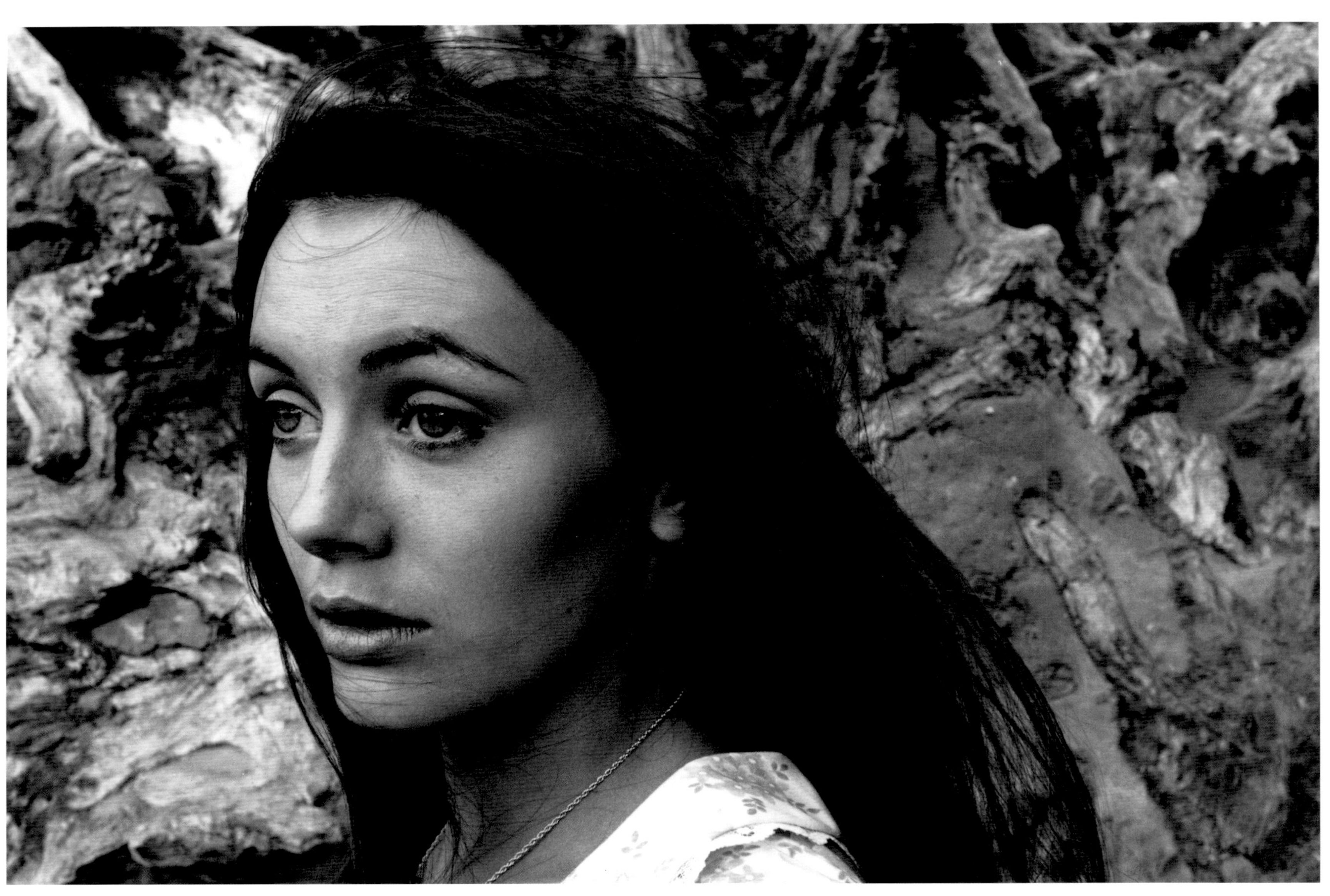

Lesley Ann Down, star in TV series “Upstairs Downstairs”

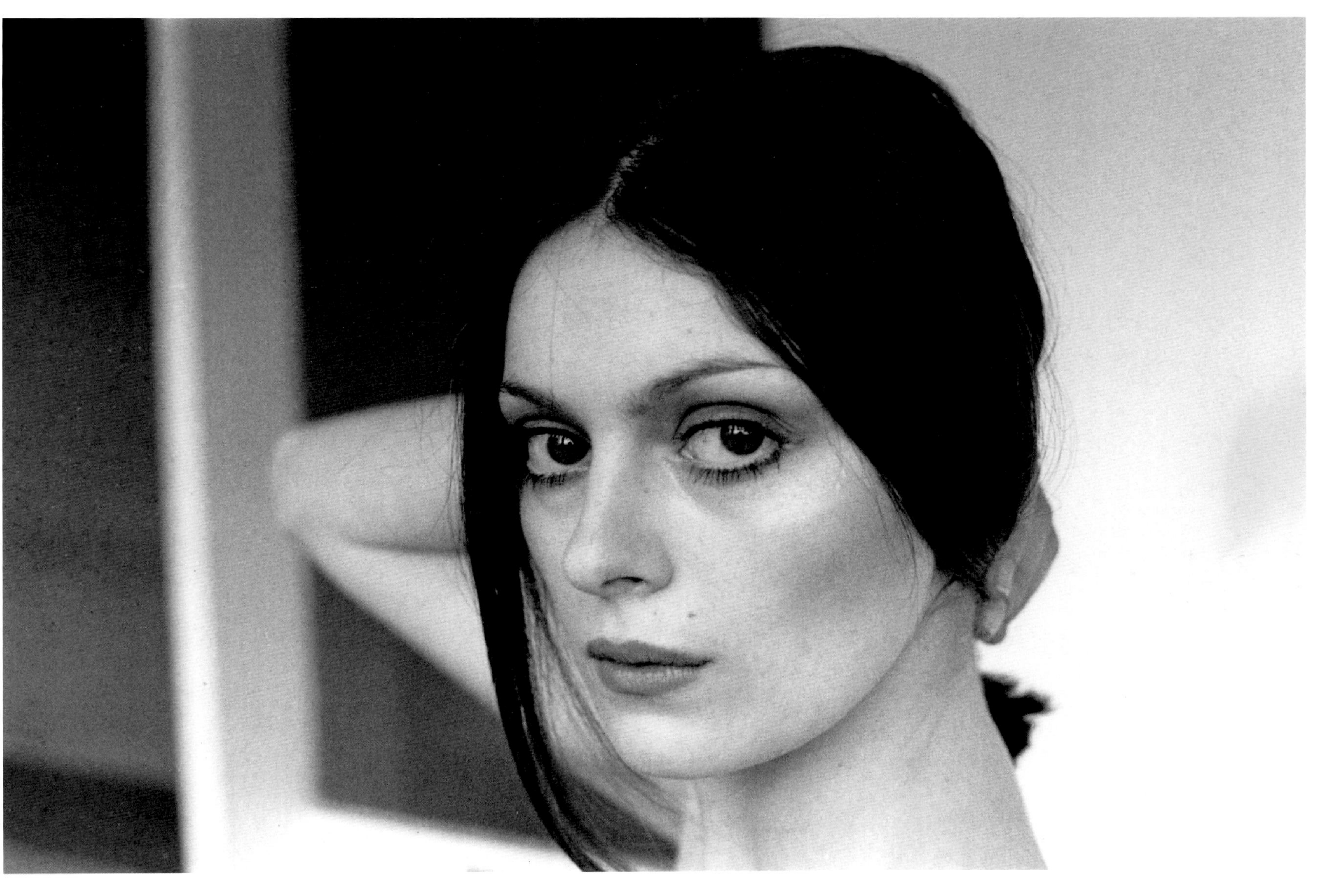

Claudine, photographer's studio, Courtfield Gardens

Next pages: Deux filles, photographer's studio

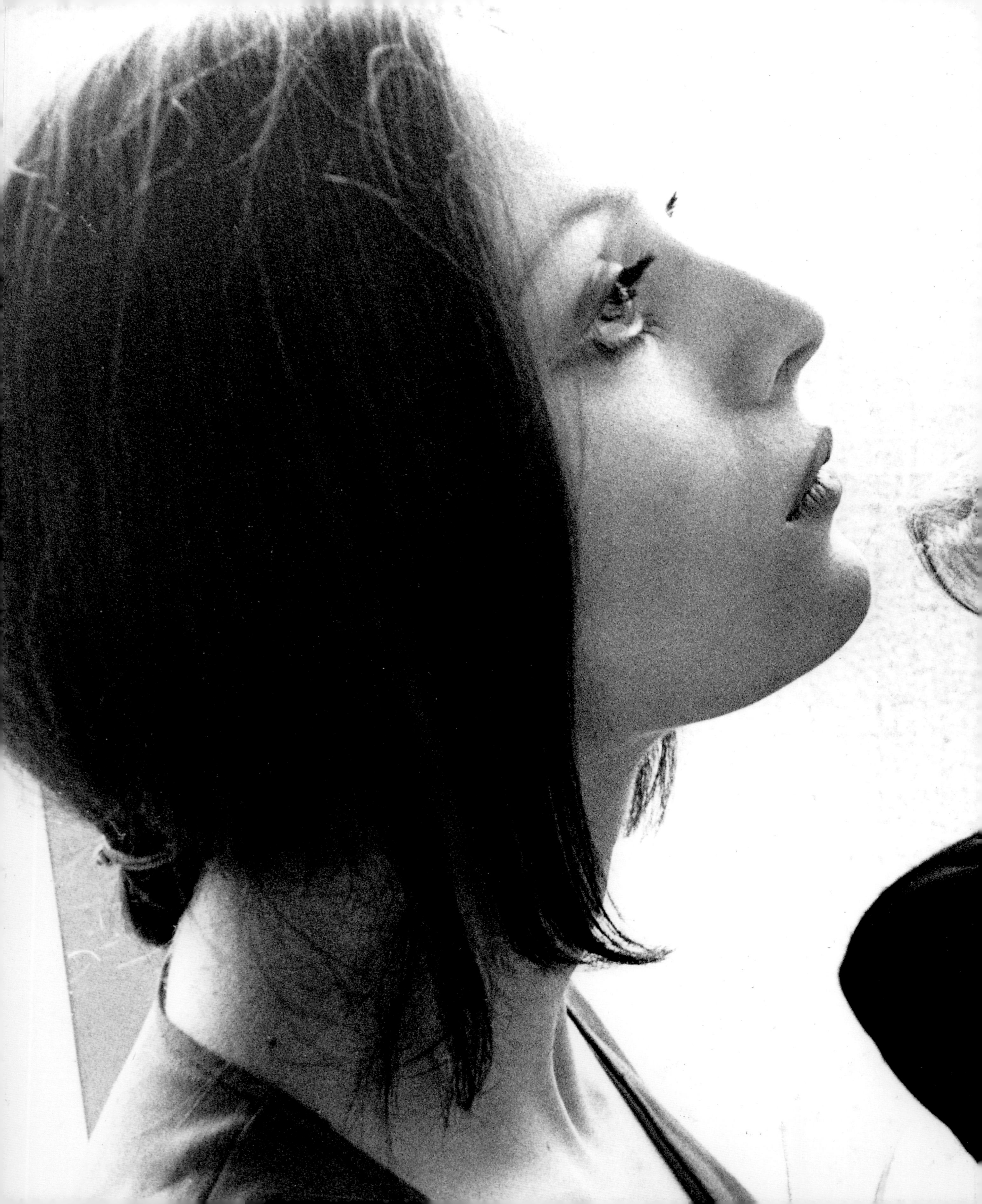

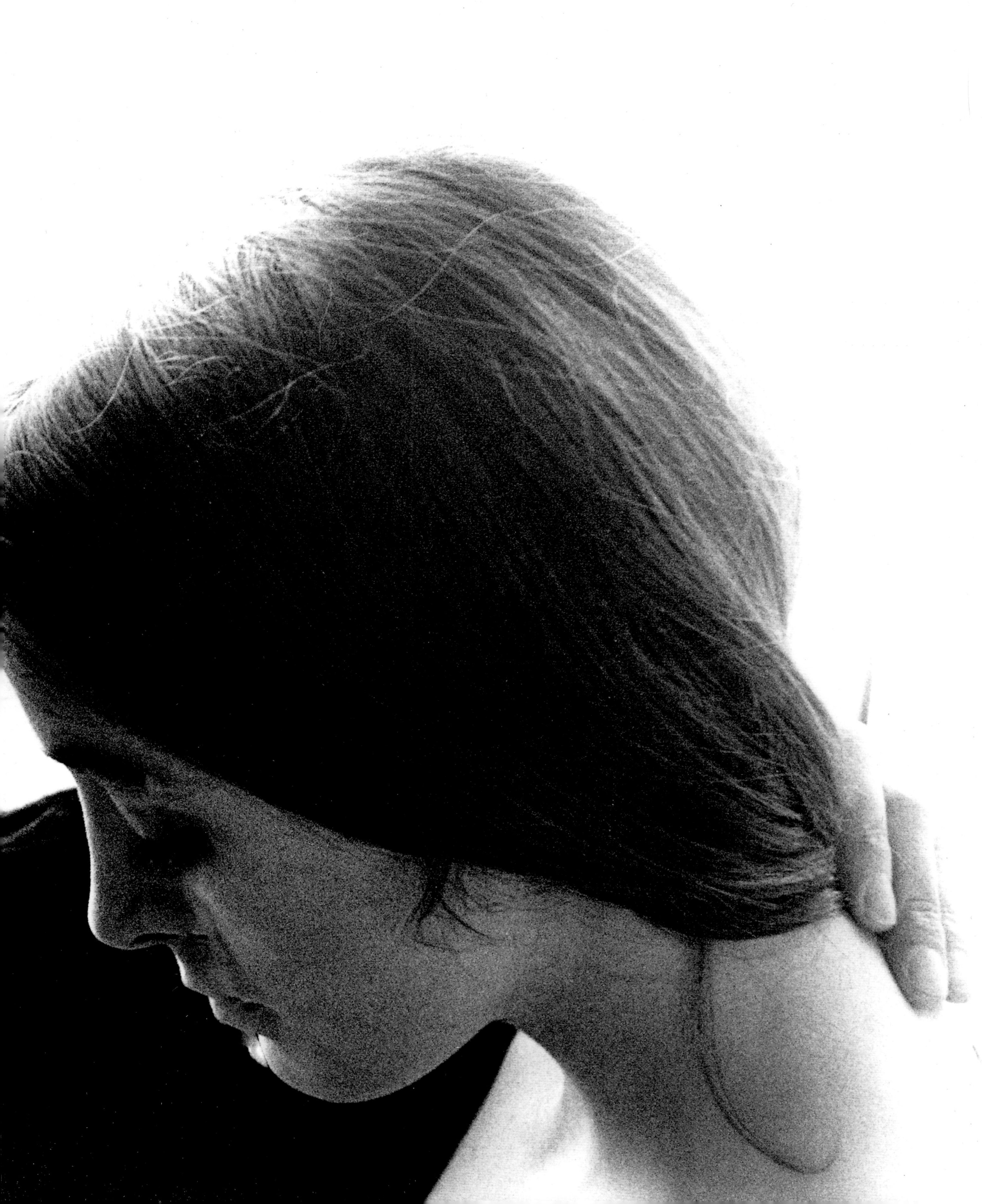

The Twen Story

In the late fifties the German magazine *Twen* was born. It was a new kind of magazine—fresh, sexy, intellectual, and targeting young readers in their mid to late twenties. The magazine was known as a stepping-stone for its emerging graphic designers, writers, and photographers.

I had the courage to contact *Twen*'s editor Willy Fleckhaus in Munich to show him some of my human-interest work for his consideration. I felt fortunate and privileged to receive an invitation from the magazine for a meeting in the summer of 1967. Some meager savings funded my flight to Munich, to the magazine's headquarters. I stayed with a friend for a few nights while I was weighing up my chances of finding work with the magazine.

The night before my appointment I ventured to a popular disco to put my mind at ease. An attractive youngish woman accepted a few slow dances. I could not keep my secret and told her what the following day might have in store for me. At the end of the night she politely declined the challenge of "meeting once again here or there in the future" and had absolutely no interest in exchanging addresses or phone numbers, not believing in brief encounters. We parted in the early hours and she wished me the "best of British luck" for my appointment.

That day, the art director's office seemed to be in an organized mess, with images of named photographers all over the floor and walls. Willy Fleckhaus glanced through my work and his eyes rested on the photograph of the pregnant girl and friend on my London rooftop. "Is she still expecting the baby in the very near future?" he asked. I could confirm that the birth was imminent, probably within a fortnight, and mentioned that the father was in prison for a drug offense. Without hesitation, the editor suggested to send his best journalist to London within the next few days to write a comprehensive story.

Willy Fleckhaus picked up the phone and summoned the journalist in question to his office. I felt short of breath, trying not to show my surprise, when suddenly standing before my eyes, with a hidden smile, was last night's encounter from the dance floor. She was *Twens'* reputed and controversial journalist Ann Thoennissen.

An eight-page story titled "We Live in London" was later published in the November issue of *Twen* 1967 and eventually resulted in George Harrap's publishing house commissioning me to compile a photographic book of London's youth in 1969 titled *Young London: Permissive Paradise*.

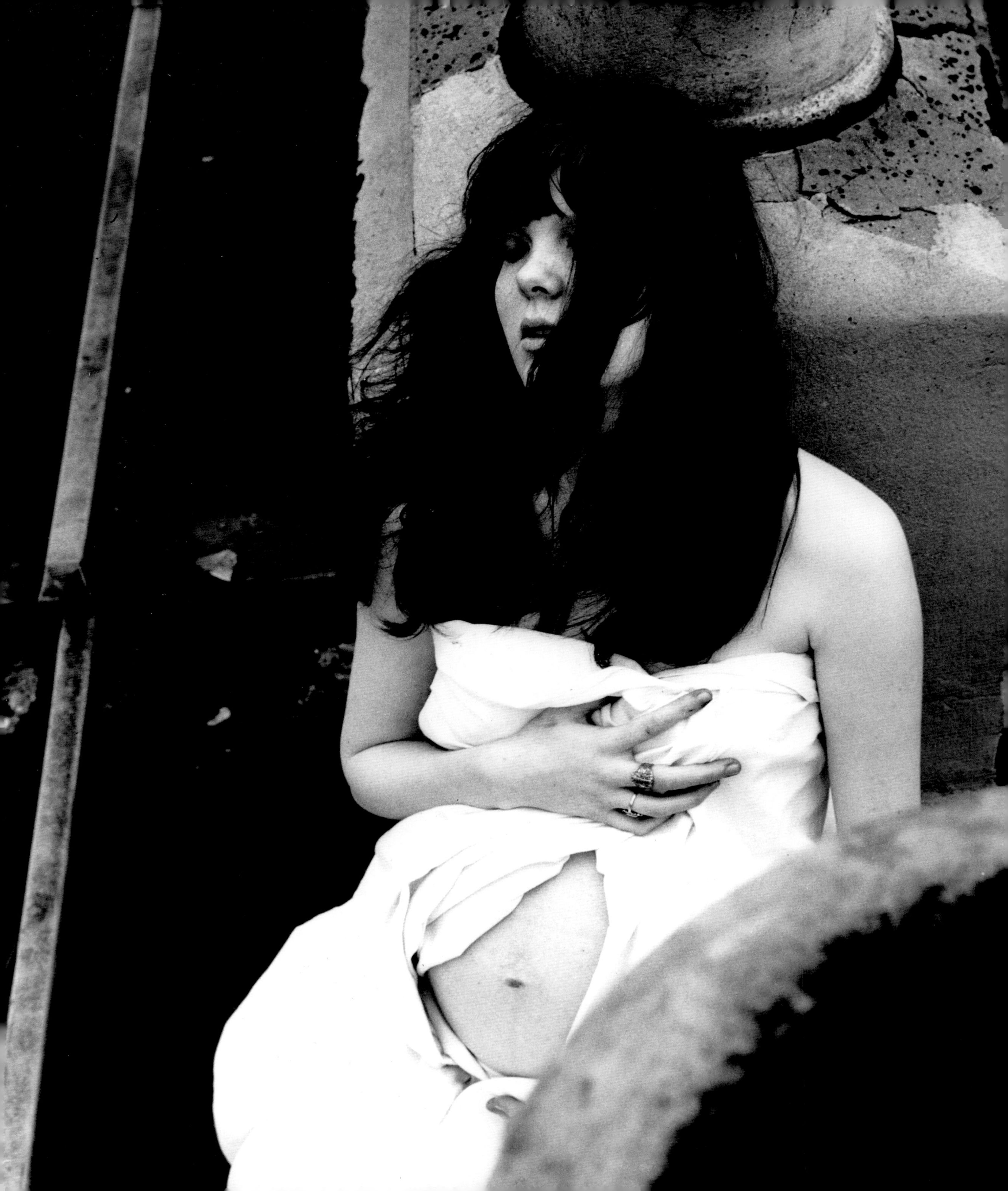

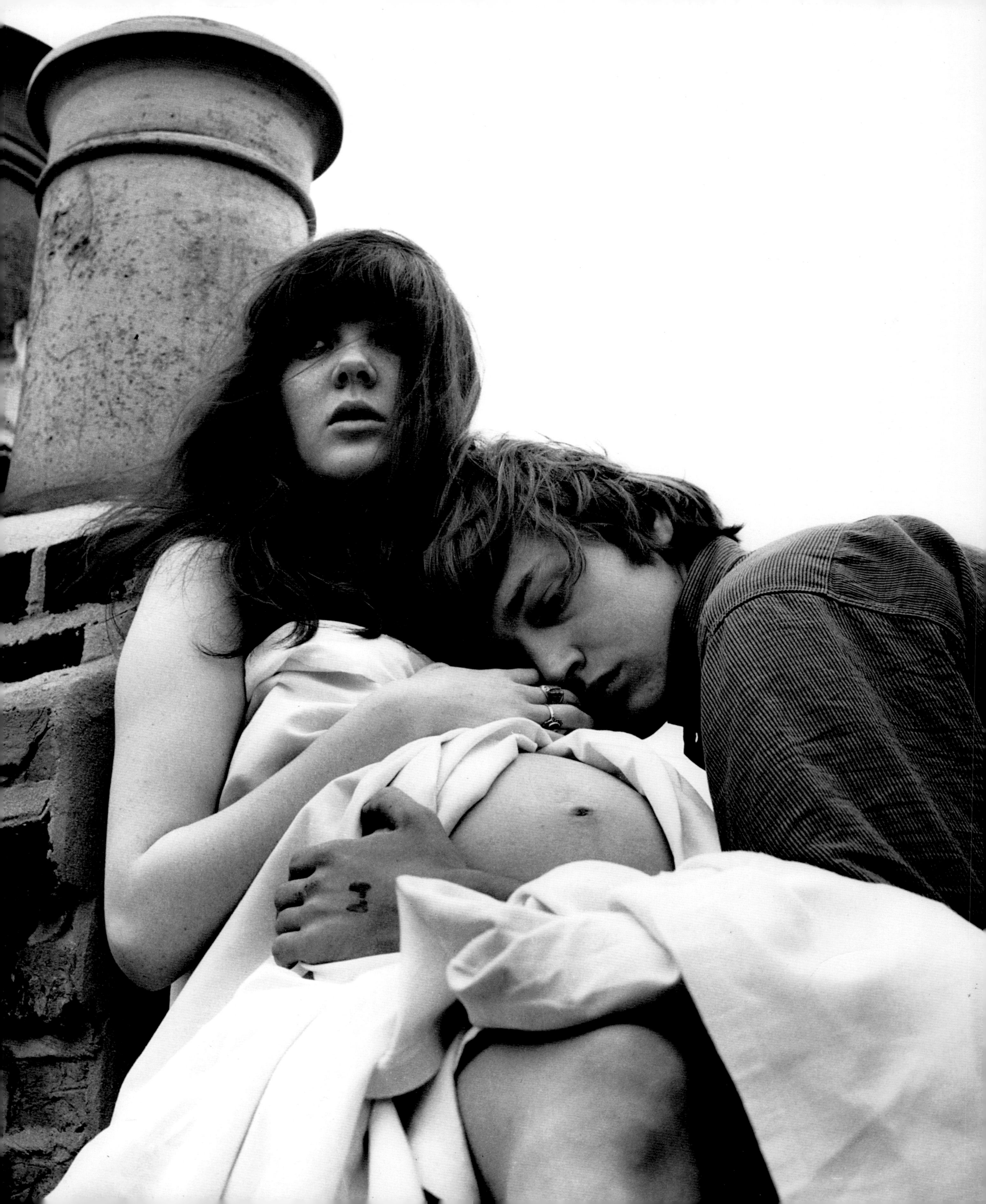

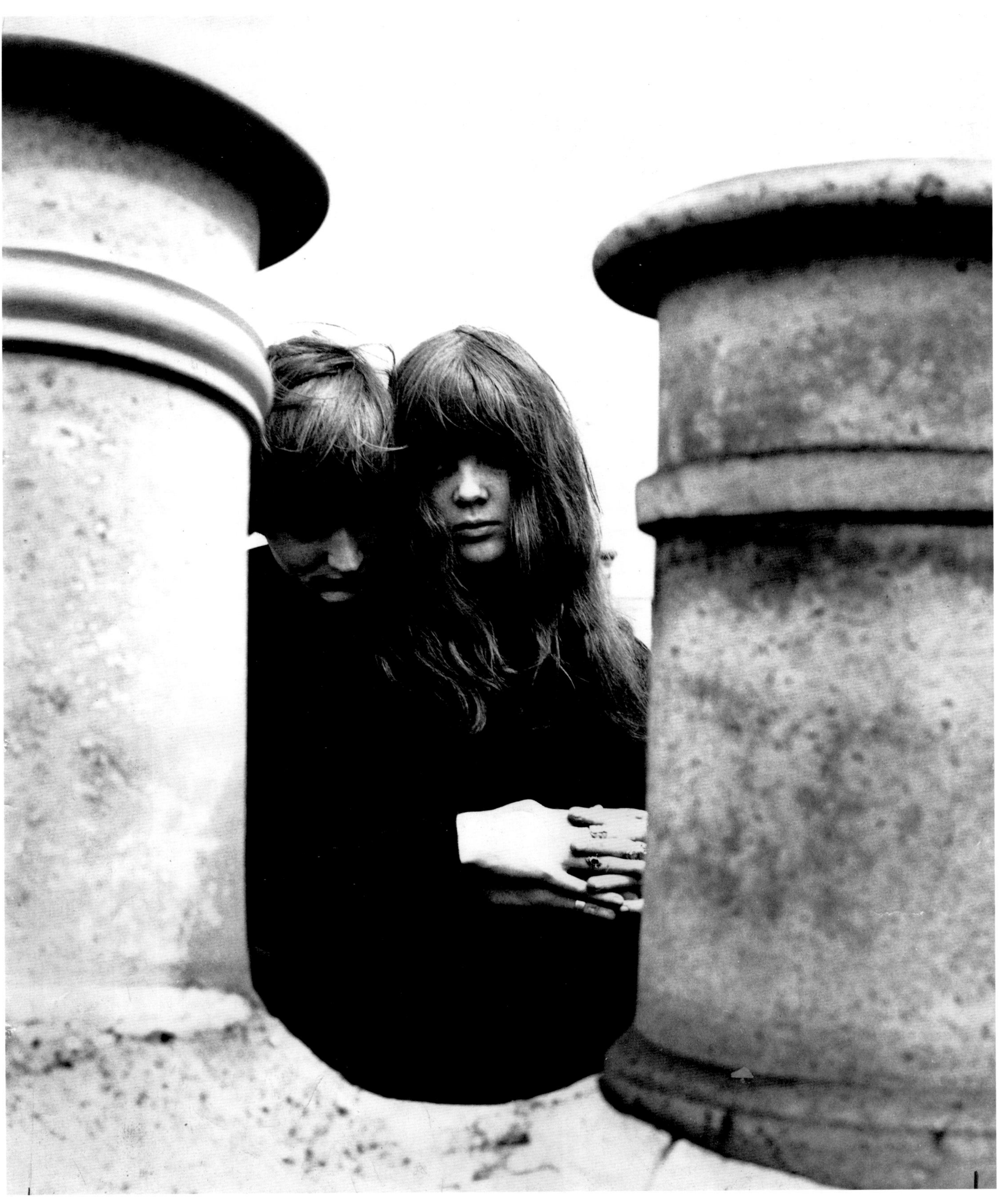

Richard and Jenny, photographer's rooftop, 1967

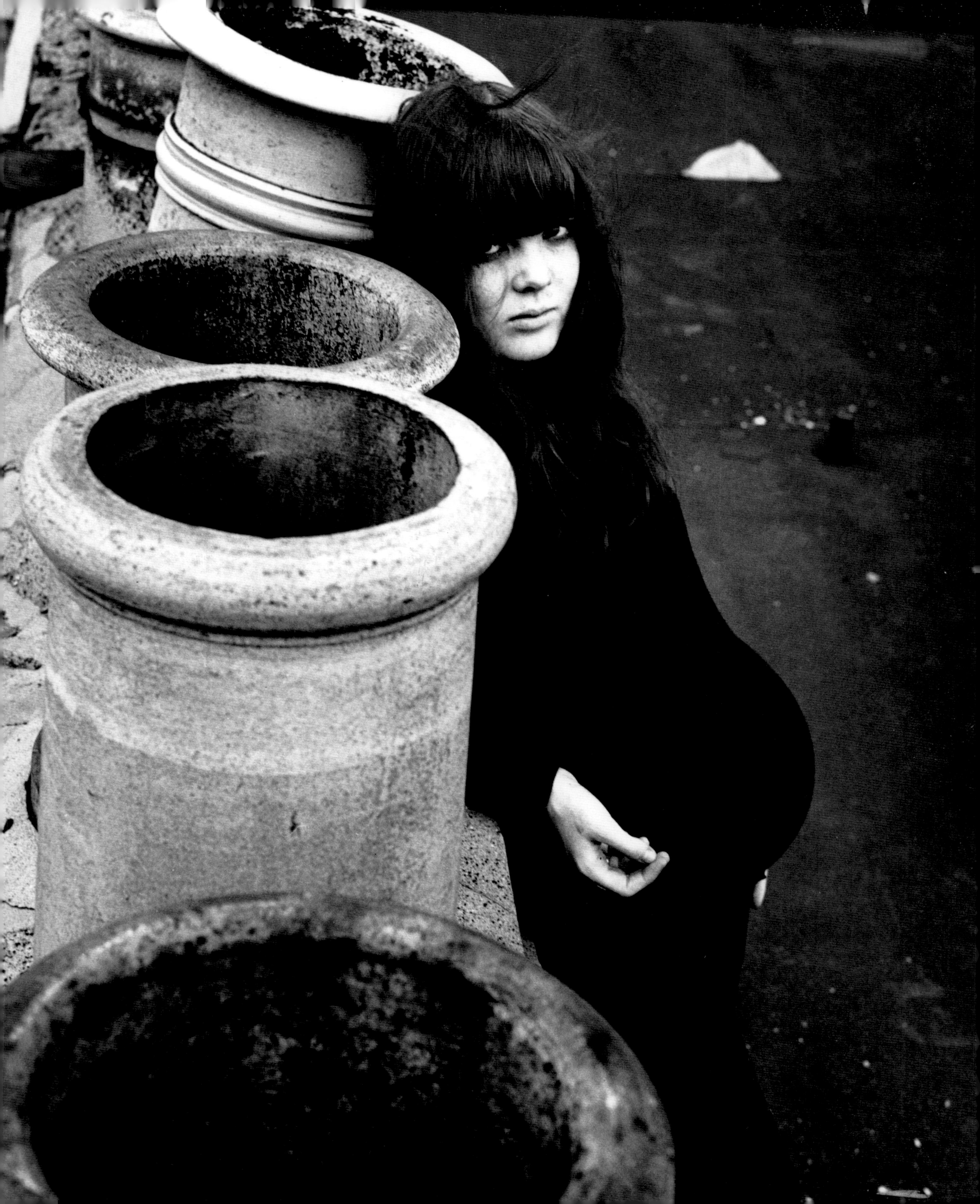

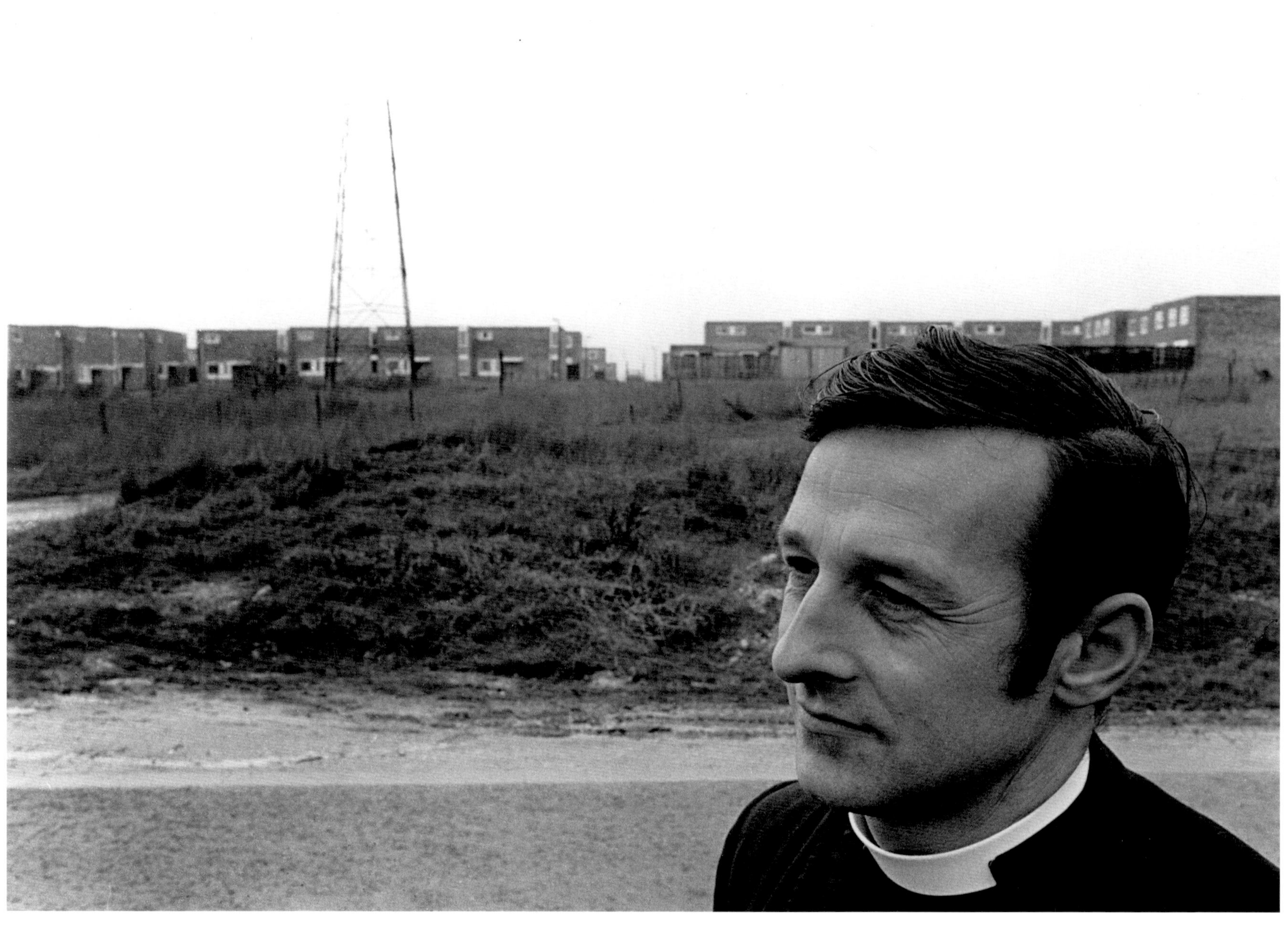

The Stones in the Park
(I Can't Get No . . . Yeah, Yeah, Yeah)

In July 1968, my agent Phillip Westgarth arranged a private photo shoot at the Rolling Stones' hideout near Marble Arch, still with their original bandleader Brian Jones. I was lucky that day that the Stones were not dressed up to impress. Their rooftop and private quarters were ideal for the shoot. They were forthcoming, relaxed, and open-minded to oblige to any poses that I suggested.

My images were published in various German magazines and helped to promote the group. In decades to come, their fame snowballed.

It was on July 5, 1969, when at least half a million revelers gathered in Hyde Park to listen to their free outdoor concert Stones in the Park. That once in a lifetime event meant the world to me.

Circumstances were inevitably emotional due to the sudden loss of Brian Jones who died two days prior to the concert. Apparently he drowned in a pool, but according to rumors, Brian was the victim of an unsolved crime.

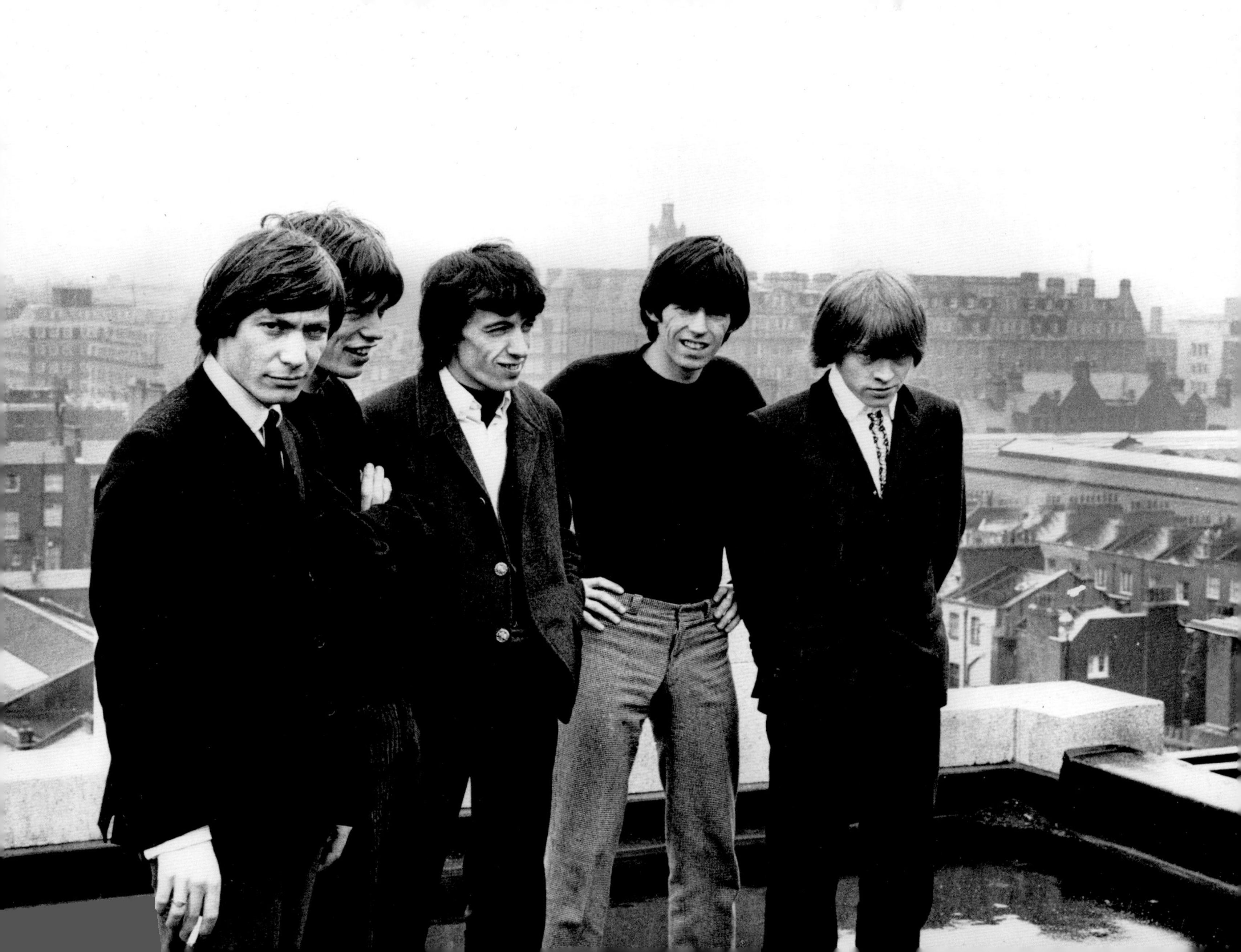

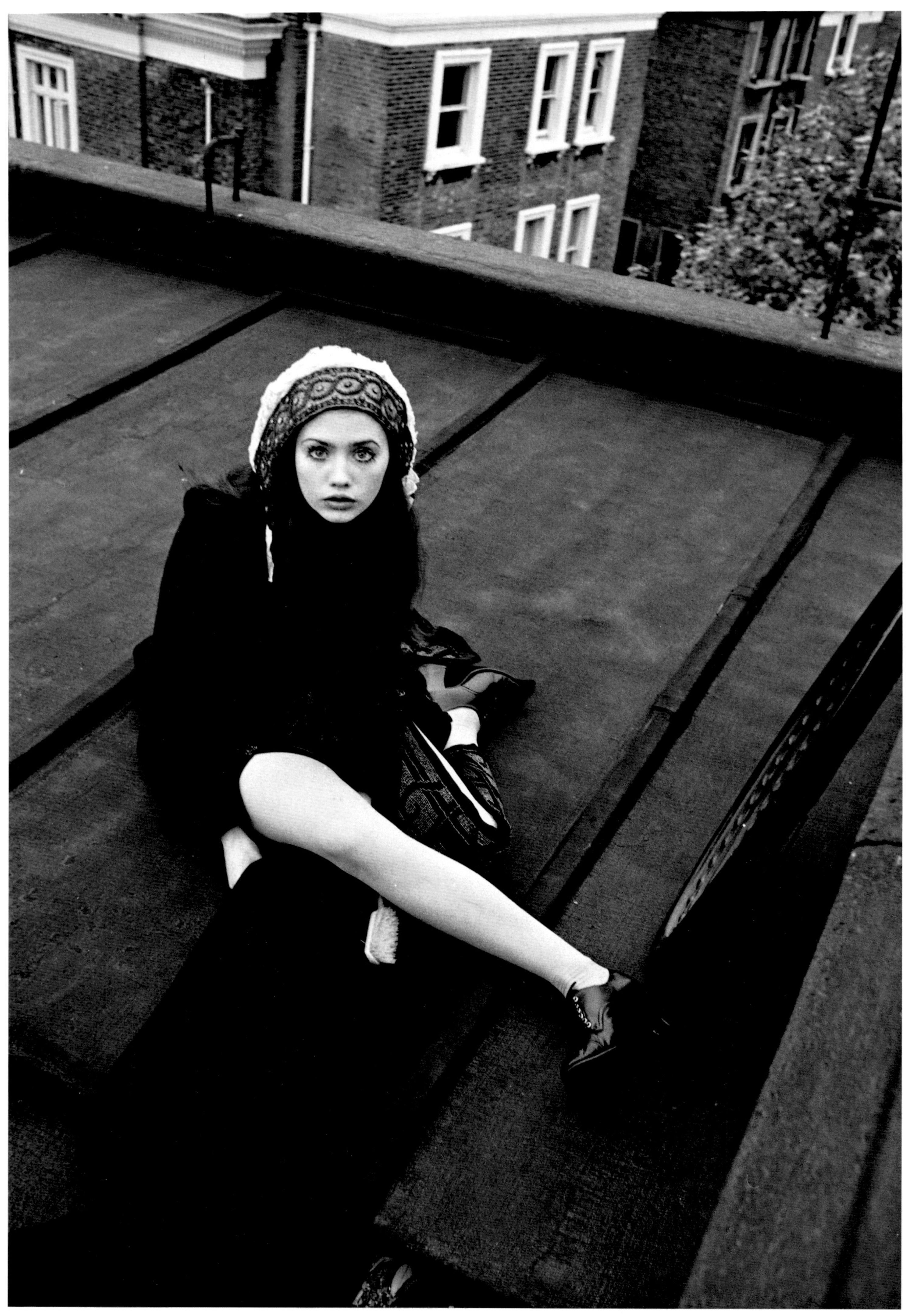

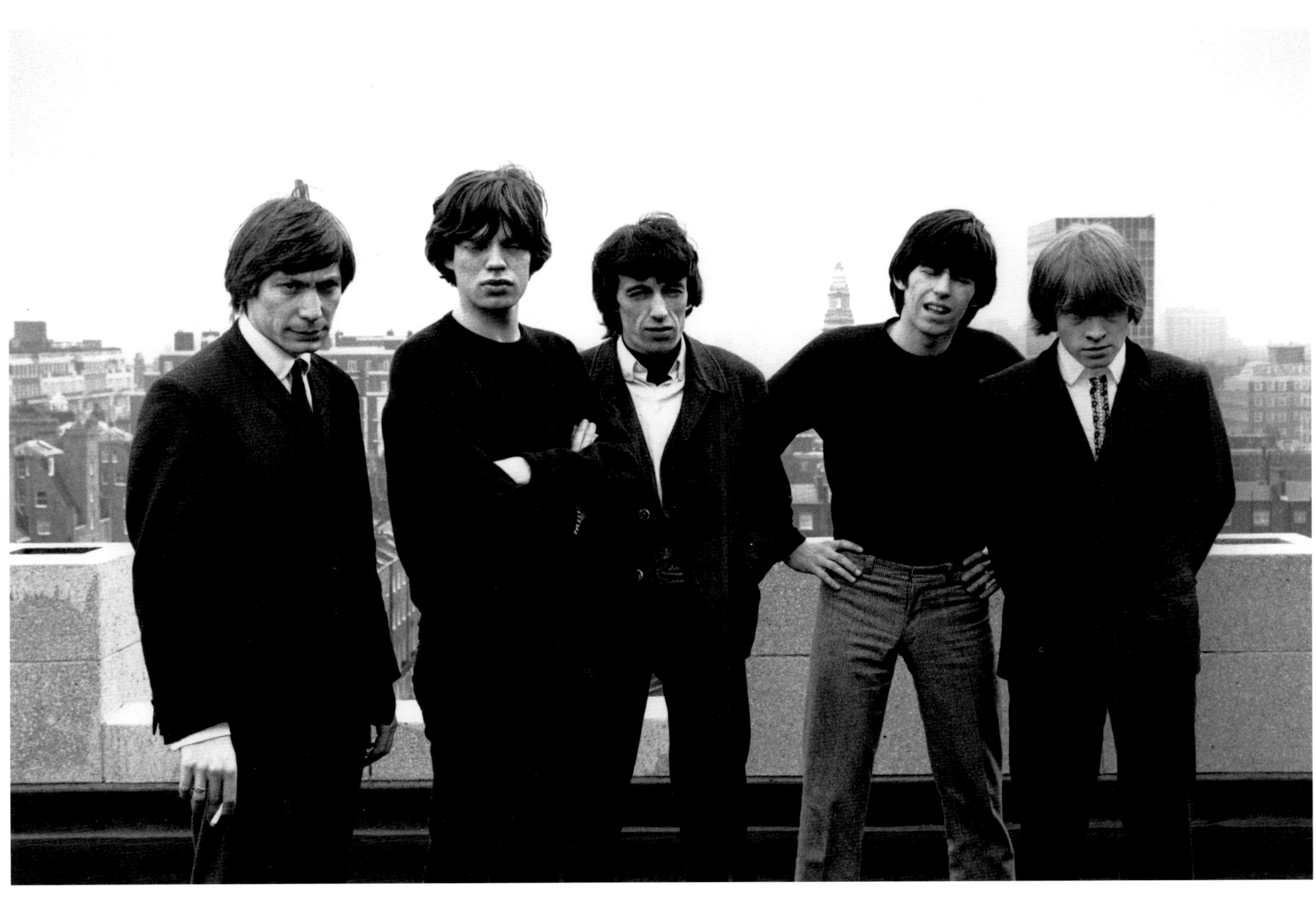

Bella, photographer's rooftop

Cooling off – The Rolling Stones, 1969

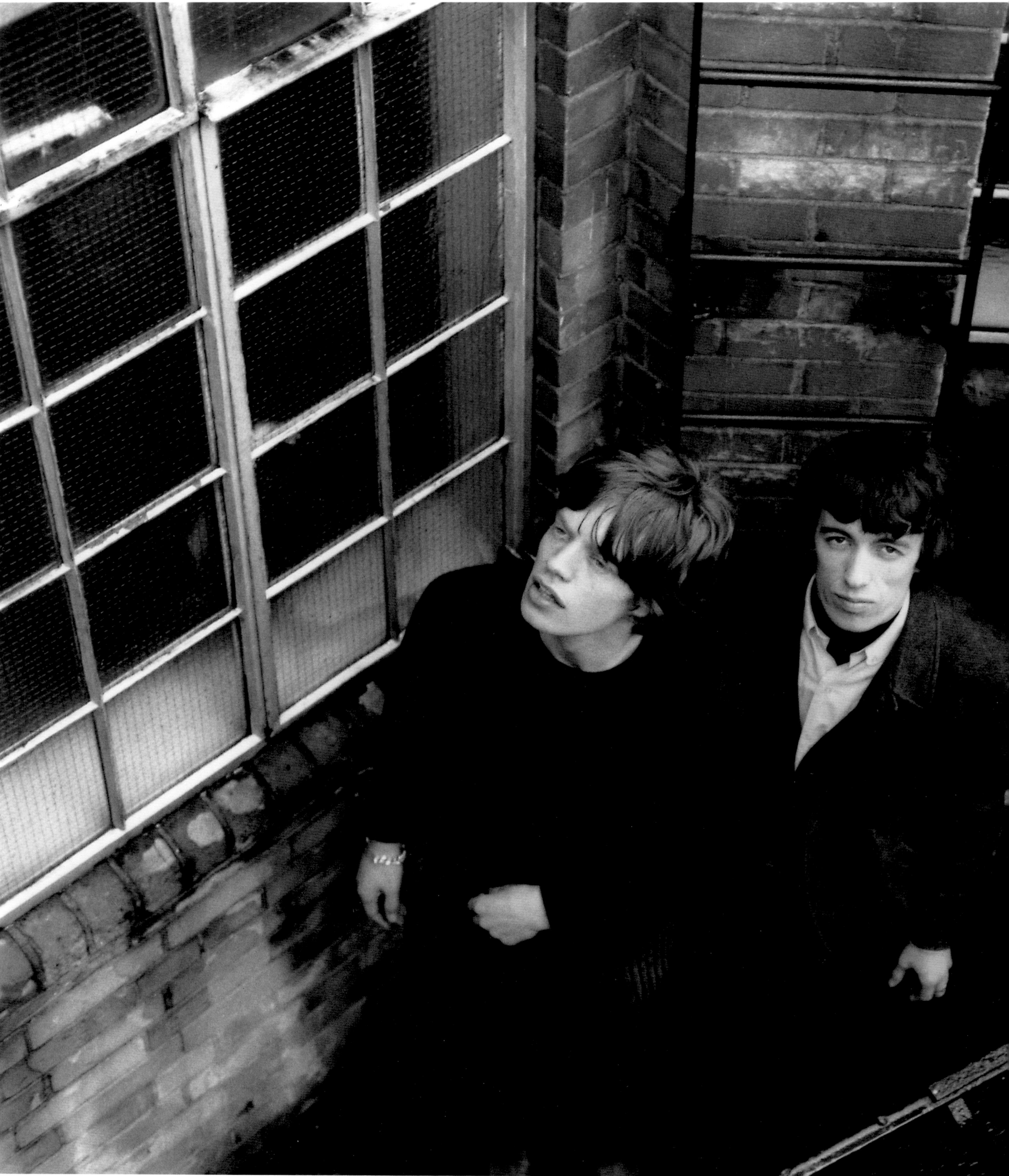

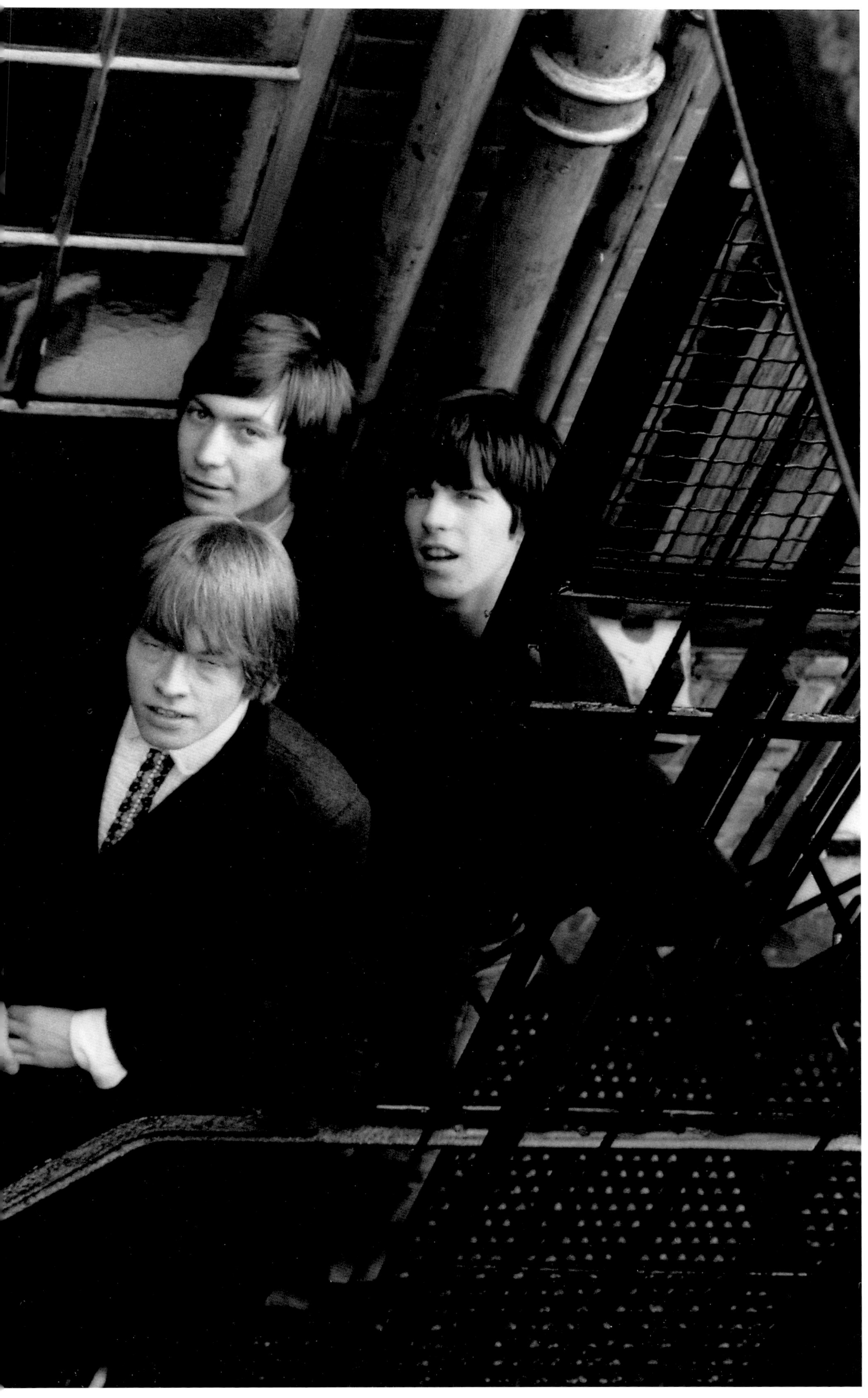

Fire escape –
Stones and former lead singer Brian Jones

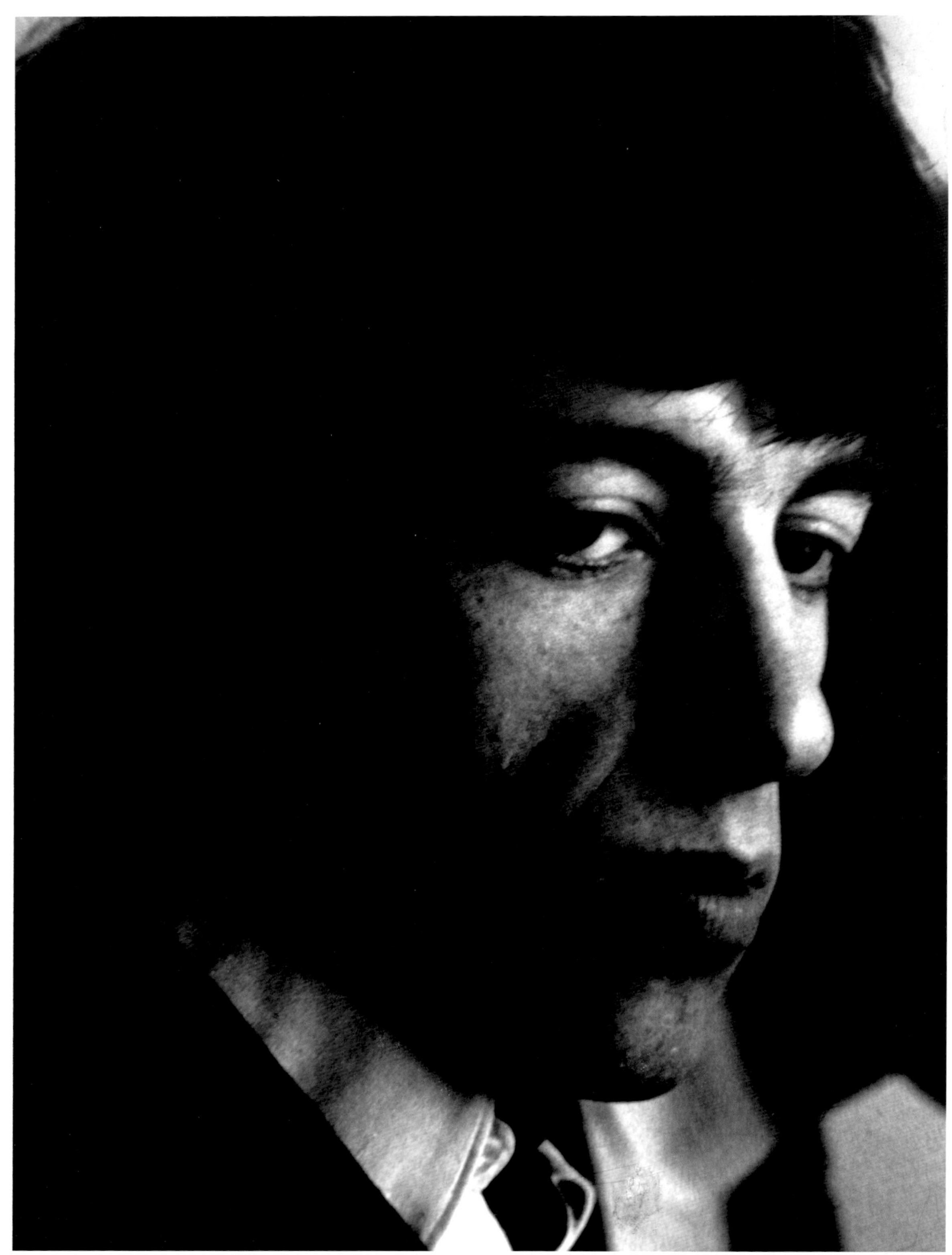

Bill Wyman, The Rolling Stones, 1969

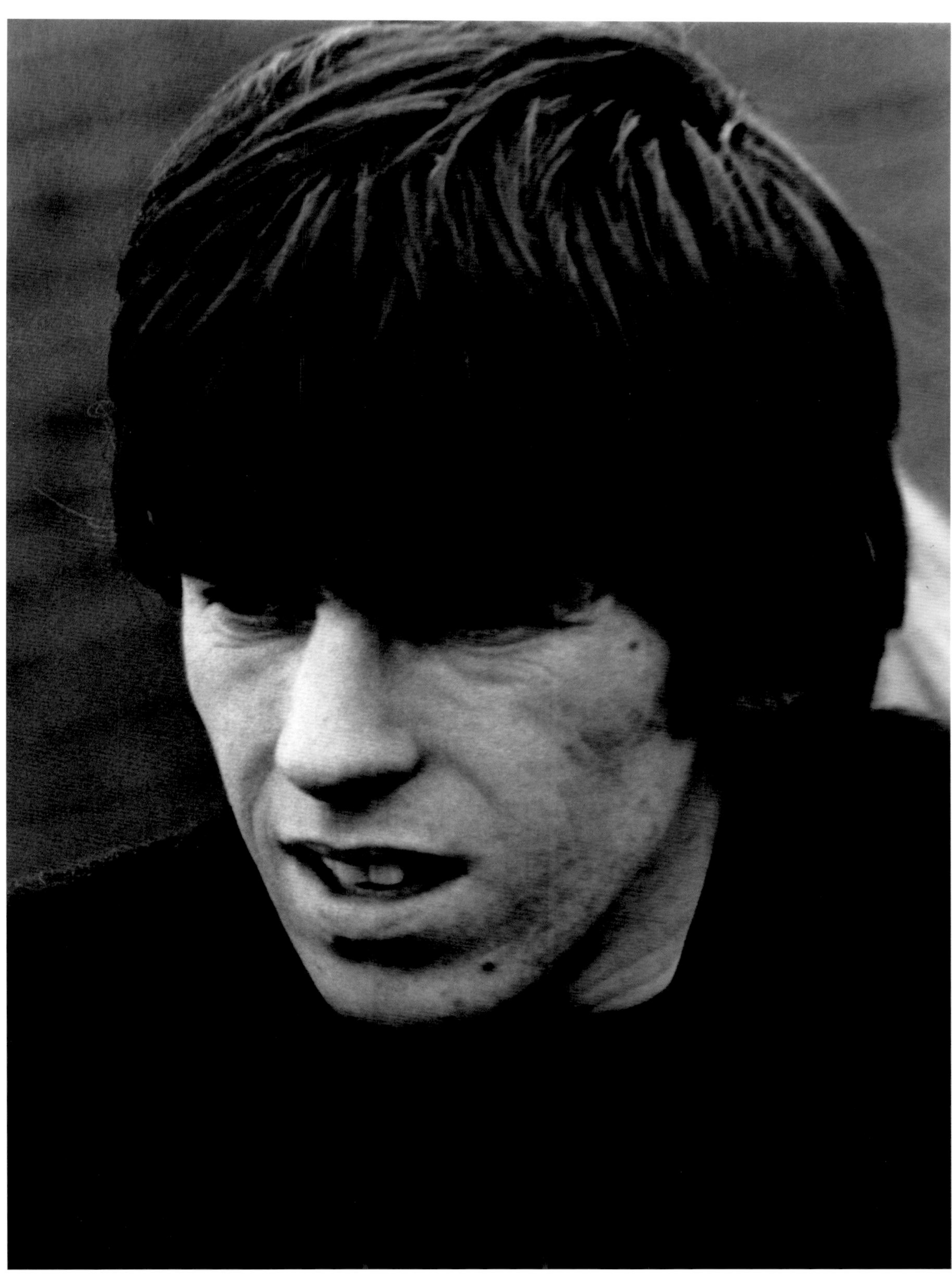

I am a Legend – Keith Richards, The Rolling Stones

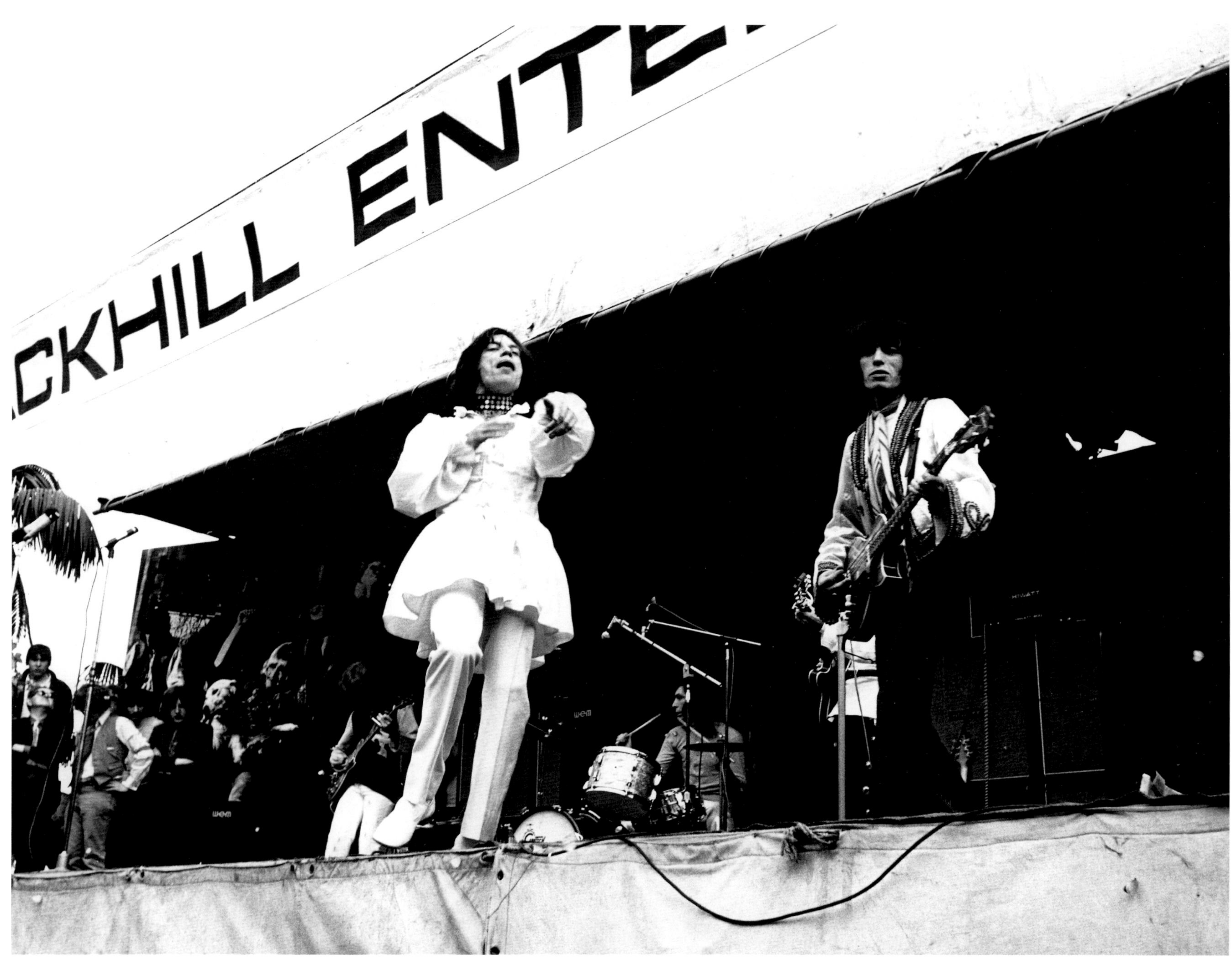

I can’t get no . . . “The Stones in the Park,” 1969

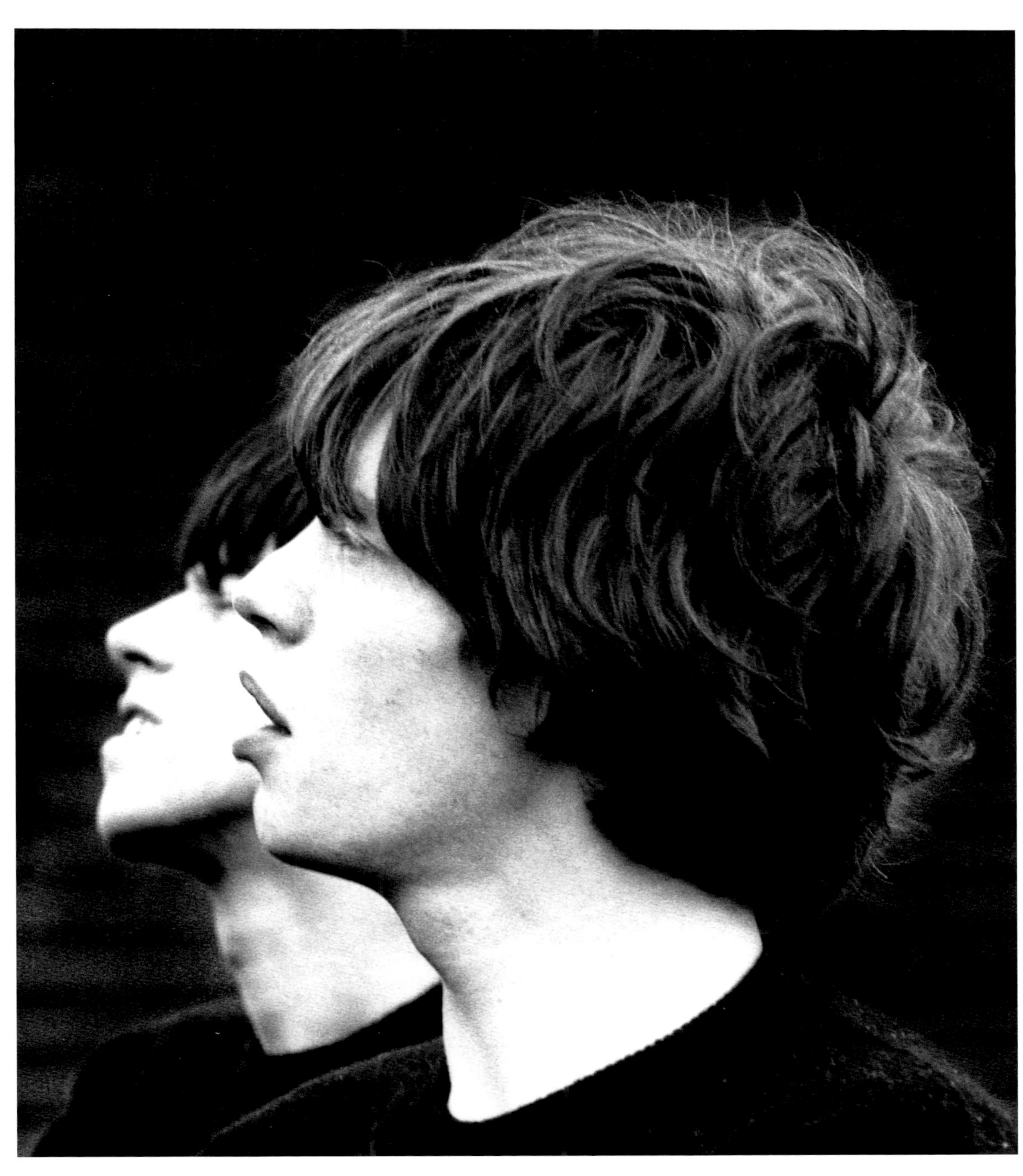

Mick and Keith

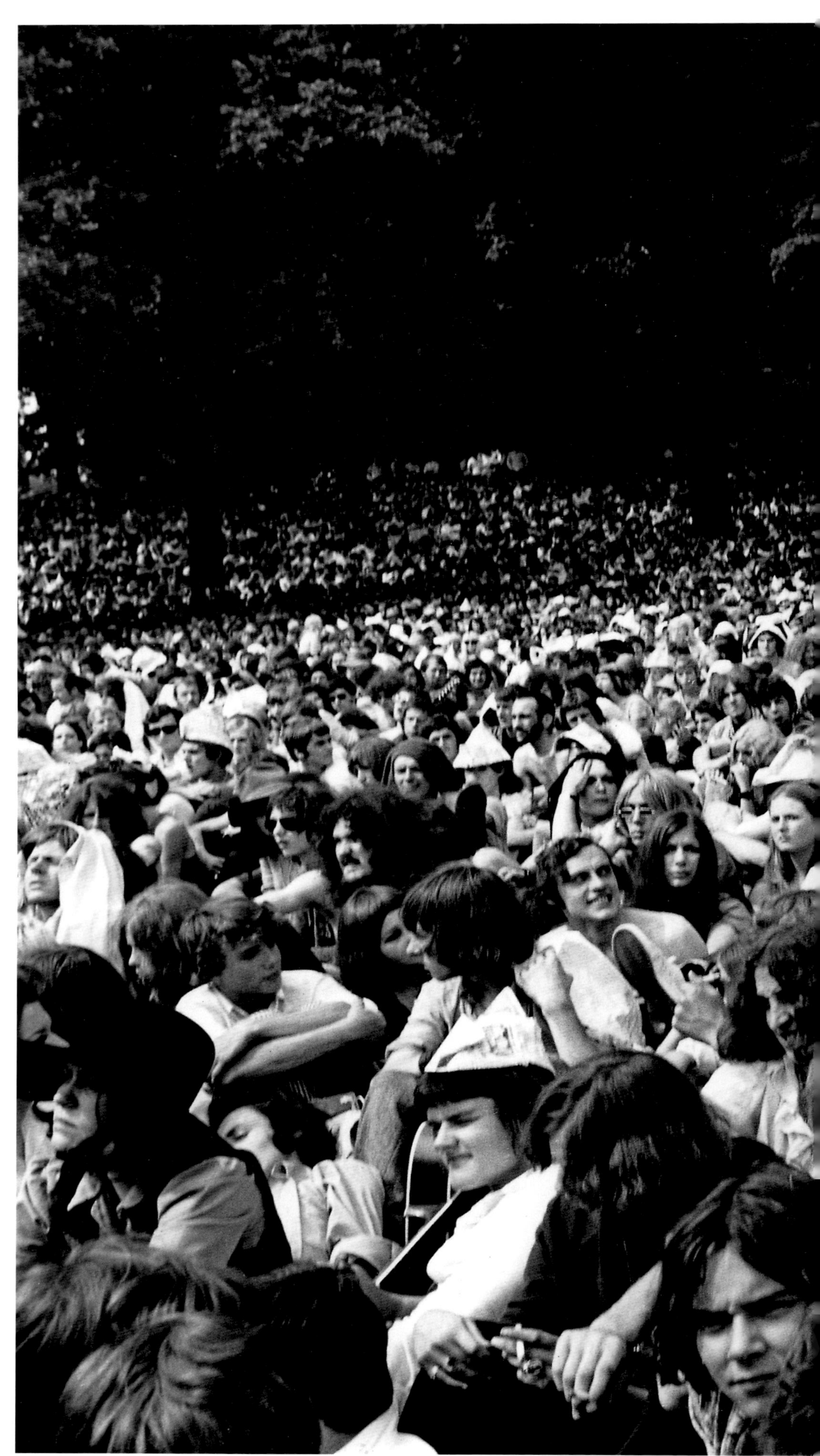

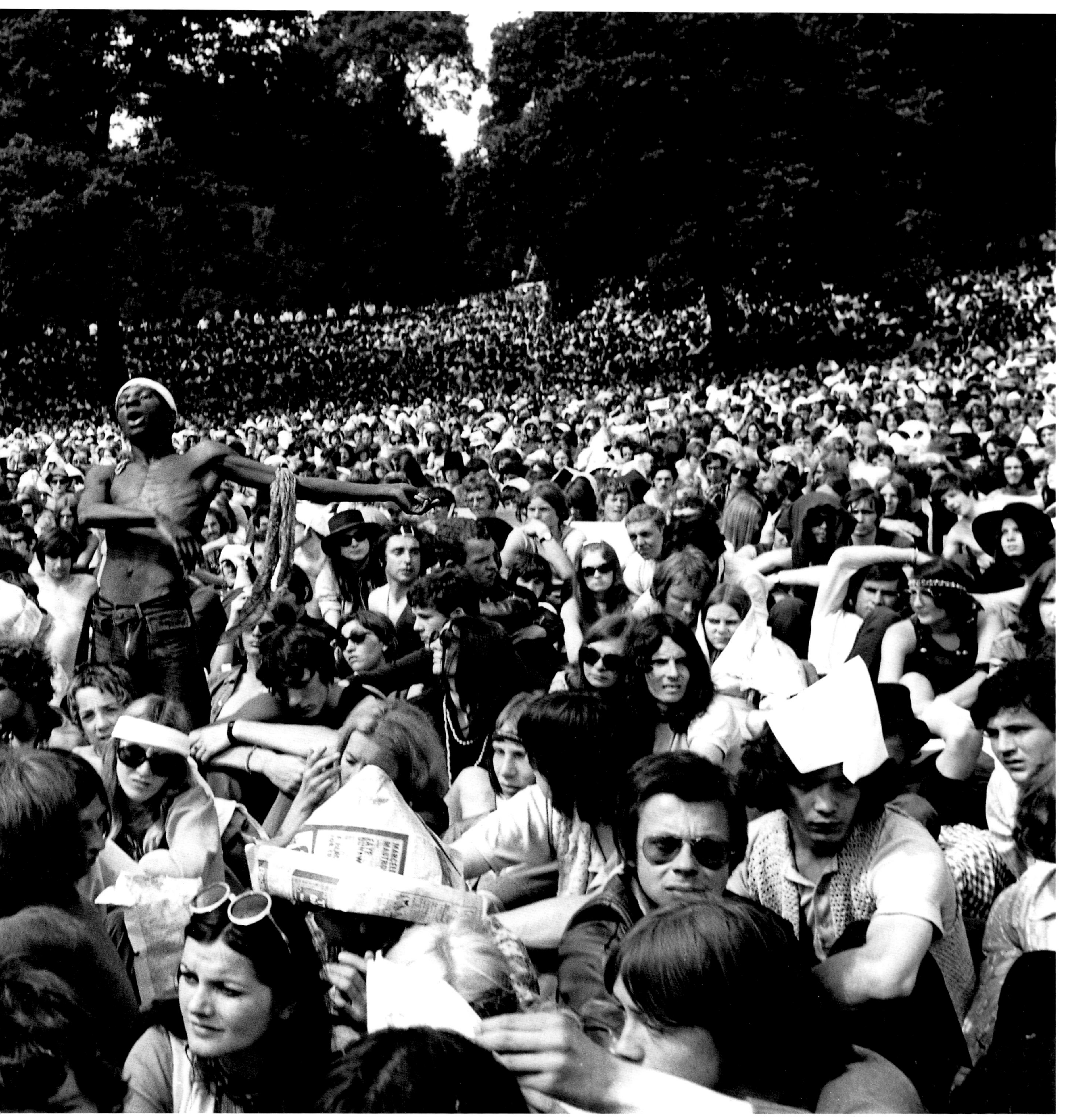

And the crowd went crazy – Stones, Hyde Park

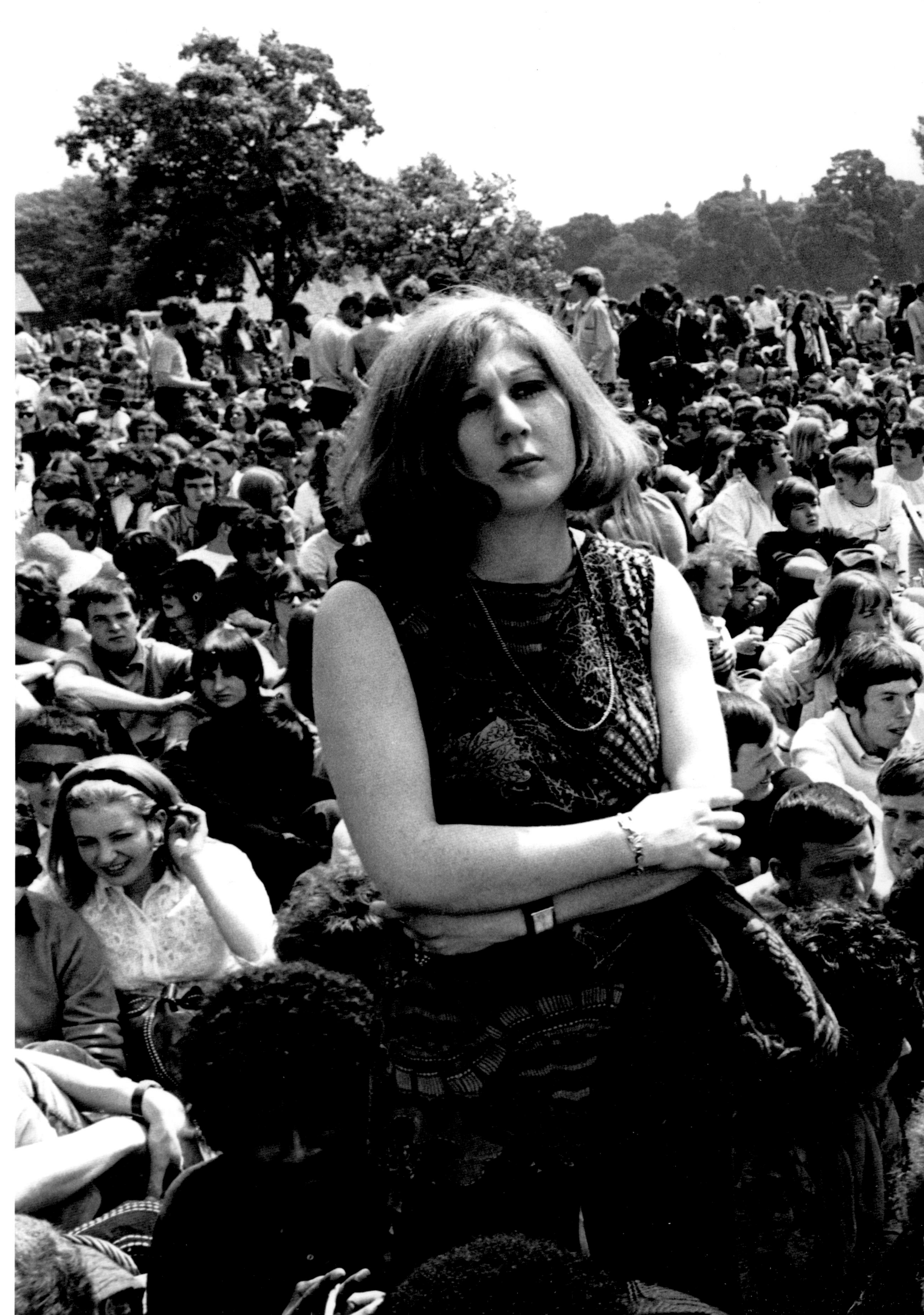

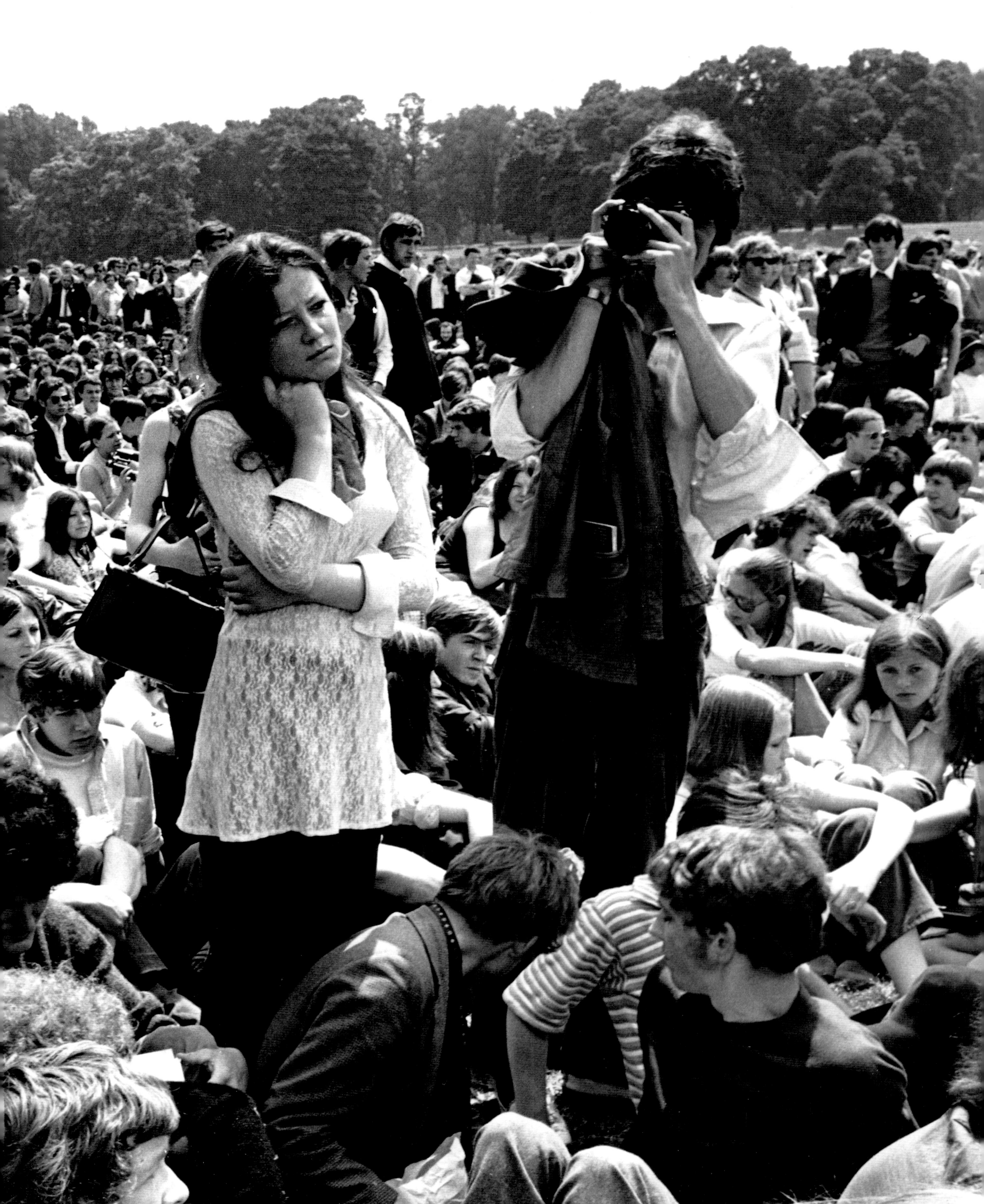

Alice In Wonderland
(Girl at Rolling Stones Concert)

On that never to be repeated day in Hyde Park in July 1969 during that Rolling Stones concert, I captured my most liked photograph ever. It was of a young woman who stood out from the rest of the revelers. She was imaginatively dressed, wearing a huge straw hat, beads, and striking eye makeup.

She immediately acknowledged my presence from the moment I directed my camera towards her, and she gave me that look with an inner smile.

Later, during the concert, I had searched the crowd in the hope of catching another glimpse of her, but it wasn't meant to be. I lost her in an ocean full of faces. I lost the girl in the park.

But I did not lose my memory of her. There was a mysterious flare about her, and it's like I was able to capture and contain part of her spirit in this photograph, like in Roald Dahl's story of *The Big Friendly Giant* where he would capture a dream and contain its essence in a jar.

In the decades to come, the photograph attracted rising attention, becoming an iconic zeitgeist image of the late Sixties. It is a collector's item, held in galleries, circulating on the Internet and celebrated as a modern day Mona Lisa.

In my heart I set "Alice" a monument. The only photograph I took of her adorns the cover of this book.

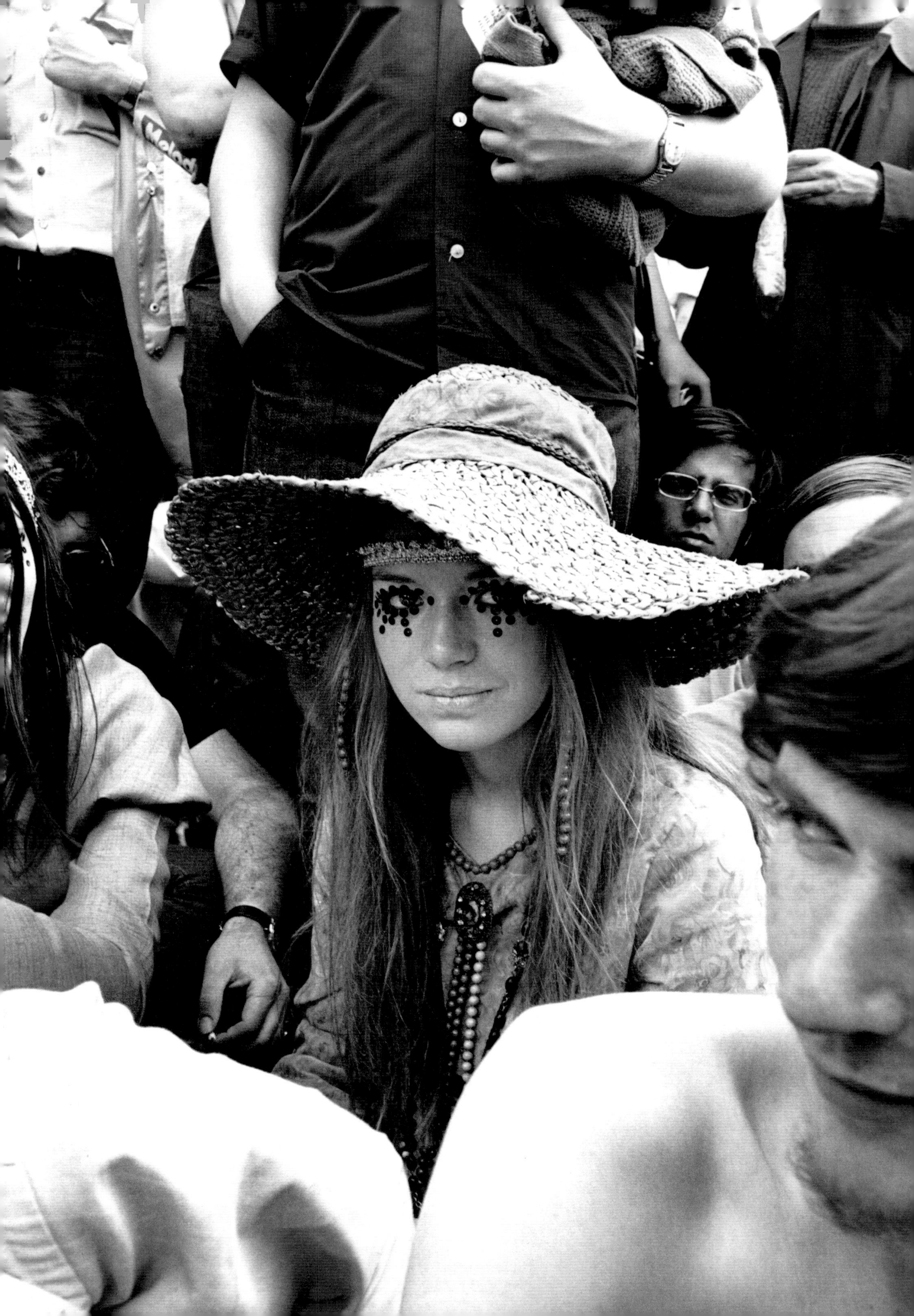

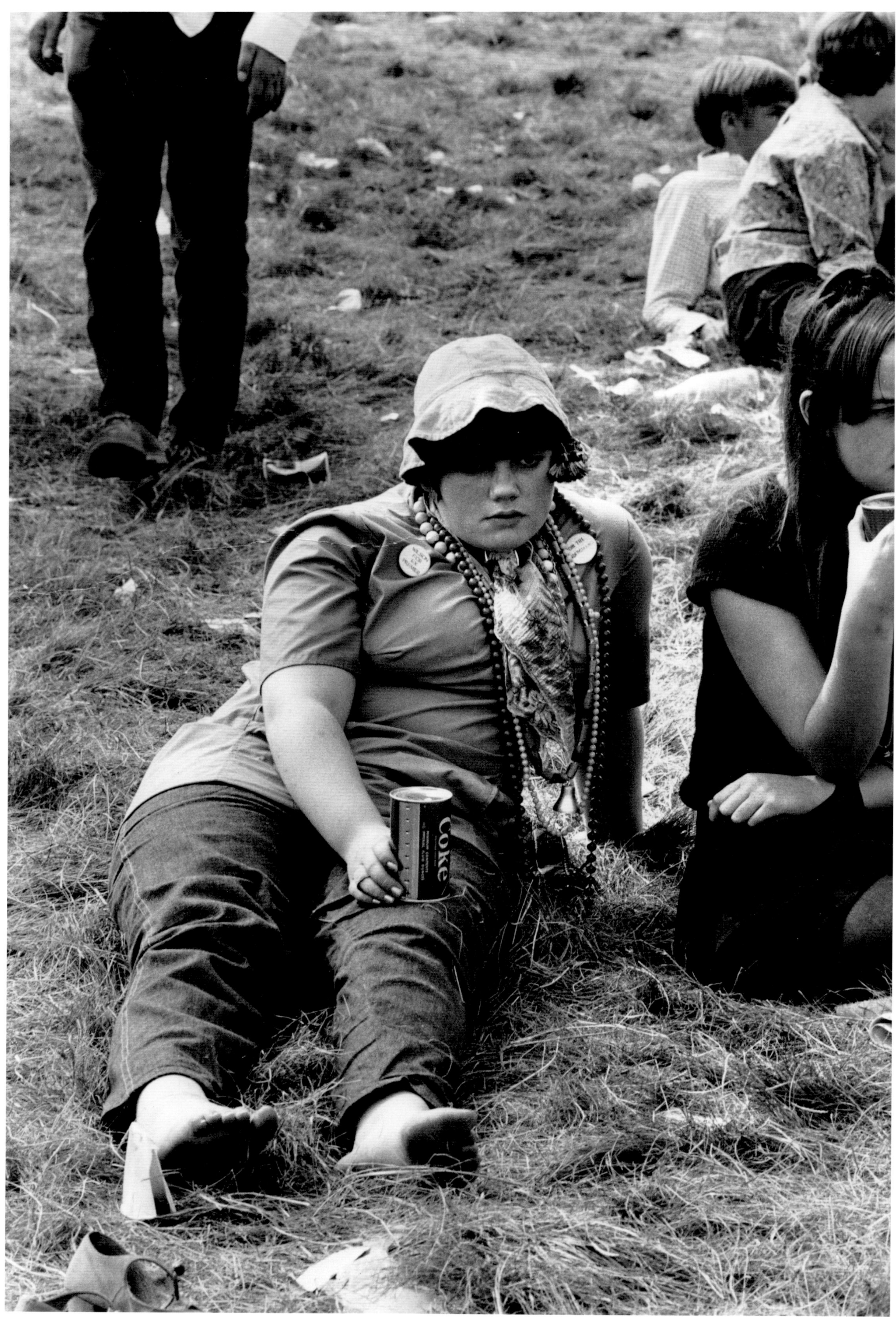
Coke

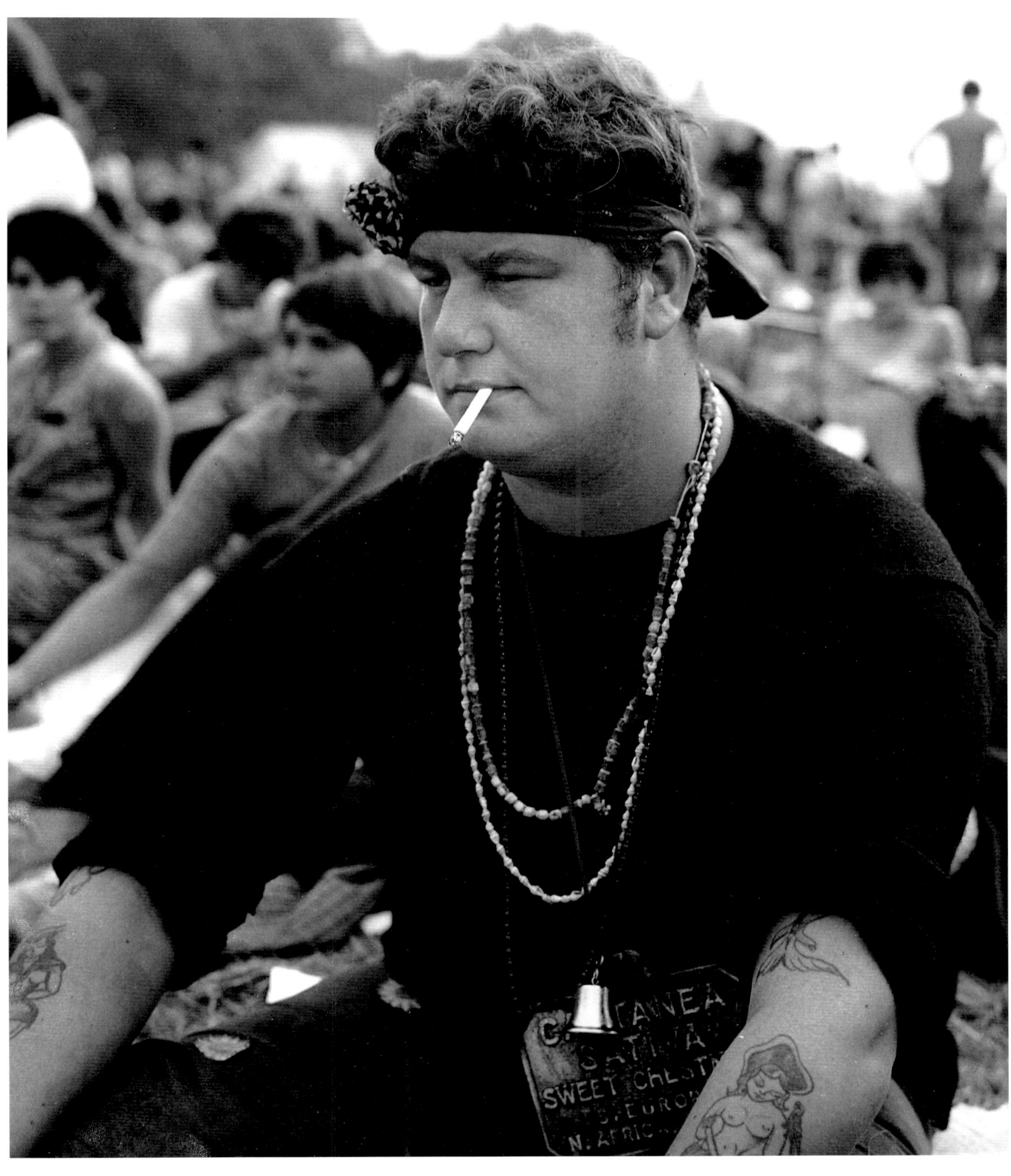

Splendour in the grass, Woburn Music Festival, 1968

Sweet chestnut, Woburn

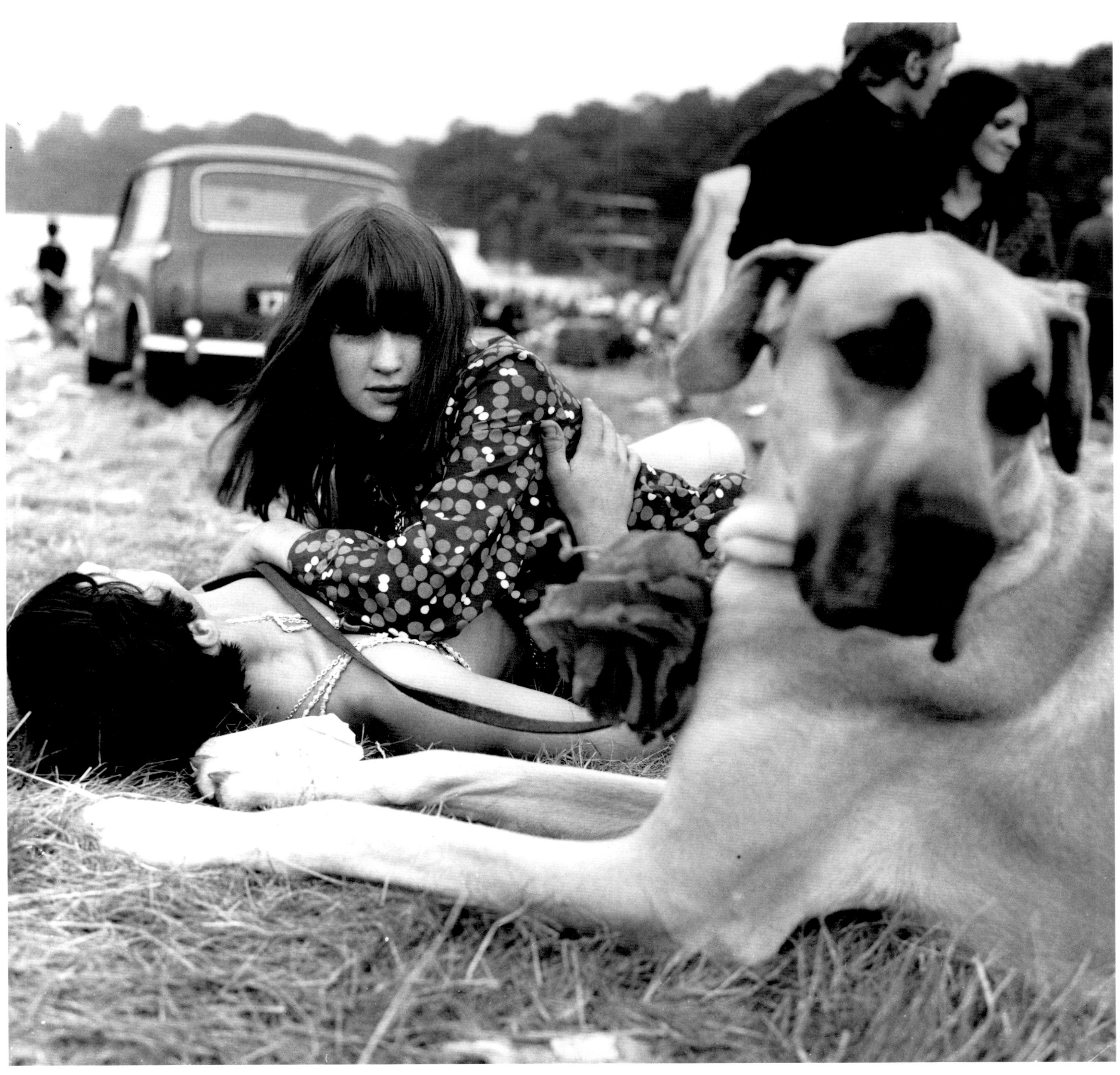

Woburn Music Festival, 1967

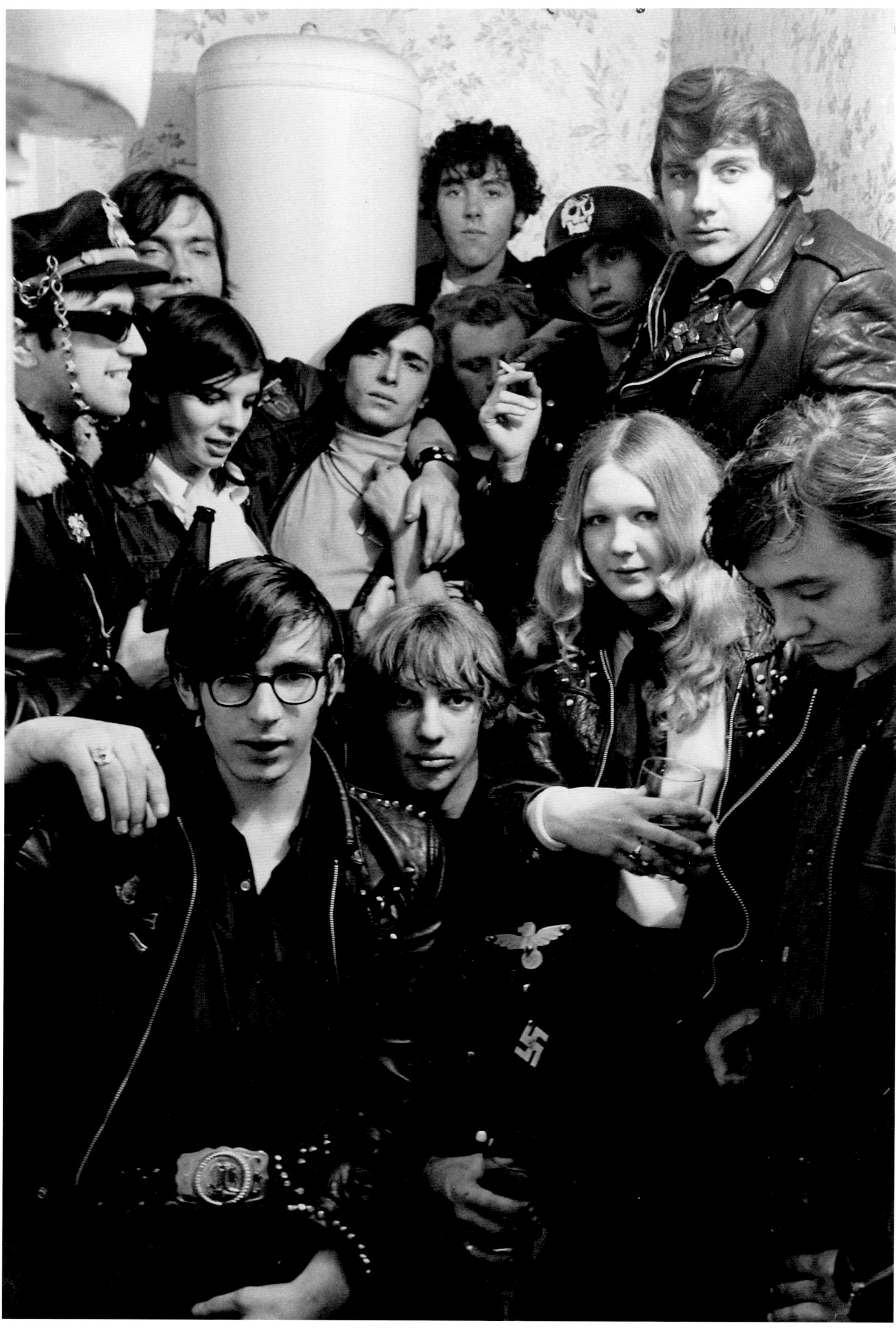

Rocker Wedding, Hells Angels, London East End, 1967

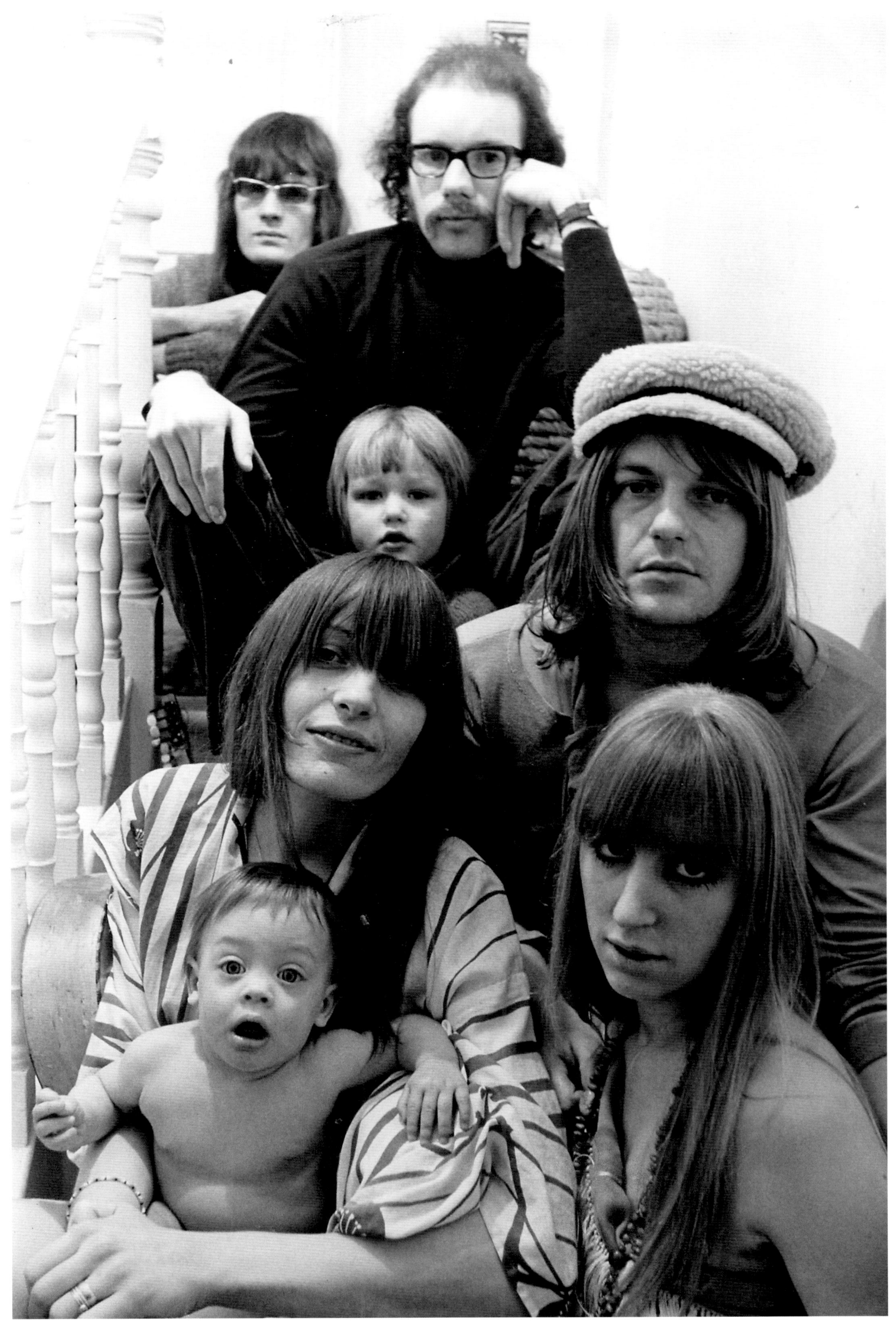

A gentle bunch – The Soft Machine, psychedelic jazz band, 1968

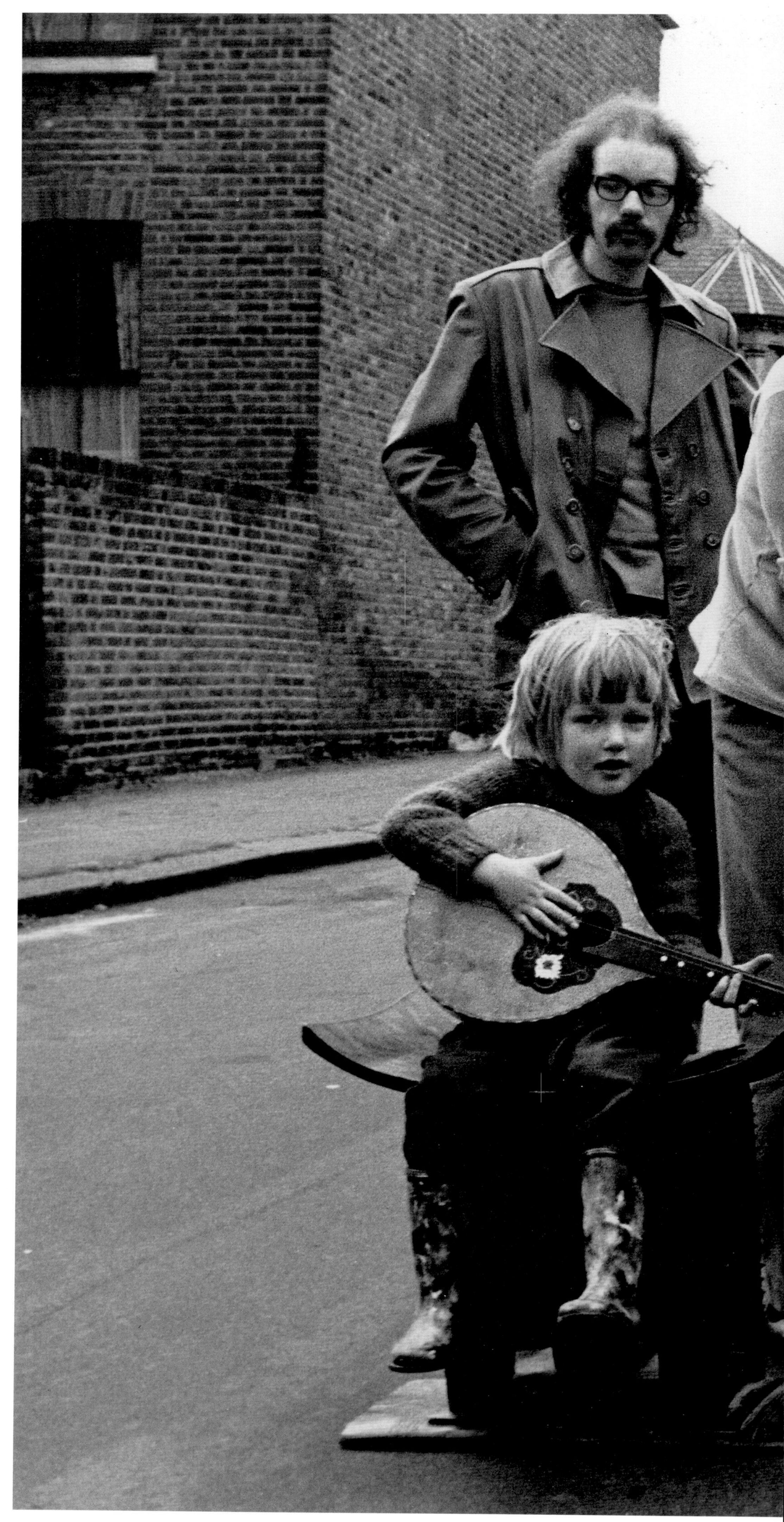

Holding down – The Soft Machine, London, mid-Sixties

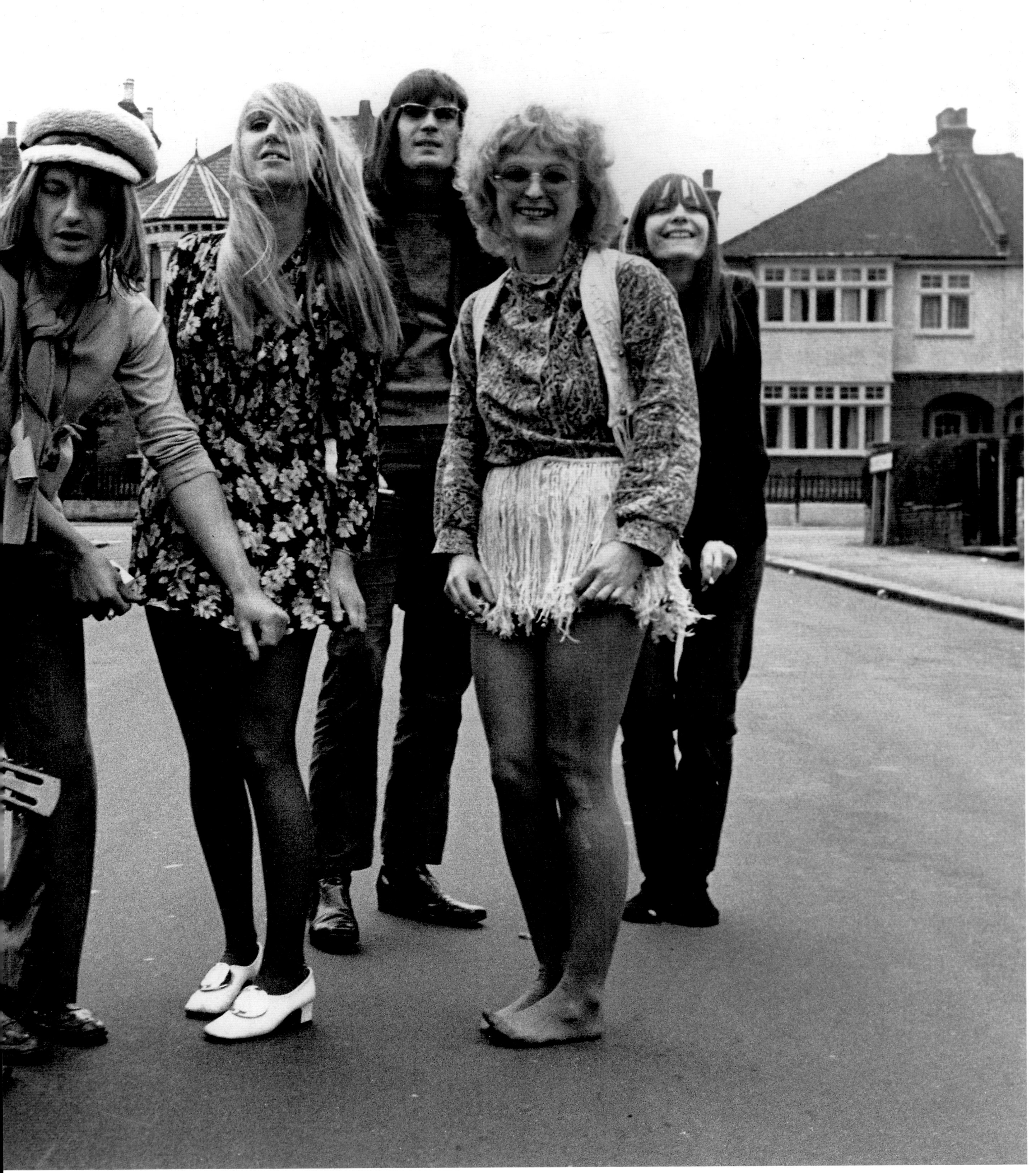

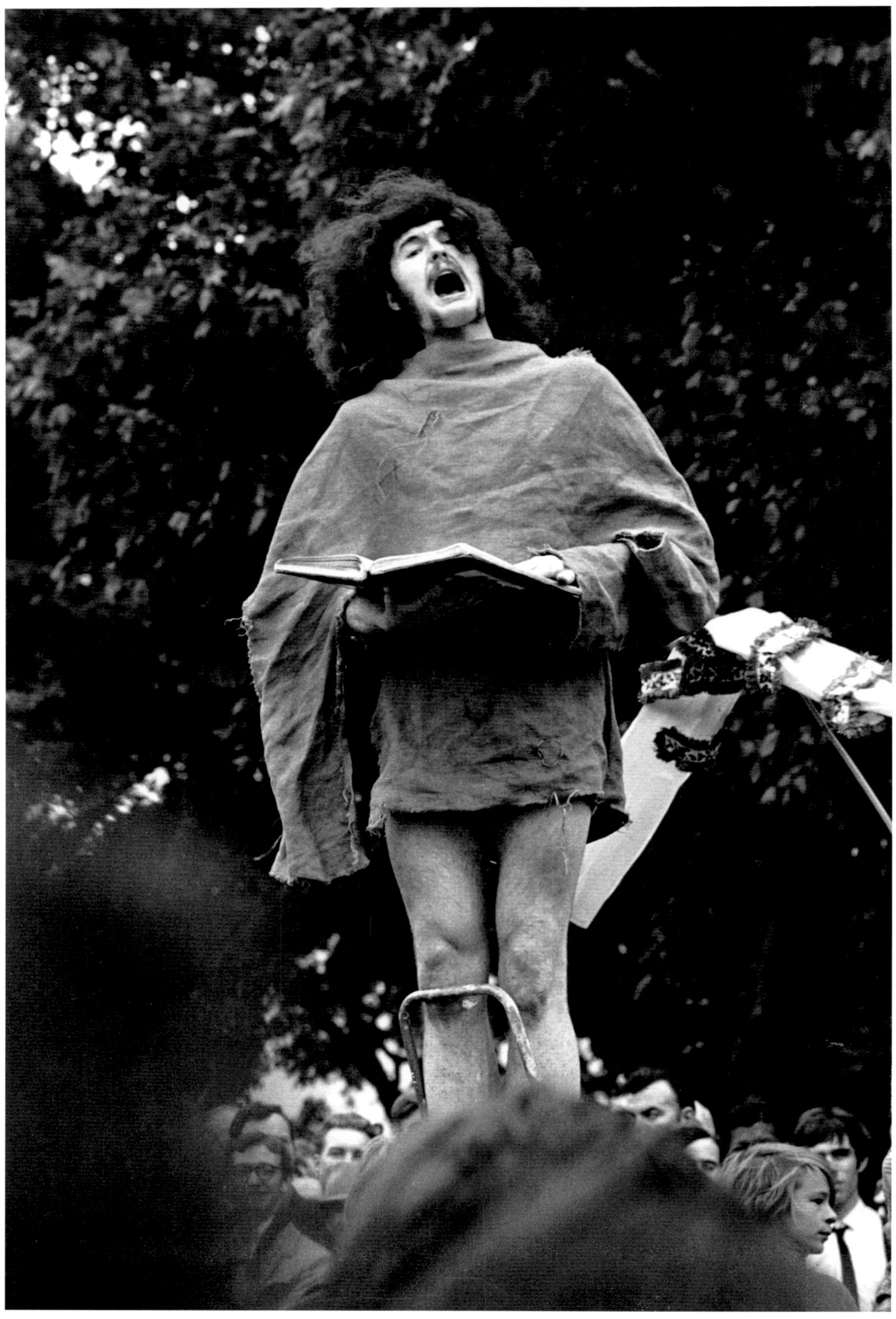

Legalise Hashish Rally, Hyde Park Speakers' Corner, 1965

I'm the Gypsy, the Acid Queen – derelict church yard near St. Paul's Cathedral

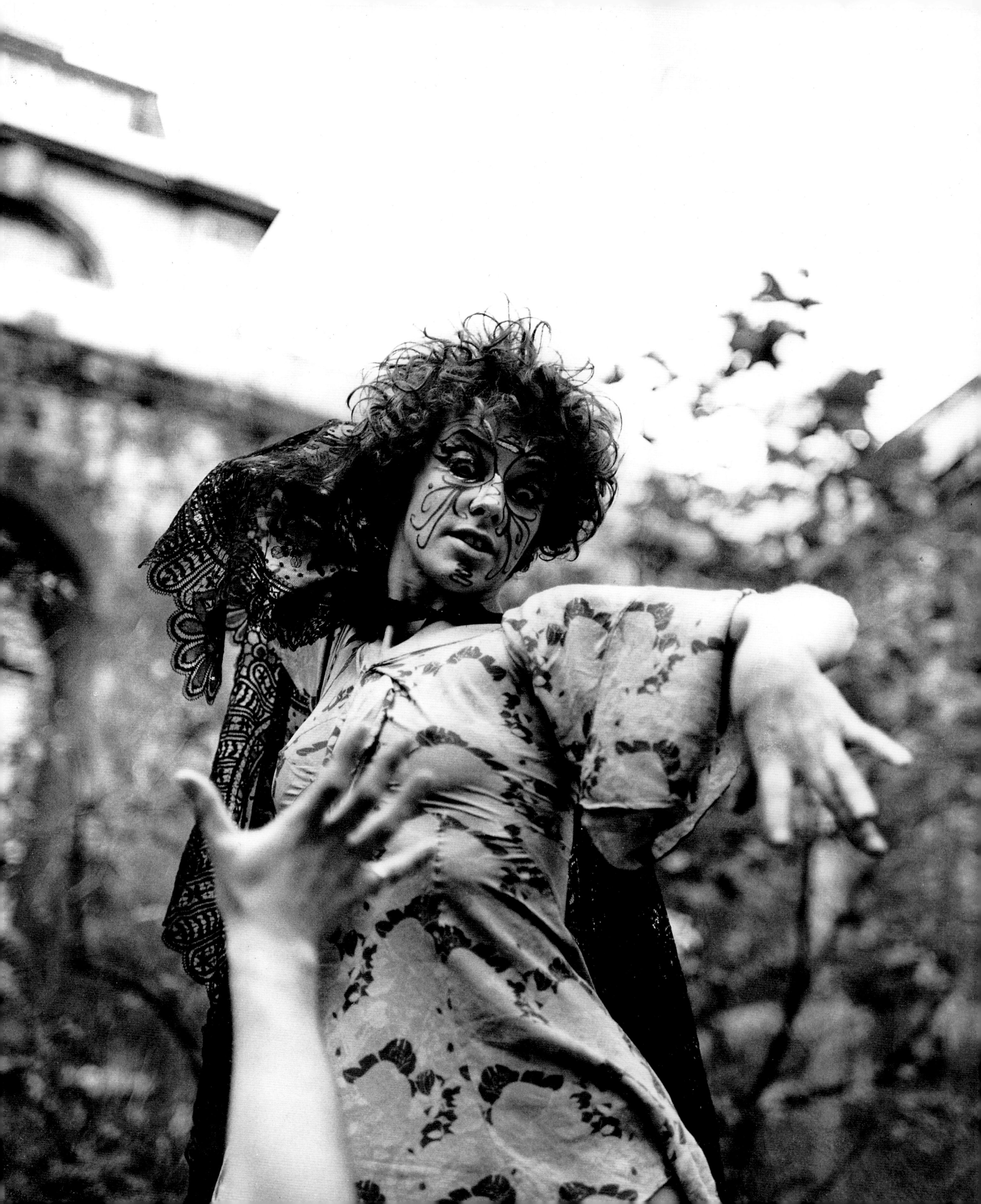

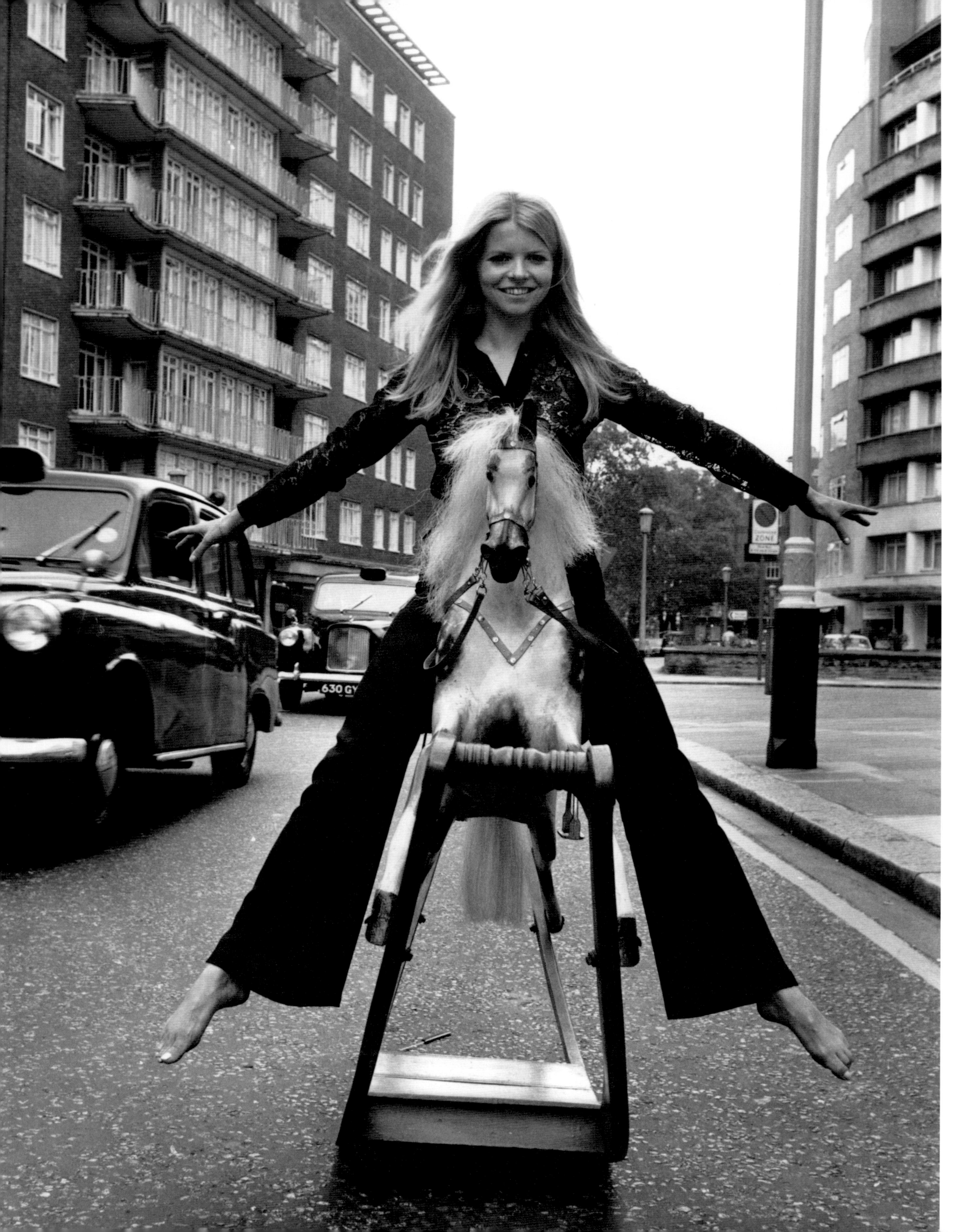
ZONE
630 GY

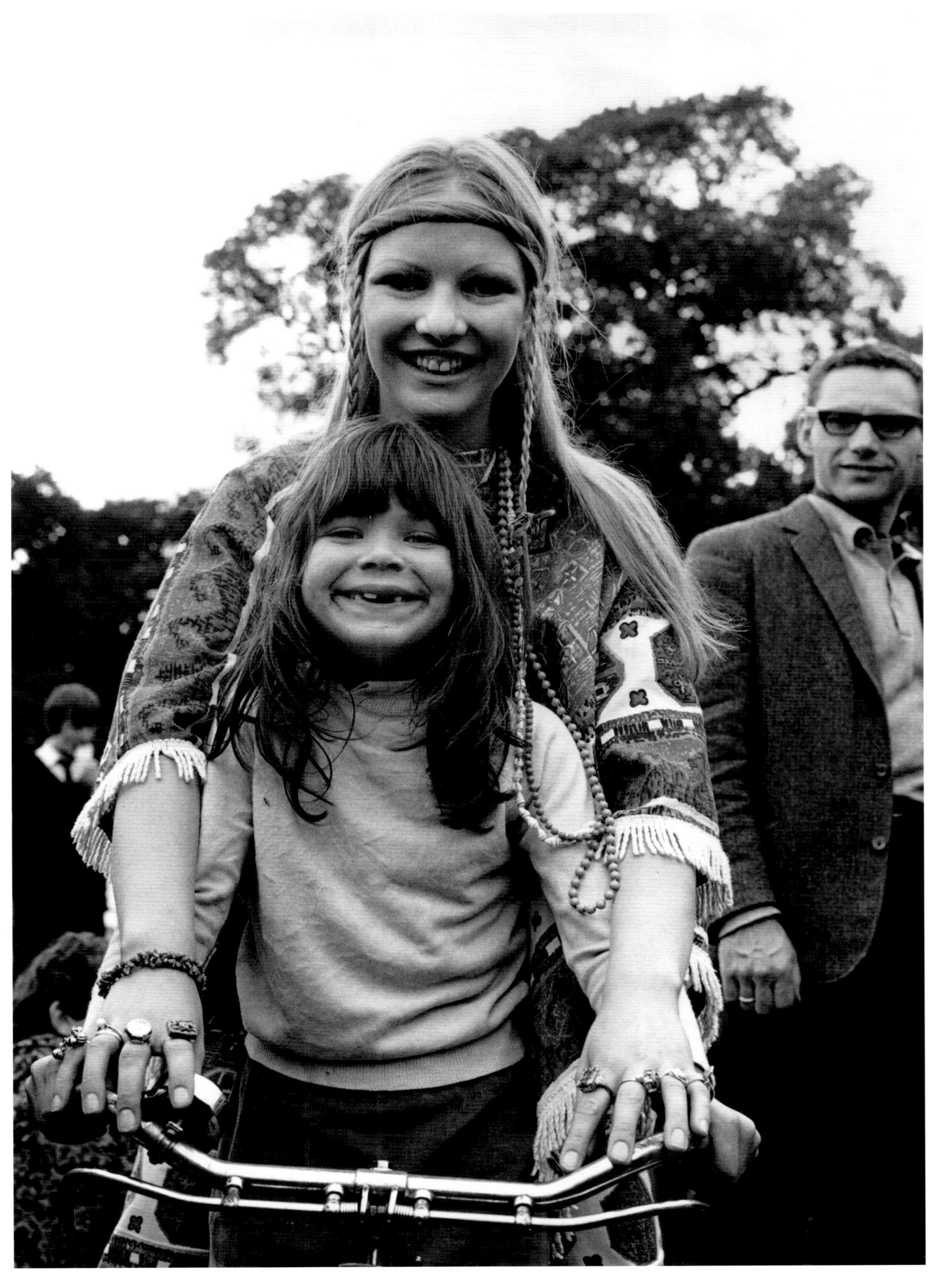

My heart fills with joy – Jane London, actress, Belgravia

In Tandem, Hyde Park

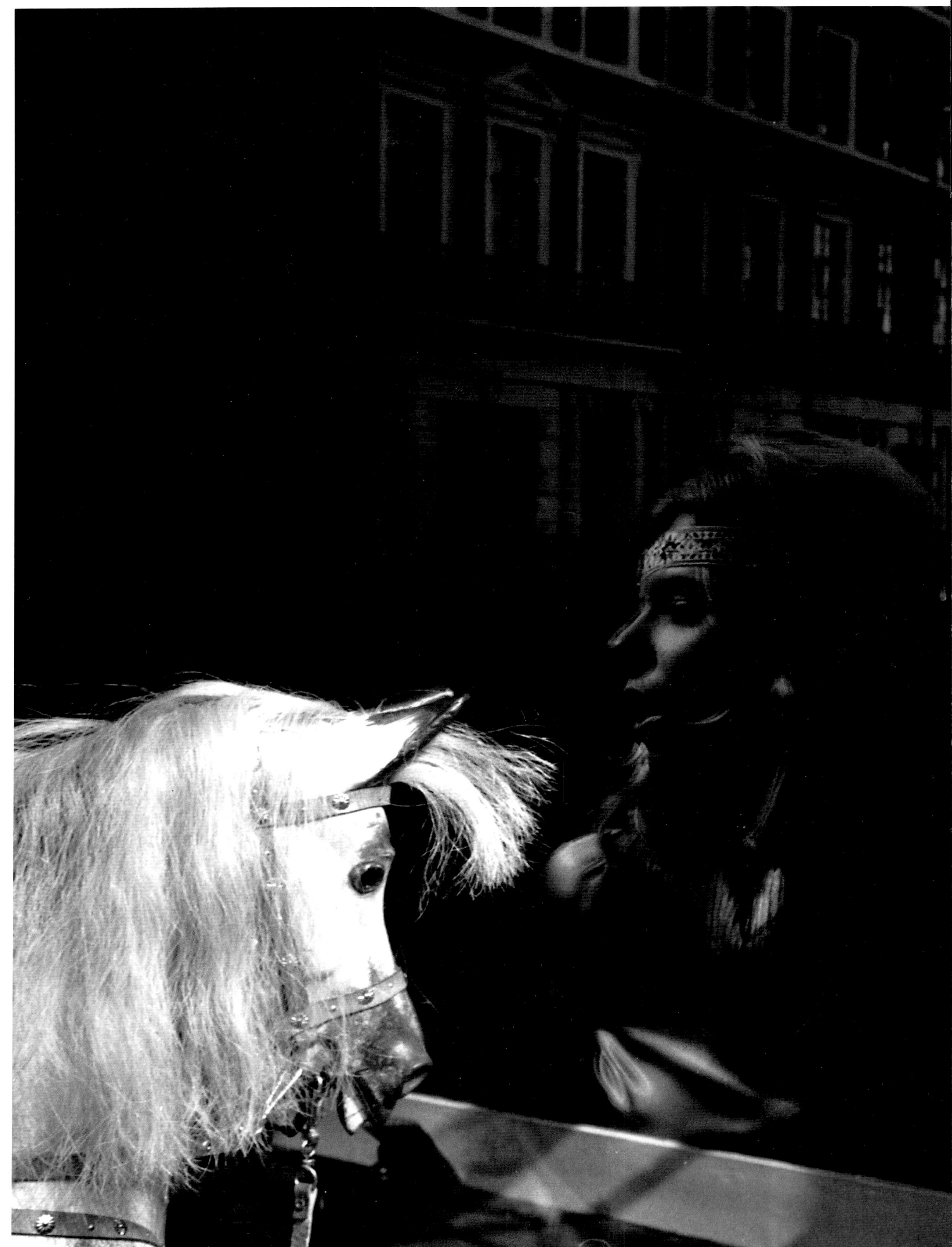

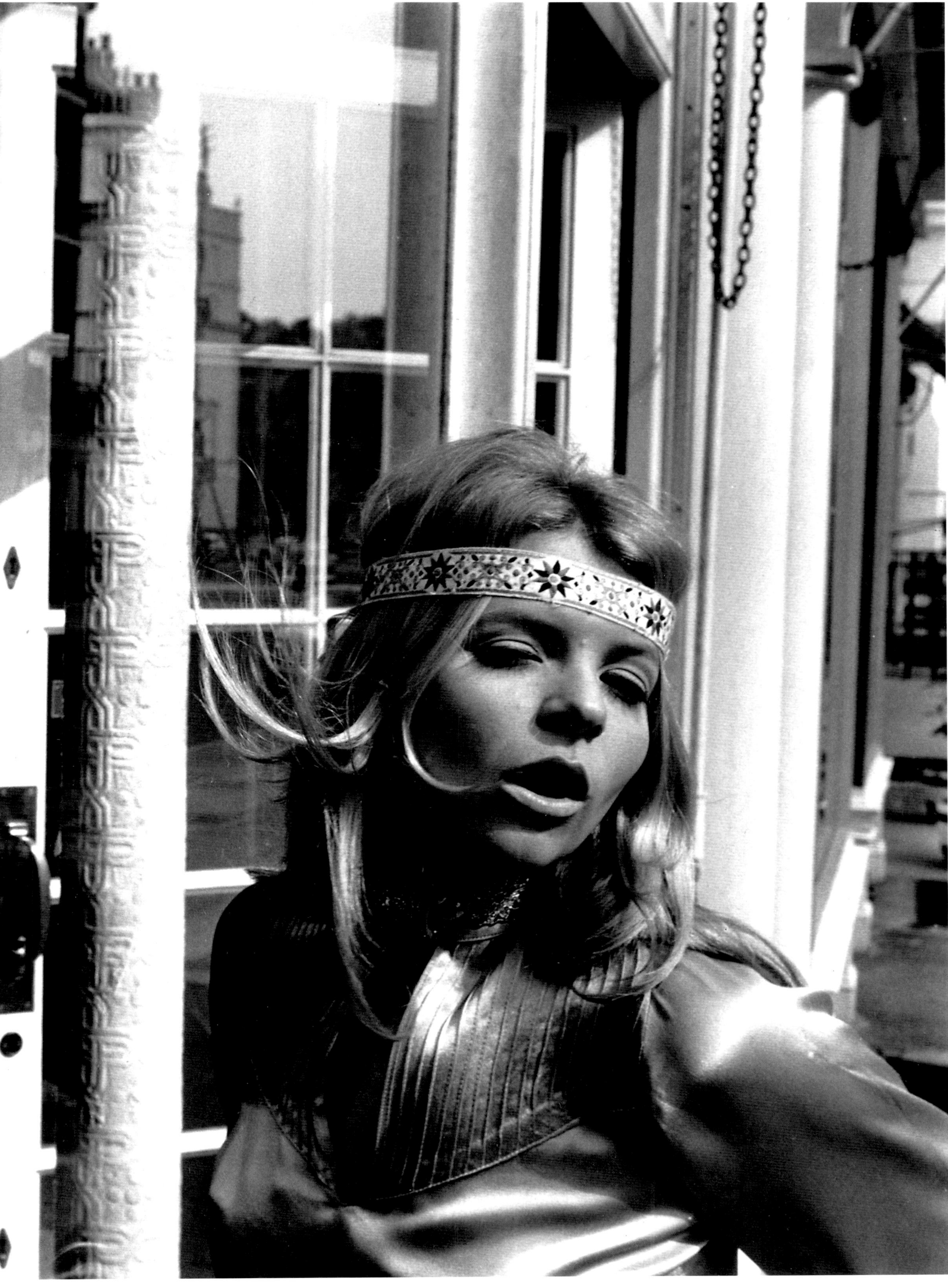

Jane London

Youth Rebellion

The years were ripe for social revolution. For the first time after the war, we felt the chains of austerity fall away. We said, "we are only young once and we intend to enjoy our youth." We were the peace loving flower children, creative not destructive. We were committed to the struggle of social justice, having to reinvent ourselves. We made our voices heard. We rejected the class structures, the "stiff upper lip environment," and the life from nine to five. Underground papers were published for entirely idealistic purposes. The Marxist-orientated *The Black Dwarf* was edited by Tariq Ali, a fierce peace activist, who organized and led the anti-Vietnam campaign under the banner "Hands off Vietnam." In March 1968 an anti-war protest began in Trafalgar Square and moved to the American Embassy in Grosvenor Square, headed by actress Vanessa Redgrave and Tariq Ali. The conservative press reported violent clashes between "young hooligans" and police, and stated that hundreds of demonstrators were arrested.

Flour bombs were pelted at police cordons instead of rocks. Today's public outcry is answered with baton charges, tear gas, and water canons. Flour bombs are a thing of the past.

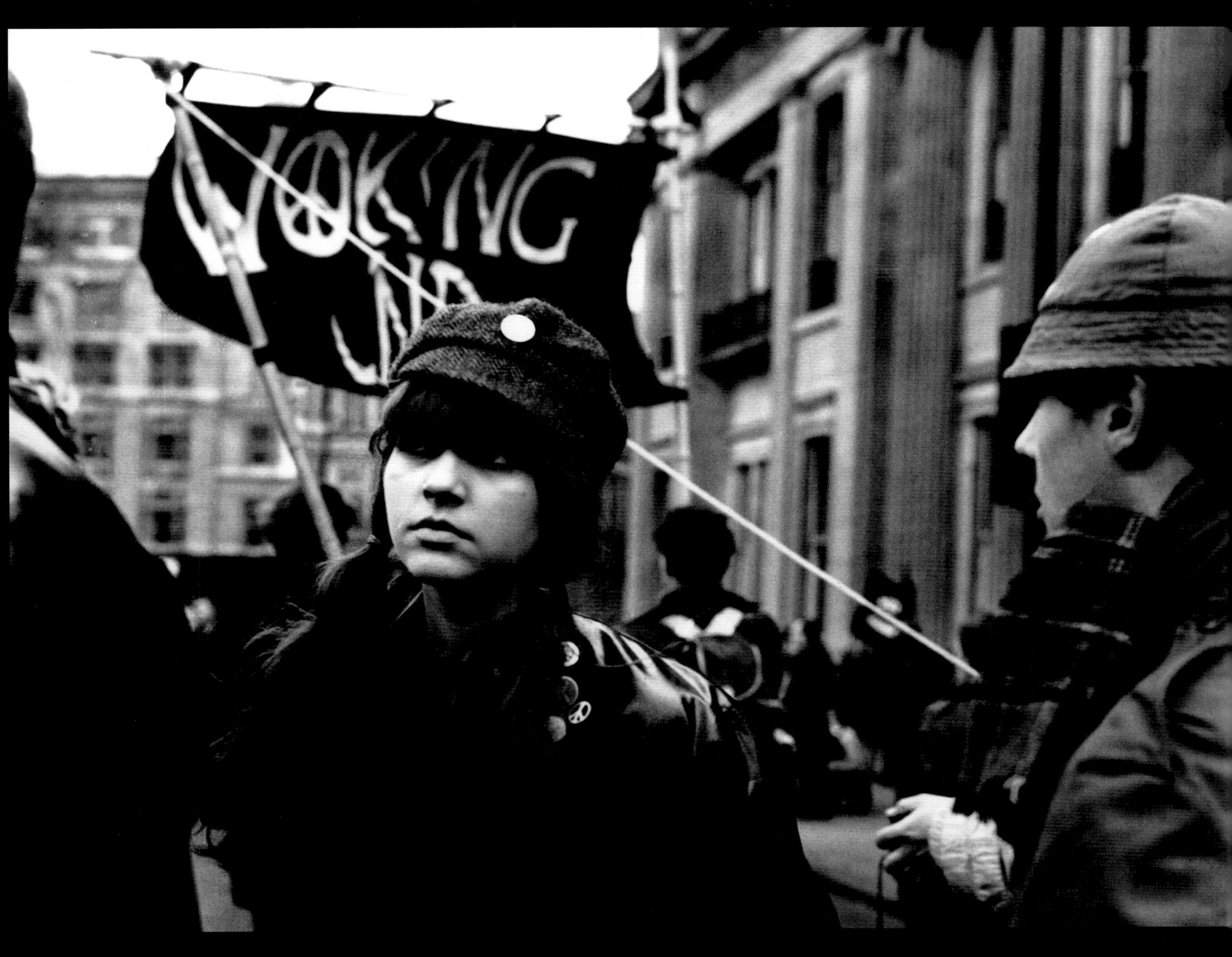

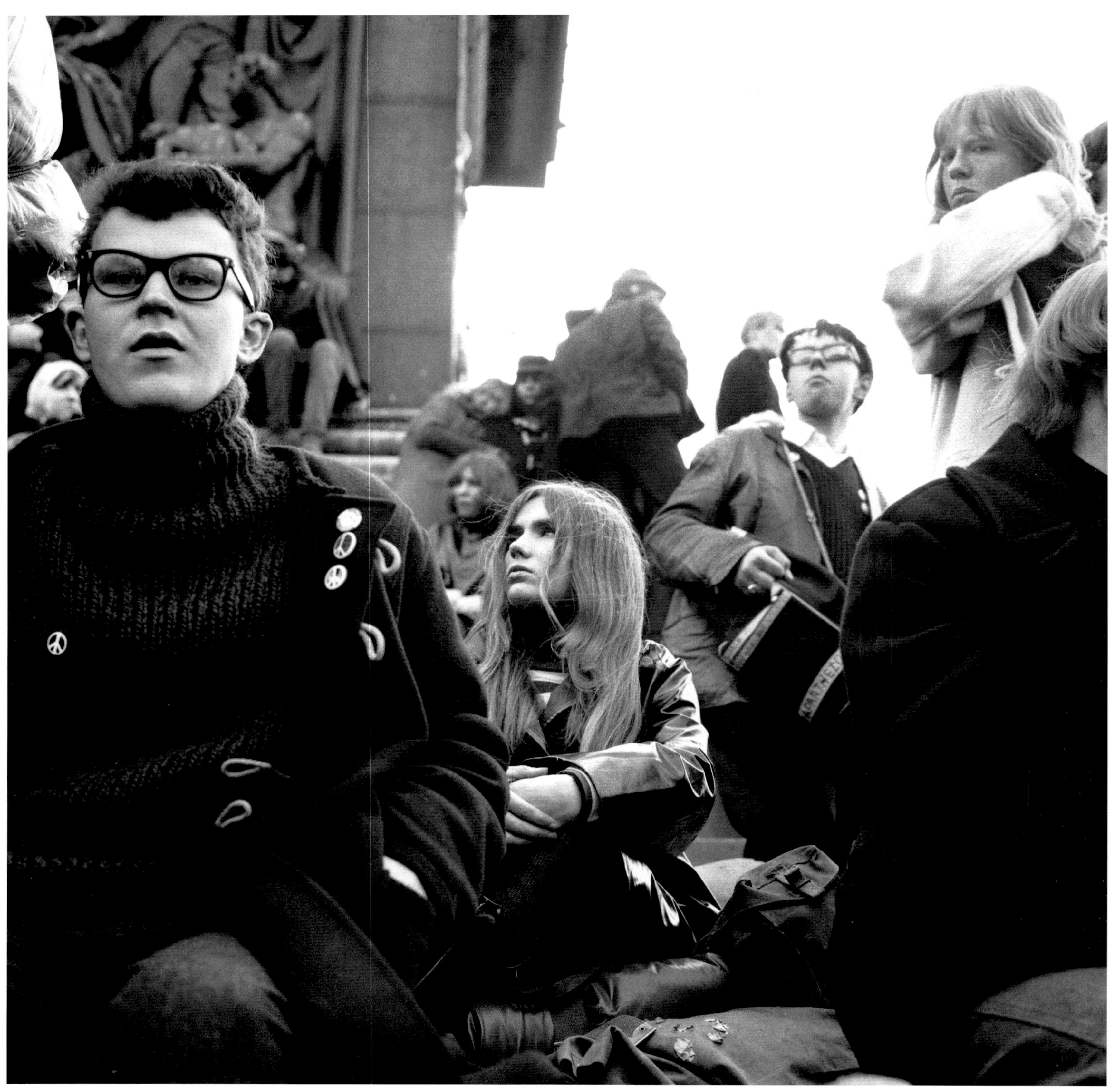

Guardians of peace, CND protest, Trafalgar Square, 1968

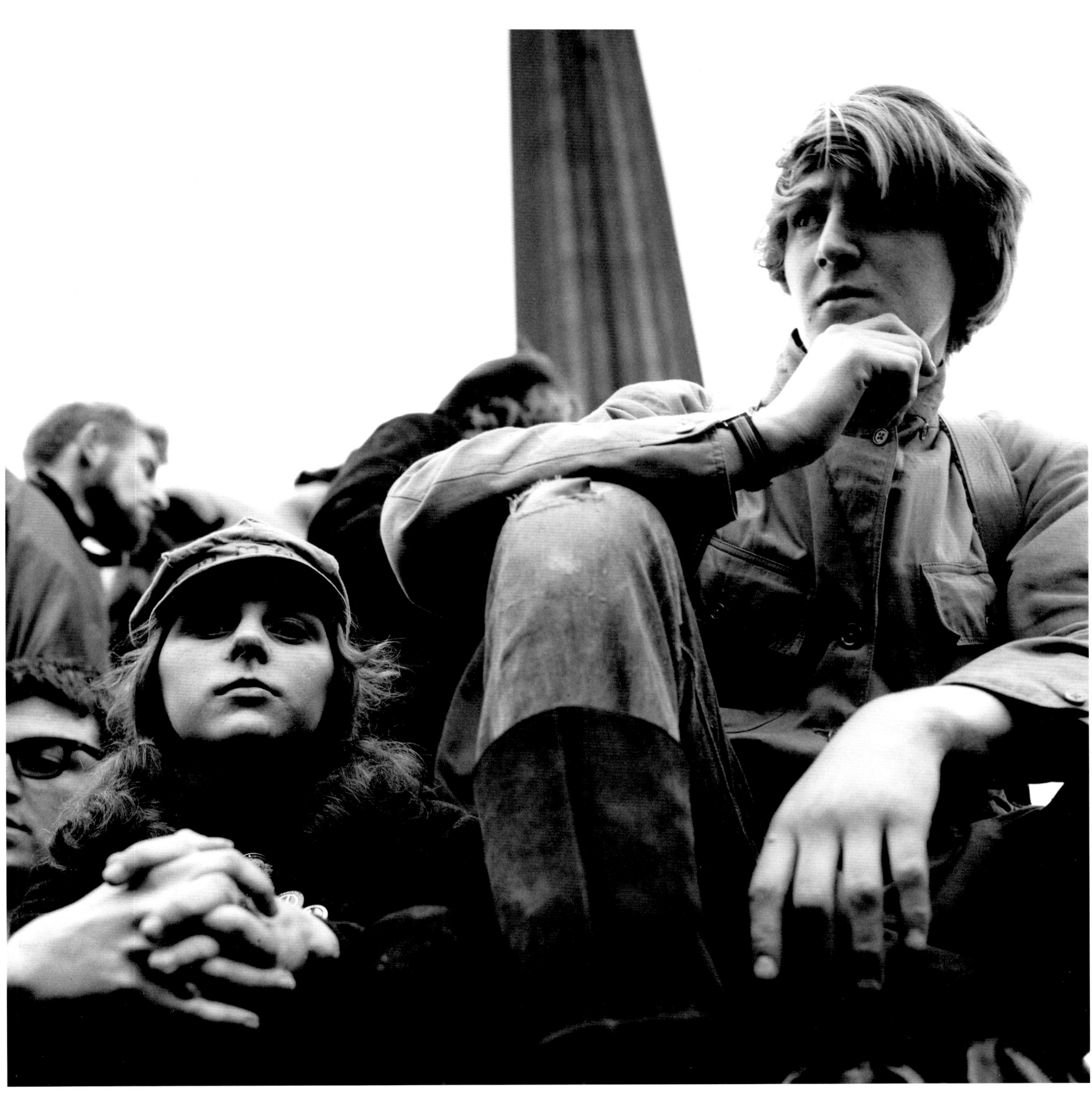

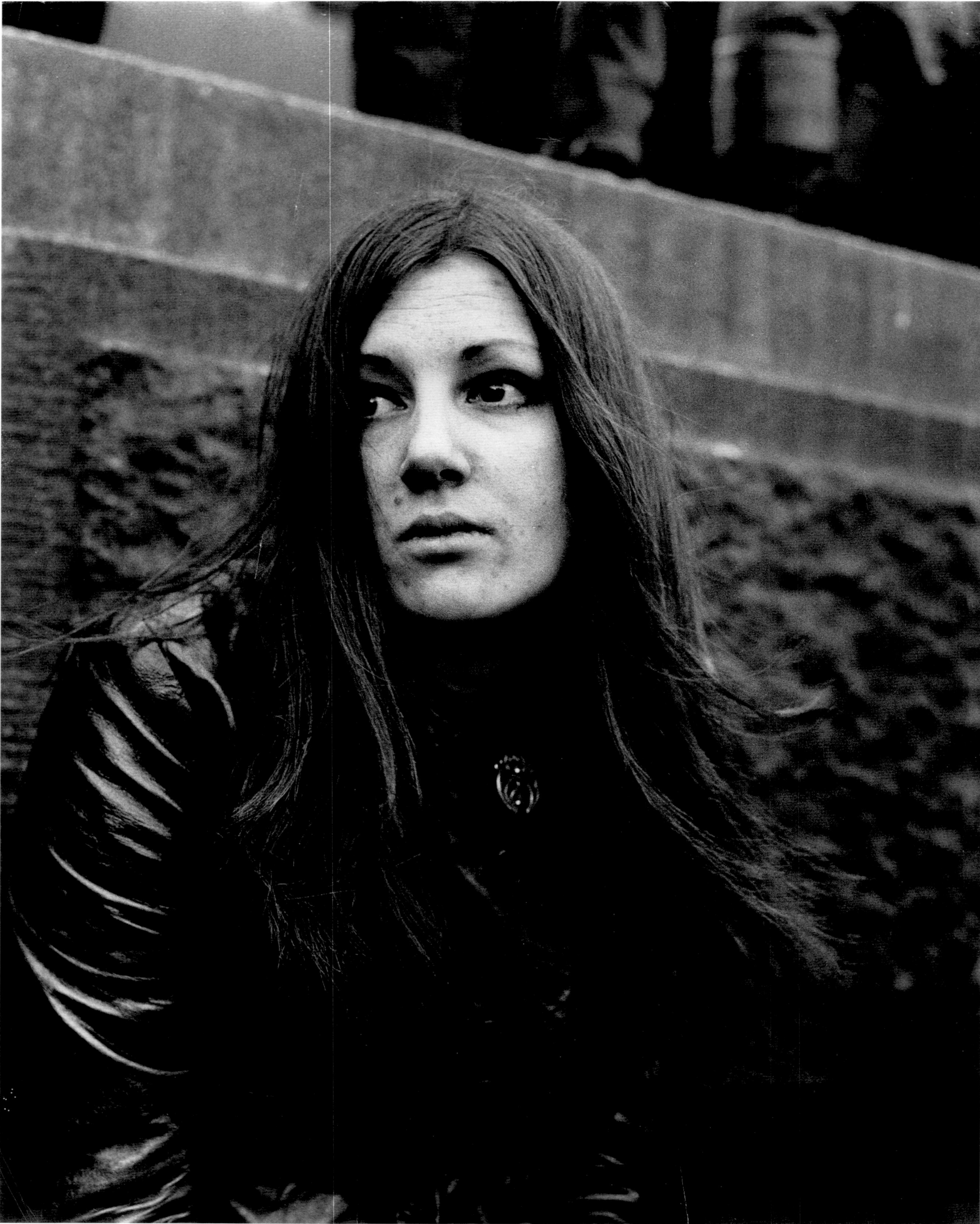

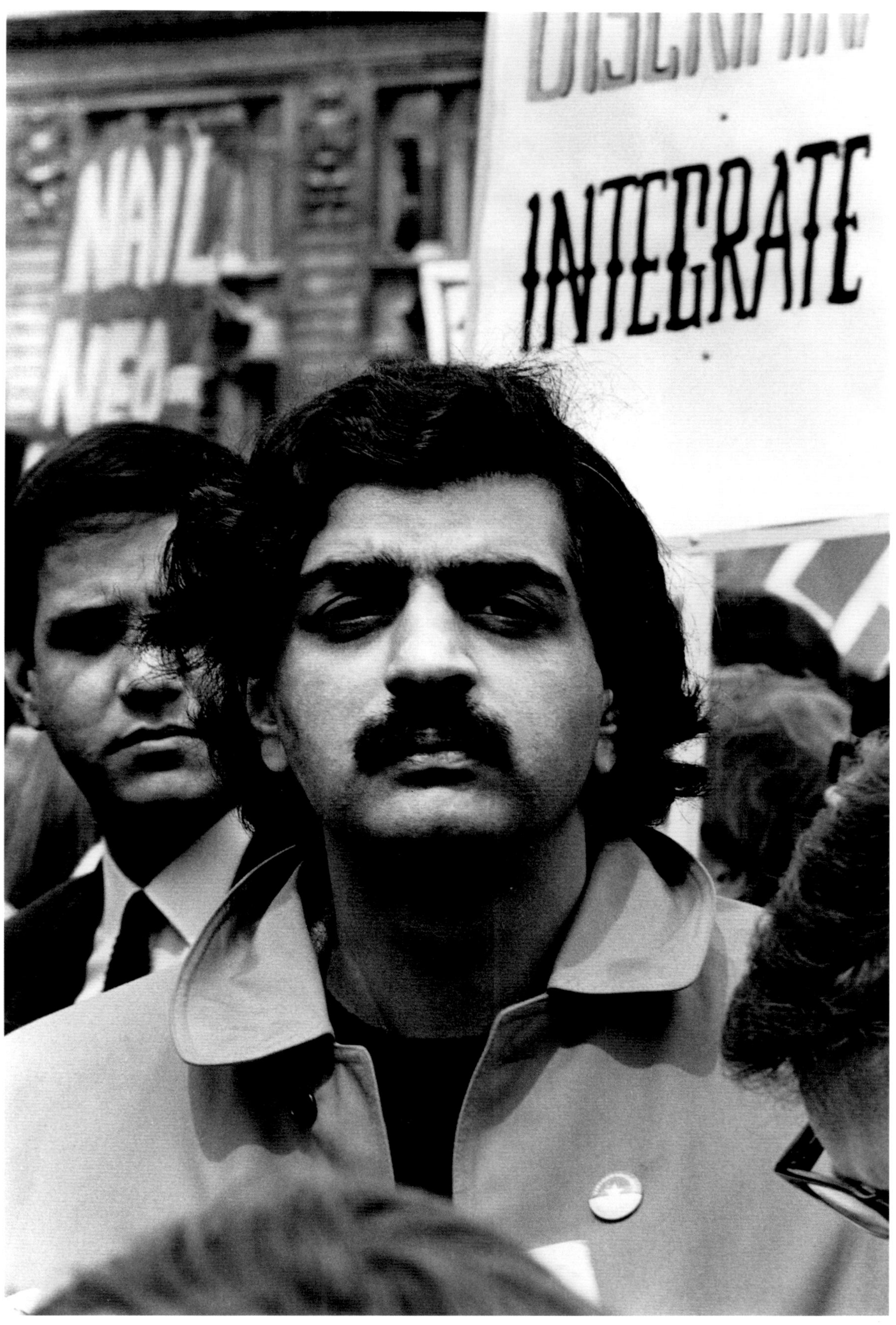

The future is ours – peace protester, 1968

In need for revolution – Tariq Ali, peace activist, writer and historian, 1968

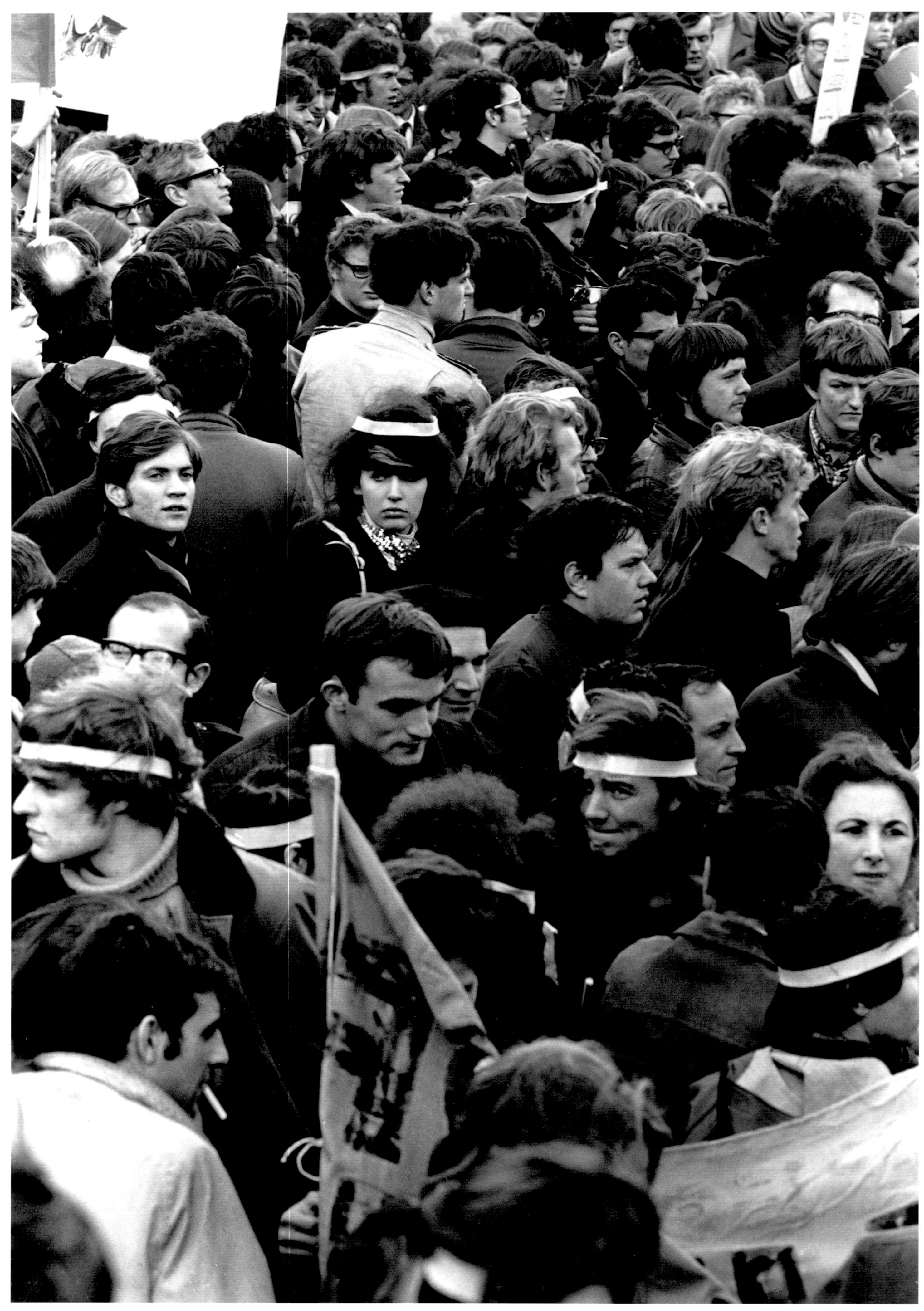

We are the people – Grosvenor Square, peace protest, 1968

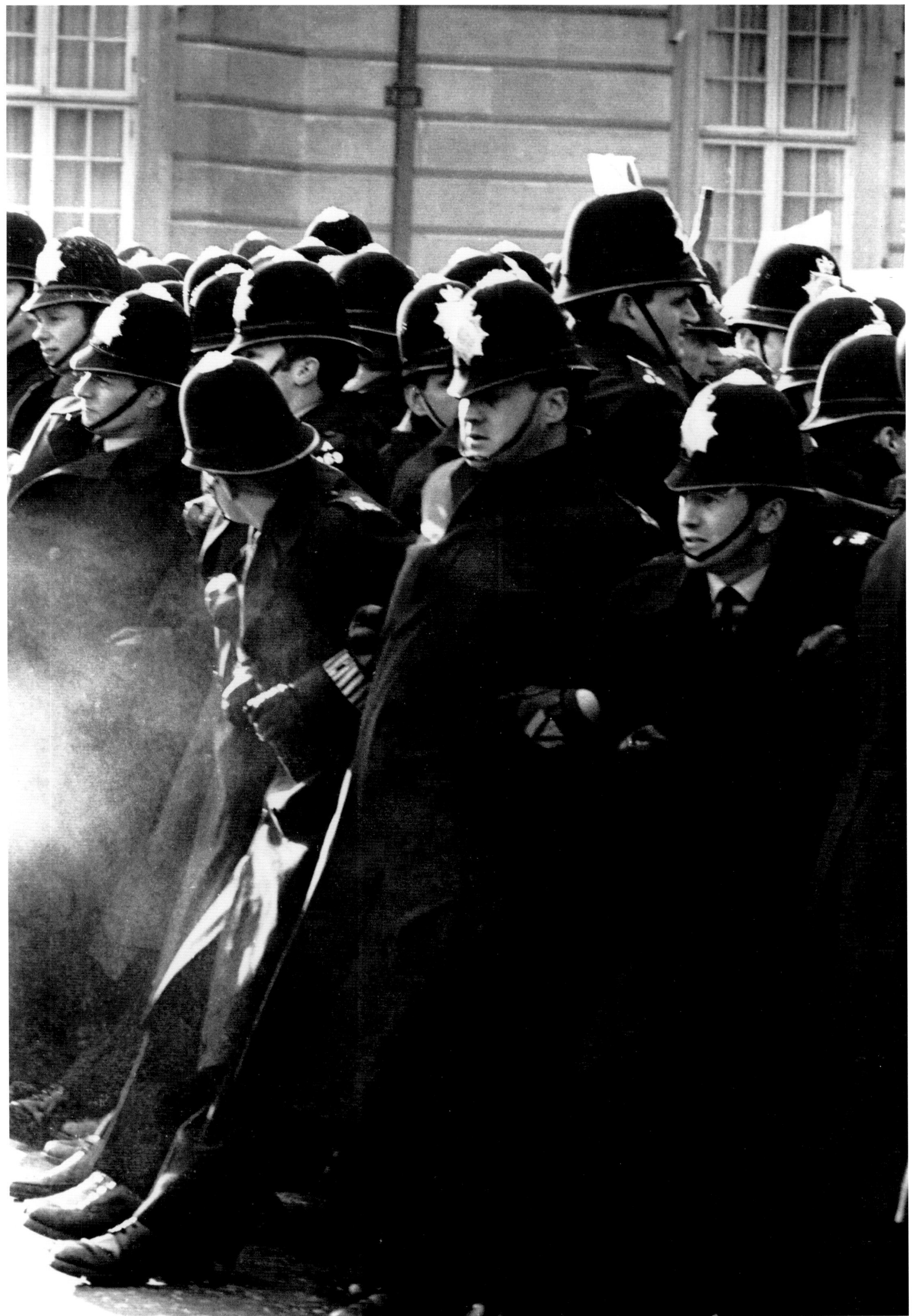

“Flour Power” – Grosvenor Square, US Embassy, 1968

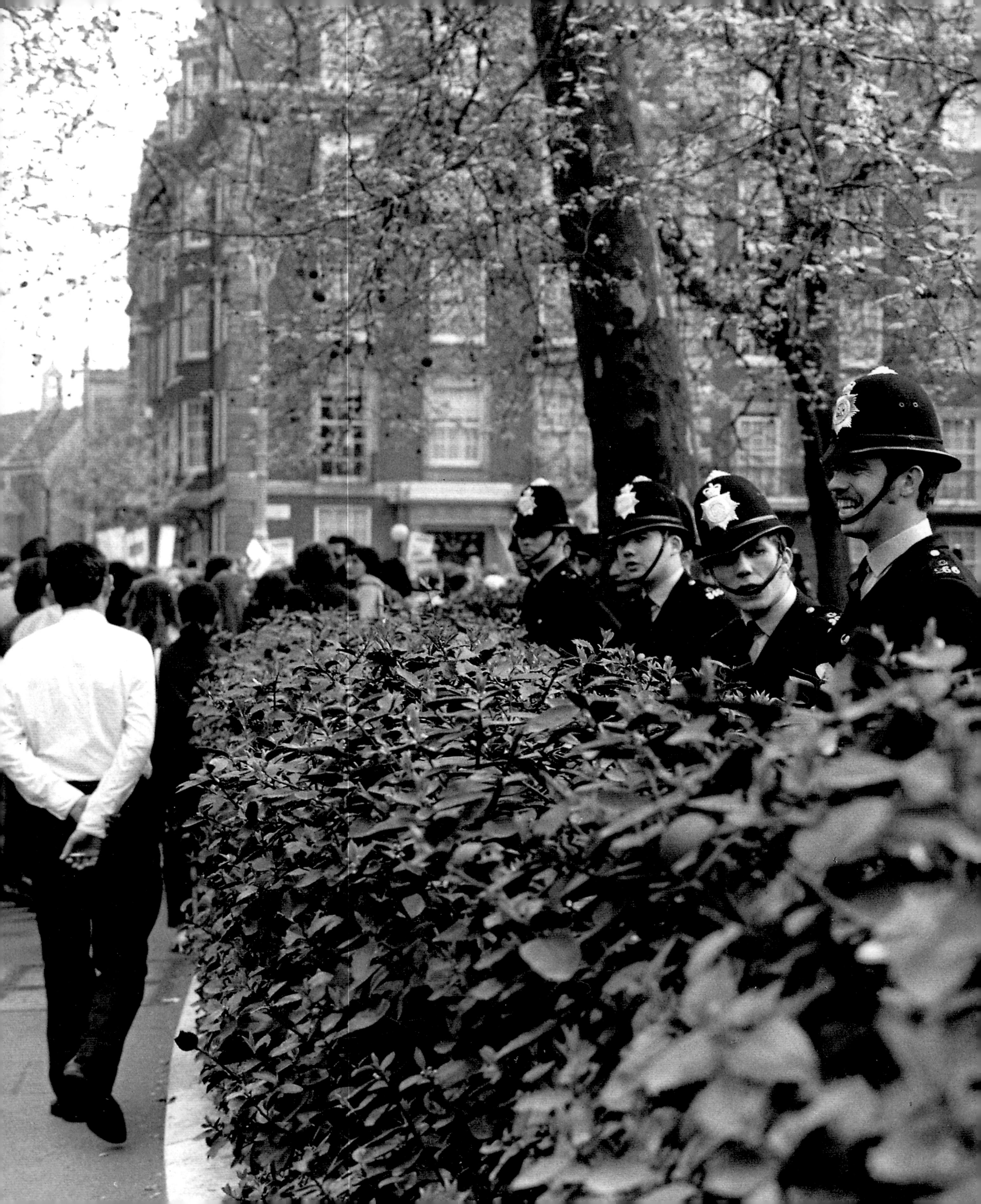

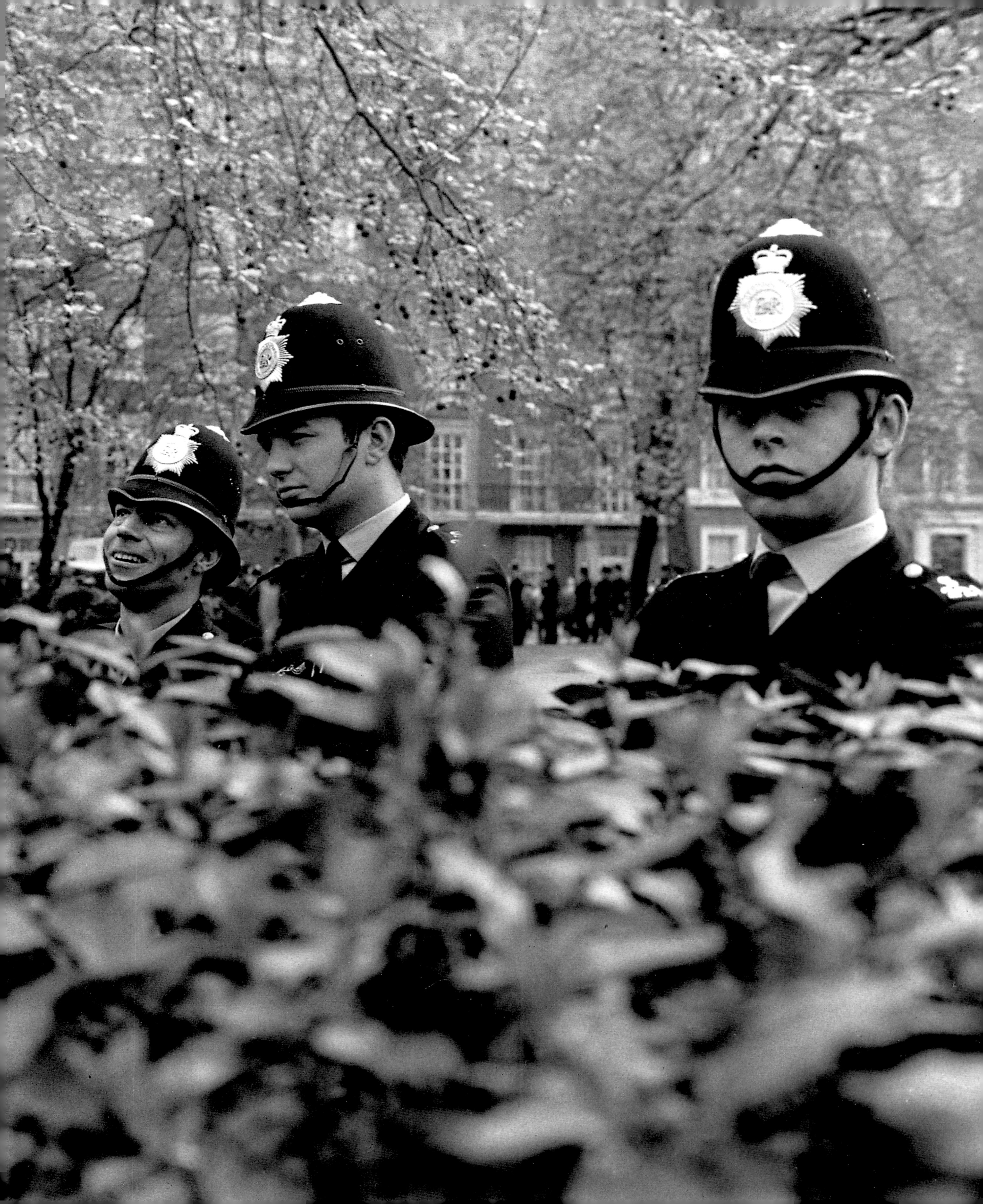

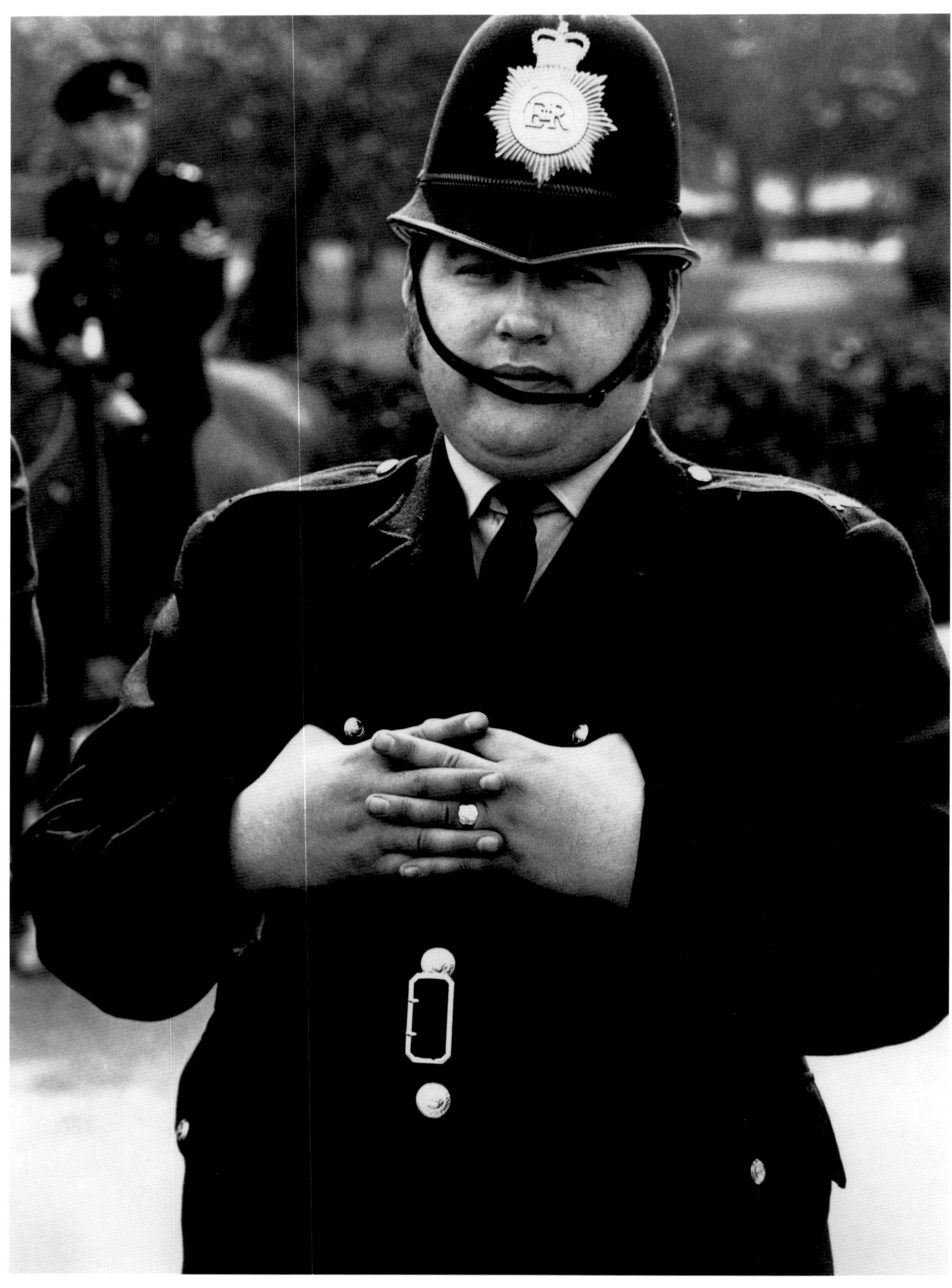

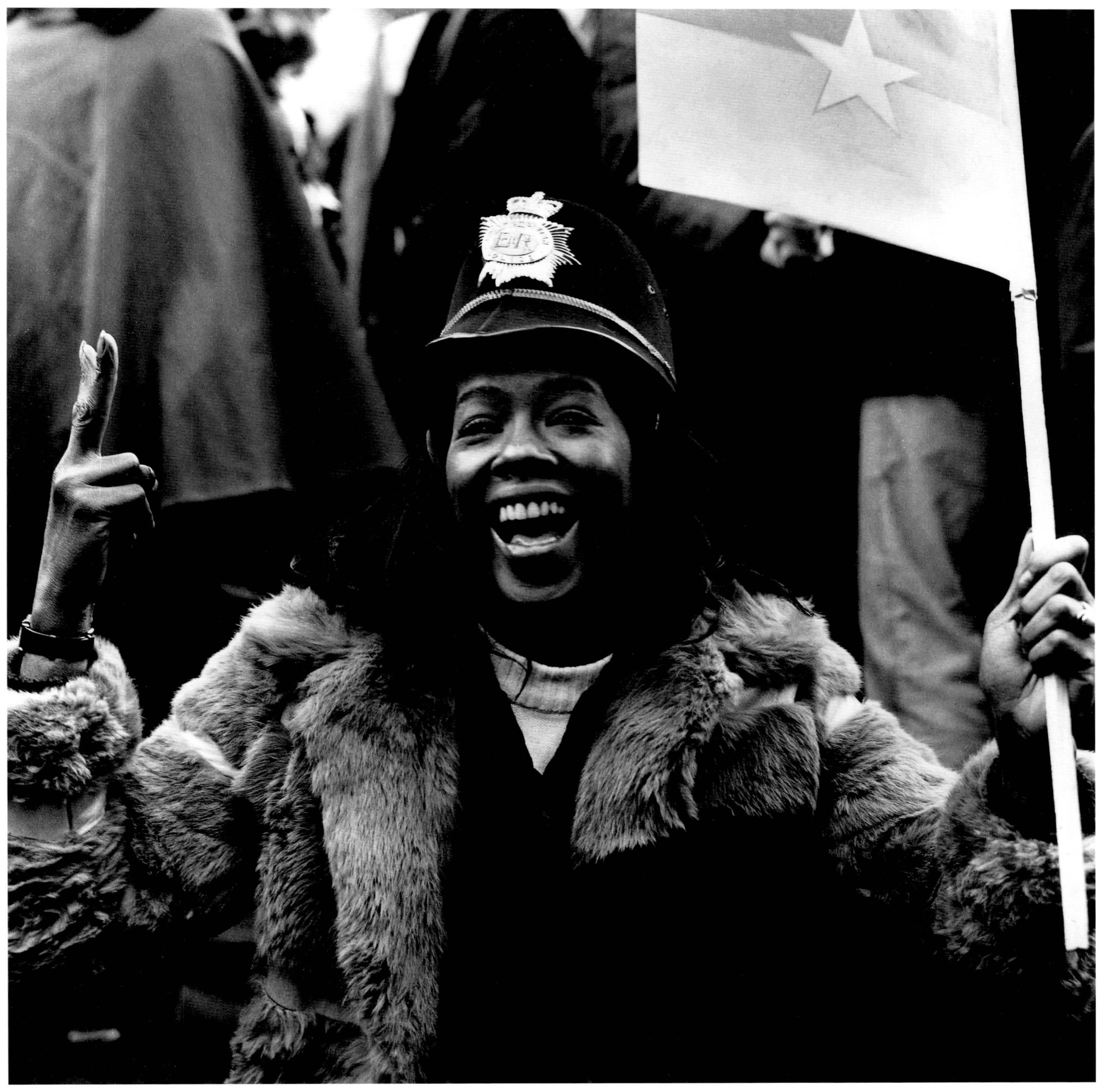

“La rouge et la noire,” Vietnam peace protest, 1968

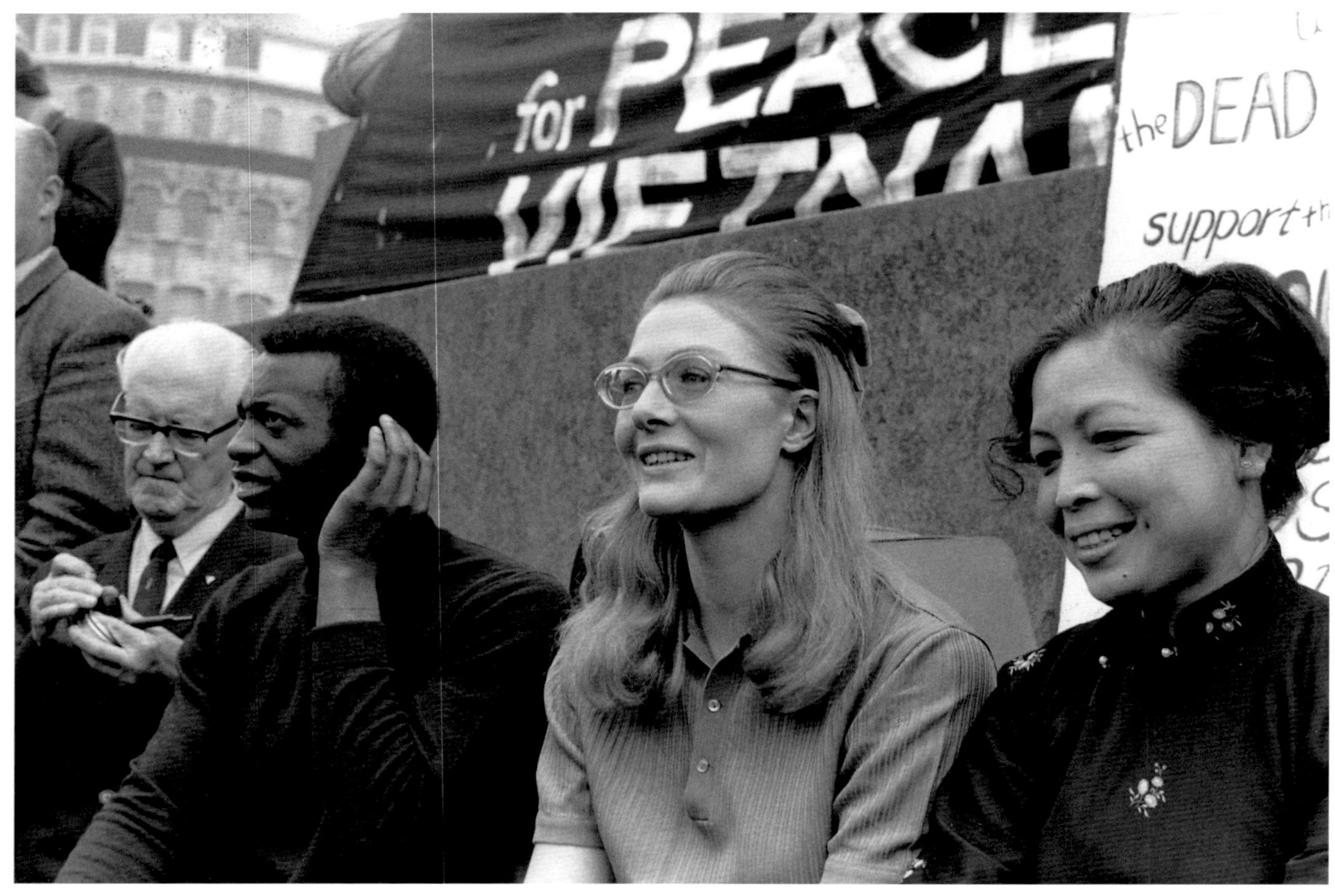

Vanessa Redgrave and like minded

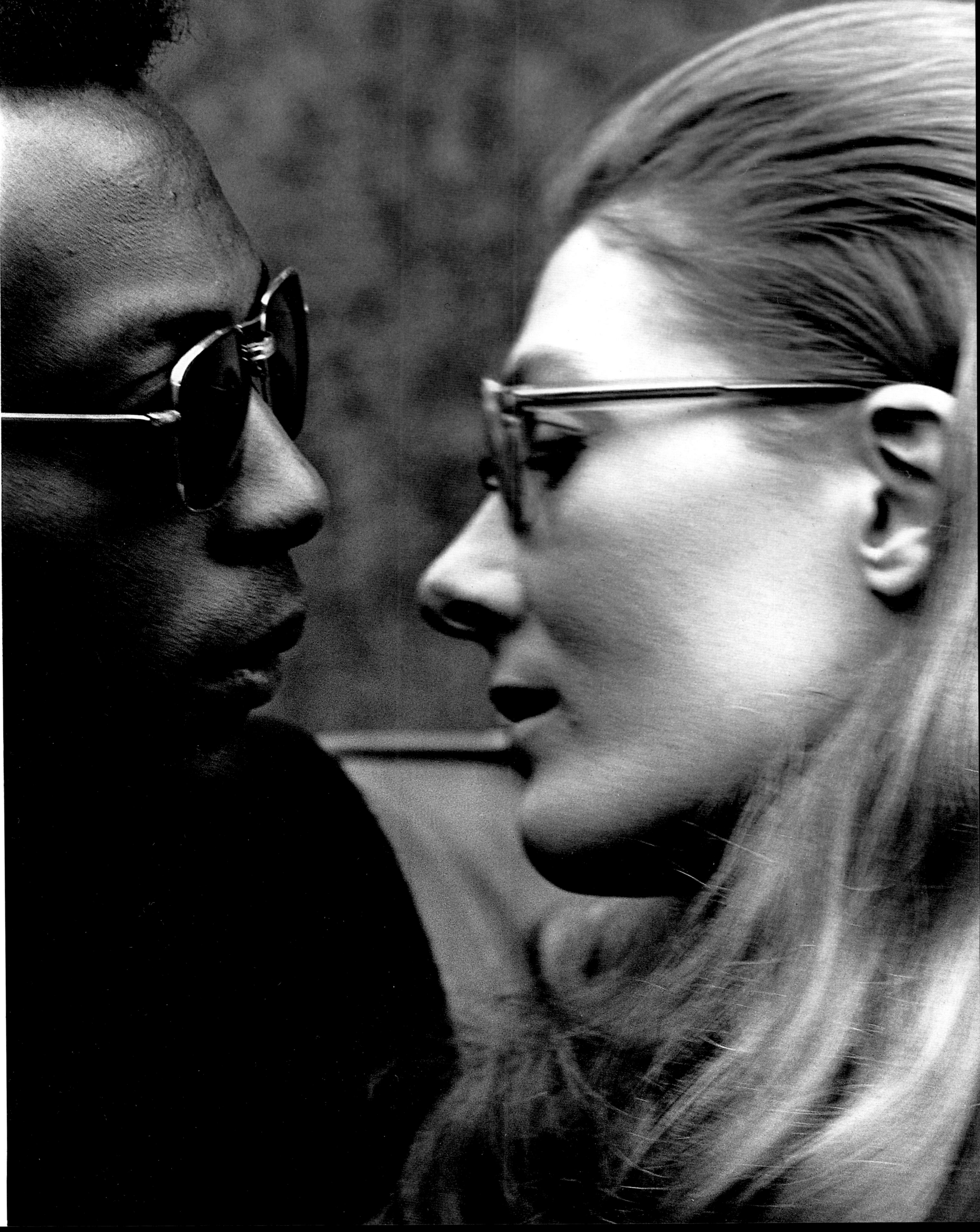

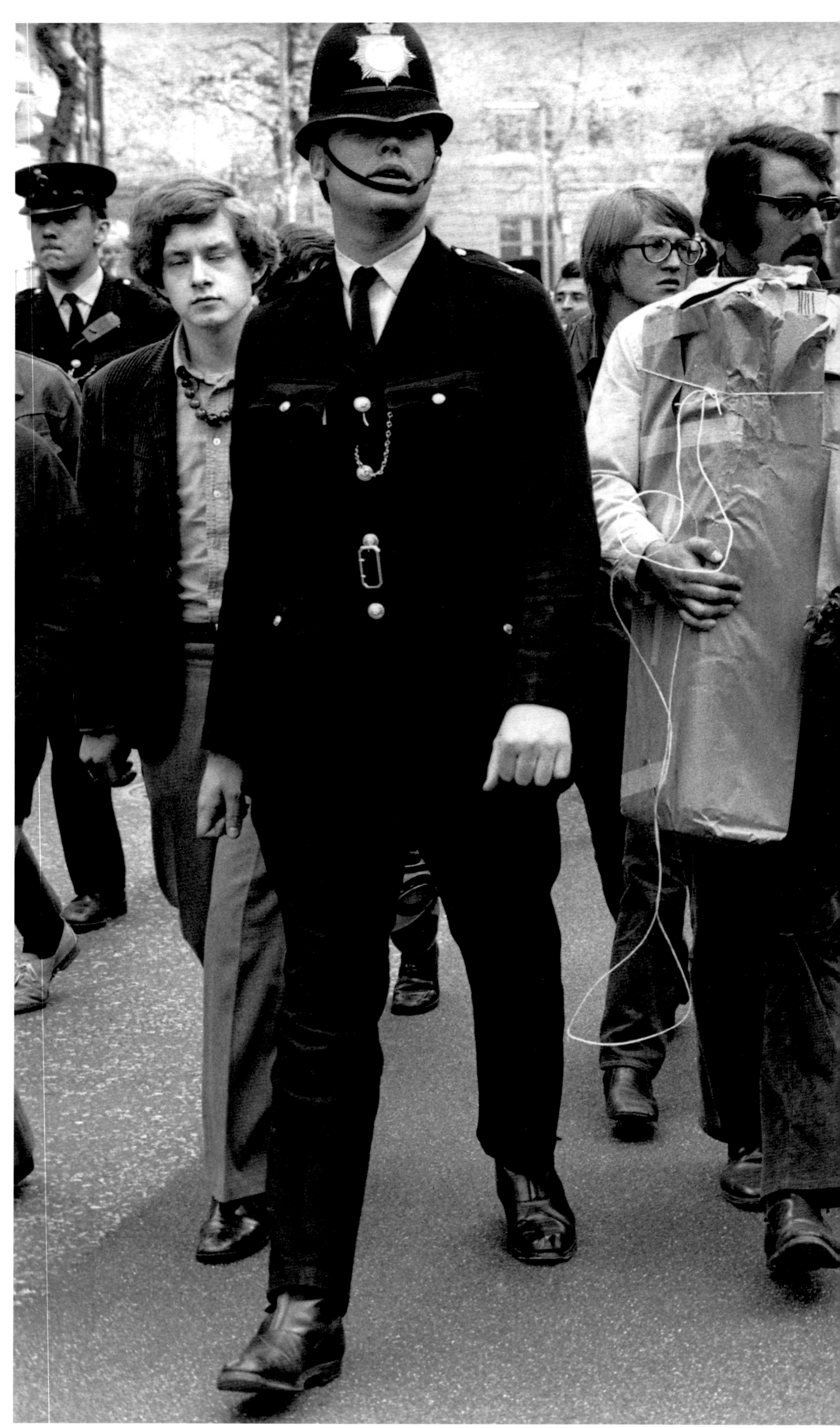

Peace message –
Vanessa Redgrave, actress and activist

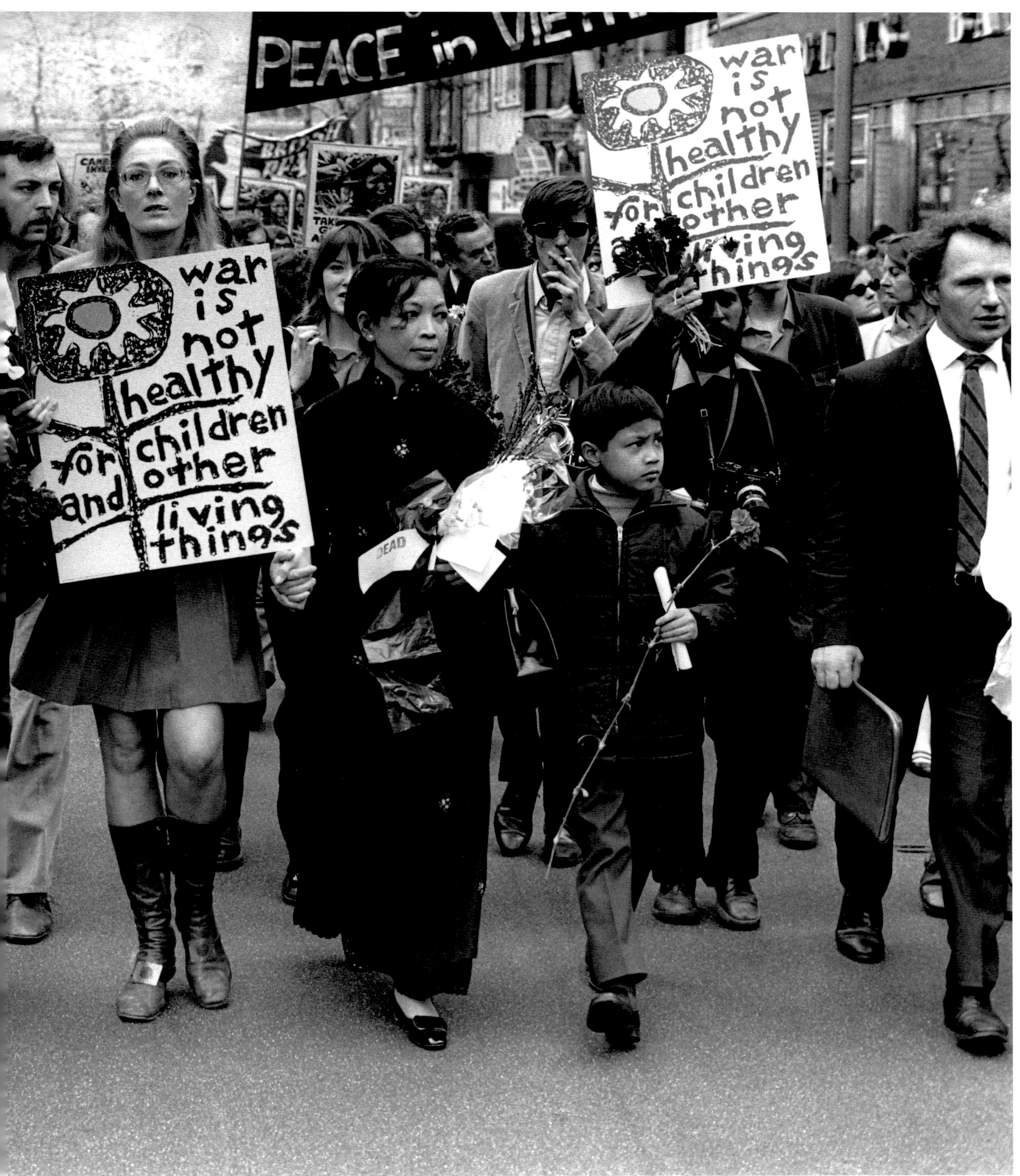
PEACE in
war is not healthy for children and other living things
war is not healthy for children and other living things
DEAD

Biography

The Sixties are synonymous with dramatic political and social revolution and change. This decade saw the conservatism and restrictions of the preceding postwar nineteen-fifties give way to a more radical libertine generation committed to fostering the utopian ideals of free love, world peace, and harmony. It was the decade that saw the Beatles and the Rolling Stones invade America, the peak of the civil rights movement, the assassination of John F. Kennedy, Martin Luther King, and Malcolm X. Widespread protests against the Vietnam War erupted while the end of the decade gave rise to hope as the world witnessed a man walking on the moon. This fertile environment encompassed Europe in the nineteen-sixties—an era that was captured through the lens of Frank Habicht.

Habicht was born in Hamburg in December 1938. He began his career as a photographer in the early nineteen-sixties attending the Hamburg School of Photography in 1962. He quickly became established as a freelance photographer and writer in Europe, submitting works to be published in magazines that included *Camera Magazine, Spiegelreflex Praxis, Twen, Esquire, Die Welt, Sunday Times* (UK), and *The Guardian.* Habicht also gained employment working as a stills photographer for film directors Bryan Forbes, Roman Polanski, and Jules Dassin, as in-house photographer for the Playboy Club in London, and as a freelance photographer for Top of the Pops. These encounters certainly provided Habicht direct access to international pop idols and film stars who became the subjects of his most celebrated photographs, and included Mick Jagger and the Rolling Stones, Jane Birkin and Serge Gainsbourg, actors Vanessa Redgrave, Marty Feldman, and Christopher Lee, director Roman Polanski and photographer Lord Lichfield.

Habicht's images capture the uninhibited spirit of the times offering a glimpse into the heady period that still manages to arrest the imagination some fifty years later. His book *Young London: Permissive Paradise* (1969), a social document on London's youth, was published in the late nineteen-sixties and in decades to come gained international recognition. Another photographic book, *In the Sixties* (1997), juxtaposed those who achieved international fame with the unnamed and unrecorded in history books.

In 1981 Habicht left a successful international career to reside in New Zealand's Bay of Islands, with his wife Christine and sons Sebastian and Florian, drawn to the country for its beauty and tranquility. He now spends much of his time devoted to creating images that celebrate the landscape and community in and around the Bay of Islands where he lives. His two books *Bay of Islands – Where the Sunday Grass is Greener,* explores the creation of New Zealand seen through the eyes of a flock of sheep. The acclaimed satirical pictorial is a collaboration with Kiki and Helme Heine. *Bay of Islands – A Paradise Found,* with a text by Bob Molloy, captures the fun and friendship to be found in this stunning part of New Zealand.

In October 2004 Habicht exhibited his *Karma Sixties* collection at Colette in Paris. Frank's fascinating images certainly captivate the wider public, both young and old alike. The images are timeless and contemporary, retaining their relevance either for those generations who experienced the Sixties firsthand or for those who are a product of them.

Habicht's Auckland exhibition, *High Tide and Green Grass,* in June 2007 at Gow Langsford Gallery, attracted nationwide critical acclaim and New Zealand's current affairs TV show *Sunday* paid homage to his work from this immortal decade.

A party in the spirit of his Sixties was held in Moscow on April 18, 2008 at the exclusive Arterium Gallery to celebrate the opening of Frank Habicht's exhibition. Funds were collected by the charitable foundation Peace Planet to aid orphaned children.

In 2011, Frank had a lead role (playing himself) in his son Florian Habicht's feature film, *Love Story.* A hybrid of documentary and fiction set in New York City.

From May to July 2016, Habicht's photographs were featured as part of *Strange and Familiar* at the Barbican Centre, London. Curated by the British photographer Martin Parr, this major exhibition looked at how foreign photographers captured UK identity. It included black-and-white photographs from the thirties to Sixties by iconic photographers such as Henri Cartier-Bresson, Bruce Davidson, and Robert Frank. *Strange and Familiar* was also shown at the Manchester Art Gallery from November 2016 to May 2017.

In July 2016, Frank's photographs were featured in *An Ideal for Living* at London's foremost commercial photographic gallery Beetles & Huxley (now Huxley-Parlour). The exhibition collated photography from the nineteen-twenties to modern day, looking at Britain's attitudes towards class and race.

Shelley Jahnke

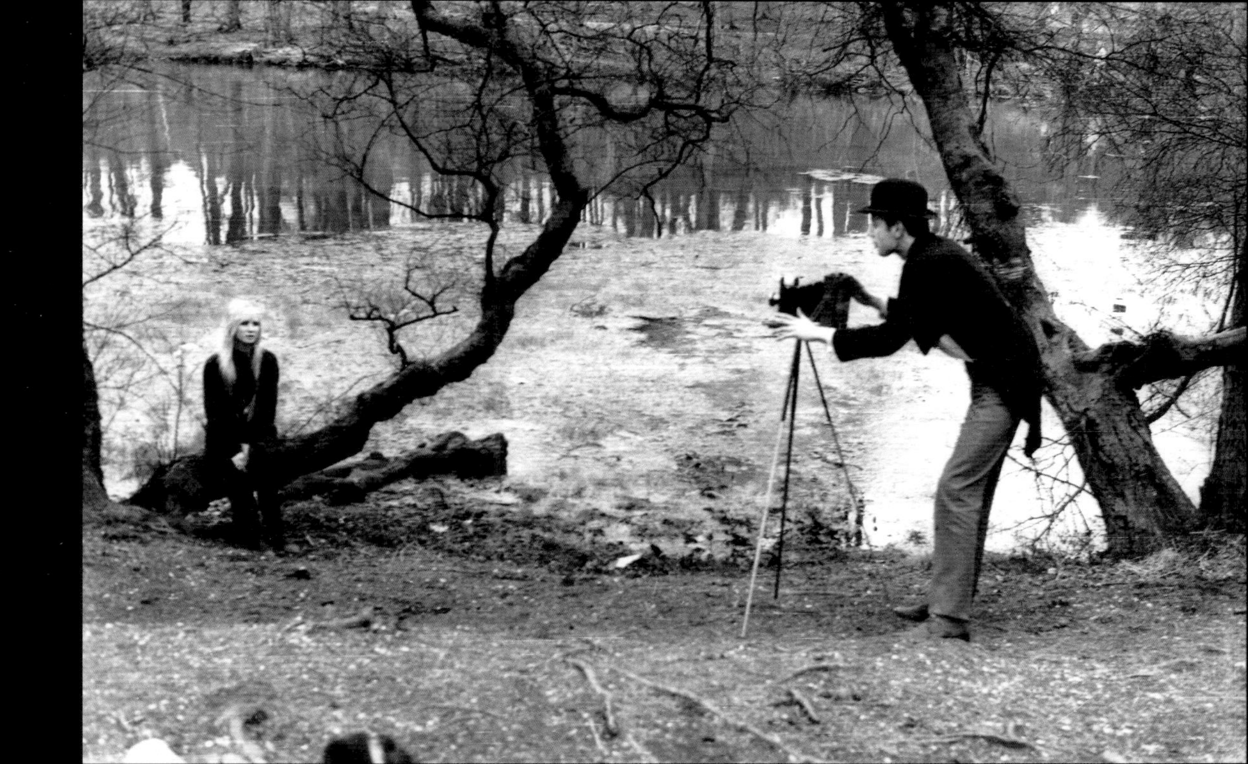

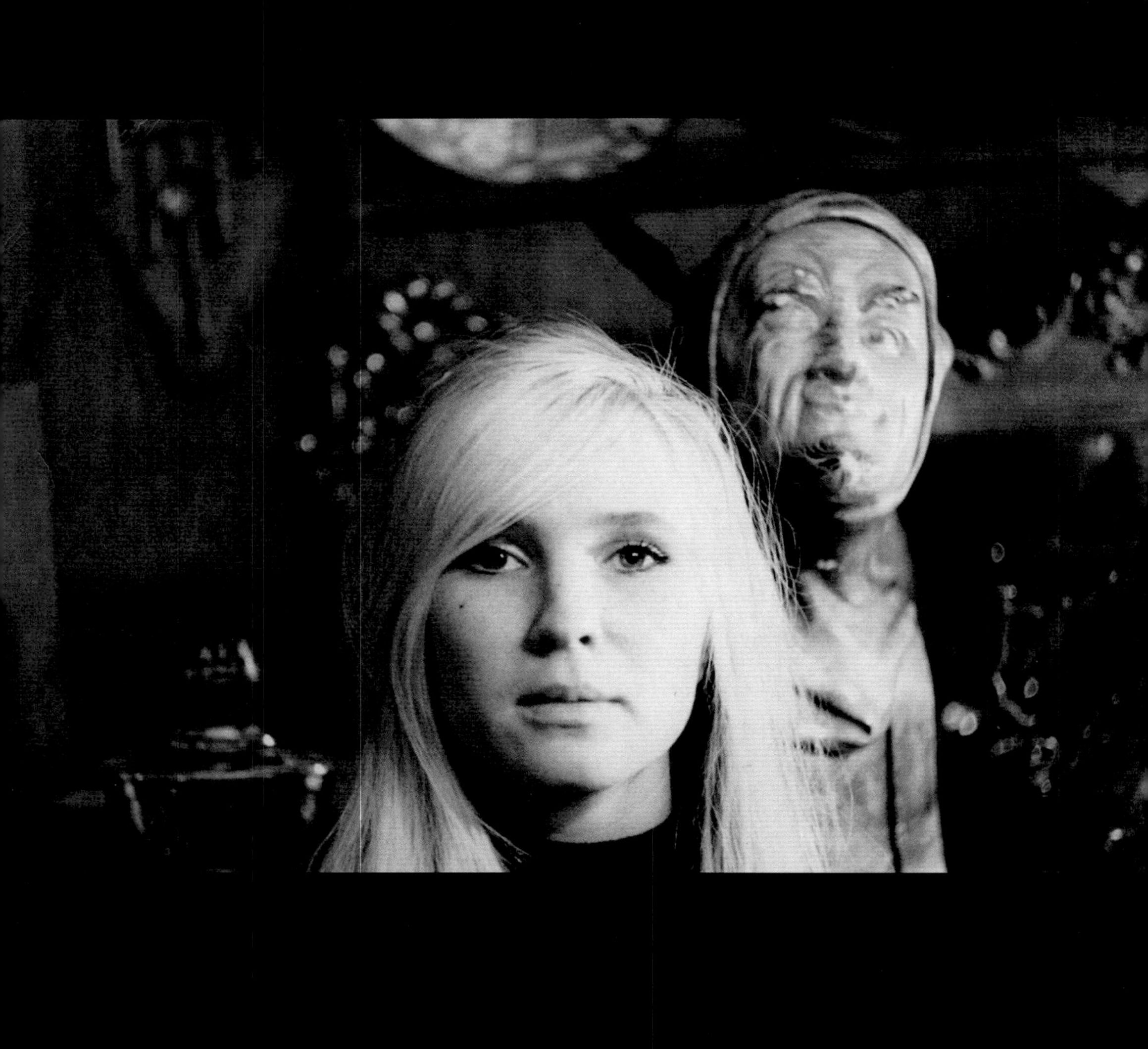

It was Uschi who inspired me to become a photographer

In the mid-fifties, during a hotel management apprenticeship in Dusseldorf I met an impulsive young woman at a disco. Her name was Uschi Weider and she would soon change my life and carreer. She was charming, youthful and outgoing. She often acted like a tomboy though never missed an opportunity to flirt. I was overwhelmed by her beauty and wanted to immortalize her. With a modest camera I took some worthwhile photos of Uschi at a local antique store. After seeing the photographs, the Antique dealer commissioned me to take more images of his objects and requested I use Uschi as the model. Uschi and I became close friends, we could "steal horses together" as the German saying goes, and that's as far as it went. I was overrun by her charm and was used as an excuse for her parents for anything and everything she got up to. All situations, anywhere, day or night, all her adventures had the name Frank attached because I could be relied upon.

Uschi married a successful German interior designer named Günter who was a jet setter and a few decades older than her. A fortnight prior to her wedding Uschi spent some time in Ibiza and wrote to me confessing that she fancied an American beau she had just met, yet I was her dearest friend. In another letter sweet seventeen year old Uschi told me I was really her intended husband to be. This innocent platonic friendship was not everlasting. While attending the school of photography in Hamburg for a year, I encountered difficulties in keeping contact. I was aware that Günter was never short of cash and he was known for obtaining recreational drugs. To my dismay, I learned that Uschi had undergone a change of personality and when I finally managed to contact her years later, she was confused and no longer knew who I was. In years to come I had to cope with the fact that Uschi passed away from an overdose.

Editor:
Florian Habicht

Managing editor:
Nadine Barth

Texts:
Heather Cremonesi, Frank Habicht,
Shelley Jahnke, Valerie Mendes

Project management:
Claire Cichy, Hatje Cantz

Copyediting:
Aaron Bogart

Art direction:
Julia Wagner

Creative consultants :
Christine Habicht, Florian Habicht, Sebastian Habicht

Typeface:
Recoleta, Neue Haas Unica

Production:
Heidrun Zimmerman, Hatje Cantz

Reproductions:
Peter Machin

Printing:
Longo SpA, Bolzano

Paper:
Condat matt Périgord, 150 g/m²

Binding:
Barizza International SRL

Visit the artist's website:
www.frankhabicht.net

Published by
Hatje Cantz Verlag GmbH
Mommsenstraße 27
10629 Berlin
Tel. +49 30 3464678-00
Fax +49 30 3464678-29
www.hatjecantz.de
A Ganske Publishing Group Company

Hatje Cantz books are available internationally at selected bookstores.
For more information about our distribution partners, please visit our website at www.hatjecantz.com.

ISBN 978-3-7757-4490-4

Printed in Italy

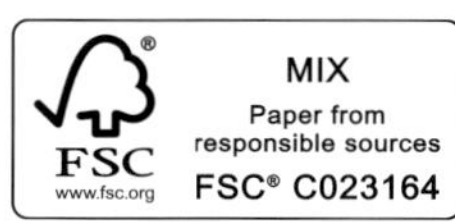

Cover photograph:
Alice, aka Girl at Rolling Stones Concert, 1969

With gratitude to Christine Turnauer and the Bonaventura Foundation